EUROPEAN UNITY

A SURVEY OF THE EUROPEAN ORGANISATIONS

OTHER PEP PUBLICATIONS

The Parliament of the European Communities

Towards a Common Economic Policy for EEC

Steel Pricing Policies

Housing in Britain, France and Western Germany

Regional Development in the European Economic Community

Aspects of European Integration

Cross-Channel Collaboration: a study of agreements between British and Continental firms

Economic Planning and Policies in Britain, France and Germany

New Commonwealth Students in Britain

Education for a Developing Region

WITH CHATHAM HOUSE

Concentration or Competition: A European Dilemma

Europe and the Developing World

Agriculture: the Cost of Joining the Common Market

The Sterling Problem and the Six

The Medium-term Economic Policy Programme of the EEC

Institutions of the European Community

Energy Policy in the European Community

Towards a European Civil Service

EUROPEAN UNITY

A SURVEY OF
THE EUROPEAN ORGANISATIONS

PEP
Political and Economic Planning
12 UPPER BELGRAVE STREET

Michael Palmer
John Lambert
et al.

London
GEORGE ALLEN & UNWIN LTD
RUSKIN HOUSE MUSEUM STREET

FIRST PUBLISHED IN 1968

Published in the U.S.A. under the title
A HANDBOOK OF EUROPEAN ORGANISATIONS

PRINTED IN GREAT BRITAIN
in 10 point Times Roman type
BY UNWIN BROTHERS LTD
WOKING AND LONDON

Acknowledgements

The first edition of this report, which was published in 1959 under the title *European Organisations*, was written by Dr Ernest Wohlgemuth and Mr Michael Palmer, under the supervision of an international research group which met regularly at PEP from September 1956 to December 1958. Chapters outlining the significance of the Treaties establishing the European Economic Community and the European Atomic Energy Community were contributed by Mrs Miriam Camps. The original project was made possible by a grant from the Leverhulme Trust.

The book has now been completely revised and brought up to date, and much new material has been added including a number of new chapters. Mr Michael Palmer wrote the chapters on the Council of Europe, the Economic Commission for Europe, the North Atlantic Treaty Organisation, the Organisation for European Economic Co-operation, the Organisation for Economic Co-operation and Development (an entirely new chapter) and Western European Union, together with the introductory chapter, European Unity since the Second World War; he was also jointly responsible with the Director of PEP for editing the complete book. The new chapter on the European Economic Community was written by Mr John Lambert, Mr Murray Forsyth contributing the section in this chapter discussing the European Parliament. Mr Lambert also revised the original chapter on the European Coal and Steel Community. The new chapters on the European Atomic Energy Community and the European Free Trade Association were written by Mr Anthony Morris and Dr Ernest Wohlgemuth respectively.

The revision of the book has been undertaken in the context of PEP's programme of European studies, the major support for which has come from the Ford Foundation.

PEP wishes to express its gratitude to the members of the Secretariats of different organisations, and others, who have given freely of their time in discussing the work of the institutions examined in the report with the authors and in commenting on the draft chapters submitted to them.

Preface

This study examines how the European Economic Community and the other European international organisations have within the last twenty years transformed the relations between the countries of Western Europe in political, defence and economic affairs. The introductory chapter, *European Unity since the Second World War*, describes the main events in the history of the postwar movement to achieve European unity and gives a brief account of the circumstances in which each of the principal European and Atlantic organisations was established.

Those readers who are already familiar with the main outline of events in Europe since 1945 may prefer to concentrate on the chapters which deal with the individual organisations, which are arranged in the following order so as to illustrate certain themes: first, the Economic Commission for Europe (ECE) which illustrates the relationship between Western Europe and Eastern Europe; second, the Organisation for European Economic Co-operation (OEEC) and the Council of Europe, which represent the attempt to establish an intergovernmental framework for all the countries of Western Europe; third the European Economic Community (EEC), the European Coal and Steel Community (ECSC) and the European Atomic Energy Community (Euratom), which represent the theme of supranational or Community Europe; fourth, Western European Union (WEU) and the European Free Trade Association (EFTA) which are the result of Britain's refusal, during the 1950s, to accompany the Six in establishing Community Europe; and finally the North Atlantic Treaty Organisation (NATO) and the Organisation for Economic Co-operation and Development (OECD), which have embodied relations between Western Europe and North America.

Each of the main European and Atlantic organisations is examined separately, with respect toi ts history and achievements. The origins and structure of each organisation and the working methods and techniques devised by them are described, and the study analyses the reasons for the relative success or failure of each organisation in carrying out the tasks allotted to it. The final chapter sets out some of the main conclusions which can be drawn from the history of European unification and of the European and Atlantic organisations in particular. A brief section summarises the role and achievements of the organisations examined in the main body of the book. Readers who wish to obtain a general picture of the process of European unification but do not wish to study the structure and work of each individual organisation in detail are recommended to concentrate on the first and last chapters and on the summary at the end of the book.

The terms 'Europe' and 'Western Europe', which appear frequently in the book, are not closely defined. They are used in the context of the membership of the organisations examined. Except in the case of the Economic Commission for Europe, 'European states' is generally used to denote those states that are not members of the Soviet bloc. When discussing the North Atlantic Treaty Organisation the scope of the report is extended to include Canada and the United States and, besides these two countries, Japan is included in the chapter on the Organisation for Economic Co-operation and Development.

The term 'European organisations' is here taken to mean those organisations working in, and centring on, Europe; thus the Economic Commission for Europe, which is a regional commission of the United Nations, is included though other United Nations agencies are excluded. The smaller organisations whose work has not yet had such a profound impact on the development of European unity, such as the European Launcher Development Organisation (ELDO) and the European Space Research Organisation (ESRO), are not included in the scope of the book.

The text of the book is basically up to date as of 1 January 1967; where major changes have occurred since that date—such as the 1967 British application for membership of the three Communities, the conclusion of the Kennedy Round and the merger of the institutions of the three Communities—further information has been added.

Contents

Detailed List of Contents

Part 1

INTRODUCTION

Chapter One

EUROPEAN UNITY SINCE THE SECOND WORLD WAR

Introduction

At the end of the Second World War the economic and industrial structure of practically all countries of Western Europe had been gravely damaged as a result of the six years of struggle between the Axis powers, Germany and Italy, and the other countries of Europe supported by the United States, the Soviet Union and many countries of the Commonwealth. Of the democratic countries of Western Europe only Britain, apart from the unattacked neutrals—Ireland, Sweden and Switzerland—had escaped invasion and occupation. Apart from the loss of millions of lives and the destruction of the European economy, the Second World War created a profound discontent with the political system under which unbridled national ambitions had twice devastated Europe within a generation. At the end of the war all the European countries which had been involved in it, whether victors or vanquished, were economically exhausted. In this situation two great powers, the United States and the Soviet Union, uneasily confronted each other across Europe, which seemed during the first postwar years to constitute a power vacuum which the Soviet Union might be tempted to fill and then, in the following years, to be an arena in which a fresh struggle might be opened.

The European peoples which had fought to defeat fascism now sought new ideas and a new political system to replace the politically and economically ineffectual governments of the 1930s. In particular, it was hoped that the postwar Europe would be organised in such a way that war between Western European countries could not recur. It was this feeling coupled with the even more urgent need to reconstruct their war-shattered economies that led the countries of Western Europe to start to work together within the framework of international organisations as a means of accomplishing in co-operation, with the financial aid provided by the United States, what they could not separately achieve.

The political weakness of Western Europe, which resulted from the collapse of democratic institutions in Germany and Italy and their replacement by fascist dictatorships, and the capitulation of other governments in the face of the attacks launched upon them by Hitler and Mussolini, meant that it was only with some difficulty that political stability and democratic practices were re-established. At the same time, the Communist parties of Western Europe established strong positions, based partly on their wartime resistance record, and for a period of several years it was feared that Communist governments might come to power in France and Italy, thus opening the way to Russian expansion and the spread of Communist control.

Britain with its prestige as the only major Western European country undefeated at any stage of the war was more strongly placed politically and economically than any of the other Western European countries which had been directly affected by the war. It was thus to Britain that the countries of continental Europe looked, in the first instance, for a lead in the building of the postwar European structure; but Britain was a reluctant leader. Protected by the Channel from invasion during the war, regarding the countries of the continental mainland as being either politically unstable or weak or both, Britain, while willing to take part in limited measures of co-operation, was not prepared to share its political and economic future with two countries which it had helped to defeat in war and a group of other countries which had in turn been defeated by Germany and Italy.

Although Britain's political prestige was at its zenith its economy was not strong. Its industry had not been destroyed but it was badly run-down by the demands of war and when faced by a major crisis such as the hard winter of 1946–47, the limitations of Britain's resources and the need for modernisation became apparent.

Landmarks in the History of European Unity

Confronted with a divided Continent, the countries of Western Europe tackled the tasks of economic recovery and common defence on a new regional basis. The Marshall Plan accelerated the reconstruction of the European economy and led to a very much higher level of intra-European trade. After the Organisation for European Economic Co-operation (OEEC) eliminated most of the quota restrictions on intra-European trade, the formation of the three communities of the Six (Belgium, France, the Federal Republic of Germany, Italy, Luxembourg and the Netherlands), in particular the European Economic Community or Common Market (EEC), has led the participating states far beyond co-operation in economic matters to the creation of a customs union and towards a full economic union. The European Free Trade Association (EFTA) has provided European countries which are not members of the EEC with a mechanism for expanding their intra-area trade and a base from which they hope eventually to negotiate their membership of the EEC.

Driven together by common ideas and common interests but most of all by common disasters and fears, the countries of Western Europe have also in the Brussels Treaty Organisation, the North Atlantic Treaty Organisation (NATO), and Western European Union (WEU) jointly organised their military resources and constructed an integrated common defence system which has effectively deterred the Soviet Union from any expansionist adventures into Western Europe. The United States and Canada have co-operated closely with the countries of Western Europe in assuring the defence of the West.

At the end of the Second World War Europe's most urgent need was to restore its economy. As early as 1943 the United Nations Relief and Rehabilitation Administration (UNRRA) had been set up with the aim of providing the relief supplies and rehabilitation services needed to restart industry and agriculture in the war-devastated countries. The European governments set up three emergency organisations of a specialised kind whose work complemented that of UNRRA. These were the European Central Inland Transport Organisation (ECITO) the European Coal Organisation (ECO) and the Emergency Economic Committee for Europe (EECE).

In 1946 the UNRRA Council decided to terminate its activities by the spring of 1947 and the Temporary Sub-Commission of the United Nations Economic and Social Council recommended that an Economic Commission for Europe (ECE) should be established to facilitate concerted action for the reconstruction of Europe and to raise the level of European economic activity as well as to strengthen the economic relations of the European countries both amongst themselves and with the rest of the world. Those who hoped that ECE, when it was established in March 1947, might succeed in achieving a substantial measure of economic co-operation on an all-European basis, especially in view of the knowledge that the three 'E' organisations would be absorbed by ECE, were quickly disappointed. The political developments in the spring and summer of 1947 already showed, in effect, that the victors of the Second World War no longer maintained their wartime co-operation. Europe was soon divided into two opposing camps. The end of the wartime links of the 'big four' was marked by the failure of the Moscow Conference of the Foreign Ministers in March 1947 and the announcement during the conference of the Truman doctrine.

The fuel crisis in the severe winter of 1946–47 increased existing economic difficulties, and the failure of European crops in the previous summer worsened the world food shortage and forced up world prices to very high levels. The resources that everyone required were available mainly in the United States. Since the outside world was not producing goods which the United States wanted urgently, the consequence was a severe dollar shortage. Sterling convertibility, which was established in the summer of 1947, had to be abandoned. It was clear that a comprehensive and sustained co-operative effort and substantial and continuing financial aid were essential to Europe's economic recovery. Against this background the United States Secretary of State, General George Marshall, speaking at Harvard on 5 June 1947, declared that the United States was willing to support a European recovery programme if the countries of Europe would first reach agreement on the steps they would take to make American aid effective.

Following the lead of the British and French Governments, representatives of sixteen Western European countries met in Paris in July to draw up such a programme. Mr Molotov, the Soviet Foreign Minister, led a delegation to Paris but it was soon clear that the Soviet Government was not prepared to take part in a joint recovery programme and wished each country simply to make a separate estimate of its own economic needs. The other countries of Eastern Europe had no alternative but to follow the Soviet lead and thereafter, except within the framework of ECE, took no part in measures of co-operation with the countries of Western Europe. These set up the Committee of European Economic Co-operation which prepared a report showing the availabilities and requirements of the sixteen Western countries for the next four years. Thus the European recovery programme was born. In the United States the Foreign Assistance Act was passed in 1948 and the Economic Co-operation Administration (ECA) was set up to administer it. After negotiations on the European side, the Organisation for European Economic Co-operation (OEEC) came into being in April 1948.

After its successful administration of Marshall aid, OEEC

succeeded in removing quota restrictions from a high proportion of intra-European trade in industrial goods and in organising a multilateral payments system within Europe which paved the way for the convertibility of European currencies at the end of 1958. Since OEEC was unable to go farther in the freeing of trade or the creation of economic union in Europe, however, the main thrust of economic organisation in Europe passed to the European Economic Community (EEC), which was established in 1958 and which soon led to the establishment of the European Free Trade Association (EFTA) by most of the other OEEC members. With OEEC split effectively into two groups, it was decided to transform the organisation into the Organisation for Economic Co-operation and Development, of which Canada and the United States were also full members. The new body started work in the autumn of 1961.

At the end of the Second World War a large number of unofficial bodies were formed to launch campaigns of education and propaganda for European unity, an idea which had already gained support from those working in the various resistance movements. These bodies joined together to hold a Congress of Europe at The Hague in May 1948. The Congress generated considerable pressure in support of the proposal that the time had come to create a European Assembly, whose task would be to discuss matters of common European concern and to devise measures to bring about the political and economic co-operation of Europe. The French and Belgian Governments in particular pressed for the adoption of this proposal but there were others, including a British one, favouring the establishment of a ministerial governing body. After six months of arduous discussions it was decided to establish a Council of Europe consisting of a Committee of Ministers, meeting in private and responsible only to the member governments, and a Consultative Assembly to deliberate and make recommendations to the Committee of Ministers, but to have no legislative functions. In addition to the five Brussels Treaty powers (Belgium, France, Luxembourg, the Netherlands and the United Kingdom), Denmark, the Irish Republic, Italy, Norway and Sweden signed the Statute of the Council of Europe in May 1949 and the first session of the Consultative Assembly was held at Strasbourg in the following August and September.

In 1947 some of the countries which had not fallen under communist domination became increasingly subjected to Soviet political pressure. It was clear that the Soviet Government would exploit any political or military weakness which might appear in Western Europe and the Eastern Mediterranean. In September 1947 the

Cominform was set up and the Council of Foreign Ministers of the 'Big Four' held its last meeting in London in November and December. The failure of the London Conference led the Western powers to draw closer together. Following proposals put forward by Ernest Bevin early in 1948 to link Britain, France and the Benelux countries (Belgium, Luxembourg and the Netherlands) more closely together, draft treaties were submitted by the British and French Governments for consideration in the Benelux capitals. On 20 February a Communist coup took place in Prague and the fear of war with the Soviet Union increased greatly. These were the circumstances under which the Brussels Treaty was signed in March 1948. The Treaty provided for joint defence against aggression in Europe, for economic, cultural and social co-operation and for the establishment of permanent consultative machinery to carry out its aims. This agreement between Belgium, France, Luxembourg, the Netherlands and the United Kingdom provided an initial Western European defence organisation which was the precursor of the North Atlantic Treaty Organisation and was later the basis of Western European Union.

In 1948 the countries of Western Europe were unable, economically or militarily, to resist the Soviet political and military threat alone. United States aid was necessary to secure Europe's defence and the American Government realised this. On the day the Brussels Treaty was signed President Truman sent a message to the United States Congress in which he referred to the Treaty as an act whose 'significance goes far beyond the actual terms of the agreement itself' and one which 'deserves our full support'. He hoped 'that the United States will, by appropriate means, extend to the free nations the support which the situation requires. I am sure that the determination of the free countries of Europe to protect themselves will be matched by an equal determination on our part to help them to do so'. On 11 June 1948 the Senate passed a resolution, proposed by Senator Vandenberg, in favour of giving military aid to defence pacts made between other members of the United Nations, if it was in the interests of the United States to do so. On 23 June the Russians began the economic blockade of Berlin by stopping rail traffic between the city and the western zones of occupation. Representatives of the five Brussels Treaty powers began to hold informal discussions with representatives of the United States and Canada in July, against the background of the tightening Soviet blockade which was maintained for nearly a year until overcome by the Allied air-lift. The North Atlantic Treaty was signed in April 1949 and in this way the nucleus of Western union created at Brussels the previous year led to an Atlantic Alliance bringing the United States and Canada into a close relationship with Western Europe.

Strenuous efforts made in the Council of Europe to reconcile the federal and functional[1] approaches to European unity were felt to have reached a dead-end when M. Paul-Henri Spaak, frustrated by the reluctance of the British and Scandinavians to move towards a United States of Europe, resigned from the Presidency of the Consultative Assembly in 1951, and from that time the idea of the supranational[2] Communities of the Six gained momentum. Although there have been customs unions in Europe in the past and although Belgium, Luxembourg and the Netherlands had agreed in 1944 to establish a Benelux Customs Union[3] which came into effect in 1948, the ideas which were put forward by the French Government in 1950 were different in kind and in degree from any previous models since they aimed at the eventual achievement of full political and economic integration between the participating nations.

When the British and some other governments had shown that they would not move beyond limited measures of co-operation to measures of integration M. Robert Schuman, the French Foreign Minister, and M. Jean Monnet, Commissaire au Plan in France, urged the introduction of the new 'Community approach'. By placing one or more sectors of the economy under the control of a supranational authority they hoped to convince the participating governments of the advantages of economic integration and thus prompt them to take further steps in other economic sectors leading ultimately to the merging of national sovereignties in a political federation. The French Government's proposals, put forward by M. Schuman in May 1950, by which the resources of the French and German coal and steel industries were to be placed under a common

[1] The 'federal approach' aimed at creating a federated United States of Europe: the 'functional approach' advocated intergovernmental co-operation over limited and specific matters, such as the liberalisation of import quotas.

[2] Throughout this study the term 'supranational' is applied to the European Communities, in which the independent executives acting jointly with the member governments together exercise certain powers previously exercised solely by national governments, and in which decisions of the ministerial body, including a number of decision of political importance, are binding on the member governments and in some cases may be taken by majority vote.

[3] In September 1944 the wartime governments of these three countries, at that time in exile in London, signed an agreement providing for the creation of a Customs Union. The Union, which came into effect in January 1948, eliminated all customs duties between its three constituent states and introduced a uniform tariff schedule for imported goods.

authority in an organisation open to other European countries, constituted a major initiative on which the subsequent development of the three Communities of the Six has been based and which introduced the new political concept of integration within a Community.

The French Government's proposals were motivated in part by the hope, expressed by M. Schuman on 9 May 1950, that 'the solidarity in production thus established will make it plain that any war between France and Germany becomes not merely unthinkable but materially impossible'. This underlying theme of Franco-German *rapprochement* became one of the main threads running through the development of the European Communities and European unification in general. The plan was also warmly welcomed by those in France who realised that, with the ending of international controls over German heavy industry, Germany could not long be denied full and equal rights to control its own coal and steel production. They were quite prepared, therefore, to make concessions of national sovereignty in these sectors to a supranational body if Germany would do the same. With the signing of the Treaty establishing the European Coal and Steel Community (ECSC) in April 1951 the Six made it clear (in the Preamble to the Treaty) that this move was only a beginning. Their joint aim was now the establishment of a full European Economic Community which, in its turn, was to be a step to political integration. The British Government was not prepared to accept either the ultimate objective of the Community or the transfer of control over the British coal and steel industries which membership of the new organisation required. The British Government's decision not to take part in this plan was to prove more far-reaching than it seemed at the time. It meant that Britain was excluded, from the very beginning, from the cumulative process of integration on which the Six were launched with the establishment of the ECSC. It marked the clear division, which was to last for many years and which has not yet been resolved, between those countries which were prepared to 'make Europe' and those which were not prepared to go beyond measures of intergovernmental co-operation.

The outbreak of war in Korea in June 1950 led to a demand by the American Government for a German contribution to the defence of the central European front. The French refused to agree to the re-armament of Germany and to its becoming a member of NATO. Parliamentary and public feeling in Britain was uneasy. The Germans, who were in any case reluctant, would not re-arm unless they had full equality of rights. As a way out of this impasse M. René

Pleven proposed, in October 1950, on behalf of the French Government, the creation of a European army to which each participating state would contribute its European military forces and which would be under joint control. The French Government convened a conference on the 'Pleven Plan' in Paris in February 1951 and by November the six members of ECSC had agreed to contribute defined forces to a European army. In December the Foreign Ministers of the Six affirmed their intention to set up a European Defence Community (EDC) under the control of a joint Defence Commission and a Council of Ministers, with an Assembly and a Court of Justice parallel to the institutions of the ECSC. The treaty was signed in May 1952. Although the British Government expressed its desire to see the EDC Treaty ratified and offered the close co-operation of its forces on the Continent, its refusal to participate in an integrated European army was one of the main reasons which led to the failure of the EDC. Successive French Governments were doubtful of their ability to secure a favourable vote for the Treaty in the French Assembly and it was not submitted for ratification until August 1954, when a combination of Gaullists, Communists and some Socialists and Radicals succeeded in rejecting it. One of the main arguments employed by those who spoke against the EDC Treaty at that time was that France could not take part in a European army which included Germany unless Britain was also a member.

The Foreign Ministers of the Six had begun to examine the possibility of setting up a European Political Community before the EDC Treaty was presented to the national parliaments for ratification. They invited the Common Assembly of the ECSC in conjunction with a number of co-opted members of the Consultative Assembly of the Council of Europe to study the creation of a European Political Authority: this became the *Ad Hoc* Assembly. In March 1953 the *Ad Hoc* Assembly made detailed proposals to the Foreign Ministers of the Six, including the establishment of a European Political Community (EPC) which would incorporate the functions of the ECSC and the EDC. Its Parliament was to be directly elected and the supreme executive authority was to be vested in a European Executive Council and a Council of National Ministers. The Assembly proposals took the form of a *Draft Treaty embodying the Statute of the European Community*. This ambitious attempt to extend the sphere of supranational control depended on the European Defence Community coming into being, and when the EDC Treaty was rejected the EPC project collapsed as well.

The rejection of the EDC Treaty by the French National Assembly was, perhaps, the greatest single setback to the 'making of Europe'. Had the treaty come into force a fully integrated European army would have been established, under single command, in the mid-1950s, and the political decisions governing its use would have been in the hands of the European Political Community. These two developments together would have implied the achievement in large measure of the final political integration aimed at by the originators of the 'Schuman Plan'. At no time since have the circumstances and the political will of the governments concerned been such as to permit the taking of such far-reaching measures.

The failure of the EDC made the problem of re-arming Germany in a manner acceptable to the French one of extreme urgency to those countries which bore the main responsibility for maintaining NATO defence. Sir Anthony Eden[1] immediately convened a conference of the powers most directly concerned and in October 1954 these negotiations resulted in the signing of the Paris Agreements. By these agreements the Brussels Treaty Organisation was modified and extended to include the Federal Republic of Germany and Italy in a new intergovernmental organisation, Western European Union, which was militarily to be an integral part of the wider NATO defence system. Germany was admitted to NATO and, as a balance to a German army, Britain agreed to maintain specified military forces on the European mainland. This commitment represented a new departure in Britain's European policy as did the agreement of the British Government to permit the Council of WEU to exercise a veto over the withdrawal of British forces from the Continent. The new WEU was also to promote European integration and to carry on the social and cultural work of its predecessor, the Brussels Treaty Organisation. Its main purpose, though, was to provide a European framework in which Germany could be re-armed and become a member of NATO, while providing also for British military participation to relieve French fears that there would be no check or balance to possible German predominance. In Eastern Europe, the Paris Agreements and Germany's admission to NATO were immediately countered by the formation of the Warsaw Pact, a treaty of friendship, co-operation and mutual assistance which provided for collective security arrangements between the Soviet Union and seven of its allies.

After the failure of the plans to establish supranational defence and political authorities, those who were anxious to extend the integration achieved in the ECSC returned to the economic sphere. In June

[1] Later Lord Avon.

1955 the Foreign Ministers of the Six met at Messina and proposed plans to establish a common market and an atomic energy pool. M. Paul-Henri Spaak, at that time Belgian Foreign Minister, was appointed Chairman of a special group to consider how these proposals could best be realised. The withdrawal in November 1955 of the British observer from the meetings of this group only served to confirm the breach which had opened up between the Six and Britain since the establishment of the ECSC. The ensuing *Spaak Report*[1] was the foundation on which the subsequent negotiations between the six countries were based. After long and complicated negotiations, which involved much hard bargaining, the Treaty establishing the European Economic Community (EEC) was signed in Rome on 25 March 1957. Ratification proceeded without setbacks and the EEC came into being in January 1958; the tariff provisions of the treaty came into operation from January 1959, so starting the process of eliminating all tariffs on trade between members of the EEC and of aligning the separate tariffs of the member states to a common external tariff to be applied to the outside world. The proposals made at Messina for creating an atomic energy pool were followed by negotiations which were carried out concurrently with those for the EEC Treaty, and which led to the signing of the Treaty establishing Euratom in Rome on the same date. In Euratom the Six aimed to develop the peaceful uses of nuclear energy jointly under supranational control.

Since its establishment the EEC has set the pace for European integration. It has moved ahead of its original time-table in the progressive elimination of tariffs on trade between its members and has simultaneously organised the progressive harmonisation of the individual national tariffs of its members on imports from the outside world, towards a common external tariff. Apart from the successful application of its customs union provisions, the EEC has, despite protracted negotiations and some setbacks, practically completed its common agricultural policy. Common transport and energy policies are being formulated and the idea of a common monetary policy is under study. The Community has, in practice, proved to be a major political force both through the decisions it has taken on issues such as the levels of target prices for agricultural products within the Community area and those that it has been called upon to take in world affairs, such as the negotiating mandate given by the Council to the Commission concerning the Kennedy Round of tariff

[1] *Comité Intergouvernemental créé par la conférence de Messine, Rapport des Chefs de Délégation aux Ministres des Affaires Etrangères*, Brussels, 21 April 1956.

negotiations in GATT. In the first nine years of its history the EEC has already created, through the application of the Rome Treaty and through its Community working methods, a new entity which is engaged in integrating the economies of its six member states. If this process is completed the Six will become one state in economic terms *vis-à-vis* the rest of the world.

When the Six started in 1955 to consider the creation of a customs union some of the other members of OEEC accelerated the studies which a group of low-tariff countries (the Benelux countries, Denmark, Sweden and Switzerland) had already begun on the possibility of cutting tariffs on products of particular importance in intra-European trade—tariffs now assuming especial importance following the 90 per cent liberalisation of quotas achieved in 1955. Tariff reductions on these products would be generalised to other members of the GATT. These countries, in common with other non-Six members of OEEC outside the Six, were anxious to avoid the adverse effects on their intra-European trade that they feared would result from the creation of a customs union of the Six inside which goods would flow freely without tariff barriers, protected by quotas and a common external tariff which would operate against them. Although the 'low-tariff club' plan was consistent with the GATT it was not acceptable to Britain, a lower proportion of whose trade was with its European partners than was the case with most OEEC countries. After it became clear that the GATT tariff negotiations, which started early in 1956, would not result in further major reductions in the near future the low tariff countries in OEEC pressed Britain to pursue the possibility of establishing a free trade area in which tariff and other barriers to trade would be eliminated on a wider European basis, and in which the participating countries would retain the right to negotiate their separate commercial policies with the outside world. After the publication of the *Spaak Report*, the Council of OEEC appointed a working party, in July 1956, to study possible forms and methods of association between the proposed European Economic Community and the other countries of OEEC. The working party proposed, in January 1957, the formation of a 'free trade area' between all OEEC countries.

In October 1957 the Council of OEEC set up an Intergovernmental Ministerial Committee under the Chairmanship of Mr Reginald Maudling, the British Paymaster-General, to negotiate a free trade agreement. Negotiations proved difficult and in particular it was impossible to reconcile the positions of the British and French Governments. In December 1958 the negotiations were terminated after the French Government had stated that it was not possible to form a free trade area between members of the EEC and the other countries of OEEC in the absence of a common external tariff and economic and social harmonisation.

In order to protect their trade in the light of the tariff and quota discrimination to which the implementation of the Rome Treaty would lead, the Swedish and British Governments took the lead in arranging discussions with Austria, Denmark, Norway and Switzerland with the aim of creating an industrial free trade area. The form and scope of a free trade association had already been thoroughly discussed in the meetings of the Maudling Committee and solutions had been worked out to the principal problems. Plans for the creation of a European Free Trade Association were completed in June 1959. Ministers from these countries and Portugal approved the plan on 21 July at Stockholm and the Convention establishing the European Free Trade Association (EFTA) was signed on 4 January 1960 and came into force on 3 May of that year. The purpose was not only to safeguard and increase the European trade of the members of EFTA but also to provide them with a common base from which to try to come to terms with the EEC, though in practice the obligations of EFTA membership have seemed to be a hindrance rather than a help to Britain, Austria and perhaps Denmark in their relations with the Six.

Once the EEC was firmly established its members began to feel the need to strengthen political consultation between the Six. General de Gaulle took the initiative, following bilateral talks with the governments of the other five member states of the Community in the summer and autumn of 1960, about the possibility of setting up a supreme authority to formulate common foreign and defence policies. A 'European Summit Conference' of the Six was held in February 1961 in Paris between the Heads of State or Government and the Foreign Ministers. After discussing the French Government's proposals the Conference established a committee to examine the problem of political co-operation under the chairmanship of M. Christian Fouchet, a French civil servant.[1] A second 'Summit' was held at Bad Godesberg, near Bonn, on 18 July 1961. The Bonn Declaration issued at the end of this meeting contained three decisions. First, to organise political co-operation between the Six on a regular basis leading to the adoption of a common foreign policy.

[1] M. Fouchet was followed as Chairman of the Committee by Signor Attilio Cattani, an Italian civil servant, and the Committee has often been referred to as the Fouchet/Cattani Committee.

Second, that the Heads of State or of Government should meet at regular intervals 'to compare their views, to concert their policies and to reach common decisions in order to further the political union of Europe, thereby strengthening the Atlantic Alliance'. Co-operation between the Six was also to be extended to the domains of education, culture and scientific research. Third, the Fouchet Committee was instructed to submit proposals on 'the means which will, as soon as possible, enable a statutory character to be given to the union of their peoples'. While formalising the French initiative for a political *relance*, the Bonn Declaration placed the development of European political and defence co-operation within the context of the Atlantic Alliance and by speaking of the unification of European peoples encouraged 'Europeans' to hope that the Fouchet Committee's proposals would be in the Community mould.

In November 1961 the French Government put forward a 'Draft Treaty establishing a Union of States' to the Fouchet Committee. The proposed Union was decidedly not of a supranational character. The decisions of its Council would be taken by unanimity. The European Political Commission which would provide the Secretariat of the Union would be composed of national civil servants. The Belgian and Dutch delegations to the Fouchet Committee objected that such a secretariat would not be independent, like the executives of the three Communities, and that because of its composition it would be subject to national pressures.

The Dutch and German delegations criticised the draft treaty since it spoke of 'a common defence policy' outside the framework of NATO. All five of France's partners criticised the vagueness of the proposals for the revision of the Treaty three years after its entry into force; they feared that at the time of the proposed revision the competence of the EEC, the ECSC and Euratom might be transferred to the ministerial body of the Union, and opposed such a move.

The French Government proposed a revised draft treaty in January 1962. The 'Five' considered the second French draft to be less acceptable than the first. They submitted an alternative draft treaty at the same time. Whereas the second French draft retained the same essential features as its predecessor, the alternative treaty stated that a common defence policy should either be carried out within the framework of the Atlantic Alliance or contribute to strengthening it. The 'Five' regarded their draft treaty as the first step to a closer form of union and emphasised that its revision should ensure the eventual development of the union in a federal direction. The text of the 'Five' proposed that the Council should eventually take its decisions by majority vote, and that there should be an independent Secretary General to be assisted by an independent secretariat.

After General de Gaulle and Chancellor Adenauer had attempted to resolve the deadlock between France and the 'Five' which had been reached in the Fouchet Committee, negotiations on the establishment of a political union ended at a meeting of the Foreign Ministers of the Six in Paris on 17 April 1962. The meeting broke down over two issues: no agreement could be reached between France and the 'Five' concerning the revision clause, and Belgium and the Netherlands refused to commit themselves to any form of political union until Britain had become a member of the EEC and could take a full part in the discussions.

On 31 July 1961 Mr Harold Macmillan had informed the House of Commons that the British Government had decided to apply to join the EEC if satisfactory arrangements could be made to meet the special needs of the United Kingdom, of the Commonwealth and of EFTA. The British application was accompanied by applications for membership of the EEC by the Danish, Irish and Norwegian Governments. Applications for association with the EEC were made, in September 1961, by Austria, Sweden and Switzerland whose anxiety not to undertake obligations incompatible with their status of neutrality precluded them from applying for full membership. Attention was concentrated on the course of the negotiations between Britain and the EEC which were in some ways to be a model for arrangements between the EEC and the other applicant countries, which felt that they were in no position to join or to become associated with the EEC without Britain.

The intergovernmental conference between the Governments of the EEC and the British Government and at which the EEC Commission was present opened on 10 October 1961. It was to last fifteen months. In his opening statement Mr Edward Heath, who led the British delegation, said that the British Government accepted without qualification the aims set out in Articles 2 and 3 of the Rome Treaty, including the elimination of internal tariffs, the adoption of a common customs tariff and a common commercial policy and the adoption of a common agricultural policy, and that Britain was ready to accept and play a full part in the community institutions. He said, however, that Britain had to negotiate special arrangements concerning British agriculture and the interests of Commonwealth and EFTA countries, though Mr Heath recognised that these arrangements must be compatible with the Common Market. In view of the rest of his long and complex statement[1] it was not, however, altogether clear whether the British Government was going to require sweeping exceptions for the Commonwealth or how far Britain was really prepared to accept the common external tariff and the common agricultural policy. In May 1962 Mr Heath stated to the Council of WEU that Britain was also prepared to take part in a European political union with the members of the EEC. When, after months of discussion, the negotiations adjourned for the summer recess in August 1962, all the points affecting the Commonwealth had been fully discussed so that the British negotiators had a good idea of the arrangements they would be able to negotiate. The principles to be applied to temperate-zone agricultural imports were settled, as were the arrangements for manufactures from the developed countries of the Commonwealth (Australia, Canada and New Zealand). The arrangements to be made for imports from India, Pakistan and Ceylon were also largely agreed. The terms for 'association' with Commonwealth countries were fairly clear, and it was also clear which of those countries would be offered association by the Six. The 'outline' agreement which the British Government sought to achieve by the recess had not, however, been achieved.

When the negotiations were resumed at the end of September it was primarily the problem of British domestic agriculture that still had to be settled. The Six insisted that deficiency payments to British farmers should end immediately Britain joined the Community, to be replaced by the Community support system at higher price levels, whereas the British proposed a progressive reduction in deficiency payments until 1970. On 14 January 1963, General de Gaulle in a press conference made it clear that he was not prepared to agree to British membership of the EEC. On 16 January the French Foreign Minister, M. Maurice Couve de Murville, called for the suspension of the negotiations on the grounds that they could not succeed. Although France's partners did not accept this view, the French Government maintained its position and since unanimity was needed if a new member was to be admitted, the negotiations were formally suspended on 29 January, together with the negotiations which Britain had also been conducting for membership of the ECSC and Euratom. The negotiations between the EEC and Denmark, Ireland and Norway also lapsed at this time as did the applications for association made by Austria, Sweden and Switzerland. The view expressed by Professor Hallstein, President of the EEC Commission,

[1] *The United Kingdom and the European Economic Community*, Cmnd. 1565, HMSO, November 1961.

when he reported to the European Parliament in March 1963, was that when the negotiations with Britain were suspended it was impossible to be certain that they would have succeeded: but it was equally certain that they had not failed.

General de Gaulle has not clarified his reasons for breaking off the negotiations in these circumstances. It is possible, though far from certain, that his decision was largely influenced or confirmed by the agreement that had been reached between Mr Macmillan and President Kennedy at Nassau on 21 December 1962, by which the United States agreed to supply Britain with Polaris missiles, to be armed with British nuclear warheads and mounted in submarines.[1] Britain and the United States had also agreed to develop 'a NATO multilateral force in the closest consultation with the other allies', to which the British Polaris submarines were pledged. This force was also to include the British Bomber Command, some American strategic forces and some European tactical forces. General de Gaulle's objections to the Nassau Agreement were plainly stated at his Press Conference in January 1963. It is equally possible, however, that the General seized upon this as a pretext to keep a rival out of the Community at a time when Britain looked like negotiating its way in.

Immediately after General de Gaulle announced his intention to exclude Britain from the Community of the Six, the French and German Governments signed the Franco-German Treaty on 22 January 1963: the sole outcome of the attempts made in the Fouchet Committee to create a European Political Union. The Treaty provided for regular consultations between the two governments concerning foreign affairs and defence and was to launch an ambitious programme of cultural co-operation. Although the Treaty was welcomed to the extent that it provided further evidence of a rapprochement between France and Germany, it aroused opposition and suspicion from many 'Europeans'[2] who saw in it the danger of a bilateral alignment that could undermine the working of the 'Community method' in the EEC and threaten the solidarity of the Atlantic Alliance. Some fears of this kind were voiced in the Bundestag, which, when ratifying the Treaty on 8 May 1963, insisted on adding a

[1] 'Mr Macmillan came to tell me that we were right to set up our nuclear striking forces. "We also have our own", he told me. "We must unite them in a European framework independent of America." He left me to go immediately to the Bahamas. Naturally what happened there changed the spirit of my press conference of 14 January.' André Passeron, *De Gaulle Parle*, Paris, Fayard, p. 199.

[2] Those who support the supranational elements of the European Communities, including those who wish to create an eventual federal United States of Europe.

Preamble stating that the Treaty's application should further the ideas of European integration and of Atlantic partnership and, in defence matters, should not derogate from NATO. Although the French Government in particular had great hopes that the Treaty would lead to close and fruitful co-operation between France and Germany in political and defence matters, its practical results have been limited.

The difference of attitude towards European integration on the part of the French Government and the five other members of the EEC was the cause of a severe crisis[1] that erupted in the Community in 1965. From the end of June 1965 to January 1966 the preparation and taking of new policy decisions in the EEC was blocked by the partial withdrawal of the French Government from the Community's institutions. This crisis was brought about by the failure of the Council to meet the deadline of 30 June set for the completion of the regulations concerning the financing of the common agricultural policy, but in reality it was due to a clash between France and the five over the political and institutional nature of the Community and its future role. The French Government wanted to ensure that, as a condition for its agreement to a resumption of progress in the work of the EEC, the Treaty should be revised so as to perpetuate the national veto on decisions of major importance. After a meeting of the Foreign Ministers of the Six at Luxembourg in January 1966 at which no final agreement was reached about the basic issues of the dispute, France agreed to resume its place in the Community and the normal work of the EEC continued.

The crisis in the EEC was swiftly followed by a crisis in NATO. For many years the French Government had criticised the structure of the Atlantic Alliance. In order to meet the widespread European desire for a more equal relationship with America, President Kennedy proposed in 1962 the establishment of an Atlantic partnership, to be based on co-operation between the United States and the 'new union now emerging in Europe'. This idea received a setback with the veto on British membership of the EEC; also the military aspect of the partnership proposal, the project for a multilateral nuclear force (MLF) in which there would be European participation but whose use would be subject to an American veto, was supported by neither the British nor the French Government. The British Government made a counter-proposal for an Atlantic Nuclear Force (ANF), but General de Gaulle decided drastically to reduce French participation in NATO. On 10 and 29 March 1966, the French Government stated in

[1] This crisis is analysed in detail in M. Camps, *European Unification in the Sixties*, New York, McGraw-Hill for Council on Foreign Relations, 1966.

two memoranda that, while remaining a member of the Alliance, France would withdraw, which it did, from the integrated command structure of the Organisation on 1 July 1966. The immediate reaction of France's fourteen allies was to declare that they would maintain the integrated military structure, although the French Government's action has raised questions about the future of the Alliance which are not yet resolved.

The breaking off of the Brussels negotiations in January 1963 had caused great disappointment in the countries which had applied for membership of the EEC, as well as leading to a bitter controversy within the EEC itself. But it was not long before there was a renewal of interest among a number of the EFTA countries in the possibility of membership of the EEC or association with it. In 1965 the Austrian Government resumed its application for association with the EEC and negotiations on possible terms are in progress. Denmark, suffering pressure on its agricultural exports to the EEC, has made clear its continuing desire for membership. 1965 and 1966 witnessed a reawakening in Britain of interest in membership of the EEC, and on 10 November 1966 Mr Harold Wilson announced in the House of Commons that the British Government would undertake a high-level approach to the EEC countries to explore the possibility of negotiations for membership. The meeting of the EFTA Council held in London, at the level of Prime Ministers, on 5 and 6 December 1966, endorsed this British initiative.[1]

Thus the future relations between Britain and the Six are, as this book is completed, again in the melting pot. This relationship has already emerged as one of the main factors underlying the development of the European organisations. Closely linked with it, and equally important, has been the controversy about the relative merits of intergovernmental and supranational forms of organisation. A third underlying factor is the relationship of the countries of Western Europe with the United States; and a fourth is the relationship of both with Russia and the other countries of Eastern Europe. The following chapters show how important these factors have been in determining the membership and structure of the European organisations and how their progress has been conditioned by the great changes in these elements that have taken place in the past twenty years.

[1] On 2 May 1967 the British Government, following the series of visits by the Prime Minister and Foreign Secretary to the capitals of the Six, announced its decision to apply for full membership of the three Communities. On 10 May the Commons endorsed this decision by a vote of 488 to 62, and the application was presented to the Communities in Brussels on the following day.

Part 2

EUROPE, EAST AND WEST

Chapter Two

THE ECONOMIC COMMISSION FOR EUROPE

The Origins

At the first meeting of the General Assembly of the United Nations in London in January 1946, it was generally realised that the reconstruction of the war-devastated countries could not wait for the development of the United Nations Organisation. Three European emergency economic organisations were already, in 1946, carrying out relief and reconstruction work in Europe. These were the European Coal Organisation (ECO), the European Central Inland Transport Organisation (ECITO) and the Emergency Economic Committee for Europe (EECE). These organisations did not include all the European member countries of the United Nations (the Soviet Union was, for instance, a member of ECITO but not of the other two) and their scope did not cover the whole range of the economic problems of the devastated areas. It seemed natural, in fact, to bring together these emergency organisations as parts of a more permanent all-European body. The case for establishing an all-European economic organisation was strengthened by the decision, in 1945, to bring the work of the United Nations Relief and Rehabilitation Administration (UNRRA) to an end by the spring of 1947. This decision was confirmed at the fifth session of the UNRRA Council in 1946. The Soviet Union was anxious that any new organisation concerned with all-European economic co-operation should be set up within the framework of the United Nations, and the USSR used the fact that it did not take part in ECO and EECE as an argument for United Nations sponsorship of such a body.

On 2 February 1946, the General Assembly unanimously passed a resolution on reconstruction which stated that:

'only full scale and whole-hearted co-operation of all Members of the United Nations can solve the urgent and grave problems of economic reconstruction of the Member countries of the United Nations.'

At the first opportunity the Economic and Social Council and one of its principal subsidiary bodies, the Economic and Employment Commission, reviewed the position, and on 21 June 1946 the Council established the Temporary Sub-Commission on the Economic Reconstruction of Devastated Areas, which was to examine all the relevant facts and report back to the Council.

After on-the-spot investigations in several European countries, the Sub-Commission drew up the *Preliminary Report on Economic Reconstruction of Devastated Areas*. This report was the first comprehensive study of the economic situation of the devastated European countries. In September 1946, the Sub-Commission recommended the establishment of a European economic commission—a recommendation which reflected the prevalent feeling at the United Nations that European problems should be dealt with on a regional rather than on a world-wide basis—and on 11 December the General Assembly of the United Nations unanimously recommended that:

'in order to give effective aid to the countries devastated by the war, the Economic and Social Council, at its next session, give prompt and favourable consideration to the establishment of an Economic Commission for Europe.'

At its fourth session the Council adopted on 28 March 1947 a resolution establishing the Economic Commission for Europe (ECE) and setting out its terms of reference.

At the time when ECE was set up it was hoped that such a body might increase the chance of a general settlement of some of the major European economic issues. The membership and terms of reference of ECE gave grounds for hope that it might prove a means for achieving all-European economic co-operation. The British Foreign Office had its doubts from the beginning whether these hopes corresponded to the political realities of the situation, while such hopes as Ernest Bevin, the British Foreign Secretary, and James Byrnes, the American Secretary of State, may have had were disappointed at the Moscow Conference of March/April 1947. Had the Soviet Union agreed to participate in a European recovery programme, following the Marshall offer, the programme later carried out through the Organisation for European Economic Co-operation might have been implemented under the auspices of ECE. At that time a variety of proposals were made linking a European recovery programme with ECE, but the United States Government, although anxious to provide a massive aid programme, did not want to entrust its supervision to ECE, in which the East–West political split was evident from the start.

The rejection of the Marshall offer by the Soviet bloc at the Paris Conference of July 1947 was the turning-point in the early history of ECE: a region-wide organisation could not administer a recovery programme for half its members only. Consequently, the work of ECE has been confined to problems considered ripe for action on this broader basis, while in both Western and Eastern Europe sub-regional organisations have been used as a means of more intensive co-operation.

The first Executive Secretary of ECE, Professor Gunnar Myrdal, commented that:

'The go-ahead signal of the Economic and Social Council in March 1947 was probably given at almost the last moment when an agreement between the World Powers to set up an all-European economic organisation was politically possible.'[1]

It was, therefore, not surprising that the work of ECE was restricted to such fields as research, the allocation of scarce materials in times of shortage and the work of the technical committees. Its very survival during the earlier years of its existence might be considered surprising in view of the political atmosphere. None of the member governments, however, wished to recognise the split between the Eastern and Western Powers as permanent. ECE was therefore kept in existence and given work to do in the hope, which later proved justified, that it might eventually help to bridge the gap.

The Terms of Reference

The opening paragraph of the terms of reference sets out the purpose and main tasks of the Commission:

'The Economic Commission for Europe, acting within the framework of the policies of the United Nations and subject to the general supervision of the Council shall, provided that the Commission takes

[1] *ECE—The First Ten Years*, Geneva, United Nations, 1957, Chapter 1, p. 10.

no action in respect of any country without the agreement of that country:

(*a*) Initiate and participate in measures for facilitating concerted action for the economic reconstruction of Europe, for raising the level of European economic activity, and for maintaining and strengthening the economic relations of the European countries both among themselves and with other countries of the world;

(*b*) Make or sponsor such investigations and studies of economic and technological problems of, and developments within, member countries of the Commission and within Europe generally as the Commission deems appropriate;

(*c*) Undertake or sponsor the collection, evaluation and dissemination of such economic, technological and statistical information as the Commission deems appropriate.'

Article 2 called upon ECE to 'give prior consideration during its initial stages to measures facilitating the economic reconstruction of devastated countries of Europe which are members of the United Nations'.

Article 3 laid down that immediately following its establishment the Commission should:

'Consult with the member Governments of the Emergency Economic Committee for Europe, the European Coal Organisation and the European Central Inland Transport Organisation with a view to the prompt termination of the first, and the absorption or termination of the activities of the second and third, while ensuring that the essential work performed by each of the three is fully maintained.'

Shortly after its establishment ECE took over the work of these bodies —the tasks of the ECO and ECITO being given to two of the Technical Committees set up by ECE.

Article 4 empowers the Commission to:

'make recommendations on any matter within its competence directly to its member governments, governments admitted in a consultative capacity . . . and the specialised agencies concerned. The Commission shall submit for the Council's prior consideration any of its proposals for activities that would have important effects on the economy of the world as a whole.'

Article 6 directs the Commission to submit an annual report to the Economic and Social Council, but does not provide for any other contact between the Commission and the Council or for the control of the Commission's work by the Council. Articles 5 and 15 empowered the Commission to draw up its own rules of procedure and to 'establish such subsidiary bodies as it deems appropriate' to carry out its functions. The looseness of the relationship between the Commission and the Council, reflected in these articles, has been primarily responsible for the considerable degree of independence and initiative assumed by the Commission. Other articles state that 'the administrative budget of the Commission shall be financed from the funds of the United Nations', and that the staff of the Commission shall be appointed by the Secretary General of the United Nations and shall form part of the Secretariat of the United Nations.

Although ECE's terms of reference have allowed the Commission great freedom to choose the means it uses to achieve its ends, these ends are limited and closely defined. ECE, alone of the organisations examined in this book, is responsible to a parent body, the Economic and Social Council of the United Nations. The Commission is empowered only to make recommendations to member governments, and its scope is restricted, like that of other intergovernmental organisations, by the requirement that it 'takes no action in respect of any country without the agreement of that country'.

MEMBERSHIP

Full membership of the Commission was originally restricted to the European members of the United Nations and the United States, but provision was made for participation of other states in a consultative capacity.

The original members of the ECE were: Belgium, Byelorussian SSR, Czechoslovakia, Denmark, France, Greece, Iceland, Luxembourg, the Netherlands, Norway, Poland, the Soviet Union, Sweden, Turkey, Ukrainian SSR, the United Kingdom, the United States of America and Yugoslavia. From 1947 certain other countries were regularly invited to participate in a consultative capacity under Article 8 of the ECE terms of reference. These were: Albania, Austria, Bulgaria, Finland, Hungary, Ireland, Italy, Portugal, Roumania and Switzerland. In 1954 the Economic and Social Council decided that certain non-member countries of the United Nations could become, on request, full members of the Commission: this applied to Austria, Finland, Ireland, Italy and Portugal. Albania, Bulgaria, Hungary,

Roumania and Spain became members of both the United Nations and of ECE in December 1955. A special decision of the Economic and Social Council in December 1955 enabled the Federal Republic of Germany to become a member of the Commission in the following February. Cyprus became a member of both the United Nations and ECE in 1960, and Malta in 1965. Attempts to make it possible for Eastern Germany to become either a member of ECE or to participate in a consultative or observer capacity were rejected. In practice experts from Eastern Germany took part in the technical activities of ECE up to 1958, but did so as experts from the 'Eastern Zone' of Germany under Art. 10 of the terms of reference, as experts from the Federal Republic of Germany had also done, as from the 'Western Zones' of Germany until 1955, under this same article.

One of the distinctive features of ECE is its membership. It is the only European organisation in which the Western powers and the Eastern European countries can discuss common problems and take joint action and the main value of ECE has, perhaps, been as a forum for discussing economic co-operation on an all-European basis.

The Institutions

The institutions of ECE consist of the Commission, the Technical Committees and their sub-organs and the Secretariat. The Commission is the policy-making and supervisory body of ECE. It reviews the economic situation in Europe and authorises and examines the work of the Technical Committees. In ECE, the Technical Committees are responsible for most of the proposals for action; the Secretariat services the Technical Committees and also, mainly through its Research Division, carries out research on its own initiative.

THE COMMISSION

The Commission, which normally meets once a year in Geneva, consists of representatives of each full member country and of Switzerland. These representatives are frequently of ministerial level though in most cases governments are represented by senior officials. The chairman and vice-chairman of the Commission are elected at its first meeting every year. Each member of the Commission has one vote, and decisions are taken by a majority of members present and voting. Besides decisions concerning its proceedings the Commission takes decisions, generally in the form of resolutions, addressed to the Economic and Social Council, or to participating governments or, in the form of instructions, to the Executive Secretary.

Although in the early years of ECE draft resolutions were quite often rejected by a majority or were adopted by a majority against a minority vote, this has become rare. Since 1957, resolutions have been adopted either by unanimity or with a small number of abstentions. In the Technical Committees and their sub-organs voting has never been the regular practice.

The only effective difference between full and 'consultative' members of the Commission is that whereas since March 1952 the latter have been able to vote at meetings of the Technical Committees they cannot vote at meetings of the Commission. As indicated above voting is, in any case, rare in the Technical Committees. The right to vote has, however, a certain significance in view of the political nature or implications of the issues voted on at the annual session of the Commission.

The Commission holds an annual public session, which lasts for about two and a half weeks. Representatives of non-governmental organisations and the specialised agencies of the United Nations are invited to attend these sessions; they may take part in the discussions, which are in three official languages, English, French and Russian, but have no voting rights. At these sessions the Commission discusses the annual *Economic Survey* and the work of the Technical Committees. It also discusses the work programme of the Commission as a whole. At these meetings governments put forward proposals for new activities. Although the Commission has the authority to control the activities of the Technical Committees, in practice it makes no attempt to lay down their policy.

Although in the early years of ECE many of the debates in the Commission served to provide opportunities for exchanges of invective and propaganda between the East and the West, since the mid 1950s this has become rare. The replacing of 'cold war' attitudes by an increasing desire on the part of governments to co-operate not only on technical but also policy matters across ideological frontiers led to more fruitful meetings of the Commission, although differences of view between governments concerning the aims and scope of ECE's development have persisted.

Originally it had been intended that the Commission should meet frequently at regular intervals like the Council of OEEC, but when the first Executive Secretary, Professor Myrdal, realised that the Commission was at that time little more than a political debating forum he persuaded the member governments to allow the Technical

Committees far greater autonomy and the pattern of annual meetings was established.

THE TECHNICAL COMMITTEES

ECE has set up twelve standing Technical Committees or sectoral organs which deal with a wide range of subjects. These are: the Committee on Agricultural Problems; the Coal Committee; the Conference of European Statisticians; the Electric Power Committee; the Committee on Gas; the Committee on Housing, Planning and Building; the Industry and Materials Committee; the Inland Transport Committee; the Committee on Manpower; the Steel Committee; the Timber Committee; and the Committee on the Development of Trade. The Committees on Manpower and Industry and Materials have been inactive, the work of the former being taken over by ILO[1] by general agreement and the work of the latter being done through expert groups on particular problems particularly on Contracts in Engineering. In addition, special meetings have been organised on energy problems, water resource problems, etc. Since 1961 there has developed a series of meetings of Senior Economic Advisers. These Committees are composed of national representatives who have full authority to make recommendations directly to their governments and to international bodies. They can thus influence policies directly. When, without passsing through the Commission, agreements are reached in the Technical Committees they can be effected by the governments without delay. The committees, like the Commission itself, cannot act with respect to any country without the agreement of its government. Recommendations are arrived at only by general agreement as it is felt that the economic problems discussed could not be resolved by majority decisions. The Technical Committees try to concentrate discussion on specific and narrowly defined issues and meetings of the Technical Committees are held in private, which is both an incentive to make progress with the work in hand and a discouragement to unnecessary political debate. In view of the highly specialised nature of their work the Technical Committees have frequently found it necessary to establish sub-groups. Member governments and international organisations have frequently made available to the Commission the services of experts and *rapporteurs*, free of charge, to help the Secretariat prepare the meetings of the Technical Committees.

Non-governmental organisations play an important part in the

[1] The International Labour Organisation.

work of the Technical Committees. Their representatives take part in the work of the Committees, and through them technical problems have often been referred to the relevant non-governmental organisations for discussion and action. For certain problems no appropriate organisations existed and ECE sponsored the establishment of new non-governmental organisations to deal with them.

THE SECRETARIAT

The Secretariat of ECE, which is housed in the Palais des Nations in Geneva, is controlled by an Executive Secretary. The Executive Secretary is appointed by the Secretary General of the United Nations, to whom he is responsible for the work of the Secretariat. Owing to the 'open' constitution of ECE the Executive Secretaries have had the opportunity, which they have in fact taken, to assume wide powers of initiative and policy-making within the organisation.

The Secretariat is part of the 'United Nations Department of Economic Affairs', but in practice it is self-contained and independent. It can address the world on its own initiative and authority. At its peak strength in 1949, the Secretariat had an established staff of 174 of whom ninety were in professional grades. The strength of the Secretariat in 1965 was 160 of whom about half were in professional grades. The Secretariat is drawn from most European countries, including the Soviet Union and Eastern European countries. The first Executive Secretary was Professor Gunnar Myrdal from Sweden (1947–57). He was succeeded by Mr Sakari Tuomioja from Finland (1957–60) and then by Mr Vladimir Velebit from Yugoslavia who was appointed in 1960. The post of Deputy Executive Secretary is traditionally occupied by a national of the USSR. The major part of the administrative and financial services, as well as translating, précis-writing, interpretation, processing and distribution of documents, is provided by the staff of the European Office of the United Nations.

The Secretariat is organised in Divisions corresponding in general to the sectors covered by the Technical Committees. The Research and Planning Division, besides being responsible for general economic analysis, services the Conference of European Statisticians and the Meetings of Senior Economic Advisers. The Technical Divisions not only service the Technical Committees but also, with the Research Division, carry out research in the sectors covered by these Committees. There are six Technical Divisions: for Commission affairs and trade development; energy; steel, engineering and housing; transport; agriculture and timber. The timber and agriculture divisions are joint FAO/ECE Divisions staffed in the main by FAO[1] professional officials. The Research and Planning Division is composed of economists who collaborate with the Technical Divisions on specialised research projects; this Division also prepares the annual *Economic Survey*, the quarterly *Economic Bulletin* and special studies.

In general terms, the Secretariat plans the agenda of ECE meetings and prepares and circulates the relevant documentation. It tries to obtain greater co-operation between the member governments of ECE and acts as a centre for the exchange of information. The Secretariat maintains contacts with the governments concerning the implementation of the Commission's decisions. The Secretariat also carries out research on the economic situation in the European region. The Executive Secretary is often asked by governments to advise them on matters under consideration before the Commission takes a decision on them, and the Secretariat may also provide oral or written statements concerning matters on the Commission's agenda.

It is clear that the Secretariat has played a crucial role in the work of ECE. In the early days because of the consistent refusal of governments to deal with problems of all-European economic co-operation the Secretariat carried a major responsibility for initiatives. The vacuum left by the governments gave the Secretariat the opportunity, which it took, of presenting proposals on its own authority. The Secretariat was able during this difficult period to put forward proposals and withdraw them without damaging the prestige of governments. The special qualities of the Secretariat which have enabled it to continue and to develop such a vital role include the traditions of independent research and initiative, the high quality of its officials and the leadership provided by its Executive Secretaries. It should be remembered, however, that the initiatives taken by the ECE Secretariat in the days of the 'cold war', valuable though they were, could not replace a positive will to co-operate on the part of the member governments. Since the mid 1950s the member governments of ECE have shown themselves readier to co-operate across East–West divisions of political, economic and social organisation and have adopted a more positive attitude to co-operation over policy as well as technical matters in the Commission. This represents a considerable advance from the situation in the early 1950s when the Executive Secretary refused on several occasions to convene

[1] Food and Agriculture Organisation.

Committee meetings which, he considered, had little chance of achieving useful work.

THE BUDGET

The gross annual budget of ECE now amounts to approximately $2 million, about two thirds of which is accounted for by the salaries of the Secretariat, and the other third by the cost of conference services. The entire cost of ECE is borne by the United Nations, as is the cost of the other United Nations Regional Commissions.

The Work of the Technical Committees

At first it was intended that the work of the Technical Committees should be under the close supervision of the Commission which, it was thought, would meet frequently. But Professor Myrdal's success in persuading member governments that the Commission should normally meet annually gave the Technical Committees virtual independence. In practice they have been free to proceed with their own work without constant reference to a hierarchy of other bodies.

THE COMMITTEE ON AGRICULTURAL PROBLEMS

This Committee was set up in 1948 to constitute a 'forum for discussion and the exchange of information' among ECE countries; it was also empowered to 'make recommendations on the best practical means of European Co-operation to develop the production of agricultural commodities and to facilitate the exchange of such commodities'. Owing partly to the wide scope of its terms of reference, and partly to the fact that it did not meet at all for a long period, the Committee took an excessive time to begin active work. Its members did not agree until March 1954 on a programme of work, previously being unable to agree on the order of priority to be given to the tasks they had to carry out.

In 1954 the Committee decided to embark forthwith on a study of trends and outlook in the market for agricultural products. Somewhat later it also agreed that delegates at its annual sessions should review jointly recent national developments in the field of agriculture.

The Committee annually discusses the short-term outlook for major agricultural products on the basis of secretariat reports. Since 1958, these reports have been published, as amended in the light of additional information furnished at the session, in the form of a *Review of the Agricultural Situation in Europe at the End of the Year.*

The Committee has also carried out work on the long-term trends in agriculture, and in 1960 published an important study *European Agriculture in 1965—A Review of the Prospects for Production and Demand* which outlined the growing disproportion between agricultural production and consumption and its effects on trade.

The Committee has set up working parties to establish uniform conditions of sale for various agricultural products and has also worked out quality standards concerning perishable foodstuffs entering into European trade. These conditions and standards have been widely accepted. Most of these 'European standards' worked out in ECE have been accepted by the European Economic Community as a basis for practice in their member countries.

Other working parties are concerned with mechanisation of agriculture, rationalisation and problems of methodology and definitions in agricultural statistics. From time to time *ad hoc* groups of experts have met to discuss special problems such as methods used in making projections.

At the request of the Committee, the Secretariat makes special studies such as the annual report on *Prices of Agricultural Products and Fertilisers* and the periodic report *Output, Expenses and Income of Agriculture in European Countries.*

THE COAL COMMITTEE

The coal shortage was the most serious of the postwar shortages which faced Europe when ECE came into being. The ECE Coal Committee took over the work of ECO together with the techniques of allocation devised by that Organisation. Between April 1948 and September 1950 the Coal Committee assigned sixty million tons of solid fuels from European sources under formulae which took into account the supply of a similar amount of fuel under bilateral trade agreements. After 1950 there was an easing of the coal shortage and allocations were abandoned. However, through its Sub-Committee on Trade, the Coal Committee continued to consider the short-term developments in the market by examining import requirements in the light of export availabilities. Adjustments were then made between the estimates of imports and exports in order to assess the tonnages required from extra-European sources to bridge any gap. In this way a reliable means of watching the market has been evolved. In the early 1950s the Coal Committee set itself three tasks: to ensure that European needs in solid fuel were met as economically as possible; to promote the rational use of fuels; and to make the coal market as stable as possible.

The Coal Committee has made many recommendations to governments to promote the more efficient use of solid fuels. As a result of this work many technical innovations have been put into effect in the member countries. One example of successful co-operation is the adoption of an international coal classification system which provides a simple procedure for the accurate identification of hard coals. The many thousands of different types of European coal can now be described in a common code.

The fierce competition between different forms of energy which emerged in the late 1950s and which still characterises the fuel market had led ECE to try to reinforce the competitive position of the coal industry through co-operation concerning modern techniques and new production and marketing methods. In particular, technical studies on the exploitation of deep seams have been carried out, since in many European coalfields the most easily accessible coal has already been mined. The adaptation of the coal industry to the increasingly competitive conditions of the world energy market of the 1960s gives considerable importance to the work of the ECE Coal Committee in its attempts to aid the modernisation of the European coal mining industry.

THE GAS COMMITTEE

The finding of natural gas deposits in Europe and the rapid expansion of oil refining which has made available a range of substances that can be used as raw materials for gas production have changed the whole nature of the gas industry since the war. With many advances in techniques of storing and using gas also being developed, the Commission became interested in the gas industry and, in 1956, set up an *ad hoc* working party on gas problems. In 1961 the working party became a committee.

The main problem of the gas industry is the need to improve availability and flexibility in the supply of gas to meet a steadily growing although fluctuating demand.

The Committee is studying ways of meeting these complex requirements: regularity in production and transmission, irregularity in demand. It examines such methods as appropriate tariff and price policies aimed at evening out demand, the large-scale storage of gas as a means of linking supply and demand, promotion of gas utilisation in sectors where consumption is regular, use of processes capable of increasing flexibility in gas manufacturing plants, etc.

Much of the Committee's work has been concerned with the problems of developing and diversifying the supply of natural gas as well as of manufactured gas of high calorific value in the European energy market, and doing this without creating major economic or social disturbances. The Committee keeps under permanent review the economics of the transport of gas and the trends of the gas market in Europe. It also seeks to facilitate the establishment of gas pipelines.

THE COMMITTEE ON ELECTRIC POWER

The postwar years have seen a rapid and sustained rise in the demand for electric power in Europe. In the early postwar period there was a serious shortage of generating and transmitting equipment. More recently the main problems to be solved on an international basis have been met by studies to see how the growing requirements for electric power can best be met and by the removal of administrative and other obstacles to the free movement of electric power across frontiers. The Committee on Electric Power was set up in 1947. In the first years of its existence its work was mainly directed to seeking the removal of shortages and bottlenecks in the supply of electricity and the development of new supplies of electricity. In the 1950s the Committee began a wide range of research studies aiming to promote international co-operation both in the field of exchange of electric power and in that of the planning and the construction of new hydro-electric developments of international importance.

One of the Committee's main concerns has been the economic analysis of the electric power situation and the factors governing it. It has published yearly and quarterly bulletins of electric energy statistics and has carried out, through working groups of experts, detailed studies of specific problems, including the determination of Europe's hydro-electric resources and their utilisation, the technical and economic aspects of rural electrification, the design and operation of thermal power plants, etc. One result of the Committee's work has been the 'Yougelexport' programme, under which Austria, the Federal Republic of Germany, Italy and Yugoslavia set up an inter-governmental research agency, whose work led to a plan for the building of four hydro-electric power stations in Yugoslavia together with a transmission network. This scheme was not put into effect on the international basis originally envisaged; however, the power plants planned in the ECE framework were built by the

Yugoslav Authorities with external financial aid. Certain studies recently initiated by the Committee concerning the problems of meeting power demands during peak-load periods and the methods and criteria used for economic selection of investments in the electric power industry are carried out by *ad hoc* working parties. On certain problems like the rationalisation of consumption of electric energy, the coverage of load during peak-load periods and problems related to the growing requirements for electric power, the Committee has sponsored international symposia.

THE STEEL COMMITTEE

The Steel Committee was set up in the autumn of 1947. Although there are other international bodies whose main concern is with European steel problems, the ECE Commission is the only one where nearly all European countries are represented. Further, it is the only UN body concerned especially with the problems of the iron and steel industry. From 1947 to 1949, when the Committee was primarily concerned with raw materials shortages, it helped to ease the scarcity of coke, scrap and ore by influencing the distribution of these materials.

Later the Committee began to prepare and publish a series of reports on consumption trends and technical problems and annual market reviews. Since 1952, the Committee has also sponsored a series of studies on major technological changes in the iron and steel industry.

At the end of 1956, the Committee undertook an investigation of the long-term trends and problems of the European steel industry. The study, which was published in 1960, made a series of interrelated forecasts of steel consumption, production and trade in finished steel products for the period 1972–75, together with an assessment of the corresponding requirements in raw materials.

Since 1959, the Committee has adopted long-term programmes of work, the main aims of which are to improve steel statistics; to provide current analyses of the European steel market; to study long-term trends in the steel market; to examine economic and technological factors influencing the main steel-consuming sectors; to stimulate technological innovations in the steel industry; and, generally, to encourage the exchange of economic and technical information among ECE countries. Two long-term inquiries on the use of steel in construction and on economic aspects of iron ore preparation were published in 1964 and in 1966. The present programme includes studies on: long-term trends in the competitive use of steel in comparison with other materials; economic aspects of continuous casting; world trade in steel and steel demand in developing countries; the world market for iron ore; and short- and long-term trends in the production and consumption of stainless steels.

The Secretariat publishes a *Quarterly Bulletin of Steel Statistics* and *Statistics of World Trade in Steel.* A Working Party on Steel Statistics advises the Steel Committee on the collection and publication of data on steel and related products.

THE INDUSTRY AND MATERIALS COMMITTEE

The Industry and Materials Committee was set up in 1947 to deal with a wide range of subjects, most of which—steel, timber, manpower and housing—were taken over by other committees. At first the work of the Committee was concentrated on relieving shortages of products that were urgently required by industry such as ball bearings, conveyor belts and high-tension insulators. The Committee facilitated the removal of several bottlenecks by helping to increase the flow of scarce materials. By 1949, shortages had largely ended in Western Europe except in the Federal Republic of Germany and for a time the Committee concentrated on how to make the best use of materials.

At the 1950 spring session the member governments failed to agree on the Committee's future. Although some governments felt there was a need for studies on specific problems within the engineering industry, the Committee was divided over the need to hold regular meetings. The Executive Secretary pointed out that it was not appropriate for the Secretariat to prepare studies unless the Committee itself was to meet and take action or was to make recommendations to governments. Subsequently the Commission established a working party on the programme of work which met in 1950 and decided that *ad hoc* working parties or study groups should be formed to study specific problems. The Committee has not met since. The working party itself took over the work previously carried out by the Committee and has prepared reports on agricultural machinery and studied the economic aspects of automation.

The Commission has carried out a considerable amount of work in the domains of mechanical and electrical engineering and agricultural machinery, including a major survey of the production and export of mechanical and electrical engineering goods which was published in April 1963. The Secretariat also publishes an annual

Bulletin of Statistics on World Trade in Engineering Products. In 1955, the Commission asked the Executive Secretary to convene an *ad hoc* working group on agricultural machinery which met three times and organised exchanges of information on combine harvesters, soil preparation machinery and agricultural tractors.

THE HOUSING, BUILDING AND PLANNING COMMITTEE

The Housing, Building and Planning Committee was originally set up in the summer of 1946 as part of EECE and was absorbed by ECE in the following year. Between 1946 and 1949 the Committee drew the attention of member governments to the gravity of the postwar housing problem at a time when, with competing priorities for investment, housing was inevitably placed low on the list. The Committee also restored and developed contacts between technicians and did its utmost to restore the production of building materials to an adequate level.

Between 1949 and 1952, the Committee's work was concerned mainly with trying to achieve greater intergovernmental co-operation on housing policy, particularly its economic aspects, but the Committee and the Secretariat lacked the financial resources to carry out the comprehensive field investigations which were required.

By the end of this period the Committee managed, however, to start preparing and publishing periodical surveys of housing trends and policies as well as periodical publications on housing and building statistics. The range, coverage and international comparability of the latter have steadily improved since then so that these statistics have become an important tool in the Committee's analytical work.

The Committee also promoted systematic arrangements for international technical co-operation which led to the establishment of the International Council for Building Documentation in 1950, which was transformed in 1953 into the International Council for Building Research, Studies and Documentation.

During the next few years the Committee concentrated on studying three interrelated aspects of government policy concerning the industrialisation of house construction and building costs. A basic study on industrialisation of construction was published in 1959 in the report *Government Policies and the Cost of Building.* The three studies which it subsequently carried out were on: house-building costs in European countries; the effect of repetition on the production cost of selected building materials and components; and the economic and technical aspects of the lifetime of houses. These three studies led to the publishing in 1963 of the report *Cost, Repetition, Maintenance: related aspects of building prices.* The Committee also organised a seminar held in Prague in 1964 on changes in the structure of the building industry necessary to improve its efficiency and to increase its output. The Committee has established a standing Working Party on the Building Industry which includes in its work programme such questions as dimensional co-ordination in building, selected aspects of industrialisation of building, construction trends and building costs.

The Committee has also studied some of the social aspects of housing policy such as the financing of housing and rent policies, housing normative needs and effective demand for housing and rural housing. A comprehensive study on major problems of government long-term housing policies was completed and published in 1966. A colloquy on problems of housing for the elderly was held in Belgium and the Netherlands in 1965.

The Committee has established a standing Working Party on Urban Renewal and Physical Planning. A seminar on the supply, development and allocation of land for housing and related purposes was held in Paris in 1965, and another was held in the Netherlands in the autumn of 1966 on the Future Pattern and Forms of Urban Settlements. Other studies in this field cover such questions as regional physical planning, methodology of appraising the quality of neighbourhoods, and the economics of urban renewal.

The Committee has been concerned to share its experience with the developing countries in other parts of the world and has made valuable contributions to seminars on housing progress and policies organised by the United Nations for the benefit of Latin American and Asian countries.

THE INLAND TRANSPORT COMMITTEE

When it was set up in 1947 the Inland Transport Committee took over the work of a postwar organisation established by the Allied Powers to deal with the problems arising from the destruction and dislocation of the European transport network. Among these problems was the return of the railway rolling stock which had been dispersed throughout Europe without reference to the ownership rights of the countries concerned. However, even in its first years of existence, the Committee had to deal with many problems of a more permanent nature. It has promoted the development of transport facilities, helped to relieve transport barriers to the movement of goods and persons across frontiers, and, generally, has worked to improve transport efficiency. In view of the wide range of problems involved the Committee set up three sub-committees as well as a number of working parties.

In the field of road transport the Committee has prepared the drafts which served as a basis for the conclusion at world level of the 1949 Convention on road traffic and the 1949 Protocol on road signs and signals. Later it concluded a European Agreement on road markings and adopted a number of resolutions aiming at a more complete unification in Europe of national regulations on traffic rules on the equipment of vehicles and on road signs and signals. At the same time it published a Declaration indicating the main European Highways and defining the standards which governments should apply in developing these main routes. In 1958 it concluded an agreement on the approval of equipment and spare parts of vehicles and on the reciprocal recognition of approvals granted in conformity with the regulations to be attached to the agreement; four such regulations have already entered into force. The Committee has also solved a number of problems concerning the international movement of vehicles, such as the mutual recognition of driving licences and registration certificates, and it has established an intra-European motor insurance against third-party risks (the green card system). As regards Customs matters the Committee concluded a Convention, called the TIR Convention, providing for the free movement of loaded vehicles across frontiers and the limitation of customs inspection to the point of departure and destination; 300,000 movements of lorries took place in 1965 under this TIR Agreement to which 22 European countries are parties. The Committee initiated also the movement towards dispensing with *carnets de passage en douane* and triptychs. In addition the Committee has concluded a European Agreement on the regulations to be applied for international transport of dangerous goods (explosives, inflammable liquids, etc.) by road.

In the field of rail transport, the main task of the Committee is to initiate work which is later carried out by the international railway organisations. It has also succeeded in simplifying customs formalities concerning rolling stock, passenger transit and goods transport, and is continuing its endeavours to arrange for the removal as far as possible of formalities hampering rail traffic.

As regards inland waterways the Committee has prepared a draft European code which will *inter alia* standardise the signalling system of inland waterways and vessels; it has also concluded three conventions which deal respectively with responsibility in case of collisions, registration and rights *in re*, and measurement of vessels. The Committee is also preparing an agreement on the carriage of dangerous goods on inland waterways.

The Committee has devoted much of its work to studies in the field of transport economics, for example the question of apportionment of track costs between road users. The Secretariat compiles and publishes each year comprehensive statistical data on all types of European inland transport and also publishes statistics of road accidents.

THE TIMBER COMMITTEE

At the end of the war, Europe faced reconstruction problems for which large supplies of timber were needed. There were three urgent tasks: to re-equip forest industries and raise production; to halt over-cutting as soon as possible; and to ensure that available supplies were sent where they were most needed. An ECE Timber Committee was established which took over the activities begun by the Timber Sub-Committee of EECE. In 1947 it was decided that ECE should deal with the first and third problems, which were the most urgent, whilst FAO should concentrate on the long-term development of European forest resources. Since 1947, the FAO and ECE have worked in close collaboration concerning timber questions and the Secretariat of the Committee is provided jointly by ECE and FAO.

Between 1947 and 1949 the Timber Committee initiated the negotiations for 'timber loans' to help re-equip industries in some of Europe's traditional timber producing countries which had suffered most from the war. European timber production soon recovered and the worst shortages were rapidly overcome. However, great concern about Europe's future possibilities of meeting requirements led the Committee to carry out a study on the longer-term trends in timber production and consumption which was published in 1953. This initiated a series of similar studies carried out in other regions.

Since its inception the greater part of the Committee's work has been devoted to assessing the supply and demand situation for the main categories of forest products in both the short and the long term. In general the Timber Committee has tried to encourage the stability of trade in forest products by reviewing and publishing information on the timber market. More recently, however, problems of productivity in the wood-working industries and of their economic aspects have received increasing attention by the Committee. Since 1951 work has also been carried out on the technical and economic aspects of forestry operations by a subsidiary body of the Timber Committee, presently named the Joint FAO/ECE/ILO Committee on Forest Working Techniques and Training of Forest Workers. Another subsidiary body, the Joint FAO/ECE Working Party on Forest and Forest Products Statistics, has helped to build up uniform statistics of production and trade in all important forest products, and has also established uniform nomenclatures and methods for dealing with statistical problems in forestry and the forest industries and related sectors. ECE's methods of international co-operation concerning forest products have been passed on to the less-developed countries through the appropriate UN regional commissions. Finally, the Committee's study *European Timber Trends and Prospects, a New Appraisal—1950–75*, published in 1964, sets out forecasts and recommendations concerning the future development of Europe's forest potential and of the production of its forest industries.

THE COMMITTEE ON THE DEVELOPMENT OF TRADE

The Committee on the Development of Trade was set up in May 1949 to 'study, consult on and submit recommendations on measures that will result in an expansion of trade between European countries and also between these countries and countries outside Europe'. The establishment of the Committee was an attempt by the member governments to promote trade and to rectify the sharp decline in East–West trade in Europe since the end of the war. The work of the Committee was considered to be vital to the effective functioning of ECE as a body for all-European economic co-operation. In the month of its establishment, however, a deadlock developed: the Western countries held that the Committee's first task should be to form a clear conception of the goods available and required for trade, whereas the Eastern European countries stressed the futility of any efforts to exchange information so long as discriminatory export licensing policies were practised against them. The Executive Secretary then took the position that no further meetings of the Committee would be justified until a foundation for agreement had been established by preliminary negotiations. However, he continued his efforts by arranging several *ad hoc* meetings at which some concrete trading possibilities, particularly for Western imports of grains, were explored. Following lengthy negotiations by the

Executive Secretary, a consultation of experts from twenty-four participating countries was held in April 1953. At this consultation lists of goods available for export or required for import were exchanged, and bilateral trade talks were organised. In April 1954 a second consultation was held; multilateral and bilateral trade talks again took place, and this consultation led to agreement on renewing the activities of the Committee on Trade.

The Committee was re-convened in October 1954; it drew up a programme of work, including a continuation of East–West trade consultations, and set up an *ad hoc* working party of financial experts to consider the possibility of multilateral payments for balances arising under bilateral agreements, and other questions relating to East–West payments.

The Committee is now the only body which discusses trade problems on an all-European basis. The Committee has also served as a forum for the discussion of trade policies and practices in the wider sense. The Committee has been used by member governments: to keep the current developments and prospects for intra-European, notably East–West, trade under close examination; to develop new trade possibilities and to improve facilities for trade between market economy and state trading countries; and to confront national commercial policies, with the aim of removing obstacles to trade and reaching greater harmony in trade relations.

Since its revival in 1954, the Committee's main achievements in the field of trade policy have been its recommendations to governments on the multilateralisation of payments, in 1959, and its recommendations to governments, in 1961, to meet together to solve trade problems arising between sub-regional economic groups. These recommendations seem to have had a positive effect on government policies and to have helped to improve the trade relations between Eastern and Western countries. In 1959 the Committee organised a special meeting of experts to improve the mutual understanding of the methods used in foreign trade by ECE countries. Each delegation submitted papers describing the organisation of foreign trade in its country and the experts replied to some 94 questions on different aspects of trade policy. Other work of this kind has served to clarify the knowledge and views of member countries concerning each other's foreign trade.

The Committee has tried to increase trade through improving trade facilities. A voluntary multilateral compensation system has been established through which governments can use the ECE Secretariat as an agent in reaching quarterly agreements on the transfer of bilateral balances among national banks.[1] Governments outside the ECE region may also take part in this multilateral balancing of trade accounts. The Committee has organised, each year, consultations on trade policy which provide the opportunity for member governments to hold bilateral talks with each other on questions of trade policy.

The Committee has carried out a considerable amount of work on simplifying the legal and administrative regulations governing international trade. In 1949 the Committee started work on trying to establish standard conditions of sale for use in commercial contracts. Conditions of sale vary from country to country and are often impossible to apply under different national legal systems. The Committee has succeeded in drawing up agreed conditions of sale for a number of products and these are widely used not only in East–West trade but more generally as well. Tens of thousands of copies of these conditions of sale are sold each year and they have greatly simplified the whole process of selling in East–West trade.

The Committee's working party on arbitration drafted an Arbitration Agreement which was concluded in 1961 and which has been ratified by most of the Eastern member countries but so far only by Austria and the Federal Republic of Germany in the West. The Agreement provides for selection of arbitrators and the place of arbitration in cases where the parties fail to agree thereon.

Traders of countries which have not signed the Arbitration Convention can use for the same purposes on an optional basis a Set of Arbitration Rules drawn up under the auspices of the Committee.

The Committee has also worked on the removal of obstacles to international co-operation on insurance and has made recommendations on administrative facilities which could be given by governments to the organisers and users of trade fairs. The Trade Committee has also done much to standardise and amplify external trade export documents as a means of expediting foreign trade operations and making them less costly.

The work of the Committee on problems of East–West trade policy has in recent years assumed particular importance. The Commission set up in 1962 an *ad hoc* Group of seven experts to study certain issues of policy hampering East–West trade. The reports of this Group are examined by the Committee with a view

[1] The total sums cleared by the beginning of 1966 amounted to some $100 million.

to the adoption of eventual recommendations for the removal of obstacles to trade.

Finally, mention should be made of the relationship between the work of the Committee and that of UNCTAD.[1] The Commission has assigned to the Committee the task of making a detailed examination of the relevant UNCTAD recommendations with a view to close co-operation in helping attain the objectives of UNCTAD. The Committee at its session in 1965 made this examination and added to its programme certain work designed to achieve the double purpose of serving ECE and assisting the activities of UNCTAD.

THE CONFERENCE OF EUROPEAN STATISTICIANS

The Economic and Social Council organised three regional meetings of European Statisticians in 1949, 1951 and 1953. At the third of these meetings the participants agreed to meet in the future as a continuing body to be known as the Conference of European Statisticians. The Conference is a permanent organisation whose members are the directors of the central statistical offices of the countries participating in the work of ECE. The Conference acts as a forum for discussion and consultation on a wide range of statistical matters.

The Conference holds plenary sessions each year and has arranged numerous meetings of specialists and experts on particular subjects. The Conference makes recommendations aimed at improving the preparation of national statistics and at making them more comparable internationally in each different subject. In practice, the Conference has found it easier to reach agreement on the formulation of standards concerning definitions of classification and methods of tabulation than on methods of collecting statistical data. The Conference works in close contact with the Statistical Commission and the Statistical Office of the UN. The Conference receives regular reports on the statistical work carried out by other European organisations such as OECD, the European Communities and the Council for Mutual Economic Assistance, and tries to avoid the duplication of the statistical work carried out by them. It draws attention to gaps in the statistical work of other European organisations and tries to obtain co-operation between them over statistical matters. The Conference has on several occasions worked directly with the technical committees of ECE on statistical matters in their fields of interest.

[1] The United Nations Conference on Trade and Development.

The Research Activities

The main concern of the Research and Planning Division of ECE is the preparation of the annual *Economic Surveys* and the *Economic Bulletins*. It is on the high standards of these documents, which are available to the public, that the reputation of ECE largely rests.

The first *Economic Survey* of Europe was published in the spring of 1948 on the initiative of the Secretariat, and received widespread attention. Since then the *Economic Survey* has been published every year. The Surveys are accurate, set out the facts clearly and without bias, and state bold conclusions; above all, owing to the fact that the Secretariat has sole responsibility for them, they are impartial, and they are accepted as such by all the member countries. The Commission's annual debate on the 'Review of the Economic Situation in Europe' is centred on the Survey. These publications and ECE's work in the research field depend on the work of a small group of economists brought together from different member countries, with a great variety of background and working anonymously. Governments have been willing to pay the price of the embarrassing things sometimes said about them in order to obtain data and analyses that are useful to them. The research work of ECE has been particularly useful to the governments of the smaller countries. In the first years of ECE's history the Soviet Union and the Eastern European countries were reluctant to provide the Research Division with information, but since the mid-1950s they have become increasingly co-operative in providing the required data and statistics.

The first *Economic Bulletin for Europe* was published in 1949. Two issues are published each year devoted respectively to a review of current developments in European trade and payments and to articles on special topics of particular interest, such as the *Economic Surveys.*

The review of the current economic situation in Europe is supplemented by special studies on more general questions which are both of long-term importance and relevant to the current formulation of economic policies in European countries. The following themes have thus been dealt with: long-term economic growth; long-term problems of economic policy or management in particular sectors; intra-European trade and integration; developments in 'problem sectors' such as agriculture; studies of Europe's present and potential trade with the developing countries; and studies of economic development problems in the less-developed regions of Europe. The most recent special study has been devoted to economic planning in Europe. The Research Division has also carried out work for and in co-operation with the Secretariats of the Economic Commission for Asia and the Far East, the Economic Commission for Africa and the Economic Commission for Latin America. Recently research has been concentrated more on large, long-term projects, as opposed to current reporting and analysis, and this trend seems likely to continue. The Research and Planning Division is also responsible for the preparation and the servicing of the meetings of Senior Economic Advisers to ECE Governments, which the Commission, at its session in 1960, decided to convene. Three meetings, which were held in 1961, 1962 and 1964, were devoted respectively to Problems of Economic Growth, Criteria for Investment Policies and Problems of Regional Economic Planning and Development. At its 20th session, in 1965, the Commission approved a long-term programme for the meetings of Senior Economic Advisers which involves the convening of annual meetings as well as the selection of topics for future meetings. The purpose of the fourth meeting, held in June 1966, was to consider the Construction and Practical Application of Macro-economic Models for Purposes of Economic Planning, Programming and Policy-Making.

The Working Methods

In the course of its growth the Commission has developed a number of special features and practices which supplement its written constitution, and enable the organisation to adapt itself to the different kinds of problem it faces. The division of labour between the Commission and its committees has followed a consistent pattern. The Commission is the directing, supervisory and policy-making body of ECE. It reviews the work of the Technical Committees at sessions open to the public and supervises their activities on the basis of their reports. In practice the committees which meet in closed sessions have been allowed great freedom to develop their functions in an independent manner and are authorised to make recommendations or requests directly to governments without asking for prior approval by the Commission. Indeed, it is in the meetings of the Technical Committees and their sub-organs that the practical day-to-day results of the organisation's work are achieved.

The most important function of the Commission is to assign new tasks to the Technical Committees and the Secretariat. In most cases the committees are authorised to choose their own problems and also to negotiate formal as well as informal agreements. There have been two main reasons for this development. In the first place most of the work of the committees has been of a highly technical character on which the need for concerted action was recognised to be particularly strong and the issues dealt with have little or no political content. Second, the committees and all other subsidiary working organs of the Commission have been composed of representatives in positions of authority in their home governments. The result has been that when an agreement is reached between governments at the committee level it is normally put into effect without delay and without any hierarchical procedure.

From the beginning ECE has been guided by the twin principles that the number of meetings of the various organs of the Commission should be kept to a minimum, and that they should be short, in order to make it possible for the most highly qualified officials in the specific fields to attend them. This has proved workable because the meetings are carefully prepared by the Secretariat often with the help of *rapporteurs* appointed by governments.

In their work the committees and sub-committees have employed a wide and flexible range of procedures for dealing with their problems. Special working parties and smaller working groups have frequently been used. Many such groups are set up on an *ad hoc* basis. Practical experience in committee work has shown that definite results can often be achieved more speedily and economically if the problem is first of all narrowly defined and then referred to a special group of experts. The structure of a number of the Technical Committees and their subsidiary organs has been changed whenever it was felt that new circumstances made this desirable.

The Technical Committees of ECE have several features in common despite their functional differences. Each serves as a forum where experts from different countries can meet and discuss common problems on the basis of the fullest possible information. The committees have developed machinery for the regular interchange of knowledge and opinion on an all-European scale. They have sponsored and participated in the preparation of fundamental economic and commodity market studies. They have done this in the belief that such studies, carried out from an international standpoint, can contribute to the development of informed and realistic national and international investment and market policies. Moreover, each of the committees has undertaken work which has contributed to improvements in technological techniques, and also to economies in the use of resources; and further, each committee offers possibilities for harmonising national policies and stimulating the solution of problems where this can be done at an all-European level.

Conclusions

ECE has not only reflected the political atmosphere of Europe but has also helped to influence it. Despite the division of Europe into two camps and the development of joint European economic activity in OEEC (later OECD), the EEC and EFTA in the West and COMECON (later CMEA) in the East, ECE has managed to achieve significant success in helping governmental co-operation on an all-European basis. In the early days, its Technical Committees helped to solve the problems caused by shortages and bottlenecks and since the mid-1950s, when the cold war attitudes have been increasingly replaced by the ideas of East–West *détente*, the Commission has succeeded in eliminating a number of the obstacles which restricted East–West co-operation in the economic field.

Even when disagreements in the annual session of the Commission have blocked intergovernmental co-operation at the political level, the technical experts have often continued to work effectively together.

In the political climate of the 1960s it is likely that ECE will continue to play a useful role in increasing co-operation between Eastern and Western European countries, both by facilitating and encouraging the development of East–West trade and by exchanges of technological information. Because of the differences in political, economic and social systems, a far-reaching harmonisation of the economic policies of all the European countries cannot at present be achieved; but for the same reason, the limited measures of co-operation which ECE can obtain at this level are of value in helping to consolidate, in a practical way, the rapprochement of the countries of Eastern and Western Europe.

Part 3

INTERGOVERNMENTAL EUROPE

Chapter Three

THE ORGANISATION FOR EUROPEAN ECONOMIC CO-OPERATION

The Origins

The severe winter of 1946–47 placed a great strain on the countries of Europe which were already faltering in their attempts to recover from the Second World War. Industrial production began to fall off and bad weather, coupled with the existing economic weakness, led to widespread shortages, industrial stagnation and grave unemployment. When the work of the United Nations Relief and Rehabilitation Administration (UNRRA) was terminated in the spring of 1947 it became generally realised that it, together with lend-lease and the initial postwar American loans, had only temporarily concealed the deep-rooted and persistent imbalance between the resources and productive capacity of the North American powers and those of the rest of the world. It was also apparent that Europe's basic industries were far weaker than had been thought. Further, Europe had enormous import needs. She was not able to export very much; consequently she was bound to incur large trade deficits for some years. With the near exhaustion of Europe's foreign exchange and gold reserves and the termination of the lend-lease and other American bilateral credits in view, new devices were needed to permit the recovery of the European economies and to allow for essential imports to continue. Britain was herself in a desperate economic position and was unable to give assistance to the rest of Europe.

The economic and consequent political weakness of Europe was driven home to the United States Administration when the British Government revealed that it would not be able to continue to provide aid to Greece beyond the end of March 1947. To some in the Administration—notably the Secretary of State, General Marshall, and Under-Secretaries Dean Acheson and William Clayton—it was clear that aid was needed not only for Greece and the other countries directly or indirectly threatened by communism but also to save Western Europe from economic collapse. Mr Acheson accordingly asked the Assistant Secretary of State, John H. Hilldring, Chairman of the State–War–Navy Co-ordinating Committee (SWNCC), to undertake a study of the problem to be presented to General Marshall or himself as quickly as possible.

On 11 March SWNCC set up a special *ad hoc* Committee to carry out a preliminary report on countries that might need emergency or long-term United States aid.

The Sub-committee in turn established groups to carry out studies on military aid, economic aid, the assistance likely to be provided by international organisations and the specific situations in different countries. When General Marshall returned from the Moscow Conference at the end of April he was convinced of the need to put Europe's economy on its feet again. The day after his return General Marshall asked Mr George Kennan, Head of the State Department's newly formed Planning Staff, to provide him with a plan of action. At this stage the American press joined in advocating a plan of aid for Europe. Mr Kennan drew widely on the studies of the *ad hoc* committee, but received his most vital contribution from the comments of Mr Clayton who had returned from a six-week visit to Europe on 19 May and who graphically described Europe's critical condition to General Marshall and Mr Acheson, urging on them the need for immediate and effective action. Thus the decision behind the Marshall speech was the result of several pressures and the work of many individuals.[1]

The Memorandum presented to General Marshall on 23 May by the Policy Planning Staff made two main points. First, there should be a distinction between the roles played by Europe and the United States in developing any programme for European reconstruction. Secondly, any European recovery programme must be a joint one.

Much of this Memorandum was embodied in the speech made by General Marshall on 5 June 1947 at Harvard, in which he invited the countries of Europe to join, with the active support of the United States, in a co-operative plan for the economic reconstruction of Europe. He said:

'The truth of the matter is that Europe's requirements for the next three or four years of foreign food and other essential products—

[1] These three paragraphs are based on information contained in Joseph M. Jones, *The Fifteen Weeks*, New York, Viking Press, 1955.

principally from America—are so very much greater than her present ability to pay that she must have substantial additional help, or face economic, social and political deterioration of a very grave character.

Apart from the demoralising effect on the world at large and the possibilities of disturbances arising as a result of the desperation of the people concerned, the consequences to the economy of the United States should be apparent to all. It is logical that the United States should do whatever it is able to do to assist in the return of normal economic health in the world, without which there can be no political stability and no assured peace. Our policy is directed not against any country or doctrine but against hunger, poverty, desperation and chaos. Its purpose should be the revival of a working economy in the world so as to promote the emergence of political and social conditions in which free institutions can exist. Such assistance, I am convinced, must not be on a piece-meal basis as various crises develop. Any assistance that this Government may render in the future should provide a cure rather than a mere palliative....

'It is already evident that, before the United States Government can proceed much further in its efforts to alleviate the situation and help start the European world on its way to recovery, there must be some agreement among the countries of Europe as to the requirements of the situation and the part these countries themselves will take in order to give proper effect to whatever action may be undertaken by this Government. It would be neither fitting nor efficacious for this Government to undertake to draw up unilaterally a programme designed to place Europe on its feet economically. This is the business of the Europeans. The initiative, I think, must come from Europe. The role of this country should consist of a European programme and of later support of such a programme so far as it may be practical for us to do so. The programme should be a joint one, agreed to by a number, if not all European nations.'

The Marshall speech clearly marked the official adoption by the United States Government of the policy of placing American economic aid to European countries on a continental instead of a bilateral basis. This was quickly appreciated in Europe and following the initiative of the British Foreign Secretary a three-power meeting to plan the main outlines of a European recovery programme was convened in Paris in June 1947 by Mr Ernest Bevin and the French Foreign Minister, M. Georges Bidault, to which the Soviet Foreign Secretary, Mr Molotov, was also invited. After General Marshall had clarified what he meant by Europe in the context of his proposals, Ernest Bevin publicly welcomed the inclusion of the Soviet Union in the offer and assured Mr Trygve Lie, Secretary General of the United Nations, that the European powers would use United Nations machinery as far as possible.

While there was still some hope in official circles in Britain and the United States that the Soviet Union might be willing to join in a recovery programme, there was little real expectation that it would do so as it had previously refused to co-operate in other international matters. In the event the Russians did decline to take part. The main objection to a joint recovery programme that they put forward at the Paris Conference was that it would mean interference with the national sovereignty of the participating states. Underlying this argument was the Soviet fear that the participation of the Eastern European 'satellite' countries in a European recovery programme would increase the influence of the West and consequently reduce the control of the Soviet Union in that area.

An agency which could possibly implement the Marshall Plan already existed in Europe: the United Nations Economic Commission for Europe (ECE). Senator Vandenberg and others advocated that ECE should be used for this purpose but this view was opposed in Britain where the Foreign Office considered that Russian membership of ECE would block rapid progress. Although it was open to Mr Molotov to suggest that ECE should draft and supervise a European recovery programme he hardly mentioned the relevance of ECE to the proposals he put forward. Moscow radio on 29 June was explicit: 'The Soviet delegation does not . . . insist that the United Nations Economic Commission for Europe should be given the task of receiving and collating estimates. It prefers that it should be done by special European committees in which Allied countries should be given first place.'

After the three-power Paris meeting invitations were sent out by Britain and France to all European countries, except Spain, to a Conference on European Economic Co-operation to be held in Paris, which began in July of the same year. Although the Eastern European countries declined the invitation, except Czechoslovakia which quickly withdrew its acceptance, sixteen Western European countries were represented at the Conference. The Conference established a Committee of European Economic Co-operation (CEEC), under the Chairmanship of Sir Oliver Franks,[1] with subsidiary technical committees whose task was to prepare a report

[1] Later Lord Franks.

outlining a joint European recovery programme as requested by General Marshall.

The work of CEEC was undoubtedly influenced by the American desire to link economic aid with progress towards European unification. At the end of August 1947 Mr Clayton and a small group of experts, joined by the United States Ambassadors to Britain and France, Mr Douglas and Mr Caffery, examined the proposals and figures that had been worked out at that stage and gave the leaders of the Committee their views on the best way of drafting and presenting them. The Americans emphasised two points in particular: first, the European countries should guarantee to be self-supporting by 1952; secondly, the CEEC must present something more than a shopping list. It should demonstrate some effort on the part of the European countries to achieve greater co-operation and unity.

The State Department also helped to shape the report by making certain suggestions designed to make the European programme acceptable to Congress. These suggestions were that:

(*a*) countries participating in the recovery programme should give specific commitments regarding the fulfilment of major production programmes;

(*b*) they should take immediate steps to create internal monetary and financial stability;

(*c*) they should express a greater determination to reduce trade barriers;

(*d*) they should consider alternative sources of dollar credits, such as the World Bank (International Bank for Reconstruction and Development), as a means of reducing the request for American assistance;

(*e*) they should give formal recognition to their common objectives and assume a common responsibility for attaining them;

(*f*) to implement the programme they should establish an international organisation to act as a co-ordinating agency.[1]

By 22 September 1947 CEEC completed its report which outlined Europe's needs for the years 1948–52 as being: (a) to increase production, especially in agriculture, energy and heavy industry; (b) to eliminate inflation; (c) to promote economic co-operation; and (d) to solve the problem of dollar payments. The report visualised a

[1] W. A. Brown and R. Opie, *American Foreign Assistance*, Washington, The Brookings Institute, 1953, p. 135.

European payments deficit of about $22,000 million with the outside world over the four-year period and suggested, following a closely reasoned case, that the United States should finance $19,000 million of this deficit. A small mission headed by Sir Oliver Franks went to Washington in October 1947 to present the report to the American Administration. The United States Government immediately set up a committee which, after close study of the CEEC proposals, suggested a four-year programme of American aid of between $12,000 and $17,000 million. A group of Representatives led by Congressman Herter visited Europe to assess the relevance of the suggested programme to Europe's problems and reported favourably to Congress. Foreign assistance bills were approved by the House of Representatives and the Senate and the Economic Co-operation Act became law on 3 April 1948.

The Economic Co-operation Act contained a declaration of policy which stated:

'Mindful of the advantages which the United States has enjoyed through the existence of a large domestic market with no internal trade barriers, and believing that similar advantages can accrue to the countries of Europe[1] it is declared to be the policy of the people of the United States to encourage these countries through a joint organisation to exert sustained common efforts as set forth in the report of the Committee of European Economic Co-operation signed at Paris on September 22, 1947, which will speedily achieve that economic co-operation in Europe which is essential for lasting peace and prosperity.'

The Act set up an agency, the Economic Co-operation Administration (ECA), to administer and supervise the aid programme, but made the grant of foreign aid conditional upon the recipient countries agreeing, in multilateral and bilateral agreements, to follow the methods of achieving recovery which were embodied in the CEEC report. The Act stated specifically that the provision of assistance was:

'contingent upon continuous effort of the participating countries to accomplish a joint recovery programme through multilateral undertakings and the establishment of a continuing organisation for this purpose.'

[1] The idea of an eventual European customs union is implicit here.

While the foreign assistance bills were being examined in Congress, the British and French Governments proposed to the other participating countries that they should take steps to set up the continuing organisation envisaged in the CEEC report of September 1947. After consultations by an Anglo-French delegation in various capital cities, CEEC held its second meeting in Paris in March 1948 to consider the creation of a continuing organisation and to decide on its structure and functions.

The OEEC Convention

CEEC submitted a draft Convention to the participating governments and on 16 April 1948 the Convention for European Economic Co-operation was signed by the foreign ministers of sixteen European countries and the Commanders-in-Chief of the Western zones of occupation in Germany. The Convention set up the Organisation for for European Economic Co-operation (OEEC) which pledged each of the member governments 'to work in close co-operation in their economic relations with one another'. As their immediate task, they agreed to undertake the elaboration and execution of a joint recovery programme. OEEC was to prepare, implement and co-ordinate measures of international economic co-operation for the better execution of the European recovery programme. It was empowered to review the actions taken by individual countries and to report its findings and was specifically given the functions of assisting the United States Government in all matters concerning the implementation of the programme.

By the terms of the Convention each member government undertook:

(*a*) 'to promote with vigour the development of production, through efficient use of the resources at their command' (Article 2);

(*b*) 'to develop in mutual co-operation, the maximum possible interchange of goods and services' and 'achieve as soon as possible a multilateral system of payments among themselves, and co-operate in relaxing restrictions on trade and payments between one another' (Article 4);

(*c*) to study the possibility of 'Customs Unions or analogous arrangements such as free trade areas' (Article 5);

(*d*) to reduce 'tariff and other barriers to the expansion of trade' (Article 6);

(*e*) 'to achieve or maintain the stability of its currency and of its internal financial position, sound rates of exchange and, generally, confidence in its monetary system' (Article 7); and

(*f*) 'to make the fullest and most effective use of available manpower' (Article 8).

The original signatory countries of the Convention were: Austria, Belgium, Denmark, France, Greece, Iceland, Ireland, Italy, Luxembourg, the Netherlands, Norway, Portugal, Sweden, Switzerland, Turkey and the United Kingdom. In October 1948 the Zone of Trieste became a member of OEEC until its existence as a separate zone was terminated. Delegates of the Federal Republic of Germany took their place on the Council in October 1949. Canada and the United States became associate members of OEEC in June 1950. Spain participated in some of the work of OEEC from January 1955 and became a member in July 1959. Yugoslavia took part in certain activities of the Organisation from 1957 onwards.

The Institutions

The structure of OEEC was based on a compromise between the opposing views of the British and French delegations attending the second meeting of OEEC in March 1948. Whereas, at that time, the French tried to introduce a certain degree of supranationalism into OEEC the British Government did not wish to give up the right of independent action. There was in Whitehall a marked fear, which lasted at least until the British Government's application to join the EEC in 1961, of participating in European international organisations which were not completely under the control of a ministerial council in which decisions were taken by unanimity. While the British Government favoured a loosely knit representative and consultative body in which the principal authority would be concentrated in the committees, staffed by officials from national delegations, the French wished to establish a more autonomous organisation with a strong executive board, that would function between meetings of the larger conference, representing all the member countries. The French also wanted an international secretariat with a Secretary General empowered to take major policy initiatives.

In the event, the structure of OEEC included no supranational characteristics. It was designed to ensure that the organisation would be under the direct control of the participating governments, so that in form and practice OEEC was an instrument of intergovernmental co-operation.

THE COUNCIL

In OEEC the power of decision was vested in the Council in which all member countries were represented and which met sometimes at ministerial level and, more often, at the level of permanent representatives—the permanent heads of national delegations stationed in Paris. Decisions of the Council, which were binding, required the unanimous assent of member governments, though if a member state abstained from voting on a decision or recommendation such an abstention did not invalidate the decision or recommendation, which was, however, not applicable to the abstaining country. The adoption of the unanimity rule was originally urged at the time of the establishment of OEEC by the Benelux countries to ensure that the interests of the smaller countries would be safeguarded. The result was that the risk of a deadlock or of an unsatisfactory compromise was always present.

In OEEC the unanimity rule was not, however, lightly used. The carefully organised process of decision-making in the organs of OEEC made governments reluctant to reject recommendations once they arrived at the stage of final decision by the Council. Considerable pressure could be built up merely by following the prescribed procedure for hearings and cross-examinations of the national teams of experts before the various committees. This procedure has been called the confrontation technique, and to a great extent OEEC's influence on national policy-making was based upon it. Although it involved the organisation as a whole, and not just the Council, it is convenient to examine the confrontation technique at this point because it played a major part in enabling the Council of OEEC to be more effective in taking decisions and more influential than might have been expected of a body based on the principle of unanimous agreement.

The confrontation technique, which has been carried over into OEEC's successor, the OECD, operates in the following way. The problem, which may affect one or more countries, is first of all defined; a report is then called for from the governments concerned, sometimes by issuing a detailed questionnaire; the replies are studied by other national delegations, as well as by their home governments and the Secretariat, and a critical analysis is prepared. The departmental experts who prepared the reply then go to Paris and are obliged to define their case against a well-briefed 'opposition', which may be, and frequently is, unanimously and vigorously expressed. In examining the economic situation and policies of member countries it is not necessary that the bodies concerned, below the level of the Council, should reach unanimity. In particular, they do not need to carry with them the representatives of the country which is being examined. When the stage has been reached where the problem in question is to be considered by the Council, ministers have to face criticism of their policies by their colleagues from other member countries, just as their officials have done at earlier stages of the confrontation procedures. Repeated 'examinations' of this kind over a number of years have done something to promote the acceptance of mutually agreed standards of financial, economic and trading behaviour. At the same time this procedure has helped to ensure that a point of view representing an international consensus is borne in mind during the formative stage of national policy-making, though, as will be seen from the chapter on OECD, the effectiveness of this process in the context of the wider organisation tends to be weaker than it was in OEEC.

The confrontation technique has thus provided a means of bringing organised persuasion to bear against discriminatory national actions or policies. It has often been successful, particularly when, as was frequently the case in OEEC, at least during the period of Marshall aid, member countries agreed that economic co-operation had to be made effective. In these circumstances, the veto was very rarely used. In many of the crises in the history of OEEC, responsible ministers felt, when it came to the test, that they could not afford to carry disagreement to breaking point. The right of veto did, of course, provide a dissenting member with a powerful lever, although any member country which sought to exploit its nuisance value to excess would find itself isolated and subject to diplomatic pressure. Indeed, normal diplomatic bargaining between meetings of the Council has been an essential part of the method by which the members have tried to reach agreement.

Although the Council alone was empowered to take decisions in the name of member governments or to make recommendations to them the responsibility for implementation rested with the member governments. The Council met once or twice a year at ministerial level and weekly at the level of permanent representatives. Although decisions of the Council were binding under the constitutions of some countries, in others they had to be ratified by the national parliaments before they became law. The Council could also adopt agreements with members, non-members or international organisations, recommendations for consideration by governments or international organisations, and resolutions concerning the work of the organisation. The recommendations and resolutions were not binding.

THE EXECUTIVE COMMITTEE

Under the Council was the Executive Committee. The larger countries were always represented on the Executive Committee, while the smaller countries took turns according to an unwritten but well understood and respected 'gentleman's agreement'.

The Executive Committee normally met once a week at the level of officials. The function of the Executive Committee was to examine and process all questions which were to be submitted to the Council, whether they related to the general policy of the organisation, the progress of its work or to its administration. The Committee was not empowered to take decisions except on the authority of the Council, and it could act only in accordance with the instructions and directions of the Council, to which it had to report. Nevertheless the Executive Committee very often played a role of pivotal importance in the Organisation, particularly during the early days of OEEC when everything depended upon the successful division of American aid. The Executive Committee has been called upon by the Council to carry out specific tasks such as the co-ordination of particularly extensive or protracted studies but its main role was to prepare the decisions of the Council.

THE TECHNICAL COMMITTEES

In OEEC the role of the Technical Committees was of prime importance. They were of two kinds: first the 'horizontal committees', which considered general economic and financial questions. There were six of these—the Fiscal Committee, the Economic Committee, the Trade Committee, the Payments Committee, the Manpower Committee and the Overseas Territories Committee. Second, the 'vertical committees' which were more specialised and were responsible for studying specific branches of economic activity, such as inland and maritime transport, the different energy sectors and the principal industries, such as iron and steel, machinery and chemical products.

The vertical committees were useful in times of crisis in the supply of essential raw materials. Thus, during the 1956 Suez crisis the possibility of the European oil shortage was foreseen and the Oil Committee had plans to deal with it. Under the auspices of OEEC an Oil Industry Emergency Group composed of the representatives of the major oil companies operating in Europe was set up to co-ordinate the flow of supplies and allocate the emergency reserve on the basis of need. The Technical Committees were wound up when OEEC was transformed into OECD.

Other committees, composed of experts chosen in a personal capacity, carried out similar work. The main committees of this kind were the Committee for Invisible Transactions, the Steering Board for Trade, the Managing Board of the European Monetary Agreement and the Steering Committee for Nuclear Energy. These Boards had seven members nominated by governments and appointed by the Council. Their role was to draw up recommendations by majority vote, if necessary, and these were passed to the Council which had the final responsibility for further action. Other important committees outside the general pattern of the Technical Committees and made up of governmental representatives were the Ministerial Committee for Agriculture and Food, the Committee of Deputies for Agriculture and Food, the Steering Committee for Nuclear Energy, the governing body of the European Productivity Agency and the Office of Scientific and Technical Personnel.

THE SECRETARIAT

The Council and the various committees of OEEC were served by an international secretariat under a Secretary General who was assisted by two Deputy Secretaries General. The Secretariat, which was housed in the Château de la Muette in Paris, employed in the latter years of OEEC's life a staff of about 1,000. The members of the Secretariat, who were drawn from all the member countries, owed their loyalty solely to the Organisation and were forbidden to receive instructions from the member governments. In the early days of OEEC the Secretariat was made up of civil servants posted into it from national administrations; later a higher proportion of its members were directly recruited as professional international civil servants.

The main power of the Secretary General was, and is in OECD, that of being able to put forward proposals of his own to the Council, though the extent to which this power has been used has depended on the personality and political authority of the Secretary General. In the past, this has enabled the Secretary General to suggest compromise solutions to settle conflicts between members. The Secretary General and the Secretariat have always maintained close relations with the national delegations to the Organisation and in many cases it has been difficult to judge how far a particular policy or decision has been due primarily to the contribution of one or the other. The Secretary General in putting forward his views could consult members of the national delegations informally in private, without committing member governments. He could circulate proposals that took account of the probable reactions and if necessary he could withdraw them without damaging the prestige of individual governments. From time to time, the Secretary General has also circulated papers on a variety of economic subjects which, although not published, have sometimes had an appreciable impact on the home governments of member countries. M. Robert Marjolin was Secretary General of OEEC from 1948 until 1955 when he was succeeded by M. René Sergent, also from France.

OEEC AND THE NATIONAL DELEGATIONS

The great strength of OEEC lay in the close relationship that was created between the Organisation and its member governments. This was largely the achievement of the permanent national delegations established in Paris, but these delegations could achieve good results only if their home governments gave them strong support. The home government had to be in a position to reconcile different departmental viewpoints and dispatch definite instructions quickly. The British delegation to OEEC was drawn from members of the Treasury, the Board of Trade and the Foreign Office.

THE BUDGET

The budget of OEEC was paid for by contributions from all member countries according to an agreed scale.

The Work of OEEC: Marshall Aid

The first and main task carried out by OEEC was to set up institutions to distribute United States aid for the recovery of Europe. The allocation of Marshall aid under the Economic Co-operation Act of 1948 laid the basis for the whole subsequent development of the movement towards European unification. Without the $11,493,800,000 which the United States Government made available[1] to the countries of Western Europe between 1949 and 1952

[1] *US Economic Assistance Programmes*, Agency for International Development, June 1964.

economic recovery from the state of postwar exhaustion in which these countries found themselves could only have been an extremely slow and laborious process. Marshall aid provided an economic basis which made it possible for European co-operation and integration to take shape.

Neither the Convention for European Economic Co-operation nor the Economic Co-operation Act of 1948 provided for machinery to determine the needs of the recipient countries for assistance, or for the methods to be used for allocating the aid made available by the United States. OEEC and ECA were left to make policy decisions concerning their respective spheres of responsibility. Mr Paul Hoffman, the first Administrator of ECA, stated: 'I try to inculcate the idea that the responsibility must be given to the Europeans themselves . . . in order to get an effective programme, each country would need to bring in its own plan and the OEEC would have to bring in a plan for co-ordination, with us not imposing a proposition on either. I have learnt from experience that if you want enthusiastic co-operation you have to get those concerned to do the planning, or at least to participate in it.'[1]

OEEC accepted the responsibility for co-ordinating the recovery programmes of its member countries and for arriving at a collective recommendation for allocating American assistance among them. ECA retained the right to screen the individual states' programmes and review the allocations agreed by OEEC. It had been feared that irreconcilable conflicts might destroy OEEC before it had begun to find its feet and thus disillusion the American people and Congress with the whole European recovery effort. Most delegations would probably have preferred to handle their aid negotiations on a bilateral basis as they had done during the war and during the first ninety days (April/June 1948) of the European recovery programme, when aid amounting to $1,300 million was distributed to the OEEC countries, but they agreed to the method proposed by the Americans.

PREPARATION OF THE 1948–49 PROGRAMME

OEEC decided to work out a programme which was not merely to be limited to imports to be financed by American aid but one that was to be a complete import programme for Western Europe. A Programme Committee, with one national delegate from each member country, was set up to carry out this task. A directive was issued to the

[1] Interview, New York, 28 January 1953, as reported by H. B. Price in *The Marshall Plan and its Meaning*, Cornell, the University Press, 1955, p. 73.

member countries on 9 June 1948 which laid down that each country's programme should contain its plans for the immediate production, consumption and export of a wide range of commodities; a forecast of the balance of payments with the dollar area; a statement of the economic policy to be followed in 1948–49; the expected results of that policy; and a justification of the amount of aid requested in support of it. The Organisation had also agreed on the principles for reviewing and screening the individual programmes and for relating them to the long-term objectives of OEEC. For many of the participating countries the collection and presentation of the extremely detailed statistical information which was required by the OEEC programme was something quite new and led directly to the wider use of modern statistical methods in these countries.

When the national programmes for 1948–49 were being prepared in May and June the total amount of United States aid that would be available was not known. OEEC therefore asked member states to prepare their individual programmes on the basis of the amount of aid shown for each country in the material the Administration had submitted to Congress when requesting an appropriation. These provisional figures were the result of the work of two committees of the United States Government, one of them using a balance of payments and the other a commodity approach. The total assistance that was tentatively proposed was $5,300 million. Early in July 1948, however, ECA gave notice that this figure must be cut to the amount available which was $4,875 million. It was at this stage that ECA asked OEEC to calculate the division of this sum. Since it was not considered possible for the Council or committees consisting of representatives of all the member states to cut down the 'bids' put in by each country a special Committee of Four was set up to work out the division, on the clear understanding that none of their recommendations would become effective until all member countries had unanimously approved them. The Committee of Four[1] was asked to examine each national programme, to discuss it with the national experts who had prepared it and to recommend a fair figure for each country. These discussions were the prototype of the 'cross-examination' procedure which became a permanent feature of the working method first of OEEC and then of OECD. It was also the first example of the use of the restricted group, a technique that was later used on several occasions in order to solve a particular crisis. In

[1] Sir Eric Roll of the United Kingdom, M. Guindey of France, Signor Stoppani of Italy, and Mr Spierenburg of the Netherlands. The four countries represented on the Committee were due to receive about 80 per cent of the aid.

making its calculations, the Committee of Four assumed that an intra-European payments scheme would be operative during the period to be covered by the 1948–49 programme. Credits granted by creditor countries to debtor countries would enable the latter to continue trade which might otherwise be threatened by the lack of a payments mechanism. A group of five was set up to supervise bilateral negotiations between all interested member countries, so that the contributions of local currencies by the creditor countries and the drawing rights of the debtor nations could be fixed. Thus the allocation of American aid became closely linked with a scheme to raise the level of intra-European trade and liberalise payments. This was necessary because one of the guiding principles laid down by the Council of OEEC concerning the division of aid was the instruction that the existence of exportable surpluses in certain European countries was to be noted and that no commodities were to be imported from the Western hemisphere which could be made available outside the dollar area.

THE LONG-TERM PROGRAMME

The genesis of the long-term programme was a visit to Paris by Mr Paul Hoffman in the summer of 1948. Mr Hoffman asked OEEC to provide an outline of its general strategy to achieve the solvency and stability of its member countries by 1952. He wanted 'not a mass of statistics but a plan of action'. OEEC accordingly invited each member to submit a plan showing how it would reach by the year 1952–53 a position from which it could maintain its own economy without extraordinary external aid. Members were also asked to show how their national economies would fit into the economy of a non-aided Europe. The programme was intended to demonstrate to Congress what could be done in the long term with a regular flow of aid over the next four years.

It was hoped that OEEC would correlate the national programmes and formulate a master plan which would show how the best use could be made of the resources of the OEEC countries as a whole. This ambitious plan was not realised. Many countries were slow in providing information about their national plans and some of it was inadequate. It was hoped that OEEC would produce a complete plan by 1 November 1948 but only the British and Icelandic plans had arrived by 1 October, the date by which national programmes should have been submitted. There were wide differences in the economic philosophy of the different OEEC countries, some of which were opposed to long-term planning, and the documents that were eventually submitted were too dissimilar for OEEC to weld them together in a coherent whole. The achievement of a generally accepted master plan depended on a greater degree of consensus than the OEEC countries possessed.

Late in 1948 OEEC realised that the immediate publication of a long-term programme was impossible and instead published, on 30 December, an Interim Report. The report did not claim to put forward a 'joint' European recovery programme but claimed that 'there lies behind it a period of co-operative activity unlike anything hitherto known in the economic relations between any group of independent states'. The report analysed the material set out in the national plans and forecast the degree of recovery that could be achieved by 1952–53. The report frankly discussed the four main aspects of the recovery of Western Europe: the expansion of production; the ability of Western Europe to pay its way with the outside world in the future; the scope for increasing Western Europe's internal trade; and the use of its resources in the best way.

OEEC saw European recovery both as an internal problem of Europe and also as one aspect of Europe's relations with the outside world. The Organisation realised that important policy changes were required on the part of its member countries and did not underestimate the difficulties. The Interim Report provided a new view of European recovery by giving OEEC members a better understanding of the ways in which Europe's position in the world economy had become weakened. The way in which experts from the different countries worked together in providing OEEC with the information which was the basis of the Interim Report was important in showing how these countries could co-operate in the future. Finally, the idea of a long-term programme provided the intellectual background for the Organisation's eventual liberalisation of trade policy.

After the publication of the Interim Report the proposed master plan slipped out of sight. Instead, in February 1949, the Executive Committee of OEEC agreed upon certain principles of co-operative action by the participating countries, thus following the lead given by Mr Paul Hoffman who had outlined a six-point plan for European recovery to Congress earlier in the month.

The Work of OEEC: Payments

From the earliest days of OEEC a payments agreement was urgently needed to plan the distribution of American aid more economically as well as to make intra-European trade, still restricted by hampering bilateral agreements, more vigorous and fluid. This was one of the principal aims of OEEC.

THE FIRST AGREEMENT

The Council of OEEC accepted the principles of a payments agreement in July 1948 but on 12 August, when the Committee of Four recommended an allocation of dollars for such a scheme to the Council, there was no agreement on the practical features of the plan. The specially created Committee of Five was therefore asked to work out an acceptable solution. The main feature of the proposed agreement was that member countries exporting more to other members than they imported from them should provide this surplus as a 'grant' by putting their own currency at the disposal of the debtor countries as 'drawing rights' in return for which they would receive an equivalent amount of dollar aid out of ECA funds, known as 'conditional' aid. The Committee of Five supervised the bilateral negotiations between each pair of the participating countries which determined the expected balance of payments between them for the coming year. This showed who would be 'creditors' and who 'debtors' in the agreement. There were many difficulties. Britain was afraid of any agreement that might make her pay out gold or dollars and Belgium, which was commercially well placed with the rest of Europe, was afraid that her aid would be dissipated by the Plan. The Committee of Five made its recommendations after a month, though it took longer for the seventy-eight sets of bilateral negotiations to be completed.

The agreement for Intra-European Payments and Compensations was accepted by the Council of OEEC on 16 October 1948. All OEEC countries except Switzerland and Portugal took part in the scheme. Each of these countries except Greece established drawing rights from at least one other country and mostly from four or more. Drawing rights made the payments agreement a 'little Marshall Plan'. They increased the credit available for the recovery of intra-European trade and thus brought about a secondary distribution of American aid besides the initial allocation of dollars, though they did not change the amount of dollars any country received from America. Thus France received $300 million worth of goods through drawing rights, almost a third as much aid as it received directly from America. Belgium on the other hand passed on 84 per cent of its dollar aid for the year. The agreement thus helped those OEEC countries whose payments positions were worst.

The Bank for International Settlements (BIS) in Basle was appointed as the clearing agency for the scheme, and it reported that drawing rights covered 37·6 per cent of the gross deficits and surpluses incurred by the member countries during the nine months of the agreement's life. Although the agreement was criticised for continuing bilateralism in intra-European trade and for providing the wrong incentives for trade, it was successful in achieving OEEC's main aim: an agreement that would stimulate trade quickly.

The weaknesses of the scheme led to heated negotiations and discussions about the revision of the agreement. ECA proposed that drawing rights should be both transferable and convertible but convertibility was strongly opposed by the British who were alarmed by their growing financial crisis and the fall of their reserves.

THE SECOND AGREEMENT

After discussing the ideas put forward for the revision of the payments agreement the Council of OEEC decided, on 1 July 1949, to agree to transferability of drawing rights of up to 25 per cent. The dispute over the second agreement, which was finally signed on 7 September 1949, was one of the biggest crises in the history of OEEC, and its solution by discussion and compromise demonstrated that the Organisation was able to overcome the most serious differences between its members, who showed themselves reluctant to force the issue to the breaking point. The main pressure to reach agreement was the possibility, in view of the attitude of representatives of the United States Administration, that the next appropriation of aid might have been endangered.

The main feature of the second payments agreement was the establishment of multilateral drawing rights. Three quarters of the drawing rights were divided among contributing countries. The other quarter could be used to cover the recipients' deficits with any other country signing the agreement, with the exception of Switzerland. BIS automatically applied the drawing rights in the same way as it had controlled the bilateral drawing rights. The new agreement provided that OEEC should 'carry out comprehensive reviews' of the working of the agreement at least twice before 30 June 1950. Mr Hoffman felt that these reviews would ensure that countries would not gain dollars from the pool of drawing rights by holding down their imports from other European countries.

In practice, the second payments agreement worked less well than the first. The 'false incentives', the failure to achieve genuine multilateralism and the rigidities of the two agreements led to discussions as to how to replace the second agreement as soon as it came into force. From December 1949 there were constant meetings of technical committees and political discussions between governmental representatives which led up to an agreement on 7 July 1950 in the Council of OEEC on the terms of the European Payments Union. The new agreement was formally signed on 19 September.

THE EUROPEAN PAYMENTS UNION

The European Payments Union (EPU) was primarily designed to be an automatic mechanism for the multilateral settlement of the accounts of its members. Its main feature was the establishment of a multilateral clearing house. During each month the payments due from one country to another were registered in the mutual accounts of the central banks and the residual balance of each country towards each one of its partners was communicated to BIS, which acted as agent for the Union, which then cancelled out the claims and debts accumulated during the month by each country with respect to all its partners. This process left only a single residual claim or debit towards EPU. This balance was settled between each government and the Union. Another main objective of the EPU agreement was to facilitate the settlement of the final monthly net payments. Mutual EPU credits financed part of these settlements and the rest was met in gold, dollars or any currency acceptable to the creditor countries. The third main objective of the agreement was to provide effective consultations between the member states on the problems arising from the growth of excessive or permanent debtor or creditor positions in the Union.

Although ECA wanted to establish a strong Managing Board (the governing body of EPU), which could exert pressure on national economic policies, Britain and the Scandinavian countries did not wish to set up a powerful international body which could interfere with their domestic planning and this view prevailed. The Managing Board was composed of seven members chosen by the OEEC Council from persons nominated by the member countries. Meetings of the Board, whose members were chosen for their personal qualifications as experts, were also attended by representatives of the BIS and of the International Monetary Fund (IMF). The Board could take decisions by a straight majority and was 'responsible for supervising the execution of the Agreement' but was to be subordinate to the Council of OEEC. In practice, the subordination of the Board to the Council scotched the ECA concept of a quasi-independent governing body with substantial influence over national policies.

EPU received $350 million of working capital from the United States Government, but once started its operations did not depend on new dollar aid and it was able to finance a large proportion of intra-European trade on its own.

EPU received more from debtors than it paid out to creditors in its first year. This led ECA to decide against a direct dollar grant to EPU for 1951–52.

There were three main features of the establishment of EPU.[1] First, monetary incentives to bilateralism in trade and payments were eliminated while, at the same time, the maximum economy of resources in intra-European settlements was attained through the multilateral clearing of all bilateral surpluses and deficits and through making fully multilateral all the means of settlement used to cover residual credits and debts. Second, OEEC member states accepted the risks involved in this system and in the concomitant trade liberalisation programme, in return for the provision of 'cushioning' credits for moderate disequilibria in intra-European payments. Third, it was intended to stimulate re-adjustment policies and to check the development of excessive permanent disequilibria in the Union.

There was a 35·4 per cent increase in trade among the OEEC countries during the first working year of EPU. It is hard to estimate to what extent EPU contributed to this, but it undoubtedly helped. During the first year of its life EPU achieved the offsetting of 65 per cent of the bilateral deficits between members. The previous payments agreements had achieved the offsetting of 2 per cent of these deficits in twenty-one months.

Intra-European trade was affected at this time by the German balance-of-payments crisis. The OEEC Council set up a Mediation Group of experts to make recommendations to Germany on fiscal policies and controls of credit and raw materials. Although the conditions imposed by the Mediation Group on the Federal Republic of Germany were resented in some quarters as 'intervention', the Federal Government had to solve its balance-of-payments difficulties either in or out of the EPU and they looked easier to solve inside.

[1] See R. Triffin, *Europe and the Money Muddle*, New Haven, Yale University Press, 1957, p. 168.

In the event it was certainly not to Germany's disadvantage to comply with the recommendations made by the Mediation Group. The solution of the German economic crisis was thus achieved by OEEC on a European basis without American intervention. During the same period the Managing Board of EPU also intervened to assist Austria, Greece, Portugal and Turkey.

The establishment and success of EPU was of great importance to OEEC. The negotiations leading to the setting up of EPU, carried out by small technical committees of experts and a small group of ministers, and the small Managing Board and Mediation Group, were proof of the effectiveness of the Organisation's policy of using restricted groups to make its whole machinery work better. The working of the two payments agreements and then of EPU demonstrated OEEC's increasing influence over European monetary and trade policies during the period 1948–51.

Later, between 1956 and 1958, the main problems facing EPU were again largely those caused by extreme debtors and extreme creditors. The Managing Board frequently reviewed the position of the so-called 'structural' debtor countries (which included Austria, Iceland, Greece and Turkey) and gave them advice. These countries received special grants from the United States and were relieved from some of their commitments under the OEEC liberalisation programme (see pp. 100–105). In 1957, together with persistent French deficits, they constituted the main problem of imbalance in the EPU system. France suspended liberalisation until its situation could be redressed. Special measures were adopted amounting to re-adjustment of the French exchange rate, and the French Government carried into effect a programme of intensive financial rehabilitation. In consequence, the French situation improved towards the end of 1957.

THE COLLECTIVE APPROACH TO CONVERTIBILITY

Following initiatives taken at the Commonwealth Finance Ministers' meeting in London in January 1952, the Prime Ministers' meeting in the summer and the Commonwealth Conference in December of the same year, it was proposed that there should be a Commonwealth approach to a wider system of trade and payments, and following the Conference the idea of such a move to convertibility was current in Britain. In February 1953 Sir Anthony Eden and Mr R. A. Butler[1] went to Washington to discuss convertibility with the new Administration but without immediate results.

[1] Later Lord Avon and Lord Butler.

Many of the members of OEEC thought that Britain was planning a move to convertibility without regard to the effects this might have on European monetary arrangements. In March 1953 Sir Anthony Eden and Mr R. A. Butler reacted by presenting the Commonwealth's ideas at a meeting of the OEEC Council, emphasising that any move to convertibility would be on a collective basis and that the freeing of payments must be linked with the maintenance of the liberalisation of trade. They also made it clear that convertibility must not be achieved at the expense of a fall in intra-European trade. The implication was that EPU would disappear. The main reaction of the OEEC countries to Britain's suggestions was that, regardless of convertibility, some kind of European clearing system should be retained. OEEC members did not want to jettison EPU in favour of a wider payments system that might collapse. They also wanted any move towards convertibility to be made slowly and under the supervision of EPU.

It was generally considered that if one country alone, or only a few, moved to convertibility there could be a serious reduction of trade and, possibly, a return to the old bilateral trading arrangements, which would be most damaging. But these dangers could be averted if a group of countries moved together towards convertibility and if the OEEC trade liberalisation programme could be preserved and strengthened. It was the combination of all these measures that became the collective approach to convertibility.

In April 1953 OEEC sent a mission to Washington to present a 'Europeanised' version of the Commonwealth plan. The OEEC mission asked the Americans for specific reforms in their commercial and foreign investment policies and in stabilising purchases of raw materials. The new administration was not, however, willing to take any action until it had assessed its own financial position and formulated a financial policy.

In March 1954 the work that had begun in OEEC on the problem of transforming EPU resulted in the setting up of a Monetary Group, under the Chairmanship of Mr R. A. Butler, to examine the problems that would arise if convertibility were achieved. Under this Group working parties discussed the technicalities of convertibility from the summer of 1954 until the difficulties were resolved in the European Monetary Agreement of the following year.

The Finance Ministers of the OEEC countries met in London in July 1954 to discuss convertibility. They decided that no member, when ready for convertibility, should retract from the level of liberalisation then prevailing. They stressed that at the same time as they moved towards convertibility members should make fresh efforts to eliminate the remaining quantitative restrictions on European trade, and should also progressively remove restrictions against dollar goods. At this meeting the Finance Ministers sketched out a system that would replace EPU after the achievement of convertibility: this was the basis of the European Monetary Agreement.

Many members of OEEC envisaged the achievement of convertibility through a gradual extension of EPU. They saw that EPU had played an invaluable part in European recovery and did not want to throw away a payments system that acted as a form of insurance in bad times. The hardening of the Union showed that member countries were already moving towards convertibility through EPU. When the EPU Agreement was renewed in June 1954 it was agreed that all settlements within quotas and the extensions to the quotas should be carried out 50 per cent in credit. When EPU was renewed in 1955 it was decided that all such settlements within the quotas and extensions should be made 75 per cent in gold and 25 per cent in credit. This was not only a victory for the creditor countries who had long wanted to harden the Union but also an important stage in moving towards convertibility.

On 10 June 1955, as a result of the discussion held by the Ministerial Group and the working parties on the skeleton plan, sketched out in July 1954, the Council of OEEC, meeting at ministerial level, adopted a decision setting out the action which should follow a return to convertibility though the actual European Monetary Agreement was not ready for approval until the end of July. The Council also took action to preserve the OEEC code of liberalisation after a return to convertibility and tightened the provisions of the code relating to the suspension of liberalisation measures by countries invoking balance-of-payments difficulties.

THE EUROPEAN MONETARY AGREEMENT

On 29 July 1955 the Council of OEEC approved the protocol extending EPU for another year and providing for the establishment of the European Monetary Agreement which was to come into force when EPU members, representing more than 50 per cent of the then existing EPU quotas, declared their intention to make their currencies convertible and their willingness to bring the Agreement into operation. This happened on 29 December 1958 when a majority of OEEC member states declared their currencies convertible in differing degrees. The European Monetary Agreement (EMA) was signed by representatives of the member countries on 5 August 1955.

The terms of EMA provided for all payments to be made on a 100 per cent convertible basis, and for the establishment of the European Fund and a multilateral system for settlements, both controlled by a Board of Management (under the supervision of the Council originally of OEEC and now of OECD, since EMA has been retained as part of the structure of the new Organisation). The Fund provides short-term (as a rule up to three years) credits to members and facilitates the settlement of monthly balances between the central banks of member states. The main difference between the working of EPU and that of EMA is that credit, which was automatic in EPU, now has to be obtained by application to the Managing Board of EMA. The Board will agree to grant a member country credit only on condition that it takes steps to rectify the conditions which made the loan necessary. The Fund was established with an initial capital of $600 million. Contributions and credits are in gold. Under the Agreement members have the option of settling their claims and debts through market channels at any time or through the multilateral system for settlements at the end of each month. Each member country is free to determine the limits of fluctuation of its currency, taking into account obligations under the IMF and undertakings to make such margins as moderate and stable as possible, but has to inform all member countries of its currency fluctuations.

The development of the collective approach was largely responsible for enabling OEEC to continue. Whereas the British saw the achievement of convertibility as a way of gaining freedom from the existing controls on European payments, other member countries were afraid of the repercussions of the liberation of sterling. Most members wished to keep such a move under the control of OEEC as an extension of EPU rather than as a replacement of the Union. The desire of these countries to retain a multilateral compensation mechanism at the same time as moving towards convertibility was satisfied by the EMA, which was intended to keep the new system of payments under the control of a Management Board and under the Council of OEEC. Little use has, however, been made of EMA since it came into operation, each country being concerned more with its overall balance of payments than with its balance with other member countries. Although after the conclusion of EMA there was a retreat from convertibility and the agreement remained dormant until 27 December 1958, a majority of OEEC countries made a concerted move to varying degrees of convertibility at that time, and the terms of agreement came into operation.

The Work of OEEC: The Liberalisation of Trade

One of the main aims of OEEC when it was set up was to reduce the restrictions on intra-European trade and to make it more flexible by attacking the import quotas which limited the amount of goods one country could import from another. Moves towards a wider European market could not be effective unless many of the then large number of quotas were removed.

The OEEC plan of action, which replaced the long-term programme in the spring of 1949, asked for a review of measures of trade liberalisation. In June of that year, during the negotiations for the first payments agreement, Sir Stafford Cripps suggested that OEEC countries should remove some quotas. At the end of June the Council of OEEC approved a programme of trade liberalisation. By October the OEEC countries had removed unilaterally quotas on about 30 per cent of their 1948 private trade with each other (all trade other than that carried out by governments or their agencies) but many of the quotas removed were obsolete or nominal and few quotas were removed on manufactured products or on farm produce.

On 31 October 1949 Mr Paul Hoffman called on OEEC to take 'really effective action to remove quantitative restrictions on trade on which you have recently made a start'. In November the Council of OEEC decided that by 15 December each member country was to remove quotas on at least 50 per cent of its 1948 imports (excluding imports for the public sector) from the other member countries in each of the three main categories: food and feeding stuffs, raw materials, and manufactures. A central group of five members was appointed to check the working of this agreement and it examined the progress made by member countries. Austria, Denmark, the Federal Republic of Germany, Ireland, Norway and Turkey failed in one way or another to meet OEEC's requirements, but in general the target was achieved without any great difficulty. The central group of five is another example of the use of restricted groups by OEEC to supervise the implementation of an important programme.

Following pressure from ECA the Council of OEEC decided, in January 1950, that, following the establishment of an adequate payments agreement, OEEC countries should remove more trade restrictions until 60 per cent of private imports in each of the three main categories were free of quotas. At this stage some member countries discriminated against others by removing quotas from only a few member countries.

Most of the discrimination in intra-European trade at this time was rooted in currency difficulties. The members of OEEC had accepted the Code of Liberalisation in August 1950 to create greater equality in intra-European trade. The Code's rules were, as soon as EPU came into effect, to end the discrimination of some countries against others when this was based solely on balance-of-payments grounds. All new liberalisation measures were to be regionally non-discriminatory within the whole EPU area, including the sterling and French and Belgian franc areas. By December 1950 all existing liberalisation measures had to be applied equally to all imports from all member countries or had to be withdrawn. After 1 February 1951 all imports from member countries had to be treated equally, whether subject to quotas or not. OEEC was to decide what was meant by 'equality' in the administration of quotas and it also provided for exceptions to these rules.

Although another decision of the Council laid down that in February 1951 member countries should remove quotas on 75 per cent of their private imports from other members, it was agreed, as a result of objections by some countries over agricultural imports, that this new level should apply to the total of imports and not to each separate category as before. It was more difficult to put the new measures into effect and no real progress was made until late spring 1951.

The strain placed on the payments position of member countries by the Korean War and the re-armament drive led several OEEC countries, including Britain, France and the Federal Republic of Germany, to evoke the escape clauses of the Liberalisation Code in 1951 and 1952, but they all returned to a policy of liberalisation within a short period.

The overall liberalisation percentage began to increase again during 1952 and was over 75 per cent at the end of 1953. By the end of 1954 the overall liberalisation percentage was over 83 per cent. In January 1955 the Council of OEEC decided, first, to raise the minimum level of liberalisation to 90 per cent of the value of imports of members and to 75 per cent of imports in each of the three principal categories. It also decided that member countries must, whatever their existing level of liberalisation, remove 10 per cent of restrictions on total private imports still in force on 30 June 1954. In view of their stringency, these decisions were accompanied by new safeguard clauses. By the end of 1956 overall liberalisation was over 85 per cent, but at the end of 1957 four countries had still not been able to fulfil the requirements of the first decision. By the time that it was transformed into OECD in 1961, OEEC had raised the degree of liberalisation to 95 per cent. Quotas in the industrial sector had by this time almost completely disappeared and the remaining restrictions were in the agricultural sector.

Parallel to its efforts to liberalise intra-European trade, OEEC wished to promote a gradual liberalisation of imports from the dollar area as soon as the problem of the dollar gap became less acute. This was in line with the commitments accepted by member countries in GATT. At the end of 1954, the Council adopted a recommendation concerning the relaxation of restrictions on imports and invisible transactions and transfers relating to the dollar area. Later on, the Organisation examined repeatedly the implementation of this recommendation, as well as the effects of the measures applied by the United States and Canada on the policies of European countries towards the dollar area. As a result of this pressure, the average percentage of liberalisation of OEEC countries *vis-à-vis* the dollar area was progressively increased. This exercise helped also to identify and alleviate certain obstacles to the expansion of European exports in North America.

LIBERALISATION OF INVISIBLE TRANSACTIONS

OEEC also aimed at easing restrictions on payments relating to invisible transactions: insurance, tourist expenditure, payments of profits and dividends, etc. In January 1950 member countries agreed not to impose new restrictions on invisible transactions. As regards tourism and business travel, the OEEC countries could agree only to 'deal in as liberal a manner as possible with applications to make payments abroad'. With other activities, they allowed the free transfer of frontier workers' wages, dividends, profits, rents, interest and other business payments. The liberalisation of insurance cover had a remarkable effect on the pattern of European insurance. In November 1955 all invisible transactions were freed, unless a member state expressly raised a reservation against a specific item which would exempt that state from liberalising it. The Committee for Invisible Transactions was set up in 1955 and was instructed to study all questions concerning invisible liberalisation. In 1957 a study by the Committee led to a decision of the Council liberalising movements of capital between member states for long-term, direct investments, making transferable the proceeds of future direct investment if liquidated, and permitting the use of non-resident blocked funds for certain types of investment and current expenditure.

GOVERNMENTAL AIDS TO EXPORTS

OEEC also tried to eliminate governmental aids to exports tending to distort international competition. In January 1955 the Council decided that member countries should abolish certain aids to exporters before 1 January 1956. The aids specified included direct subsidies to exporters, currency retention schemes involving a bonus on exports, and remissions of direct and indirect taxes. Member states also undertook that they would not introduce new measures which would distort international competition. This decision was quickly carried into effect by most member countries though it left some of the special problems relating to agriculture unsolved.

TARIFFS

OEEC's liberalisation activities were highly successful, although there still remained barriers to trade in the form of restrictive business practices, administrative rules and technical regulations. But the more successfully OEEC eliminated quotas the more tariffs became the main obstacle to freer intra-European trade. When imports were completely subject to quotas, tariffs did not constitute a significant barrier to international competition. When imports were 90 per cent liberalised, tariffs assumed far greater importance. Low tariff member countries felt that they stood to lose by eliminating quantitative restrictions when other member countries, although abandoning quotas, retained their high tariff walls. The high tariff countries, having lost one means of protecting their industries in the form of quotas, were very chary of the increased competition with which tariff reductions would face them. The British Government, in particular, was opposed to OEEC becoming a framework for tariff reductions. Some member countries felt, as a matter of principle, that tariffs should be treated in GATT, the appropriate world-wide organisation. The members of the EEC have by now nearly eliminated their national tariffs and established their common external tariff. Those countries which are members of the European Free Trade Association eliminated national tariff barriers on industrial trade within the EFTA area on 1 January 1967, though they have not undertaken the harmonisation of their tariffs towards third countries. The creation of the European Economic Community as a customs union has presented problems, concerning the commercial relationship of the Six with the other OEEC member states, which are still unresolved.[1]

[1] Whereas imports into high tariff members of the EEC, such as France, from countries outside EEC have tended to benefit from the downward alignment of

THE RAW MATERIAL SHORTAGE

Owing to the Korean War and the ensuing re-armament drive, shortages of raw materials occurred during the second half of 1950 and became worse throughout that year and the beginning of 1951. The price of wool, copper, nickel, zinc and other raw materials rose rapidly within a few weeks of the outbreak of hostilities. The cost of European imports rose sharply in consequence and inflationary pressures were built up. In September 1950 M. Marjolin, Secretary General of OEEC, published *Urgent Economic Problems, Memorandum by the Secretary General,* which emphasised the need for close co-operation between member countries in their approach to the shortage.

The most urgent of the problems facing the OEEC countries was the allocation of available raw materials. Except for coal, timber, pulp and a few other commodities, Western Europe depended heavily on imports from the rest of the world. In October 1950 the Council of OEEC agreed to call for studies of restrictions on the use of these materials and of the allocation of certain goods using them.

OEEC committees on coal, iron and steel, non-ferrous metals, pulp and paper, textiles, chemical products and miscellaneous products played a certain role in trying to harmonise the internal rationing methods which it was recommended that member countries of OEEC should employ to ease the shortage. These committees also exchanged information on action taken by member countries and the United States and Canada to increase production.

The worst of the crisis was over by the summer of 1951 but the Council of OEEC decided, in March 1951, to call for additional long-term measures to overcome the shortage. Agreements were reached concerning copper and other scarce materials in the summer of 1951 at a time when the position concerning most of these materials was easing, and they were, therefore, never fully tested. Useful work was carried out by the OEEC Coal Committee which, in co-operation with the ECE Coal Trade Sub-Committee, created a coal pool from a small percentage of the coal exports of member countries for distribution among the countries with weaker bargaining power. The same technique of distributing a proportion of available supplies was later used by the OEEC Oil Committee at the time of the Suez crisis. Although OEEC succeeded in easing some of the problems of the shortage of raw materials and achieved considerable success in the

high tariffs towards the common external tariff, trade between low tariff members of the EEC, such as the Federal Republic of Germany, and third countries has suffered from the upward alignment of tariffs to the Community level.

case of the Suez crisis when full co-operation prevailed with the United States and the major international oil companies, on the whole the experience of the organisation in trying to deal with some of the major problems affecting the member countries showed that its effective role was limited when the economic problems requiring attention were world-wide in their scope.

The Work of OEEC: The Free Trade Area Negotiations

When the six members of the European Coal and Steel Community seriously began, in 1955, to consider the formation of a customs union some of the other members of OEEC accelerated the studies they had already begun concerning the formation of a 'low tariff club' in which tariffs would be cut on products of particular importance in intra-European trade. These reductions would be generalised to the other members of the GATT. This plan was not acceptable to Britain but after it became clear that the GATT tariff negotiations which had begun early in 1956 would not succeed, the low tariff countries in OEEC pressed Britain to pursue the possibility of establishing a free trade area on a wider European basis. This the British Government did.

Following the publication of the 'Spaak Report',[1] which was accepted by the foreign ministers of the Six in the spring of 1956 and which made definite proposals for the drafting of treaties establishing European atomic energy and economic communities, the Council of OEEC appointed a special working party, in July 1956, to study the possible forms and methods of association between the proposed European Economic Community and the other OEEC countries. In January 1957 the working party submitted a *Report on the possibility of creating a Free Trade Area in Europe*[2] stating that despite technical obstacles, a possible solution would be to form a 'free trade area' between all OEEC countries. In this area, while eliminating tariffs and other barriers to trade between themselves (as in the European Economic Community), member countries would retain the right to regulate their individual commercial policies with the outside world.

In October 1957 the Council of OEEC established an intergovernmental ministerial committee under the chairmanship of Mr Reginald Maudling, at that time British Paymaster-General, to negotiate a free trade agreement.

[1] See pp. 31 and 171.

[2] OEEC document C(57)5, Paris, 1957.

At the beginning of the negotiations, the British Government published a White Paper suggesting a loose form of association between the Common Market and other OEEC member countries in a free trade area. Tariff reductions and the abolition of quotas would be limited to industrial products. Members of the free trade area other than the Common Market countries would retain their own external tariffs against non-members, the British Government being unwilling to adopt a common external tariff, owing mainly to its desire to be entitled to continue to apply an independent low tariff policy to Commonwealth trade.

Negotiations in the Maudling Committee proved difficult. The Six agreed on a common position, which was set out in a *Memorandum from the European Economic Community*, more generally known as the Ockrent Report.[1]

Although the British Government made certain concessions towards the desire of France and Italy to provide for agricultural free trade in compensation for their acceptance of industrial free trade, the French Government wanted a greater harmonisation of tariffs and of commercial policies than the British Government was prepared to accept. Further, the British Government was unwilling to accept the institutional system which the French Government proposed.

In December 1958, negotiations in the Maudling Committee came to an end after the French Minister of Information, M. Soustelle, had announced to the press that it was not possible to form a free trade area between the Six members of the EEC and the eleven other countries of OEEC without a common external tariff and without harmonisation in the economic and social spheres, a view which had already been expressed in June by the EEC Commission.

Had the free trade area negotiations succeeded, it is probable that OEEC would have played a very important role in supervising the working of the area. In the event, intra-EEC trade has been subject to the institutions of the Community which also deal with trade agreements between the EEC as a group and third countries, and the intra-area trade of the seven members of the European Free Trade Association (EFTA), which was established in 1960, has been subject to its own institutions, thus leaving OEEC, and later OECD, in a marginal position concerning intra-European trade.

[1] M. Ockrent, from Belgium, was Chairman of the Co-ordination Committee of the Six members of EEC.

Other activities of OEEC

The European Productivity Agency (EPA) was set up in June 1953 by the Council of OEEC to

'draw up a European productivity programme, with a view to preparing and implementing the collective action and co-ordinating the individual action of the Member countries in the field of productivity.'

In practice, EPA co-ordinated the National Productivity Centres which had already been set up in member states to improve productivity at the national level. The EPA was controlled by a Governing Board composed of representatives of all the member countries, together with Spain and Yugoslavia, which was responsible to the Council of OEEC. It was assisted by an advisory board consisting of representatives of the Council of European Industrial Federations, the Joint Trade Union Advisory Committee and European agricultural organisations.

EPA was an operational body which tried to raise levels of productivity by stimulating national action through the exchange of techniques, experience and information, and by common action where this was advisable for reasons of economy. The Governing Board developed close links with the national productivity centres and gave advice indirectly through national organisations and professional bodies rather than directly to industrial firms themselves.

EPA extended its interests to cover the needs of the less developed areas of Europe, both through providing training facilities and by pilot demonstration schemes. It was responsible for projects in Sardinia, Turkey and the North of Greece, aimed at demonstrating the possibilities of development prospects to the local inhabitants, local and national authorities, and to other bodies that could provide capital for more extensive schemes later on.

EPA also carried out work in the scientific and educational domains and this, together with its work in the less developed areas of Europe, transformed it, in practice, into an operational agency of OEEC. EPA was considered to have achieved its work before OEEC was transformed into OECD and it was wound up in 1961.

OEEC also carried out work in the domains of energy, agriculture, transport and manpower: activities in these sectors which continue under OECD are described in the chapter on OECD (see pp. 405–456).

OEEC, NATO AND THE ECONOMY DRIVE

The development of NATO, which was established by the signing of the North Atlantic Treaty in April 1949, as an organisation endowed with economic as well as political and military competences[1] led the Council of OEEC to decide, at the beginning of 1952, that the time had come to reconsider the role of the Organisation. At this time Britain was anxious to put its major effort behind NATO and the Atlantic concept. The problems of European economic co-operation were considered by Britain to be of secondary importance at this time and the political objectives centring on the Atlantic Alliance were given pride of place.

The British Government decided that the scope of OEEC's work could be reduced in view of the work of NATO in distributing American military aid. It therefore proposed cutting the administrative budget of OEEC by 50 per cent, but the continental member countries insisted that some purely European body should continue to work in the economic field and this point of view won support from the United States Government. The British Government then changed its proposal to a budget reduction of 28 per cent and in view of the cuts, which were agreed, the Council decided to reduce the Secretariat from 949 to 633, and the Organisation's budget was cut by one third between 1951–52 and 1952–53. The Council also decided to merge some of the commodity committees and abolish the Committee for Miscellaneous Products. These decisions were preceded by a detailed examination of all the activities of OEEC and before they were made the Council was reassured that none of the fundamental activities of the Organisation would be impaired.

The result of the economy drive was to cut down the secondary activities of OEEC and to place the Organisation on a more economic basis. The British desire to reduce the scope of OEEC and to rely more on NATO had been successfully resisted by the continental countries and the United States, though the Americans went part of the way with Britain in wanting to use NATO as the chief instrument of their policy. It was generally held by the OEEC countries that the work carried on by OEEC after the end of the Marshall Plan was too important to be discontinued.

[1] Article 2 of the North Atlantic Treaty states that the partners shall 'promote conditions of stability and well-being' and 'seek to eliminate conflict in their national economic policies, and to encourage economic collaboration between any or all of them'.

Conclusions

OEEC had four major achievements to its credit. It administered the distribution of Marshall aid. It freed intra-European trade from wartime and some prewar restrictions. It created a multilateral European payments mechanism. And, after being established as a 'crisis organisation', it became Western Europe's first permanent organisation for economic consultation and co-operation. These achievements not only restored Western Europe's war-shattered economies and enabled it to secure great increases in production and trade and to eliminate what had once seemed likely to be a lasting dollar gap: they also provided a springboard for subsequent developments in European co-operation and integration.

OEEC's success was due largely to the fact that, in the years of its most important achievements, its members had the will to co-operate. Most of them faced the same immense problems of economic reconstruction. Their approach to these problems had much in common, because most of them shared many characteristics of political, economic and social structure. Most important of all the factors that led them to work so closely together, however, was the condition, laid down by the United States Government, that they must collaborate if they were to receive Marshall aid.

A second major factor that made for effective co-operation, especially during the years of Marshall aid, was that OEEC evolved working methods which were very well adapted to the task of securing ministerial unanimity in an intergovernmental organisation. These were developed largely from the methods which were used to carry out the first division of aid, notably the use of the small 'restricted group', the questionnaire and the 'confrontation' techniques. One of the principal lessons to emerge from the work of OEEC was the utility of a small group of from three to six experts, instructed to work out difficult multilateral agreements affecting all the member countries and requiring their assent. Another factor which contributed to OEEC's success was its provision of a permanent mechanism for the multilateral discussion and negotiation of problems to be settled on a multilateral basis. Within this framework, the habit of consultation was developed at many different levels, among financial and technical experts, government officials and politicians. The national delegations and the Secretariat developed a particularly close relationship in which the main strength of OEEC lay. National delegations acquired the habit of considering problems from an 'OEEC point of view' which made it much easier to obtain genuine co-operation between the member countries. Through the national delegations the 'OEEC point of view' constantly influenced home governments.

Despite this, OEEC was not entirely successful. It was effective so long as its members had a powerful motive for reaching agreement, such as the need to qualify for Marshall aid, or when it handled crises and short-term problems. But its member governments did not encourage it to deal with deep-seated and continuing problems such as the reduction or elimination of tariffs, the promotion of trade in agricultural products, and the co-ordination of its members' general economic policies and planning. As an intergovernmental organisation, it depended on continuing unity of view among its larger members at least, and this proved in general insufficient after the Marshall aid period. The deepest rift was that between Britain and the six countries that formed the ECSC and later the EEC. The British and some of the other members of OEEC did not at that time want to deal with problems of trade and of general economic co-ordination at the European level, holding that world-wide bodies such as the International Monetary Fund (IMF) and the GATT provided the proper forum, whereas the Six were determined to press ahead with the unification of Europe. After this split within Europe had become institutionalised with the establishment of the three Community organisations of the Six, followed by that of EFTA, OEEC was transformed into OECD in 1961.

Chapter Four

THE COUNCIL OF EUROPE

The Origins

In October 1942, Sir Winston Churchill wrote to the War Cabinet:

'Hard as it is to say now I trust that the European family may act unitedly as one under a Council of Europe. I look forward to a United States of Europe in which the barriers between nations will be greatly minimised and unrestricted travel will be possible. I hope to see the economy of Europe studied as a whole. I hope to see a Council of perhaps ten units, including the former Great Powers. . . .'[1]

In March 1943, in a BBC broadcast, he outlined the plan for a Council of Europe which would be:

'A really effective league, with all the strongest forces concerned woven into its texture, with a High Court to adjust disputes and with forces, armed forces, national or international, or both, held ready to impose their decisions and prevent armed aggression and the preparation of future wars. This Council, when created, must eventually embrace the whole of Europe, and all the main branches of the European family must some day be partners in it.'

After the British general election of July 1945 Sir Winston Churchill continued to urge the creation of a 'United States of Europe'. His wording often indicated, however, that he saw Britain and the Commonwealth countries as collaborating in such developments from the outside rather than directly participating in them. Churchill's speeches met with an enthusiastic response from the members of the voluntary organisations which aimed at the achievement of European

[1] F. L. Schuman, Council of Europe, *American Political Science Review* No. 45, 1951.

unity, most of which had sprung up in the countries of Western Europe after the war. These included groups such as the United Europe Movement, the European Union of Federalists and the European League for Economic Co-operation. In December 1947 these organisations formed the International Committee of the Movements for European Unity which organised the Congress of Europe held at The Hague in May 1948.

The Hague Congress adopted a series of resolutions calling for the merging of certain national sovereign rights, preparatory to the creation of an economic and political union, the establishment of a European Consultative Assembly and the creation of a European Court of Human Rights. Following the Congress its organising International Committee founded the European Movement in October 1948 as an unofficial organisation to further European union. Results followed quickly. In the same month the Consultative Council of the Brussels Treaty Powers (Belgium, France, Luxembourg, the Netherlands and the United Kingdom) set up a committee for the study of European unity which was known as the 'Committee of eighteen', composed of distinguished politicians and private individuals including M. Edouard Herriot, who was its chairman, and M. Fernand Dehousse, later President of the Assembly. The Committee examined a proposal originally put forward by M. Paul-Henri Spaak and M. Georges Bidault in July 1948, and accorded the official support of the Belgian and French Governments in August, for the creation of a European parliamentary assembly, which would meet twice a year, take resolutions by majority vote and have considerable powers including the power to legislate. A Committee of Ministers would prepare and implement the Assembly's resolutions. It also examined a British counter-proposal for an Assembly of governmentally chosen delegates responsible to an intergovernmental ministerial body which would control the work of the organisation. The committee continued to deliberate throughout the winter of 1948–49 during which period it was in continual contact with the Consultative Council and the Permanent Commission of the Brussels Treaty Organisation. In January 1949, after complex negotiations, the foreign ministers of the Brussels Treaty Powers agreed in principle to the establishment of a Council of Europe, based on the intergovernmental pattern preferred by Britain rather than the supranational system desired by Belgium and France, and composed of a ministerial committee and a consultative assembly. They convened a conference of ambassadors, to which Denmark, Ireland, Italy, Norway and Sweden were also invited, to draft the Statute of the Council of Europe. On 5 May 1949, the Statute was signed at St James's Palace in London by the foreign ministers of the ten countries.

The Statute

In the Preamble to the Statute the signatories state their

'devotion to the spiritual and moral values which are the common heritage of their peoples and the true source of individual freedom, political liberty and the rule of law, principles which form the basis of all genuine democracy.'

They also state their belief in the 'need for a closer unity between all like-minded countries of Europe'. The aim of the Council of Europe as expressed in Article 1 of the Statute is

'to achieve a greater unity between its members for the purpose of safeguarding and realising the ideals and principles which are their common heritage and facilitating their economic and social progress. This aim shall be pursued through the organs of the Council by discussions of questions of common concern and by agreements and common action in economic, social, cultural, scientific, legal and administrative matters and in the maintenance and further realisation of human rights and fundamental freedoms.'

The only matter which was excluded from the scope of the Council was national defence. Article 1 (*d*) of the Statute states

'Matters relating to national defence do not fall within the scope of the Council of Europe.'[1]

Although the word 'political' is not used in the Statute, this omission is of little importance, since the Council has been actively interested in political questions from its inception and is clearly a political body, its two main organs being composed of Foreign Ministers and

[1] There were two reasons for this: first, the NATO Treaty had been signed in April 1949 and the members of NATO wished that organisation to have an undisputed competence in defence matters; second, as M. Robert Schuman, the French Foreign Minister, explained to the French National Assembly on 9 July 1949, 'the neutrality to which certain present or future members [of the Council of Europe] are devoted will be completely respected'.

parliamentarians respectively. Moreover, from the very beginning one of the committees of the Consultative Assembly has dealt exclusively with political matters. This committee, at first known as the Committee on General Affairs, became the present Political Committee in April 1957.

Membership of the Council of Europe is open to any European state 'which is deemed to be able and willing to fulfil the provisions of Article 3 of the Statute'. Article 3 states that each member

'must accept the principles of the rule of law and the enjoyment by all persons within its jurisdiction of human rights and fundamental freedoms and collaborate sincerely and effectively in the realisation of the aim of the Council.'

Until their regimes are modified, Article 3 implicitly excludes the authoritarian governments of the Iberian Peninsula and Central and Eastern Europe from membership of the Council of Europe.

Besides the ten original member states eight other countries have become members of the Council of Europe: Greece and Turkey in 1949, Iceland in 1950, the Federal Republic of Germany in 1951, Austria in 1956, Cyprus in 1961, Switzerland in 1963 and Malta in 1965.[1] The Saar was for a time an associate member of the Council until it became part of the Federal Republic of Germany in January 1957.

The most important articles of the Statute as far as the working of the Council of Europe is concerned are those defining the functions of its two principal organs: the Committee of Ministers and the Consultative Assembly. Many of those who had attended the Hague Congress hoped for the establishment of a European constituent assembly charged with drafting a European constitution, but the opposition of the British and Scandinavian Governments to participation in a purely parliamentary body, even of a less ambitious kind, ensured that the supervisory and executive body of the Council of Europe, as defined in Articles 13–21 of the Statute, was to be an intergovernmental committee of ministers. The role of the Assembly on the other hand, as laid down in Article 23, is confined to discussing

[1] Observers represented Austria in the Assembly for several years before Austria regained its independence with the signing of the State Treaty in 1955. The entry of the Federal Republic of Germany into the Council in 1951 was of great political and psychological significance for the German people and the West since it symbolised the acceptance of a democratic Germany as an equal political partner of the other democracies of Western Europe.

and making recommendations upon matters within the competence of the Council. The implementation of recommendations made by the Consultative Assembly depends on the approval of the Committee of Ministers.

Articles 36 and 37 of the Statute state that the Secretariat, which serves both the organs of the Council, is to be headed by a Secretary General 'appointed by the Consultative Assembly on the recommendation of the Committee of Ministers' and that 'the Secretary General is responsible to the Committee of Ministers for the work of the Secretariat'. The Statute also provides that 'the expenses of the Secretariat and all common expenses shall be shared between all members in such proportions as shall be determined by the Committee [of Ministers]'.

The Institutions

The Council is, as explained above, a two-tier structure consisting of the Committee of Ministers which is the organ of intergovernmental co-operation where agreements are reached on courses of common action by governments, and the Consultative Assembly, which is the deliberative body drawn from the parliaments of member countries. The creation of this two-tier structure represented not only a new political concept, on account of the participation for the first time of parliamentarians in the work of an international organisation, but also a momentary compromise between opposing political forces, the Assembly being the driving-force created by the 'Europeans', the Committee of Ministers being the check inserted by the anti-federalists. These two bodies have quite distinct functions and pursue largely independent lives. Relations between the Assembly and the Committee of Ministers have not, on the whole, been close or fruitful. The Bureau of the Assembly (see p. 125) once put the matter bluntly in a report which stated:

'It [the Bureau] has been led to conclude that the "Fifteen" have no common political will on the questions to which the Assembly devotes most of its time.'[1]

Throughout the early years of the Council of Europe its member governments showed little interest in its work. It was a widely held

[1] *Report on the Institutional Reform of the Council of Europe presented by the Bureau of the Assembly*, Rapporteur M. Teitgen, Assembly Document 763, 20 December 1957.

view, even in official circles, that the Council was nothing more than a debating society for European parliamentarians with an inter-governmental body somewhat incongruously attached to it. The remark '. . . an organisation somewhat unhappily combining the characteristics of an unending diplomatic conference and of a House of Lords' is a typical comment.[1] This view is based on the fact that until recently the Council has lacked an executive with a defined working programme[2] and that its Assembly lacks the characteristic powers of a national parliament. An international assembly is, however, a very different kind of body from a national parliament and has different functions. Governments and lesser powers have also found that in many cases co-operation can be more effectively promoted in other organisations, notably in the North Atlantic Treaty Organisation and the Organisation for Economic Co-operation and Development. Politically it is easier for governments to hammer out their differences in these other organisations than in the Council of Europe's Committee of Ministers.[3] The result of the Committee's activity often takes the form of an agreed statement of policy in a ministerial resolution or an agreed report to the Assembly, though the conclusion of international conventions often results from the Ministers' non-political work. Thus, although the aims of the Council of Europe as set out in the Statute and many of its discussions have been primarily political, the Committee of Ministers has usually found it easier to reach agreement on technical matters on which its member countries have been less divided.

In recent years member governments have been led to take a greater interest in the Council of Europe in the light of the continuing division of Western Europe into two groupings, the European Economic Community and the European Free Trade Association. The breakdown in December 1958 of the negotiations which were held in the framework of OEEC for the establishment of a free trade area in Europe, the creation of EFTA in November 1959 and the breaking off in January 1963 of the Brussels negotiations concerning Britain's application to become a member of the EEC have led the parliamentarians of the Assembly and some member states to attach a greater value to it as the one framework in which they can meet

[1] R. R. Baxter, *British Yearbook of International Law, 1957.*

[2] The Committee of Ministers approved a programme of work, prepared by the Secretariat, in May 1966; see pp. 144–45.

[3] Since there have been considerable differences of emphasis and approach between the members of EEC and of EFTA, and between the NATO members and the neutral states, this is, perhaps, not surprising.

together to discuss the political and economic problems with which these developments have confronted them. Many governments take considerable interest in the differing degrees of association with the Council of Europe achieved by some Eastern European countries and Spain and some people think that the Council may yet become a grouping of all Europe, loosely encompassing both its present members and Eastern European states.

THE COMMITTEE OF MINISTERS

The Committee of Ministers is the executive organ of the Council of Europe. It alone has powers of decision. Although many of these decisions must be taken by unanimity, decisions on questions concerning the findings of the Commission of Human Rights, notably in cases of violation of the European Convention for the Protection of Human Rights and Fundamental Freedoms, may be taken by a two-thirds majority as can certain other decisions on matters such as the establishment of committees of experts, the adoption of the Council of Europe's Budget and other points of administration.[1] Most of the decisions voted on by the Ministers' Deputies are taken by a simple majority vote. On many occasions, however, particularly in the early years of the Council, insistence on unanimity has prevented the adoption of views and measures supported by a substantial majority of the Committee. This led in 1950 and 1951 to much criticism in the Consultative Assembly of the virtual 'power of veto' in the Committee of Ministers. As a partial remedy the Assembly at that time proposed that the Committee of Ministers might conclude agreements in which it would not be necessary for all member governments to participate. In 1951 the Committee of Ministers adopted a statutory resolution on the conclusion of partial agreements which makes this possible, but only after a unanimous decision of the Committee to permit this solution in each case. In this way it was hoped to modify the rigours of the unanimity rule and permit the development, within the general framework of the Council of Europe, of activities towards further European integration in which some member governments did not wish or felt unable to participate. This procedure is intended to make possible in the Council of Europe the practice which had already been established in OEEC of allowing a member country to abstain if it does not wish

[1] Decisions of the Committee of Ministers concerning the application of the European Social Charter and the European Code of Social Security will also be taken by a two-thirds majority.

to take part in a given decision, or declares itself not to be interested in its adoption. The procedure on the conclusion of partial agreements was used for the first time in April 1956 for the creation of the European Resettlement Fund.

The principal function of the Committee of Ministers is to consider what action is required to further the aim of the Council of Europe, which is to bring about greater unity in Europe. Two ways of achieving this are mentioned in the Statute: the conclusion of conventions or agreements and the adoption by governments of common policies with regard to particular matters. To this end the Committee of Ministers, when it has reached a decision on the desirability of either form of action, may make a recommendation to the member governments requesting them to take the necessary action and to keep it informed of such action. The powers of the Committee are in effect limited. The Committee, after its deliberations, is empowered only to make recommendations to member governments and cannot take decisions which are binding on them. The member governments are free to accept or reject these recommendations as they see fit. Many recommendations of the Committee have remained a dead letter and, owing to political implications and problems or to the apathy of some of the member governments, several of the conventions concluded under the auspices of the Council have not been fully ratified. Certainly the legal effect of the decisions taken by the Council of Europe and OECD is not the same, and also in practice the Committee of Ministers has not taken decisions of a binding character in substantive matters. In accordance with its Statute the Council of Europe may, of course, draw up conventions which are intergovernmental agreements and therefore binding on their signatories. For a number of years it has been felt within both the Consultative Assembly and the Secretariat that the Committee of Ministers should have the power to take decisions binding the governments. This is one of a number of recurring suggestions made for the institutional reform of the Council of Europe.

The Committee of Ministers consists of one representative of each member of the Council. In principle it is the Foreign Ministers themselves who are the members of the Committee, but each of them is entitled to nominate an alternate who shall be, whenever possible, a member of his government. Ambassadors and senior officials may also be nominated to act for the Foreign Ministers. The absence of a number of Foreign Ministers from the meetings of the Committee is a frequent occurrence. The practice regarding substitutes for Foreign

Ministers is different in the various member countries. If the British Foreign Secretary is unable to come, the Minister of State or Parliamentary Under-Secretary will take his place. The Italian practice is similar. The French Government usually sends another minister and if the Foreign Minister of the Federal Republic of Germany is unable to attend in person he is usually represented by one of the two State Secretaries, the senior officials of the Ministry of Foreign Affairs. The Foreign Ministers of Iceland, Sweden and Turkey have frequently sent their diplomatic representatives in Paris or in Bonn as alternates. At an early stage the Assembly pressed for meetings of the 'technical' ministers concerned with the work of the Council of Europe, a suggestion which has borne fruit in the creation of special conferences of technical ministers, such as that of Ministers of Justice.

According to the Statute the Ministers are required to meet only once a year immediately before the opening of a session of the Assembly. The original expectation was that the Committee would meet for one or two days some two or three times a year. From the early days of the Council it has, however, been the practice to hold meetings of officials of the various foreign offices immediately before each session of the Committee of Ministers in order to prepare the work of the Ministers. After the Council had been in existence for a year, the increasing volume of work made it necessary to hold these meetings regularly and since October 1950 they have taken place almost every month. This committee of senior officials was first known as the 'Ministers' Advisers' and its function was limited to that of making recommendations to the Committee of Ministers. In March 1952, its title was changed to that of 'Ministers' Deputies' and it was empowered to take decisions.

Each government has now appointed a Permanent Representative to act in the capacity of Minister's deputy. About half of these representatives are actually resident in Strasbourg. The others combine these duties with other functions and although they are not resident in Strasbourg they go there almost monthly to attend the various meetings. The Committee of Ministers' Deputies is the body in which the majority of decisions at intergovernmental level are now taken. The character of the Committee of Ministers, at both its levels, is in effect that of a permanent diplomatic conference.

The Ministers' Deputies, as officials of the various foreign offices, are naturally not experts on technical subjects. The Committee of Ministers, however, is often called upon to take decisions on technical proposals. It has thus felt the need, foreseen in Article 17 of the Statute, for organised technical advice, which the Ministers' Deputies are not themselves competent to provide. This has led to the practice of convening committees of governmental experts who are normally senior officials of the various government departments concerned with the subjects in question. The intergovernmental committees of experts include the committees on educational, cultural, social, science policy, public health, crime and legal questions. Some of these committees are convened on an *ad hoc* basis, but most of them are now permanent bodies of the Council and correspond on the governmental side to the various parliamentary committees of the Consultative Assembly. In this way there has grown up an elaborate machinery of intergovernmental co-operation for use by member governments. Another way in which the Committee of Ministers obtains expert advice on problems submitted to it is by consulting other international organisations which are competent in the relevant technical field. OECD in its past and present forms has been the organisation most frequently consulted. Expert advice has also been sought from the International Labour Organisation on social questions, the United Nations Educational, Scientific and Cultural Organisation on educational matters and the General Agreement on Tariffs and Trade on tariff problems.

The Committee of Ministers meets then at two levels: at the ministerial level when the Ministers themselves are present, and at the level of officials when the Ministers' Deputies have power to take decisions by virtue of the authority given to them by the Ministers. In this respect, therefore, the practice of the Council of Europe is in line with that of OECD and NATO. One direct result is that the Committee of Ministers now meets less frequently than it used to do in the first three years of the Council's existence. Since 1952 it has met twice each year in sessions of one to two days. Usually the Committee tries to arrange its winter meetings either immediately before or after, and in the same place as, the meetings of the ministerial organs of NATO or OECD, and for this reason it has, during the last few years, met in Paris as well as in Strasbourg, where its May meetings are held. The Committee of Ministers and its expert committees meet in private and the Committee itself decides what information shall be made public regarding its work. The chief source of information on its activities are the reports which the Ministers present to the Assembly as required by the Statute at the opening of its part-sessions. In its reports the Committee of Ministers gives an account both of the action it has taken on the recommendations presented to it by the Assembly and of its other activities, but it is under no obligation to give reasons for its decisions or to explain why it has not accepted any of the recommendations addressed to it.[1] The Assembly debates the report of the Committee of Ministers, which is personally presented to the Assembly by the Chairman of the Committee or his alternate, usually another minister in the same government. In October 1957 when no member of the Committee of Ministers was present to introduce the Committee's report, the Assembly refused to take cognisance of it. Under the amended rules of procedure of the Committee it is now possible for any minister of a member government to address the Assembly in his individual capacity without first obtaining the agreement of the Committee of Ministers. The original procedure, which required the authorisation of the Committee by a simple majority vote, was first used to enable M. Robert Schuman to address the Assembly on his proposals for the pooling of European coal and steel production in August 1950. The practice of ministers addressing the Assembly in their personal capacity is now well established. M. Robert Schuman, Count Carlo Sforza, Chancellor Adenauer, Sir Anthony Eden, Signor Alcide de Gasperi, M. Pierre Mendès-France, M. Paul-Henri Spaak, M. Maurice Couve de Murville, Mr Edward Heath, Mr Joseph Luns, Chancellor Klaus, Mr Michael Stewart, Signor Amintoro Fanfani, and Mr Harold Wilson have been among the ministers who have taken part in the political debates of the Assembly. U Thant, Secretary General of the UN, addressed the Assembly in May 1966. Members of the Committee of Ministers, however, are not entitled to sit as representatives from their national parliaments in the Consultative Assembly although, particularly in the early days of the Council, ministers other than foreign ministers have come to Strasbourg as members of their national parliamentary delegations.

Since 1961 the Committee of Ministers, following the practice previously adopted in the European Communities, has held an annual colloquy or joint meeting with members of the Assembly. This meeting is, in effect, an enlarged meeting of the Joint Committee (see p. 131). It provides an opportunity for members of the Assembly to question the foreign ministers or their alternates on outstanding political and economic issues.

[1] One of the main functions of the Assembly's Working Party on Parliamentary and Public Relations is, in consequence, to persuade members of the Assembly to ask questions about the governmental attitude of each country concerning recommendations of the Assembly, in their home parliaments. From 1 July 1964 to 1 July 1965, for instance, 523 questions were asked or interventions were made by members of the Assembly in their national parliaments concerning Council of Europe affairs.

THE CONSULTATIVE ASSEMBLY

It is the existence of an international assembly of national parliamentarians that distinguishes the Council from the international organisations which had been set up in the past. With the creation of the Consultative Assembly, members of national parliaments from member countries were enabled for the first time to play an official and permanent, though limited, part within an organisation devoted to international co-operation between sovereign states—a process that has been called 'parliamentary diplomacy'.[1] In 1949 an international assembly of parliamentarians was an innovation for which there had been no precedent. But although the Assembly is a forum for the frank discussion of European political, economic and other problems it is not (except indirectly)[2] a European legislature. Direct comparisons with elected national legislatures which have the powers to make laws, to vote money and to bring down governments, though often made, are inappropriate.

The Assembly consists of 147 representatives from the eighteen member states of the Council.[3] The delegates to the Assembly of the seven WEU member countries are also normally the same parliamentarians as constitute the WEU Assembly. No country has less than three representatives, which makes it possible for the principal democratic parties to be represented,[4] and the four largest countries are each given eighteen seats. Each 'Representative to the

[1] This phrase is also frequently used to describe organisations of a primarily diplomatic nature in which civil servants adopt parliamentary techniques of open debate.

[2] The Assembly has, however, contributed to the creation of a corpus of 'European law' by initiating and helping to draft some sixty European Conventions, which, when they come into effect, have the force of law in the signatory states.

[3] France, the Federal Republic of Germany, Italy and the United Kingdom have eighteen representatives each; Turkey has ten; Belgium, Greece and the Netherlands have seven; Austria, Sweden and Switzerland have six; Denmark and Norway have five; Ireland has four; Cyprus, Iceland, Luxembourg and Malta have three representatives each. Israel has sent observers to the Assembly since 1961.

[4] In April 1964, when the Cyprus House of Representatives had sent a delegation consisting of three Greek-Cypriot representatives and three Greek-Cypriot substitutes with no Turkish-Cypriot representative or substitute, the Assembly, after receiving a report from its Committee on Credentials, ruled that it recognised the validity of the mandate of only two Greek-Cypriot members of the Cyprus delegation and two Greek-Cypriot substitutes (since it considered that the Cypriot delegation to the Assembly should consist, in accordance with the Constitution of Cyprus, of two Greek-Cypriot members and one Turkish-Cypriot member).

Assembly' may have a substitute who may, in his absence, vote in his place. Representatives must either be elected by their parliament or be 'appointed in such a manner as that parliament shall decide . . .'. Representatives to the Assembly are elected or selected by their national parliaments and appointed for an annual term by their government or parliament as the case may be. Their mandates may be, and often are, renewed. Their total length of service on a national delegation varies from country to country. Communists, the Nenni Socialists (PSI) and some other parties have been excluded from the process of the selection of delegations in the national parliaments. Representatives enjoy certain immunities, including freedom from arrest, when engaged in those duties or when travelling to and from meetings.

There is no rule prescribing that representatives must be members of their national parliaments. The selection or appointment of non-parliamentarians is, however, very rare, though they have contributed to the work of the Assembly. Mr Per Federspiel remained Chairman of the Assembly's Economic Committee during a period in which he was not actually a member of the Danish Parliament. Another Danish representative, Mr Hermod Lannung, was Chairman of the Assembly's Legal Committee while no longer a member of his national parliament. The strength of the various democratic political parties within each parliament is roughly reflected in their representation in the Assembly. The seats in the Assembly Chamber are arranged in alphabetical order without regard to nationality or party.[1] On some issues, particularly concerning relations between the EEC and the non-Six, representatives tend to vote either along national lines or together with other representatives of the EEC and EFTA groupings as the case may be. On other issues voting is primarily along party lines. In the Assembly there was at first little organisation along party lines but between 1954 and 1956 the three main parties, Christian Democrats, Liberals and Socialists, established formal party groups. In 1958 a fourth party group of independent representatives began to take shape. This group, which has since formally become known as the Group of Independent Representatives, consists mainly of members of conservative parties from the United Kingdom, Ireland and the Scandinavian countries.

These political groups hold regular private party meetings in rooms provided by the Council and they are given financial assistance, which is charged to the budget of the Assembly, and which

[1] In the European Parliament the parliamentarians sit with their political colleagues in party groups (see p. 180).

provides for translating, stenographic, typing and duplicating services. The structure of the political groups in the Assembly of the Council of Europe is less formal and developed, however, than that of the party groups in the European Parliament. At group meetings the parties define their attitude to the subjects to be discussed in the Assembly. Of these groups the Socialists[1] are the most highly organised and they initiated the practice which has since been adopted by the other groups of sometimes presenting agreed statements to the Assembly through an official spokesman on behalf of the group as a whole. At the Socialist group meetings the procedure is more formal than at those of the other groups: proceedings of these meetings are fully recorded and minutes are taken. Since 1956 the Socialist Group has maintained formal contacts with the equivalent Group in what was the Common Assembly of the European Coal and Steel Community and with that of its successor body, the European Parliament. The Socialist Group also maintains contacts with the Socialist International and exchanges observers with these two bodies. The Socialist Group has, in recent years, become increasingly active at the level of Assembly Committees. It sometimes instructs spokesmen to intervene in Committee Meetings on subjects which particularly interest it and it has succeeded in obtaining, in several instances, the appointment of its nominee as *rapporteur* following proposals made on behalf of the Group as a whole. Despite the development of party groups, party discipline at Strasbourg is not strong. Even if the Assembly is now less of 'an assembly of individuals' than when it was so described in the House of Commons in November 1949 by Mr Ernest Bevin, representatives are free to speak and to vote as they wish and there are no 'Party Whips'.

The Assembly holds one session each year which, under the terms of the Statute, may not last for a total period of more than a month unless the Committee of Ministers agrees to an extension. Since 1950, the Assembly session has been divided into two, three and, on one occasion, even four part-sessions usually of between five and ten days' length. Generally, each part-session centres around two main debates on political and economic affairs while, since 1964, on the initiative of the President of the Assembly, M. Pierre Pflimlin, debates relating to the work of all committees of the Assembly other than the Political and Economic Committees have been grouped to be

[1] Who, under the leadership of Mr John Edwards, the first British President of the Assembly, were the first political group to emerge in the Assembly, following the example of the party groups in the Common Assembly of ECSC.

held once a year. M. Pflimlin's scheme has led to a rationalisation of the Assembly's working programme and it is hoped that this will result in greater interest being focused on the work of the more technical committees of the Assembly such as the Legal, Cultural and Social Committees.

At the beginning of each session the Assembly elects by secret ballot its Bureau consisting of its President[1] and eight Vice-Presidents. The Bureau is responsible for: suggesting the reference of motions and other documents to the relevant committee of the Assembly for study and report, drawing up the daily working programme of the Assembly during its part-sessions and representing the Assembly in negotiations with other international and national parliamentary assemblies and organisations.

The normal procedure which governs the work of the Assembly is that a proposal for the placing of a question on the agenda (which must be in the form of a motion for a recommendation or for a resolution, signed by ten representatives) is laid before the Assembly or, between sessions, before the Standing Committee. The Bureau then proposes the reference of the motion to a committee of the Assembly for study and report and possibly to a second committee for its opinion. When a subject has been referred to a Committee for report it remains inscribed on the 'register of the Assembly' until the eventual report is disposed of by the Assembly.

The committee to whom the motion is referred then appoints a *rapporteur* who prepares a report and a draft recommendation or resolution which is submitted to the committee. *Rapporteurs* are often given considerable assistance by the Secretariat in preparing their reports. After examining the draft recommendation or resolution together with the explanatory memorandum the committee will then submit this to the Assembly, sometimes in an altered form. The practice has grown up of regarding the text of the explanatory memorandum as being the responsibility of the *rapporteur*, expressing his own views on the subject concerned, whereas the draft recommendation or resolution represents the formal proposals of the committee as a whole. The Assembly then disposes of the draft recommendation or resolution and report as it sees fit, by amending, adopting or (very seldom) rejecting it.

[1] Presidents of the Assembly have been M. Paul-Henri Spaak (1949–51), M. François de Menthon (1952–54), M. Guy Mollet (1954–56), M. Fernand Dehousse (1956–59), Mr John Edwards (1959), M. Per Federspiel (1960–63), M. Pierre Pflimlin (1963–66) and Sir Geoffrey de Freitas, who was elected in 1966.

One of the weaknesses of this procedure is that committees tend to prefer to submit a compromise draft recommendation or resolution in the hope of obtaining the unanimous approval of the Assembly rather than put forward controversial texts which risk dividing members of the Assembly, particularly on political issues. Thus the discussion of political or other controversial subjects is often livelier in Committee than in the subsequent debate in the Assembly.

Most of the work of preparing the part-sessions of the Assembly is carried out in committee. The Assembly's Committees carry out detailed studies of motions or of other documents, such as the reports of other international organisations which are referred to them, and they draft texts on a large variety of subjects for submission to the Assembly for debate. The Committees of the Assembly include, first of all, the Standing Committee which consists of the members of the Bureau, the chairmen of the permanent committees of the Assembly, the chairmen of the party groups, in an advisory capacity, and other members elected on a geographical basis, totalling in all over thirty. The Standing Committee's main task is to act on behalf of the Assembly between its part-sessions. In cases of urgency it can adopt recommendations or resolutions on behalf of the Assembly which have the same force as those adopted by the Assembly itself and it can also act on behalf of the Assembly in referring motions to committees in cases of urgency. The Standing Committee is responsible for deciding on the Assembly's agenda for each part-session. There are twelve permanent committees of the Assembly: Political, Economic, Social, Legal, Cultural, Science and Technology, Local Authorities, Agricultural, Non-Represented Nations, Population and Refugees, Rules of Procedure and the Committee on the Budget. There is also a permanent Working Party on Parliamentary and Public Relations. An *ad hoc* Credentials Committee, whose members are chosen by lot, meets at the very beginning of each session of the Assembly to endorse the validity of the credentials of the members of the Assembly. The number of members of each committee varies from fifteen to thirty-two. Committees meet in the intervals between sessions, usually in Paris though sometimes elsewhere. It is usual for the more important committees to hold at least one or sometimes two meetings between each part-session of the Assembly to discuss and adopt the texts of the reports and to draft recommendations or resolutions which they wish to submit to the Assembly. Each week, on average, there are about two meetings of Assembly committees. Several of the Assembly committees have appointed sub-committees and working parties which either carry out preliminary studies of subjects referred to the parent committee or keep a watching brief on subjects in which the parent committee maintains a special interest. For instance, the Political Committee has set up sub-committees which deal with co-operation with developing countries and the South Tyrol question.

The Assembly is free to discuss any matter within the wide limits of the Council's competence. The original text of the Statute, however, provided for ministerial control of the Assembly's agenda. The Assembly was not to be master of its own agenda since the permission of the Committee of Ministers was required before any subject could be debated. The difficulties experienced in drawing up an agreed agenda for the first session of the Assembly led it to recommend, at the first opportunity, that the Ministers should relinquish their right to control the agenda. This they agreed to do and the Statute was amended in May 1951. At this time there was another important amendment to the Statute when the Ministers recognised, in a resolution, the right of the Assembly to discuss the political aspects of defence though they specified that the Assembly was not competent to address recommendations to them on this matter.[1] The Assembly has taken advantage of this resolution, albeit with reservations on the part of representatives from the neutral countries, to include references to the political aspects of defence problems in resolutions addressed to the Committee of Ministers and to examine these questions in reports and in debates.[2] Any matter referred to the Assembly by the Committee of Ministers for an opinion must be debated by the Assembly which may also make recommendations on it. The powers of the Assembly have not been extended to autonomous control of its own budget or the work of the Office of the Clerk, which, although responsible to the Assembly for the work which it does on its behalf, is under the administrative control of the Secretary General. The official languages of the Assembly are English and French. All its documents are produced in these two languages. Speeches in the Assembly may also be made in German and Italian. The Italian Government bears the expense of simultaneous interpretation into Italian. The German, Austrian and

[1] This decision followed the adoption of a recommendation by the Assembly in 1950 calling for the creation of a European army under the command of a European Minister of Defence. The first reaction of the Committee of Ministers was to remind the Assembly that it was not competent to discuss such matters.

[2] The Assembly's right to discuss the political aspects of defence was re-affirmed on 6 June 1956 in the agreement between the Bureaux of the Consultative Assembly and the Assembly of WEU (see p. 336).

Swiss Governments share the expense of simultaneous interpretation into German. As in the British Parliament, representatives normally speak from their own places, but there is a 'Tribune' which can be used by speakers on special matters, for Ministers who are addressing the Assembly and for other speakers who are not members of the Assembly—usually representatives of the international organisations which submit annual reports to the Assembly. The debates consist largely of formal speeches: interruptions and repartee are comparatively rare. The practice of addressing oral questions to the Chairman of the Committee of Ministers or to representatives of other international organisations when presenting their reports has grown up and has proved a useful method of obtaining information.

The usual outcome of a debate in the Assembly is the adoption of a Recommendation which is addressed to the Committee of Ministers asking it to take certain action in pursuit of the aims of the Council. A Recommendation requires an absolute majority of the representatives present and voting for its adoption which must total at least one-third of the Assembly's members. This is not the only form in which the Assembly can present its conclusions. It can also adopt a Resolution, Opinion or Order, each of which requires only a simple majority for its adoption. The first of these gives formal expression to the opinion of the Assembly on a particular matter which does not call for action by the Committee of Ministers. On several occasions, the Assembly has adopted resolutions addressed not to the Committee of Ministers but to a limited number of member governments or other international organisations which transmit reports of their activities to the Assembly. The replies which the Assembly makes to the reports it receives from OECD, the International Labour Organisation and the World Health Organisation fall within this category. An Opinion contains the view of the Assembly in answer to a formal request from the Committee of Ministers for the expression of such a view on a matter specifically referred to it, such as the application of a state for membership of the Council of Europe. An Order of the Assembly deals with matters of internal procedure such as the reference of a question to the appropriate committee of the Assembly (supplementing the procedure already outlined) or instructions to the Secretariat.

Quite apart from its normal work the Assembly has sometimes voiced democratic opinion on political and moral questions on which the voice of Europe as a whole can be expressed. Thus the Assembly has condemned the methods employed by communist regimes in Central and Eastern Europe, and expressed its horror at the brutality with which the Hungarian Revolution of 1956 was suppressed. In January 1965, while the Federal German Parliament was considering what action to take concerning the extension of the period during which Nazi war criminals could be brought to justice, it declared its conviction that crimes against humanity are not subject to prescription and shortly afterwards the German Parliament voted in favour of the extension of the time limit within which Nazi war crimes could be prosecuted. In May 1965 the Assembly adopted a resolution appealing to the Soviet Union to end discriminatory measures directed against the Jewish community in Russia. Shortly after, this matter was also raised in the United Nations and an agreement was reached in the summer of 1965 between leaders of the Jewish community in the Soviet Union and the Soviet Government by which certain discriminatory measures were ended. The moral force of the Assembly's recommendations and resolutions on subjects of this kind has been considerable and has, perhaps, been seen to best advantage during its discussions of matters of principle which affect human dignity.

Relations between the Consultative Assembly and the Committee of Ministers

The effectiveness of the Council of Europe in obtaining concrete results from its work depends to a large extent on the successful co-ordination of the work of the Committee of Ministers and the Consultative Assembly. Initially the Statute contained no provisions for such co-ordination nor for the reconciliation of their points of view in case of disagreement. The excessive formality in the relations between the two organs, resulting in much wasted effort and irritation, has been a persistent problem affecting the progress of the Council since its inception. The unsatisfactory nature of these relations soon led the Assembly to make a number of proposals aimed at improving the method of co-ordination. The first attempt along these lines was made in 1950 when the Assembly adopted a recommendation asking the Committee of Ministers to refer back to the appropriate Assembly committee, with a statement of its reasons, any recommendation made by the Assembly which is not, or is only partially, acceptable to the Committee of Ministers. The Committee agreed in substance with this idea and the new rule was introduced but it has seldom been invoked. The usual procedure is for the Committee of Ministers to give indications of the reasons why proposals have not been accepted in their statutory reports to the

Assembly. These have been generally very brief and have not contained the detailed explanations necessary for re-consideration of the question by the Assembly and its committees. Thus even if the Committee of Ministers may sometimes consider recommendations of the Assembly to be ill-judged or insufficiently prepared the replies given by the Committee to the Assembly do not explain the Ministers' views. It has been suggested that representatives of the Assembly might sit with the Ministers and their Deputies at their meetings to insist on action being taken by the Committee of Ministers when the Assembly has expressed its wishes strongly. On some occasions the chairmen and *rapporteurs* of certain committees have attended meetings of the Deputies to explain recommendations originating with their committees. Another method of contact between the representatives and the Ministers that has been developed is the right of representatives to put written questions to the Committee of Ministers. The Ministers, when agreeing to this procedure, decided that the Deputies should deal with these questions on their behalf. This procedure was at first used very little but recently the number of questions asked has increased.

In 1950 the Joint Committee, described as the 'Organ of co-ordination of the Council of Europe', was set up. Its job was intended to be the discussion of problems common to the Committee of Ministers and the Assembly and the examination of the means of giving political effect to the recommendations adopted by either body. The Joint Committee consists of eight members of the Committee of Ministers and eight representatives of the Assembly including its President who convenes its meetings and acts as chairman. The Joint Committee is a liaison body. It cannot take formal decisions and consequently there is no voting. The Committee meets once or twice a year depending on whether the President of the Assembly considers that there are subjects of sufficient mutual interest to be discussed between the two sides. Because the Joint Committee was not very successful in carrying out its original task a change was made in 1956, when the Committee was allowed to meet at the level of the Ministers' Deputies on the governmental side, in the hope that greater progress on points at issue between the Assembly and the Committee of Ministers could be made at a lower level. A further change took place in 1961 when the practice was introduced of holding an annual meeting of the Joint Committee in its expanded form (the Colloquy) to obtain, within a confidential context, information about the policy of member governments concerning such issues as East–West relations, the development of a

European political union and Atlantic partnership, rather than to attempt to settle differences of approach between the Assembly and the Committee of Ministers on particular issues. In some cases, however, the Assembly's representatives in the Joint Committee have used meetings of the Joint Committee to try to persuade the Committee of Ministers to take action on matters about which the Assembly has been deeply concerned, such as the development of the situation in Cyprus during 1964. Although the Joint Committee cannot be considered to have been successful in co-ordinating the work of the Committee of Ministers and the Consultative Assembly it has, in the form of the Colloquy, been a useful method of keeping members of the Assembly in close touch with thinking in the governments of the member states on major issues in international affairs.

THE SECRETARIAT

The Secretariat works in La Maison de l'Europe, a large and functional modern building in Strasbourg. Its head is the Secretary General, who is appointed by the Consultative Assembly on the recommendation of the Committee of Ministers. The Committee of Ministers submits a short list of recommended candidates to the Assembly which then elects the Secretary General by secret ballot. The Secretary General is responsible to the Committee of Ministers for the work of the Secretariat, which serves both organs of the Council. The powers and initiative of the Secretary General (which are not defined in the Statute) have, in the past, been limited mainly to the internal administration of the Council though the Secretary General has the right to place, on his own initiative, matters on the agenda of the Committee of Ministers and can, at the request of the Assembly, carry out studies embodying initiatives or proposals for action to be taken. Article 57 of the Convention for the Protection of Human Rights and Fundamental Freedoms states that signatory governments 'shall furnish an explanation of the manner in which [their] internal law ensures the effective implementation of any of the provisions of the Convention' when requested to do so by the Secretary General. The Secretary General is assisted by a Deputy Secretary General and by the Clerk of the Assembly, in charge of the work of the Assembly services, who also holds the rank of Deputy Secretary General.[1]

[1] The Secretaries General of the Council of Europe have been M. Jacques-Camille Paris (1949–53), M. Léon Marchal (1953–56), Count Lodovico Benvenuti (1956–64) and Mr Peter Smithers, who was appointed in 1964.

The strength of the Secretariat is just under 500 of whom about 140 are in administrative grades, but during sessions of the Assembly this number is swollen by the recruitment of some 300 temporary staff. The Statute lays down that all members of the Secretariat shall 'perform their duties conscientiously, uninfluenced by any national considerations . . . [or] instructions in connection with the performance of these duties from any government or any authority external to the Council.'

The Secretariat is composed of nationals of all the member countries according to a rough national quota system[1] and is divided into: the Office of the Clerk of the Assembly; the Political Directorate, which serves the Committee of Ministers; and other Directorates responsible for Human Rights, Legal Affairs, Educational, Cultural and Scientific Affairs, Economic and Social Affairs, Press and Information, and Administration. The Secretary General and the Deputy Secretary General are helped in their work by a small private office and a planning unit. The budget of the Council of Europe is paid for by member countries, their shares being determined by the Committee of Ministers.[2]

THE SPECIALISED CONFERENCES

Apart from the methods of co-operation provided for in its Statute the Council of Europe has developed the method of sponsoring specialised conferences to further co-operation between the participating countries in specific fields. Some of these conferences, which are held at ministerial level, correspond to the Assembly's recurrently expressed wish that the Committee of Ministers should at the level of specialised or technical ministers meet to discuss particular issues.

The Deputy Secretaries General have been Mr Aubrey Halford (1949–52), Mr Anthony Lincoln (1952–55), Mr Dunstan Curtis (1955–62) and M. Polys Modinos, who was appointed in 1962. The Clerks of the Assembly have been Lord Campion (1949), Prince Filippo Caracciolo di Castagneto (1950–54), M. Arnold Struycken (1954–55) and Herr Gerhard Schloesser, who was appointed in 1956.

[1] Based on national budgetary contributions.

[2] The Council of Europe's budget for 1966 amounted to about £2·5 million and was divided between the member states in the following proportions: France, the Federal Republic of Germany, Italy and the United Kingdom 17·06 per cent each; Turkey 10·21 per cent; the Netherlands 4·05 per cent; Belgium 3·08 per cent; Austria, Greece and Sweden 2·59 per cent each; Denmark and Switzerland 1·79 per cent each; Norway 1·30 per cent; Ireland 0·97 per cent; Cyprus 0·32 per cent; and Iceland, Luxembourg and Malta 0·16 per cent each.

Typical of the Assembly's requests on this subject was Recommendation 358 of May 1963 which proposed that the Committee of Ministers should 'draw up annually a list of special meetings, organised on an *ad hoc* basis, for which the Ministers for Foreign Affairs will delegate their powers to Ministers responsible for other departments, who will examine questions within their particular province (justice, education, social affairs, agriculture, etc.).'

Although these proposals were not implemented as such, the Conference of Ministers of Education, which first met on a Dutch initiative in 1959, and the Conference of European Ministers of Justice, which was established in 1961 in reply to proposals made in the Council's expert committee on crime problems, largely respond to the Assembly's concern to see action of this kind taken. These two ministerial conferences provide guiding lines for the work of the Council in educational and legal matters and their close connection with the Council is emphasised by the fact that the Council provides the Secretariat for these meetings and that the Committee of Ministers is responsible for drawing up the agenda of the Conference of Ministers of Justice.

Close links exist between the Council and other European specialised conferences, which although autonomous were established following initiatives taken by the Council. These are: the European Conference of Ministers of Transport, the European Civil Aviation Conference and the Conference of European Postal and Telecommunications Administrations.

Conferences of experts on particular subjects have also been established by the Council of Europe. Following an initiative taken by the Assembly in 1955, the European Conference of Local Authorities was set up in 1957. Subsequent meetings of the Conference were held in 1958 and 1960, when the Committee of Ministers agreed that it should meet every two years and approved the Charter of the Conference. The aim of the Conference is to gain the informed support of local authorities and those engaged in local government for the progress of European unity. The European Parliamentary and Scientific Conference,[1] composed of parliamentarians and scientists, was established in 1961 as an attempt to bridge the gap between parliaments and scientific progress. The European Conference on Wines and Spirits was established in 1960 following proposals of the Assembly's Committee on Agriculture and has, so far, held three meetings of representatives of the appropriate trade associations together with national officials and parliamentarians to review the

[1] For details of this Conference see p. 157.

work carried out by a committee of experts, established previously, which has been preparing a European convention on the production and marketing of wines and spirits. In order to give political impulsion to its work the Marquis Lucifero d'Aprigliano, a member of the Assembly, was made Chairman of the Conference. Further examples of the specialised conference method are: the Tripartite Conference to examine the Social Charter convened by ILO in 1958, the European Conference on Road Safety organised by the Economic Committee of the Assembly in 1962 and the European Conference on Air Pollution which was held in 1964. A Conference on Demographic Problems was held in 1966.

The Political Work of the Council

At the first session of the Assembly in August 1949, the agenda included: 'Consideration of any necessary changes in the political structure of Europe. . . .' The Assembly appointed a Committee on General Affairs (now the Political Committee) to consider this item and this has proved to be the most prominent of the Assembly's committees.

THE ATTEMPT TO CREATE A POLITICAL AUTHORITY

At the first session of the Assembly many suggestions were made advocating changes in the political structure of Europe. Most of these proposals lay outside the limited powers granted to the Council by the member governments in the carefully drafted Statute. One proposal, among many similar ones, which was in the form of a motion put forward by Mr R. W. G. Mackay[1] and which secured virtually unanimous support, was that 'the aim and goal of the Council of Europe is the creation of a European political authority with limited functions but real powers'. This became the dominant political theme of the Council between 1949 and 1951. During 1949–50 it became evident, however, that the Assembly contained one group (mainly from France and Italy) which wished to create a European organisation with real powers, governed by a central authority, and another group (mainly composed of British, Irish and Scandinavian representatives) which preferred to try to achieve a measure of intergovernmental co-operation in various fields. These groups became known at Strasbourg as the 'federalists' and the 'functionalists' respectively.

In May 1950, M. Robert Schuman launched his plan for the

[1] Then a Labour Member of Parliament. See *Official Report*, 5 September 1949, pp. 1032–6. See also Document 61, 1949.

pooling of French and German coal and steel production under a High Authority in an organisation open to other European countries. In August 1950, M. Schuman addressed the Consultative Assembly on his proposals. These were warmly welcomed by the 'federalists' who saw the Coal and Steel Community as the first step towards a European government, which would be established by setting up 'specialised authorities' for industrial, agricultural, transport and military purposes, and by providing that the Council of Europe, as 'the organisation best qualified to supply the general framework', should act as a European parliament to which these authorities would be responsible. The British and Scandinavian representatives, on the other hand, were not prepared to delegate governmental powers to supranational institutions. Despite the divergence of aims between the 'federalists' and 'functionalists' the latter countries did not discourage the Six from forming new institutions of a supranational character. Recommendations were adopted suggesting that such new authorities should be created within the framework of the Council of Europe, that each member should be free to accede or not to one or more of them, and that they should all be open to all members of the Council.

Dissatisfaction with the existing powers of the Council led the Committee on General Affairs, whose *rapporteur* was M. Guy Mollet, to make a series of proposals for the amendment of the Statute. These proposed that the aims and functions of the Council should be extended to include those of OEEC and the Brussels Treaty Organisation, whose administrative organs should be taken over by the Council: executive authority and legislative power should be granted to the Council, which would become a European political authority with a parliament of two houses. The Assembly and the Committee of Ministers would have power to pass European acts binding on all member states without parliamentary ratification. The 'La Malfa Proposals' put forward by an Italian member of the Assembly, Signor Ugo La Malfa, stated that the member governments, by ratifying the Statute, had created a Consultative Assembly and that it should therefore be obligatory for them to consult it about relevant decisions. Governments should be statutorily bound to inform the Committee of Ministers of 'any project or proposal with European implications' so that the Committee might transmit it to the Assembly for the expression of its views. The Assembly would thus be able to give member governments guidance on all proposals of a European character before these were implemented.

The various constitutional proposals made in 1950 were examined by a special Committee on the Revision of the Statute, set up by the Committee of Ministers in November of the same year. Although the Committee of Ministers adopted a resolution providing that 'the Council of Europe may take the initiative in instituting negotiations between Members with a view to the creation of European Specialised Authorities' and also adopted a number of formal and minor amendments to the Statute, it refused to give its assent to the proposals of the Assembly to make the Council into a political authority. In December, 1951, the Assembly adopted a recommendation containing the proposals made by M. Guy Mollet on behalf of the Committee on General Affairs, but by this time it was clear that neither the United Kingdom nor the Scandinavian Governments would be prepared to accept any such proposals. This was the end of the attempt to increase the powers of the Council so as to turn it into a 'political authority with limited functions but real powers'.

THE COUNCIL OF EUROPE AND THE SIX

The failure of the Council of Europe to extend its powers, and its caution in moving towards European unity, led to the resignation of M. Spaak as President of the Assembly in December 1951. In the period 1952–53 the main political task of the Council was to develop a satisfactory relationship between the Six and the other members of the Council. This relationship and its effect on the Council as a whole prompted a British *aide-mémoire* to the other member countries, known as the 'Eden Proposals', in March 1952. These proposals stated that the Council should be remodelled

'... so that its organs could serve as the institutions of the European Coal and Steel Community, the European Defence Community and any future organisations of the same structure and membership. ... Mr Eden is confident that a satisfactory "two-tier" system could be evolved which would enable the Council of Europe to continue its work as an organisation for intergovernmental co-operation in Western Europe. On occasions the Committee of Ministers and the Assembly could meet on a six-Power basis to transact business connected with the Coal and Steel Community, the Defence Community and any future organisation of the same type and membership. At the same time both the Committee of Ministers and the Assembly would continue to meet on a fifteen-Power basis[1] as at present for the purposes defined in Article 1 of the Statute.'

[1] The number of member states at that time.

Although part of the 'Eden Proposals' were approved by the Assembly, which (in September 1952) adopted an opinion stating what organic links should be established between the Council and the ECSC and although these proposals were also agreed to by the Committee of Ministers, they were never put into practice.

The plans for the creation of the European Defence Community (EDC) and its relations with the other member countries of the Council of Europe were major issues confronting the Assembly during 1952 and 1953. After the signing of the EDC Treaty in May 1952, the Assembly adopted resolutions calling for

'the closest possible association therewith of Great Britain and those other Member States of the Council of Europe which may desire to be associated.'

In 1953 the Assembly urged the six parliaments to ratify the Treaty without delay. Owing to the exclusion of questions of national defence from the competence of the Council under the Statute, and because certain members (notably neutral Ireland and Sweden) were unwilling that the Council should concern itself with military matters, the proposals made for forming a close association with the EDC were aimed at linking the EDC with the other member countries of the Council rather than with the Council itself. Although certain governments took steps to follow these recommendations they came to nothing when the EDC Treaty was rejected by the French Assembly in August 1954.

The proposals for associating the Council of Europe with the Communities of the Six also extended to the proposed European Political Community (EPC), which would have given political and further economic powers to the institutions of the Six. The Foreign Ministers of the Six did not wait for the EDC Treaty to be ratified before starting work on a constitution for EPC. At the request of the Foreign Ministers the Coal and Steel Community set up the *Ad Hoc* Assembly (see p. 31), in which nine members of the Consultative Assembly from the member countries of the Six were co-opted and other members of the Council of Europe were represented by observers, to prepare the draft treaty for the Political Community.

In January 1953, the Consultative Assembly held an extraordinary session to examine the proposals of the *ad hoc* assembly, and in May of the same year it adopted two recommendations and one resolution concerning the *Draft Treaty embodying the Statute of the European*

Community, which had been presented to the six Foreign Ministers in March. The Assembly held that

'the success of the European Community will in large measure depend on the extent to which links are maintained and reinforced between that Community and the States not members thereof, on the one hand, and between that Community and the Council of Europe, on the other.'

Various suggestions were made by the Consultative Assembly for strengthening these links, and a protocol to the Treaty, containing provisions for close association, was approved. In the event the failure to ratify the EDC Treaty also entailed the breakdown of the EPC negotiations.

During the next phase of its history the Council of Europe's political work centred on an attempt to establish the Council as 'the general framework of European Policy'.[1] This form of words was also accepted and used by the Committee of Ministers on several occasions. In the report which he presented on this subject, Herr Karl Mommer, *rapporteur* of the Committee on General Affairs, distinguished five aspects of this proposed role for the Council:

(*a*) the regrouping of European intergovernmental organisations around the Council;
(*b*) the association of non-member States;
(*c*) the establishment of close links with the specialised communities;
(*d*) the consultation of the Council by member countries on all European proposals;
(*e*) the co-ordination of the foreign policies of member states within the Council.[2]

The Council of Europe has in fact become the main international European parliamentary forum for the expression of opinion on major European and Atlantic problems. Even though the representatives who attend these meetings have no mandate and represent no

[1] *Preliminary report of the Committee on General Affairs commenting on the Special Message of the Committee of Ministers relating to the Programme of Work of the Council of Europe*, Assembly Document 264, 10 August 1954.

[2] While the Council may perhaps be considered as having succeeded over points (b) and (c), and partly succeeded over (a), it has made no progress with points (d) and (e).

electorate they take the opportunity provided by the major political and economic debates mounted in the Assembly to hold confrontations of national and regional viewpoints concerning the main issues of European integration. Thus, following a debate held in 1953 on 'the policy of the Council of Europe in the light of recent developments in the international situation', the Committee of Ministers itself adopted a resolution

'to approve the broad lines of the policy defined and express its earnest hope that the Assembly will continue to debate major political questions of this kind and so guide European public opinion.'

Political debates have become a permanent feature of the Assembly's agenda and Foreign Ministers of the member states have taken a prominent part in them.

In 1956, in an attempt to reconcile the Six and the other countries of Western Europe, Mr Selwyn Lloyd, then British Foreign Minister, proposed a 'Grand Design' in which a single European Assembly would be set up with committees dealing with defence and political, economic, social, cultural, legal and administrative affairs. The Italian Government then made a counter-proposal that the existing European assemblies—the Consultative Assembly, the Assembly of Western European Union and the Common Assembly of ECSC—should maintain their independent existence but that there should be identical membership in the national parliamentary delegations to these assemblies. Neither of these projects met with any success.

In 1957 the Assembly recommended the merging of the Council of Europe and OEEC but this idea was rejected by the member governments.

After the initial attempt to become 'a political authority with limited functions but real powers', which ended in failure, the political work of the Council of Europe has been divided into several phases. First, during a period when Western Europe has been divided into the Six-power European Communities and the European Free Trade Association of the Seven, the Council of Europe has been the meeting place in which members of both groups can explain and defend their national and collective policies and demonstrate the problems that have arisen as a result of the formation of these groupings. Ever since 1955, when the Foreign Ministers of the Six met at Messina and outlined schemes for the creation of economic and nuclear energy communities of the Six, the Council of Europe has closely followed the evolution of the European Communities. The Council backed both the establishment of the European Economic Community and the European Atomic Energy Community in 1958 and also the plans discussed in OEEC for the establishment of a European Free Trade Area. With the breakdown of the Free Trade Area negotiations in December 1958, the Council of Europe took on a greater importance for those of its member states which remained outside the nascent Communities. Discussions in the Assembly were increasingly focused on relations between the Six and the non-Six and the Assembly repeatedly emphasised the need to avoid the creation of permanent economic divisions in Europe which could, in turn, it felt, lead to political divisions. The creation of EFTA in November 1959 in no way reduced the value of the Council of Europe since EFTA itself provided no platform for discussion between its members and the Six and those countries which were outside both organisations. The British Government's application for membership of the EEC in July 1961 was followed by the protracted negotiations which continued until January 1963, when they were broken off by the French Government. During this period the Consultative Assembly acted, together with WEU, as the parliamentary forum for the Brussels negotiations. As each major step in the negotiations was taken its significance was anxiously debated by the Assembly, particularly by the representatives of those countries which had also applied for membership of or association with the EEC.

The breaking off of the Brussels negotiations not only ended Britain's hopes of immediate entry into the EEC but also meant that Danish, Norwegian, Irish, Swedish, Austrian and Swiss hopes of membership of or association with the EEC were, at least, postponed for a time. Under these circumstances the Council of Europe proved the one international meeting place to which all the interested countries could turn to minimise the political and economic split which had now appeared in Western Europe.

In May 1963, the need for closer political co-operation between the members of the Council of Europe following the abrupt ending of the Brussels negotiations led the Committee of Ministers to adopt a Resolution[1] stating its resolve:

'to make full use of each of its sessions, to hold comprehensive discussions on the major political problems of European unification, in the light of the opinions expressed by the Consultative Assembly.'

[1] Resolution of the Committee of Ministers (63) 6 of 6 May 1963.

Following this Resolution the Ministers' Deputies have prepared exchanges of views on major political themes to be held by the Foreign Ministers themselves at each subsequent meeting of the Committee of Ministers at ministerial level. The Ministers have held frank and useful discussions on such topics as the Kennedy Round of GATT negotiations, Atlantic partnership and East–West relations, and now inform each other of developments in the bilateral relations of their countries with Eastern European states.

POLITICAL UNION

Since the *relance politique* of the Six in February 1961, when the Foreign Ministers of the EEC countries set up a committee under the chairmanship of M. Christian Fouchet to examine the problem of political co-operation, the Council of Europe has followed closely all moves towards the establishment of a European political union.

The breakdown of the negotiations between the Six on the French Government's proposals concerning the establishment of a political union in April 1962, was deplored by the Assembly which returned to the study of this question in January 1964, when Lord Grantchester presented a motion for a recommendation suggesting 'the implementation of a plan on the lines of the Fouchet Plan which would aim at achieving, among the members of the Council of Europe, the beginnings of a European Political Union'.[1] The Political Committee studied Lord Grantchester's proposals and M. Etienne de la Vallée Poussin, in the detailed report[2] on this matter which he presented to the Assembly in April 1964, set out the reasons why the Council of Europe could not itself provide the framework for a European political union:

'The experience of the last fifteen years seems to indicate that the construction of Europe can progress at a reasonable speed only if the States have come to an agreement on a definite aim and have set up an international or supranational body to achieve these aims, suitable to the work to be done. OEEC and the Six-power Communities met those requirements, and have been successful. The Council of Europe, WEU and the present OECD do excellent and essential work on the level of studies and conferences of officials, but from the point of view of political decisions, for lack of a precise programme and an effective structure, they achieve with great difficulty results that might be gained by any well-organised international conference.

[1] Assembly document 1715. [2] Assembly document 1741.

They may yield good fruit, but they have neither the energy nor the possibilities for survival that one expects of a true European union.'

The Recommendation which the Assembly adopted on the basis of this report[1] requested the Committee of Ministers to 'set out the views of their several governments as to the main lines on which they believe a form of European political unity can most appropriately be achieved and refer this document to the Assembly for an opinion'. There was no positive response by the Committee of Ministers to this request.

The initiatives taken by the Belgian, Federal German and Italian Governments between September and November 1964 to relaunch informal discussions concerning the creation of a European political union led to the Political Committee's carrying out a further study of this subject (the *rapporteur* was again M. de la Vallée Poussin), which was submitted to the Assembly in January 1965. Following a lively debate between representatives of the Six and the other member countries, which involved the adoption of several substantive amendments to the text of the draft recommendation presented by the Political Committee, the Assembly adopted Recommendation 408 which invited the Committee of Ministers 'to take advantage of every opportunity available to it to conclude agreements and pursue a policy which will pave the way for the political union of all Europe'.

ATLANTIC PARTNERSHIP

The Council of Europe has displayed a lively interest in the achievement of Atlantic partnership. As early as 1951 a joint meeting was held in Strasbourg between delegations from the Assembly and from the Congress of the United States. In a report which he presented to the Assembly in September 1962, on behalf of the Political Committee, M. Pierre Pflimlin gave a warm response to President Kennedy's speech of 4 July 1962, in which he advocated the idea of an Atlantic partnership,[2] and in Recommendation 337 which accom-

[1] Recommendation 390.

[2] In his Independence Day Speech at Philadelphia, President Kennedy stated: 'I will say here and now, on this Day of Independence, that the United States will be ready for a declaration of interdependence, that we will be prepared to discuss with a united Europe the ways and means of forming a concrete Atlantic Partnership, a mutually beneficial partnership between the new union now emerging in Europe and the old American union founded here 175 years ago.' On the European side the Action Committee for the United States of Europe had already issued a declaration on 26 June 1962, stating: 'While the economic unity of Europe is being consolidated and a start made on its political unification, the co-operation that has already grown up between the United States and European

panied this report the Assembly recognised the 'historical importance' of President Kennedy's declaration, affirmed that 'the principles defined in the declaration of 4 July 1962 correspond to the aspirations of the peoples represented in the Consultative Assembly' and recommended the Committee of Ministers 'to study the problems raised by the declaration'. In this Recommendation the Assembly was the first European body to respond to the American offer of interdependence.

The breaking off of the Brussels negotiations between the EEC and the British Government in January 1963 ended any prospect of the construction of this partnership in the near future since the achievement of the partnership depended on the prior construction of a united Europe based on an enlarged EEC of which Britain and the Scandinavian countries would be members. The Assembly has, nevertheless, repeatedly expressed its concern that European unity should be built up within an Atlantic context and has advocated Atlantic solutions for the nuclear defence of the West and for the co-ordination of aid policy towards the developing countries. It has emphasised the necessity of a successful outcome of the 'Kennedy Round' of tariff negotiations in GATT,[1] which opened in Geneva in

countries should gradually be transformed into a partnership between a united Europe and the United States. The partnership between America and a united Europe must be a relationship of two separate but equally powerful entities, each bearing its share of common responsibilities in the world. This partnership is natural and inevitable because the peoples of Europe and America share the same civilisation based on freedom, and conduct their public life in accordance with common democratic principles.'

[1] The United States Trade Expansion Act of 1962 was the first concrete step towards the achievement of partnership in the economic and commercial domains. It empowered the President to negotiate reciprocal linear tariff reductions of up to 50 per cent and it was originally hoped that the main partners to the negotiations, to be held in GATT, would be the United States and an expanded EEC including Britain. In view of the expected enlargement of the EEC to include Britain and other European countries the Act gave the President further authority to negotiate with the EEC greater reductions in, or even the elimination of, tariffs on products where the United States and the EEC together accounted for 80 per cent or more of world trade. With the ending of the Brussels negotiations in January 1963 the European countries which had been excluded from membership of the EEC hoped that a successful Kennedy Round would ameliorate their increasingly difficult trade problems resulting from their remaining outside the EEC's tariffs and to some extent quotas. Such problems have been especially difficult for countries like Austria and Sweden, a high proportion of whose exports have traditionally gone to the Federal Republic of Germany whose formerly low tariffs have been rising sharply with the progressive alignment of the individual national tariffs of the members of the EEC towards the common external tariff.

May 1964, in the hope that substantial tariff reductions would, as part of a 'pre-partnership' relationship, result amongst other aims[1] in increased trade between North America and Western Europe and accelerated economic growth on both sides of the Atlantic.

Some of the supporters of the idea of partnership have advocated the establishment of a formal Atlantic Assembly. Feeling in the Consultative Assembly has, however, been that while an eventual move of this kind should not be excluded it is better during the 'pre-partnership phase' not to formalise parliamentary relations at the Atlantic level. Meanwhile the Assembly has itself started to develop closer contacts with the Congress of the United States. In November 1964, Congressman Wayne L. Hays was invited to address the Assembly. He returned to Strasbourg during the Assembly's part-session of May 1965 with a delegation from Senate and the House of Representatives which included Senator J. William Fulbright (Chairman of the Senate Committee on Foreign Relations), to engage in a day's debate on Atlantic problems with members of the Assembly.[2] This procedure was repeated in 1966 and if continued will permit the development of Atlantic parliamentary discussions[3] of political and economic matters on an *ad hoc* basis, a development which could have far-reaching consequences for the Assembly.

PROGRAMME OF WORK

At the beginning of 1963 the Council of Europe started to work on the problem of drawing up a coherent working programme into which activities of both the Committee of Ministers and the Assembly could be fitted. Recommendation 358 of May 1963 proposed that the Agenda of the Assembly should include 'questions put down with the agreement of the Committee of Ministers'. This was followed up by Recommendation 376 which proposed the establishment of a programme of work. After the Assembly had received the Committee of Ministers' reply to Recommendation 358 the President of the Assembly submitted a list of eighteen subjects to the Committee of

[1] The most important of the other aims of the negotiations is to increase the export earnings of the developing countries.

[2] A joint meeting between members of the Assembly and of the United States Congress had already been held in 1951.

[3] The North Atlantic Assembly (formerly the NATO Parliamentarians Conference) brings together parliamentarians from the NATO countries once a year but parliamentarians of the European non-NATO countries (Austria, Sweden, Cyprus, Ireland, Malta and Switzerland) do not take part in those meetings, which are concerned primarily with military questions and problems of the Alliance. It is described in more detail on p. 418.

Ministers with a view to these subjects being placed on the Assembly's Agenda with the agreement of the Committee of Ministers. In response to an invitation from the Committee of Ministers that he should draw up a working programme, the Secretary General established a Programme Unit within the Secretariat at the beginning of 1965 to compile a single coherent plan of activities for the intergovernmental work of the Council to be submitted over a period of years to the Committee of Ministers. Addressing the Assembly in May 1965, he proposed 'a planned programme of harmonisation' which would both take account of recommendations from the Assembly and proposals from member governments.

The Secretary General made a similar suggestion to the Committee of Ministers in the same month, and he received from the Committee a mandate to draw up a comprehensive programme of work covering all the organisation's intergovernmental activities. A draft was referred to the Ministers' Deputies for examination, and in May 1966 the Ministers themselves approved the programme, the first of the comprehensive reviews which will now take place. The aims of the programme are to give the Council's work more impetus, to rationalise existing and new activities and establish an effective system of priorities. In the first review it was not possible to do very much more than classify and organise work already sanctioned by governments on an *ad hoc* basis, and to allot priorities by fixing terminal dates for each activity. Even so new items have been included and some existing proposals abandoned. The annual revision of the programmes of work should help to ensure that the activities of the Council become better balanced and more effective.

FUTURE PERSPECTIVES

At the world level there are signs that the Council of Europe may develop increasingly close relations with the United Nations over the next few years. In particular the present Secretary General, Mr Peter Smithers, has put forward the idea that the Council of Europe might become a regional organisation of the United Nations.[1]

Another idea which was developed in the Secretary General's inaugural address to the Assembly was that the Council of Europe should in the coming years explore the possibilities offered by the East–West *détente* and the recent political and social developments in the Iberian Peninsula to 'keep open the door to the whole of the European family if and when that family is able to qualify in terms

[1] In his inaugural statement to the Assembly in April 1964.

of the Statute'.[1] This suggestion could, possibly, at first find practical expression in agreements between the Council of Europe and the less rigid communist regimes of Eastern Europe. After its meeting of 19 December 1964 the Committee of Ministers stated in a most significant communiqué that its discussions 'had brought out clearly that the Council of Europe does not form a "bloc" and remains open towards the outside world within the limits set by its Statute'. In the press conference which was held at the end of the Assembly's part-session of May 1965, M. Pierre Pflimlin, the Assembly's President, stated: 'The participation of representatives of communist countries of central and Eastern Europe in the technical bodies of the Council of Europe is desirable, in particular in order to start on co-operation in economic, social, legal and cultural matters. If we move in this direction, this does not mean that we abandon the principles on which our institution is founded.' Since then some Eastern European countries have taken part in certain technical activities of the Council of Europe; Russian observers have taken part in some of the work of the Patents Committee, and various Eastern European countries were represented at the Demographic Conference held in September 1966.

Other Work of the Council

ECONOMIC

The Council of Europe's concern that Western European political and economic unity should be achieved within the broadest possible framework has, since the breakdown of the free trade area negotiations in December 1958, meant that the political and economic work of the Council has overlapped to a considerable extent. In the Assembly, in particular, the political and economic debates have since the end of 1958, as has been described earlier, been concerned largely with the relations between the Six and the other member states of the Council. A good example of the Council's concern over this problem was the attempt launched by the Assembly in September 1963 to link those member states of the Council which were not members of the EEC more closely with some aspects of the integration achieved by the Six. Recommendation 376 of the Assembly, which accompanied a report proposed on behalf of the Political Committee by M. Marc-

[1] It was Mr Harold Macmillan, when Foreign Secretary, in a speech to the Assembly in July 1955, who first mooted the idea of an 'opening to the East' by suggesting that the Council was perhaps too exclusive and should consider enlarging its membership to include, for example, observers from Yugoslavia.

Antoine Pierson, recommended the Committee of Ministers '. . . to convene, as soon as possible, committees of senior civil servants who would be charged with the preparation of agreements extending to some or all of the member countries of the Council of Europe the arrangements adopted by the European Economic Community with regard to workers and the right of establishment, services, capital and transport'. Since then, the Council of Europe has kept in contact with the EEC Commission about the possibility of extending specific regulations of the EEC to those member countries of the Council which might be willing to accept them.

Apart from its role as a contact body between the Six and its other member countries, the Council of Europe keeps a watching brief on European economic policy as a whole, though, owing to the existence and work of OEEC (and later OECD) as the major European organisation dealing with economic affairs, the Council's possibilities to take action in economic matters have been limited. OECD submits an annual report to the Council (as did OEEC), which is generally presented by the chairman of the Ministerial Council of OECD and which is the subject of a full debate in the Assembly. The Assembly takes the opportunity provided by the annual debate to address a comprehensive Resolution to the Ministerial Council of OECD making specific recommendations on all the different aspects of OECD's work, including the work of its Development Assistance Committee in the field of aid to the developing countries. Liaison committees, in which representatives of both the ministerial and the Assembly sides of the Council of Europe meet heads of delegations and senior members of OECD, hold joint meetings. These formulate proposals for improving the co-operation between the two bodies and press for the implementation of these proposals. The Secretary General of OECD addresses the Political, Economic and other Committees of the Assembly from time to time to outline developments in the work of OECD. Although Portugal, Spain, Canada, the United States and Japan are members of OECD but not of the Council of Europe, the Consultative Assembly has in practice become, even if on an *ad hoc* basis, a parliamentary assembly for OECD affairs in which the major problems of Atlantic economic relations are publicly debated.

The annual joint meeting of the Assembly with the European Parliament,[1] together with the debates on the annual reports of the EEC, Euratom and ECSC,[2] provides the Assembly with the

[1] The joint parliamentary assembly of the three European Communities.

[2] The Assembly also debates the annual reports of EFTA.

opportunity to hold an annual confrontation with parliamentarians representing the Communities of the Six concerning the economic and commercial policies of the EEC and EFTA, and allows representatives of those member states of the Council which are not members of the EEC to pose the problems which the development of the Common Market is causing them. The utility of discussions of this kind has been twofold. First, they have had an educative effect on parliamentarians from those countries (in particular the 'neutral' countries, Austria, Sweden and Switzerland) which have been reluctant to accept the underlying political aims of the EEC. Secondly, they have helped to bring home to the parliamentarians of the Six the responsibilities of the EEC in its tariff and trade policies towards its fellow members of the Council in the light of its own spectacular commercial success.

The Assembly has given considerable attention to agricultural problems. The European Agricultural Conference of 1953 was convened in response to proposals made by the Council. A convention on the production and marketing of wines and spirits in Europe is in preparation. Transport has been another continuing interest of the Assembly. The European Conference of Ministers of Transport was established as a result of a special Conference which was organised by the Council in 1953. The Conference transmits an annual report to the Council. The Council was also instrumental in convening the first European Conference of the International Civil Aviation Organisation in 1954, which has been followed by further meetings at two-yearly intervals. The Conference of European Postal and Telecommunications Administrations was convened after requests had been made in the Council. The desire to check the growth of road accidents has led the Council to start work on the preparation of a European Highway Code. Several Conventions on industrial patents have come into force and work in this field continues.

The Assembly's Economic Committee keeps certain problems under constant review. These include: intra-European economic relations; economic relations between Western Europe and North America; East–West trade; aid to the developing countries; monetary policy; and transport and energy problems. Some of the detailed studies carried out by the Economic Committee, with the help of the Secretariat, such as the 'Strasbourg Plan' of 1951 (which made proposals for the linking of the economies of the European countries with those of their overseas dependencies), have achieved wide attention. 'The Present State of the Economic Integration of Western Europe', a study proposed in the spring of 1955, was used as a basic document for the negotiations held between the Governments of the Six, under the chairmanship of M. Paul-Henri Spaak, at the Château of Val-Duchesse in the summer of 1955 concerning the establishment of the EEC.

HUMAN RIGHTS

The most notable single achievement of the Council of Europe is the European Convention for the Protection of Human Rights and Fundamental Freedoms which was initiated by a recommendation of the Assembly in September 1949, signed by representatives of all member countries in Rome on 4 November 1950 and came into force in September 1953. The Convention both defined the rights of the citizen in a democratic society and provided for international machinery to ensure the protection of those rights. The rights and freedoms guaranteed in the Convention are: the right to life; freedom from torture; freedom from slavery and servitude; the right to liberty and security of person; the right to a fair trial; protection against retro-activity of the law; the right to privacy; freedom of thought, conscience and religion; freedom of expression; freedom of assembly and freedom of association; the right to marry; and the right to an effective legal remedy. In March 1952, a first protocol to the Convention was signed; this extended the terms of the Convention to cover the rights to the peaceful enjoyment of property, to education, and to free elections at reasonable intervals by secret ballot. The Convention has been ratified by all member states except France,[1] and new member countries such as Switzerland and Malta. The first protocol came into effect in May 1954, and has been ratified by the same member states. Three further protocols were signed in 1963 but none of these has yet entered into force. The second protocol will give the Court the competence to give advisory opinions. The third will amend the Commission's procedure and the fourth will guarantee certain additional rights not at present protected. The fifth protocol will slightly amend the provisions of the Convention governing the length of terms of office of members of the Court and the Human Rights Commission.

After the coming into force of the Convention, the European Commission of Human Rights was set up. The Commission may

[1] France took a leading part in drafting the Convention and was one of the original signatories in 1950 but has still not ratified it. During a debate in the National Assembly on 17 November 1964, the Minister of Justice described the Convention as having been drawn up in terms of Anglo-Saxon law, and consequently as not being suitable for ratification.

receive complaints or 'applications' from both states and individuals.

State applications may be received from any 'High Contracting Party' (any state which has ratified the Convention) which alleges a breach by another High Contracting Party. The Commission has received and investigated complaints made by Greece against the United Kingdom concerning events in Cyprus before Cyprus became independent. The Commission was seized of complaints made against the Greek military Government by the Netherlands and the Scandinavian Governments in September 1967.

Individual applications may be received from anyone within the jurisdiction[1] of any High Contracting Party which has also made a declaration (under Article 25) accepting the 'right of individual application'. Seven countries have not yet done so: Cyprus, France, Greece, Italy, Malta, Switzerland and Turkey. The British Government recognised the right of individual petition and the jurisdiction of the Court in January 1966. The complaints received (since 1955, these number 2,500, of which 500 have not yet been examined) have to satisfy certain conditions before being declared 'admissible' by the Commission (so far only forty have been found admissible).

When an application is declared to be admissible the Commission's first duty is to try to find an agreed settlement.[2] Only if it fails to do so must the Commission decide upon further action. It must in any event submit to the Committee of Ministers a report and an opinion as to whether or not the facts disclose a breach of the Convention, and it may accompany its report with 'such proposals as it thinks fit'. Then if the Commission decides not to submit the case to the Court, it is for the Committee of Ministers to decide upon the case. A two-thirds majority is required. All member states are entitled to vote.

The Commission first met in July 1954, and at present consists of fifteen members (one for each state which has ratified the Convention). Members are elected on their individual capacity by the Committee of Ministers from lists of names presented by each delegation to the Assembly. They serve for six years, with the possi-

[1] This means that besides nationals of that state anyone who is for any reason within the territory of the state may benefit. The protection of the Convention is thus not confined to 'Europeans' only.

[2] 'The primary duty of the Commission is to conduct confidential negotiations with the parties and to try to set right unobtrusively any breach of human rights that may have occurred. It was not primarily established for the purpose of putting states in the dock and registering convictions against them.' Speech made by Sir Humphrey Waldock, first President of the Commission, at the World Exhibition at Brussels on 3 September 1958. A great deal of the useful work accomplished by the Commission is thus never brought to light.

bility of re-election. The Convention also provides for a European Court of Human Rights. The Court was set up in April 1959, and has so far dealt with only two cases. Another case (the Belgian linguistic affair) is now being considered by it. The Court consists of a number of judges equal to that of the member countries of the Council of Europe, sitting however as a chamber of seven for the consideration of any particular case.

The jurisdiction of the Court extends to all cases concerning the interpretation and application of the Convention which are referred to it. Only the Commission and the High Contracting Parties may refer cases to the Court, and the power of the Court to pronounce judgement on the case depends on whether the states concerned have accepted the jurisdiction of the Court in advance, under Article 46 of the Convention (Austria, Belgium, Denmark, Germany, Iceland, Ireland, Luxembourg, the Netherlands, Norway, Sweden and the United Kingdom have done so), or at the time the case arises by a special agreement.

A case concerning an individual application can thus come before the Court only if the state concerned has accepted both the right of individual petition and the jurisdiction of the Court.

Although a state may present a case to the Court at any time, the Commission may do so only within three months of its sending its report on the case to the Committee of Ministers. Until now all cases have been referred to the Court by the Commission.

The first case brought before the Court was that of Gerald Lawless, an Irish national who was detained by his government without charge or trial on suspicion of being a member of an illegal organisation: the Irish Republican Army. The Court decided that this did not constitute a violation of the Convention since, at the time of Lawless's detention, a state of emergency existed in Ireland which justified the government in making derogations from certain Articles of the Convention, as permitted under Article 15. Another case concerned Raymond de Becker, a Belgian journalist who had been condemned by the Belgian courts for wartime collaboration. He was released on undertaking to live abroad and not to exercise his profession of journalism. His application was declared admissible by the Commission which, however, failed to obtain a friendly settlement. A hearing was held by the Court in July 1961, but the Belgian Government then informed the Court that the relevant article of the Penal Code had been amended and that a new article had been promulgated, in June 1961, which was in conformity with the Convention. A further case, decided by the Court in December 1966, concerned a German, Armin Poerschke, who had, in confused circumstances, been over-sentenced by his national courts for robbery. He was set free at the end of 1966, following the Court's decision, gaining a remission of four months' imprisonment. Proceedings before the Commission have led to member governments either changing their constitutions or making alterations in their internal legislation in cases where infringements of the Convention have caused hardship or injustice to individuals. The Court was seized in 1965 of a series of cases concerning the language problem in Belgium which it is still considering.

Under Article 57 of the Convention, the Secretary General of the Council of Europe may request any High Contracting Party to 'furnish an explanation of the manner in which its internal law ensures the effective implementation of any of the provisions of the Convention'. This request was sent to all such states for the first time in November 1964, and was so phrased as to include *all* the provisions of the Convention. At their meeting in Rome, in 1962, the European Ministers of Justice characterised the Convention as 'the very basis of any legal or political construction of Europe'. Outside Europe nine newly independent states have included parts of the Convention in their constitutions: Cyprus, Jamaica, Kenya, Malawi, Nigeria, Sierra Leone, Trinidad and Tobago, Uganda and Zambia. In addition the Inter-American Council of Jurists (the legal organ of the Organisation of American States) have prepared a draft Convention on Human Rights inspired largely by the Council of Europe's Convention.

The Convention has already proved itself to be a valuable instrument for the protection of the rights of the individual, at both the national and international levels, against infringements of human rights, particularly by governments. The events which occurred in Cyprus between 1964 and 1966 showed, however, that the machinery for enforcing human rights is not easily applied in times of political unrest.

LEGAL

The legal side of the Council's activities has proved one of the most productive. 'Human Rights' apart, no less than forty-six treaties or conventions have been drafted on a wide range of subjects.

The procedure for drafting these treaties is unique. Both the Committee of Ministers and the Consultative Assembly take part, and whereas the former has the last word, the latter very often has the first. In fact many of the matters dealt with in these treaties were suggested by the Assembly, and sometimes even worked out in first draft by its Legal Committee.[1] This process of mutual consultation is continued when a Committee of Experts is set up by the Committee of Ministers to produce a final draft. When this final draft has been approved by the Committee of Ministers it is recommended to governments by a Resolution of the Committee of Ministers. The Resolution also names the day on which the Treaty will be 'opened for signature'.

Conventions normally specify whether they need to be ratified, and if so how many states must do so before they can 'come into force'.

Even where treaties give governments the option of becoming a Party by signature 'without reserve as to ratification', whether they do so or not depends upon their own constitutional requirements. These vary from country to country. The general rule in Britain is that agreements requiring ratification must be laid before Parliament for twenty-one days before the Instrument of Ratification can be deposited. In addition, any legislation necessary to give effect to an agreement must be passed before Britain becomes bound by the agreement. At this stage the drafting procedure shows its value since the parliamentarians who suggested or even helped to draft the treaty are present in Parliament to support its ratification.

Conventions have been drawn up on a wide range of subjects. Leaving aside those in the social and medical, and educational and cultural fields, there are two groups of more obviously 'legal' treaties.

There are, first, treaties which create obligations between states without affecting the rights and duties of individuals. These are the traditional subject matter of treaties, including, for example, the peaceful settlement of disputes, consular functions, extradition (with an extension on mutual assistance in criminal matters), and multiple nationality. The majority of the conventions, however, deal with matters of direct concern to their nationals or, in some cases, anyone resident within their territory. Such conventions achieve the additional purpose of creating a corpus of 'European laws' on specific matters, for, the convention being more in the nature of a 'uniform national law', any state becoming a Party to it must then change its internal law to meet the requirements of the 'uniform law'. Into this category fall such matters as 'the liability of inn-keepers', the compulsory insurance of motor vehicles, the punishment of road-traffic offences and the supervision of offenders. One very important

[1] This was the case for instance with the Convention on Human Rights.

convention, which entered into force in 1965, is the Establishment Convention, the object of which is, eventually, to permit the nationals of one Party to set up in business in the territory of another on equal terms with the nationals of the latter.[1]

Other treaties deal with patents, frontier formalities, television and, more recently, the prevention of 'pirate' radio stations. Any matter, indeed, on which national laws are made can, in theory, become a 'uniform law' type of Treaty. Naturally priority is given to matters of international concern.

Two committees have been set up by the Ministers to guide the legal work of the Council: the European Committee on Crime Problems, in 1958, and the European Committee on Legal Co-operation, in 1963. They have terms of reference which together cover most of the Council's legal work, and there is every sign that this will increase in the future.[2]

Since so much of the Council's legal work falls within the competence of the Ministers of Justice rather than that of the Ministers of Foreign Affairs, the practice of convening a Conference of European Ministers of Justice has developed. First held in Paris in 1961, other meetings have taken place in Rome in 1962 and Dublin in 1964.

EDUCATION, CULTURE AND SCIENCE

The educational and cultural activities of the Council, in which Spain and the Holy See take part, have been extensive. At the first session of the Assembly a series of recommendations were adopted calling for the development of a programme of cultural co-operation in Europe. In response the Committee of Ministers set up a Committee of Cultural Experts which then proceeded to work out and put into effect a cultural and educational programme. A European Cultural Convention, which entered into force in 1955, provides for general co-operation in cultural matters and for the free movement of cultural material. A Cultural Fund was established in 1959 'to promote and prosecute cultural activities'. Contributions were shared between member states in the same proportion as contributions to the Council's general budget. The Fund, which gave a

[1] In view of the provision in the Rome Treaty on the right of establishment, it is interesting to observe that of the six states who have become a party to the Establishment Convention, three (Italy, Belgium and Germany) are Common Market countries and three are outside the EEC (Greece, Norway and Denmark).

[2] One indication of this is that the Ministers, when setting up the European Committee on Legal Co-operation, charged it with the implementation of an 'expanded legal programme'.

measure of financial autonomy to the cultural experts, was governed for three years by an Administrative Board. In 1961, in response to an appeal from the European Ministers of Education to set up machinery for educational co-operation, the Committee of Ministers decided to establish a Council for Cultural Co-operation (CCC) which came into being at the beginning of 1962 and took over the functions previously exercised by the Committee of Cultural Experts and the Administrative Board of the Cultural Fund. In order to deal with new responsibilities in the educational field the CCC was empowered to set up permanent committees dealing with: higher education and research; general and technical education; and out-of-school education (youth, physical education and sport, and adult education). In 1965 a fourth permanent Committee was set up to deal with the problems of educational and cultural films.

In the educational field the Committee of Cultural Experts, together with the Assembly's Committee on Cultural and Scientific Affairs, prepared the European Convention on the equivalence of university entrance examinations, which was signed in December 1953, and which came into force soon afterwards. This Convention provides for students who have passed university entrance examinations in their own countries to have access to the universities of other member countries. In 1956 it was agreed that periods of study spent by students in certain faculties in universities of one member country should be counted for degree purposes in the universities of other member countries. A further convention on the academic recognition of university qualifications entered into force in October 1961. Under this convention each member country undertakes to grant academic recognition to university degrees awarded by a university in another member country.[1]

Following the transfer to the Council of Europe of the exercise of the social and cultural activities of WEU, in 1960, the Council's work in the field of higher education has been consolidated under a Committee for Higher Education and Research, which has abandoned the former legal approach in favour of establishing agreed norms for university curricula in the different disciplines. The work of the former European Universities Committee, which originated under WEU, has been taken over by this committee. The Council of Europe provides the staff of the Conferences of European Ministers of Education, which meet periodically but have not been institution-

[1] The British Government is not committed to do more than commend its provisions to British universities, which are not government controlled and are not obliged to act in accordance with the Convention.

alised, and the CCC examines the possibility of giving effect to their recommendations when drawing up its annual programme.

With regard to general and technical education the Council for Cultural Co-operation organises comparative research on teaching methods to spread the use of modern techniques, identifies current trends and common problems in the European countries, tries to improve standards in such fields as school guidance and teacher-training and has launched a campaign to ensure that all school children follow courses in citizenship containing a European element. The Council's work in the field of out-of-school education is concentrated in three directions: adult education and leisure pursuits; youth activities, including co-operation with non-governmental youth organisations and the training of youth leaders at a centre at Strasbourg; and physical education and sports, including the training of instructors, the establishment of a European Athletics Diploma, the study of equipment needs and attempts to prevent the doping of athletes.

To permit research workers, teachers, scientists and artists to benefit from free or reduced-rate admission to university facilities, museums, libraries and theatres, the Council of Europe has issued, since 1954, a Cultural Identity Card, replacing that previously issued by the Brussels Treaty Organisation. Over 30,000 of these cards have been issued. A programme of Council of Europe fellowships (originally awarded jointly with the ECSC) was instituted in 1953 but was terminated at the end of 1964 in favour of commissioned research on problems relevant to the programme of the CCC. The Council has encouraged exchanges of professors and teachers and carried out work on the revision of history and geography text books and atlases in the hope of eliminating nationalist prejudices. A number of art exhibitions have been organised by the Council to illustrate European cultural unity during different periods of history, and audio-visual material such as travelling exhibitions, slides and illustrated catalogues have been produced for educational purposes.

The Council has tried to interest schools in the process of European unification by sponsoring and helping to finance a 'European Schools' Day' competition which awards prizes for drawing and essay writing.

Since the establishment of the CCC, the cultural work of the Council has tended more and more to adopt the methods of technical co-operation applied in the educational field under the general heading of 'the protection and development of the European cultural heritage'. Such activities vary from studies of the cultural facilities of towns to the revival of craftsmanship. The Council has been active in the field of television. Agreements have been signed on programme exchanges of television films and the protection of the rights of broadcasting organisations concerning the retransmission, distribution or public performance of their television broadcasts. The Technical Committee for Film Activities of the CCC is promoting the co-production of educational and cultural films and tackling the problems of film distribution.

At the invitation of the British Government, a European Parliamentary and Scientific Conference was held in London in March 1961. This was organised by the Parliamentary and Scientific Committee of the British Parliament while the Consultative Assembly provided the parliamentary delegation from the European countries and OEEC arranged the participation of the scientists. Following this successful meeting the Council of Europe and OECD were instructed to arrange a further conference of the same kind, which was held at Vienna in May 1964. In Recommendation 400 the Assembly called for the appointment of a Minister in each member country charged with 'the promotion and co-ordination of science policy in all its aspects'; in Resolutions 284 and 285 the Assembly has proposed a programme to follow up these conferences and the holding of periodic debates 'to consider . . . the activities of the international and European organisations playing a role in the field of scientific co-operation' in order to 'contribute to better co-ordination of the efforts being made in the field of European scientific co-operation'.

SOCIAL AND PUBLIC HEALTH ACTIVITIES

In social matters the Council aims at ensuring that the citizens of one member state who are resident in another receive, as far as possible, the same social benefits and protection as nationals of the country in which they live. The Council also aims at the harmonisation of social security and welfare standards to the highest possible level throughout its member countries. Initial steps towards the realisation of the first aim were taken in 1952 with the signing of two interim agreements on social security and a convention on social and medical assistance. They provide that any member country shall give to nationals of other member states resident or working in its territory the same social benefits as it gives to its own citizens.

The signature of the European Social Charter in Turin in October 1961 was an advance towards the second aim. The Charter, which supplements, in social matters, the Human Rights Convention, lays down the following economic and social rights: the right to work; to just conditions of work; to security and hygiene in the place of work; to a fair remuneration; to form trade unions; to engage in collective bargaining and to strike; to protection of children and young persons in work; to protection of employed women; to vocational guidance; to vocational training; to assistance; to benefit from social services; to vocational training, rehabilitation and resettlement of the disabled; to the protection of the family; to the protection of mothers and children; to engage in a gainful occupation in the territory of other contracting parties; to protection and assistance for migrant workers. These rights are embodied in nineteen articles which describe in some detail the corresponding undertakings on the part of the Contracting Parties. However, the Parties need not subscribe to all the undertakings immediately, provided that they accept a specified minimum of them. The Charter provides machinery for the supervision of its implementation by independent experts, by governments, the Assembly, workers and employers.

A European Code of Social Security was signed on 13 May 1964. It defines the general principles and standards on which social security schemes should be based. An Additional Protocol establishes standards higher than those of the Code itself. The implementation of these instruments is also subject to international control.

The Social Committee, composed of high-ranking government officials, is undertaking studies of such subjects as the social aspects of regional development policy, and the role, training and status of social workers. A fellowship scheme for the benefit of social workers enables a large number of people working on social matters to go abroad to improve their professional knowledge.

The seven members of WEU have undertaken to provide certain guarantees concerned with the rehabilitation or re-employment of disabled persons. In 1960 the exercise of the social activities of WEU was transferred to the Council of Europe.

Among other achievements of the Council in social and public health matters are agreements on: the exchange of war cripples for medical treatment; the exchange of therapeutic substances of human origin, concerning, in particular, the supply of blood and blood products; and the temporary duty-free importation of medical, surgical and laboratory equipment for use on free loan in hospitals. There are also more recent agreements on: an international book of vouchers for the repair of prosthetic and orthopaedic appliances (for disabled people travelling in those member countries which have accepted the agreement); material assistance concerning special medical treatment and climatic facilities (cures); and the exchange of blood grouping reagents. More than 800 fellowships have been awarded by the Council to doctors to enable them to study new medical techniques employed in member countries.[1] Research has been organised on transfusion, camping hygiene, noise abatement, the repercussions of automation and the problems of old age. The Council has held a conference on air pollution in order to co-ordinate the different attempts being made to remedy this problem. A conference on water pollution is being prepared to supplement this work.

The Council of Europe has actively concerned itself with the problems of refugees and over-population. In 1953 it appointed a Special Representative, M. Pierre Schneiter, to examine these problems. In 1953 he made certain recommendations, which were approved by the Assembly and received the assent of the Committee of Ministers in 1956. In 1956 the Ministers set up a European Resettlement Fund which has given loans to governments to help them absorb refugees and surplus population into their economies, notably by financing small businesses and housing to an extent of some $10 million. The Special Representative was to 'impart political impulsion' to ensure that the commitments undertaken by governments would be effectively carried out. In December 1956, the Fund provided a special grant of £100,000 to the Austrian Government to assist in supporting the refugees who had fled from Hungary to Austria during the Hungarian revolution. Since the United Nations is responsible for 'international refugees' the Council of Europe has restricted its activities to the problem of 'national' refugees. In recent years the Council has been particularly concerned with the assimilation of population surpluses. Special attention has been given to the vocational training of migrant workers, the establishment of training centres and welfare facilities for migrants.

THE PARTIAL AGREEMENT

In 1960, following an arrangement made in 1959 between the Council of Europe and Western European Union, the Council of Europe took over the 'exercise of the social and cultural activities' of WEU. In doing so it developed the technique of a Partial Agreement between a number of member states which are prepared to embark in particularly close co-operation in specific matters.[2] In practice this has meant especially close co-operation between the seven members of WEU in

[1] Finland takes part in the medical fellowship scheme and in certain other public health activities.

[2] This procedure had been used for the first time in April 1956 for the creation of the European Resettlement Fund.

the social and medical domains with, from time to time, the participation of one or more other member states. The co-operation achieved between Britain and the Six within the framework of this Partial Agreement, albeit the subject matter is in every case non-political, has had a certain political importance in the light of the breaking off of the Brussels negotiations concerning Britain's application for membership of EEC. The method of work employed, which was transferred from WEU, is an interesting one. The Committees which prepare agreements consist of representatives of the participating governments who make recommendations to the Committee of Ministers by unanimity, on the harmonisation of the laws of their member states concerning the social and medical matters dealt with. The administrative arrangements made between the participating governments are implemented directly, following an agreement, by the member governments, and require no intermediary international machinery for their application. One of the most interesting developments under the Partial Agreement is a convention to establish a European Pharmacopoeia. The seven members of WEU and Switzerland participate in this scheme. These countries are in the process of establishing monographs—definitions of drugs and medicines—which will become standard in those countries taking part in the pharmacopoeia. The Partial Agreement is one of the most interesting working methods devised by the Council of Europe and its use is likely to be extended to other fields in the future.

LOCAL AUTHORITIES

The Council of Europe is the only intergovernmental organisation dealing specifically with local authorities. After the establishment of the Council of Europe, it became clear that the association of local authorities with its work, and a close and permanent contact between the Council and the European peoples, would be useful and serve European interests. In 1952, a Committee on Local Authorities was set up within the Consultative Assembly. In 1956, the European Conference of Local Authorities was established, a body which brought together representatives of municipalities. Since then, the Conference has met every two years and has become a permanent organ of the Council of Europe.

Both bodies aim at establishing a link between municipalities and the process of European unification and they endeavour to preserve and stress the principle of local autonomy. Their main activities can be described in the following way: propagation of the European idea through the medium of local authorities and other associations;

association of local authorities with the work of the Council of Europe and promotion of co-operation among European municipalities; and promotion of intergovernmental co-operation with regard to local authorities in spheres within the legislative or executive competence of states.

While the Committee and Conference have succeeded very well in the first task and the Conference has proved useful, intergovernmental co-operation has been limited to a small number of subjects owing to the differing structures of local authorities in each country and also to the fact that some federal states, such as the Federal Republic of Germany and Switzerland, even have different municipal systems within one country.

The Committee on Local Authorities awards each year a 'Europe Prize' to the European town which has made the greatest efforts in propagating the European idea; further awards are given to other towns. The movement of European town twinning has been fostered and a European Inter-municipal Exchange Plan has been instituted and operated jointly by the Committee and the Conference. 'Europe Day', which is celebrated every year on 5 May, the anniversary of the establishment of the Council of Europe, was instituted following a resolution of the European Conference of Local Authorities.

Some subjects with which the Committee and the Conference on Local Authorities have dealt during the last few years include: the work and interests of local authorities in the process of regional planning and development; evolution and adaptation of local structures to modern requirements; the work of local authorities in the cultural field with special regard to leisure problems; the promotion of international exchanges and the possibility of setting up a European Youth Exchange Office within the Council of Europe.

Conclusions

The Council of Europe has failed to achieve its principal original aim: the political unity of Western Europe. There have been two main reasons for this. First, the powers of the Council's institutions are not sufficient to achieve this end. In particular the fact that the Committee of Ministers is limited to making recommendations to member governments or making resolutions (which sometimes carry greater weight) and cannot itself take binding decisions has been a continuing obstacle to political progress by the Council. Secondly, and more fundamentally, the member governments of the Council have shown little common political will to use the Council as an instrument to achieve greater political unity. Indeed, the very aim of 'greater unity' has been interpreted since the beginning in differing and even contrary ways. The Six countries which eventually established the three European Communities found little response to their initial desire to use the Council as a means of moving towards a federal union of European states. Until the EEC had been established and was demonstrably successful, the British and Scandinavian governments regarded this eventual aim as extravagant and impractical, refusing to agree to proposals which led in this direction. It was because of this lack of common political will on the part of the member governments of the Council that the Six created their own institutions in which they could move further and faster towards European integration outside the framework of the Council. Having once established their own separate Community institutions designed to achieve 'an ever closer union' the Six have, since then, placed much greater emphasis on the work of these institutions than on the co-operative activities of the Council.[1]

The Council has nevertheless considerable achievements to its credit. The Assembly has served as the only official meeting place where parliamentarians from all the democratic countries of Western Europe can debate the guiding-lines of European political and economic affairs and in which they can consider their national and bloc problems together with their neighbours. As such it has had a special value for those countries which were excluded from the EEC by the breaking off of the Brussels negotiations in January 1963.

Their work in the Assembly has influenced the thinking of representatives both from the Six and from the other member countries. There is no doubt that British, Scandinavian, Austrian and Swiss parliamentarians, for instance, have been greatly influenced by their experience of this work and that this has helped to modify national attitudes towards European unification. The Assembly has not only enabled the countries which are not members of the EEC to gain a better comprehension of the aims and methods of the European Communities, but has also brought home to the members of the EEC the problems which confront the other European countries. Moreover, the discussions held in the Assembly on the legal and political aspects of neutrality[2] set off an intensive public debate in Austria and

[1] Apart from the annual joint meetings between the Assembly and the European Parliament.

[2] On the basis of two memoranda presented to the Assembly by M. Paul Struye, the Chairman of the Political Committee, in May 1962 and in April 1963; Assembly Documents 1420 and 1581.

Switzerland and led to a rethinking of traditional views concerning neutrality in these two countries.

The Assembly has been the dynamic organ and the proposal-making body of the Council, and has acted as the spokesman of European democratic opinion on certain political or moral issues on which all of its members have been agreed, such as threats concerning Berlin or crimes against humanity. The Committee of Ministers has, on its side, built up through the work of some sixty committees of experts a complex structure of European co-operation covering an enormous range of subjects which has made the Council the principal framework for European co-operation—in contrast to the more closely knit and further-reaching integration of the Six—in the educational, legal and social fields. Through the Partial Agreement and the specialised conferences established under its auspices, the Council has developed new techniques of co-operation. Over the years the Council has, indeed, become an effective machine for working out agreements between Western European governments in the form of conventions in the legal, cultural and social fields. By means of its conventions the Council has harmonised national practice and standards in many different domains and has started to build a growing corpus of commonly applied European laws. The Council has, moreover, taken the lead in implementing the United Nations Declaration of Human Rights through the European Convention and the machinery established to implement it.

In addition to the Council's functions concerning the relations between Western European countries, there have in recent years been developments in relations between the Council and other parts of the world. Progress is being made in building up contacts on a multilateral basis, within the framework of the Council, between Western European countries and those of Eastern Europe. There has been a tendency towards closer co-operation with the United Nations. And the visits of North American Congressmen and parliamentarians have opened up the possibility that the Council might play a more direct role in relations between Europe and North America.

Part 4

COMMUNITY EUROPE

Chapter Five

THE ORIGINS OF THE THREE COMMUNITIES

The European Community comprises at present three distinct organisations: the European Coal and Steel Community, founded in 1952, and the European Economic Community and Atomic Energy Community (Euratom) which came into being in 1958. They group the same six countries: Belgium, France, the Federal Republic of Germany, Italy, Luxembourg and the Netherlands. The EEC and Euratom, which were modelled on the experience of the ECSC, are based on similar organisational principles. The use of the name Community reflects the difference in kind between these three organisations and others described in this book. The present Communities are seen by many of those most closely concerned with them and by other 'Europeans' as a step on the way towards a full economic and political union of the present and future member countries. Thus, whilst the three Treaties set up 'organisations' whose structure and activities are described below, they also set in motion a fundamental economic, and at the same time political, process by which it is hoped the destinies of the member countries will become inseparably linked. Through its institutions the Community (the three organisations taken together) is the instrument of a structural change. The nature of the tasks carried out by the institutions is thus perpetually evolving: they have been charged not only with functions, such as the dismantling of tariffs, which were laid down in detail in the Treaties, but also with a continuous policy-making process at the Community level.

The original undertaking on which the six countries embarked, the European Coal and Steel Community (ECSC), was limited to two sectors of the economy. It had, however, political aims, clearly stated in the preamble of the Treaty: 'to substitute for their historical rivalries a fusion of the essential interests' of the members; 'to establish by creating an economic Community the foundation of a broad and independent Community among peoples long divided by conflicts; and to lay the basis of institutions capable of giving direction to their future common destiny'.

The steps by which this progress towards full political union was to be achieved were never clearly spelt out. Following the success of the ECSC, projects were launched for a European Defence Community and for a European Political Community. The first was approved by the six governments in 1952 but was not ratified by the French Government, and the second was abandoned in consequence. In 1956 and 1957 the six governments went on to negotiate the Treaty setting up the European Economic Community, covering the whole range of economic and social activity in the six countries. At the same time Euratom was set up to bring about a pooling of the member countries' work concerning the peaceful uses of atomic energy. The EEC Treaty is less explicit about political aims, referring to a shared determination 'to establish the foundations of an ever closer union among the European peoples'; but the founders of the new Communities continued to think in terms of a long-term process leading to political union.

Legally three communities have existed since 1 January 1958, when the two Rome Treaties, establishing the European Economic Community and the European Atomic Energy Community, came into effect. The Court of Justice and the European Parliament became common institutions operating under the terms of all three Treaties. With the successful development of the EEC, certain anomalies have, however, emerged resulting from the fact that the coal and steel sectors were subject to provisions very different from those of the Rome Treaty, which had been negotiated five years later in very different circumstances. Some problems, whose solution is vital to the long-term success of the EEC, above all those of energy policy, cannot be satisfactorily solved whilst the products involved are subject to widely different systems. As a result pressures developed for a merger of the three Communities. A treaty negotiated in 1963 and 1964 and finally signed in May 1965 provided for a merger of the executives of the three Communities; ratification was however delayed by the agricultural and institutional crisis of that year.[1] The merger Treaty institutes a single Commission and a single Council of Ministers functioning under the terms of the three Treaties. The full merger of the Communities, requiring the negotiation of a single Treaty to replace the three existing ones, is planned for two years later. In practice, however, the three Communities

[1] The merger finally took effect on 1 July 1967.

can be regarded as facets of one basic experiment, stages in an unfinished process, the future development of which cannot yet be foreseen.

The new and essential fact common to the three organisations is the 'Community method' of decision-making, applying in the fields covered by the Treaties. This involves a limited pooling of sovereignty in a system where both the interests of the whole and the interests of the individual parts are represented. A dialogue takes place in which the executive body charged with furthering the Community interest makes proposals which are debated in the Council where ministers represent the interests of each country: the Council then takes a decision applying to the whole Community. The smooth and effective working of this system in a wide field of economic and social policy requires a political commitment to achieving the aims laid down in the Treaties and a consequent readiness to accept the necessary rules and procedures.

Whilst the basic institutional pattern remained the same, with a body representing the Community interest, there was a major shift of institutional emphasis between the ECSC and the EEC Treaties. In the former the High Authority was clearly intended to be predominant, having considerable powers of direct action, and needing the agreement of the Council of Ministers only in specific areas of policy or matters not fully covered by the Treaty. In the latter, the most important decisions are taken by the Council of Ministers, and the influence of the Commission, as spokesman of the common interest, derives from its independence and from its right of initiative as the only body empowered to put forward the proposals on which such decisions are based. This change in the institutional balance, giving greater weight to the Council, was due largely to the fact that the EEC Treaty covers the whole field of the economy: over such a wide area states were less willing to surrender sovereignty to an independent body. In practice, however, the greater political weight of the EEC Commission has more than compensated for its lesser constitutional powers.

As will be seen from the detailed description which follows of the EEC's activities, these are coming more and more to have political implications, as is to be expected in major questions of economic policy. Yet no progress has been achieved towards a 'political union' covering the other great political domains of foreign policy or defence. Almost the entire period of the EEC's existence has been marked by a fundamental disagreement between France and her partners about the nature and aims of political union. Formal negotiations on the establishment of a political union took place after a declaration of intent made at a meeting of the Heads of Government of the Six in July 1961; but they broke down in April 1962. Five countries were not prepared to enter a political and defence union without obtaining assurances of its later evolution in a federal direction and without a commitment that any defence integration would be carried out within the framework of NATO obligations. France was not willing to accept these commitments. The negotiations have not since been resumed.

A similar and related clash occurred over the extension of the Community to new members. The willingness of the Six to extend their Community to take in other European states had been stated in the Treaty, but in January 1963 negotiations on British membership were ended by a unilateral French decision with no prior consultation of France's partners. The Community of the Six described in the following pages may well, nevertheless, embrace a wider area in the future through the admission of other European countries. It also seems likely, despite the difficulties that have been encountered, ultimately to become the nucleus of a full political Community.

Chapter Six

THE EUROPEAN ECONOMIC COMMUNITY

Despite the failure of the European Defence Community project in 1954 and the consequent abandonment of the plans for a Political Community, leading politicians in the six countries remained determined to work actively for closer union. They felt that the next step had to be taken in the economic field, and were convinced that the Community system offered advantages over traditional intergovernmental formulae. The European Economic Community was thus the sequel to the success of the formula of economic integration worked out in the ECSC. The decision to launch a new initiative was taken at a meeting of the Foreign Ministers of the Six at Messina in June 1955. Preparatory work on the idea of a customs union was done in the summer and autumn of 1955 by an intergovernmental committee under the chairmanship of M. Paul-Henri Spaak, Belgian Foreign Minister, and the report it produced was approved by the ministers at Messina in May 1956. Negotiations, also under M. Spaak's chairmanship, led to the signing in Rome, on 25 March 1957, of a Treaty which, after parliamentary ratification in the six countries, came into force on 1 January 1958.

The Institutions

Before dealing with the contents of the Treaty, and what has been achieved in the first eight years, it is necessary to describe the institutions of the Community and their working. The decision-making and executive functions are fulfilled by two bodies: an independent Commission, and a Council of Ministers on which the member governments are represented. There is a parliamentary assembly known as the European Parliament, and an Economic and Social Committee made up of representatives of economic interests. Legal disputes are subject to final ruling by a Court of Justice.

THE COMMISSION

Until the merger the Commission consisted of nine members. Appointments are made unanimously by the member governments; a meeting of the foreign ministers may be held to take the decision, but written procedure has been used on occasion for individual appointments. Their term runs for four years and is renewable. The mandates of the President and the three Vice-Presidents are subject to renewal every two years. The Treaty provides that the members of the Commission should be chosen for their 'general competence', and they take an oath of independence from their national governments and of loyalty to the Community. Some are former ministers of member countries, others had held senior international posts.[1] The staff of the Commission totals over 3000, of whom more than 600 are in the administrative grade. By tacit agreement there is a balance of nationalities amongst the staff. The Community has four official languages (Dutch, French, German and Italian) and all four are used (with simultaneous interpretation at meetings) as working languages. Within the services of the Commission a simpler pattern has tended to emerge, with working documents circulating in French and German only; for personal contacts French has become the principal working language. The staff is organised in nine Directorates-General, for each of which one member of the Commission is primarily responsible: external relations, economic and financial affairs, internal market, competition, social affairs, agriculture, transport, overseas countries, and administration. In addition there is an Executive Secretariat, and a Spokesman's Group responsible for relations with the Press. The EEC Commission shares with the High Authority and the Euratom Commission a Joint Legal Service, Statistical Office, and Information Service.[2]

The Commission meets regularly once a week for a whole day.

[1] Professor Walter Hallstein was German State Secretary for Foreign Affairs at the time of the negotiations, Dr Sicco Mansholt and M. Henri Rochereau had been Ministers of Agriculture in the Netherlands and France respectively, M. Jean Rey had been Minister of Economic Affairs in Belgium and M. Lambert Schaus Minister of Agriculture in Luxembourg; M. Robert Marjolin was formerly Secretary General of OEEC, and Signor Colonna de Paliano is a former Deputy Secretary General of both OEEC and NATO.

[2] The merger Treaty lays down that the European Commission is to have nine members; but it was agreed that for an initial period of three years there should be fourteen. The staff of the merged Commission totals over 7,000. The entire administrative structure will be remodelled, making the separate administrations of the three executives into a coherent whole, to include the joint services.

All important decisions of policy including the adoption of draft regulations or decisions to be submitted to the Council are taken by the Commission as a whole after full discussion, and if necessary by a simple majority vote; numerous minor questions are settled by written procedure.

When preparing its proposals on major issues of Community policy the Commission holds far-reaching discussions on the general line to be followed. To ensure that all factors and points of view are known and can be taken into account at this stage, unofficial consultations are held with representatives of the national administration, with both sides of industry (as represented at the Community level) and with other interested parties. Once the major choices have been made, one member of the Commission is responsible for establishing a detailed draft on the basis of which the Commission can adopt the proposal in its final form. In the case of technical proposals, for the implementation of existing policies, there is regular consultation with groups of experts from the six national governments, called together under chairmanship provided by the Commission: without committing their governments the experts can help to pinpoint problems and thus enable the Commission to establish proposals which embody practicable solutions. Well over a thousand such meetings are held each year, thus bringing a very large number of national civil servants and experts into direct contact with the affairs of the Community.

The Commission has three main tasks in the Community. It is the initiator of almost all policy decisions, and plays the role of honest broker in the Council in promoting the necessary compromise between the different national interests involved. Secondly, it is the executive organ of the Community, and powers are vested in it to carry through the decisions taken by the Council of Ministers. Lastly it is the watchdog or custodian of the Treaty, entrusted with ensuring that the basic text and all subsequent Community legislation are correctly observed.

THE COUNCIL OF MINISTERS

Under the Treaty the Council consists of one minister from each member government. In practice many senior ministers attend the Council sessions, which have come to be held with increasing frequency. Sessions at which the foreign ministers are present, often accompanied by ministers of finance, of economic affairs and of agriculture, take place once a month, and it is at these that major decisions are taken. Departmental ministers represent their countries at sessions devoted to specialised aspects of Community policy—agriculture, transport, social affairs: at times during the elaboration of the common agricultural policy the ministers of agriculture were spending nearly half the working days of the month in session in Brussels.

The Council normally meets in Brussels. The groundwork is done at meetings of national experts, convened by the Council Secretariat, and by the permanent representatives in their regular weekly sessions. All decisions are officially taken at ministerial level. Procedural or highly technical matters, which have been agreed between the permanent representatives following the meetings of national experts, figure in a list for formal approval at each Council session; all other questions are debated by the ministers themselves.

RELATIONS BETWEEN THE COMMISSION AND THE COUNCIL

The dialogue between the Commission and the Council lies at the heart of the Community system. The Commission takes part in the Council sessions and plays a full and active part in the deliberations. It is accepted by the ministers on a footing of equality and its views carry a great deal of weight. The strength of the Commission's position stems from two main elements: its right of initiative, and the implications of the voting rules.

The Commission has the right to put forward such proposals as it thinks fit on any matter covered by the Treaty, and save where the Treaty lays down specific requirements may choose its own timing. Except in a few rare cases, the decision of the Council of Ministers must be taken on the basis of a proposal of the Commission. This gives the Commission considerable scope in shaping policy. The Council can itself amend a Commission proposal against the latter's wishes only by a unanimous vote. The Commission proposals initiate the dialogue between the members of the Council, who defend their own national interests, and the Commission itself, which must seek to promote the solution in the best interests of the Community as a whole.

The general rule established in the Treaty for decision by the Council of Ministers is that of majority voting, which eliminates the national veto and makes the process of decision-making more efficient. The votes are weighted: each of the three larger countries, France, Germany and Italy, has four votes, Belgium and the Netherlands two each, and Luxembourg one. The weighted majority needed to pass a decision is twelve votes out of the total of seventeen. The result is that a large country alone cannot block a measure but needs the support of at least Belgium or the Netherlands. For the first eight years very considerable exceptions to this rule were established in the Treaty (the application of the majority rule being partially extended from the start of the second stage of the transitional period in January 1962). Thereafter unanimous decisions were required in only a limited number of fields. In the case of decisions requiring unanimous approval, the role of the Commission has proved to be essentially that of an 'honest broker', seeking to ensure that unanimity could be obtained on an acceptable text. In this its standing with the Council enables it to press effectively for the solutions which it considers to be politically and technically realisable and in the best interests of the Community. The Commission is empowered to amend its proposals at any time, and this gives it considerable flexibility in finding compromises between national positions whilst at the same time defending a 'Community' approach.

With the expiry on 1 January 1966 of many exceptions to the majority voting rule, the Commission's constitutional position was strengthened. If its assessment reveals that the position of a member country is markedly divergent from that of its partners and the compromise that the Commission holds best for the Community, it is less bound than it would be under the unanimous voting system to make allowance for the extreme position. Experience has shown that on an issue where recourse can be had to majority voting, the delegation concerned will tend to make the first move towards a compromise, hoping to encourage similar concessions from the Commission and the other delegations and thus to avoid being isolated and consequently having either to make big concessions or to see itself outvoted.

The possibility of a majority decision is thus a potent instrument in obtaining agreement, and above all in obtaining it more rapidly. Its importance is not to be judged simply by the number of majority votes actually taken: during a representative part of the second stage of the transitional period it was found that of a group of decisions falling potentially under majority voting, very few in the end required the application of the procedure, but that they were settled far more rapidly than an equivalent group of decisions still falling under the unanimous voting rule.

Although majority voting was under fire from General de Gaulle during the 1965–66 constitutional crisis, its resolution turned not on the question of majority voting, as such, but on the possibility of its being used where a vital national interest was at stake. All agreed that majority voting would not be used in such cases; but whilst

General de Gaulle insisted that each national government should decide for itself when such a case arose, the other five governments held that the possibility of deciding by majority vote must be maintained intact.

On a number of occasions a group of important Community decisions, requiring political concessions all round, have been taken together. The wide range of subjects covered by the Treaty has made this almost inevitable; and it can greatly facilitate the taking of decisions, because countries are readier to make concessions on one issue if they are at the same time securing advantages with respect to another. When lengthy debates at ministerial level have narrowed gaps but exhausted the limit of unilateral national concessions, the Commission is asked to present a 'package deal' representing an acceptable balance of advantage for all countries. A strong desire to reach agreement, coupled on occasions with both a time limit (self-imposed by the Council or resulting from a Treaty requirement) and the psychological pressure built up in long hours of debate, has made it possible for ministers to adopt solutions which in other circumstances would have been difficult to accept.

Experience has shown that even allowing for these factors, compromise would usually prove impossible without the intervention of the Commission. Because the issues involved in Council decisions are often technically complex, the intervention of an independent body strong and able enough to master such matters is particularly necessary. Sound political judgement is essential to assess the weight of national objections and the concessions which can be expected. The six countries were able to appoint to the Commission men of the required ability and political experience, and a staff of sufficiently high calibre to cope with the intricacies of the six sets of national interests in the various complex fields has been attracted to serve in Brussels.

The Commission's right of initiative is also important in ensuring continuity, since the general Community interest defended by it is a more constant criterion than would be any shifting pattern of compromise between national interests. This advantage has been reinforced by the relative length of service of members: appointed for four-year terms, most have been renewed in office on at least one occasion.

A final comment on the Council's decision-making concerns the interests of the smaller countries. These are protected both by the requirement that the Council shall act always on a Commission proposal, and the provision that it can only amend such a proposal unanimously. In the rare cases where the Council can decide by a weighted majority, other than on the basis of a Commission proposal, the twelve votes must include those of at least four member countries—thus ruling out the imposition of a solution by the three larger countries. The small countries have been the most ardent advocates and defenders of the decision-making procedure and of the role of the Commission, in which they see some assurance that solutions will be found which take their interests sufficiently into account.

THE EUROPEAN PARLIAMENT

Since its establishment in 1958, the European Parliament has been an institution common to all three European Communities, a distinction it shares with the Court of Justice alone. The Parliament's roots go back beyond the Rome Treaty, however, for it is the successor of the former ECSC Common Assembly, set up in 1952. The EEC and Euratom Treaties, establishing the new body, refer to it simply as the Assembly and it was not until 1962 that the name European Parliament was formally adopted by the institution itself (though, at the French request, French texts in the Council retain the Treaty designation). The Parliament holds its meetings in the Assembly Chamber of the Council of Europe in Strasbourg;[1] the offices of its Secretariat are in Luxembourg.[2]

The Parliament is composed of 142 members nominated by the parliaments of the six member states. Germany, France and Italy provide thirty-six members each; Belgium and the Netherlands fourteen each; and Luxembourg six. The method of nomination varies. The Dutch and Belgian members are nominated on a proportional basis from both houses of parliament; the German members are nominated on a proportional basis from the Bundestag alone; the French and Italian members are chosen by a majority vote in both houses; and the Luxembourg members are nominated by the parliamentary committee for foreign and military affairs.

The chief distortion produced by these divergent methods of nomination is that the Italian and French Communist parties are not, and have never been, represented in the Parliament. As these parties

[1] Though a new departure was made in 1967 when the Parliament held one of its meetings in Luxembourg.

[2] The Presidents of the Parliament have been: M. Robert Schuman (1958–60), Herr Hans Furler (1960–62), Signor Gaetano Martino (1962–64), M. Jean Duvieusart (1964–65), M. Victor Leemans (1965–66) and M. Alain Poher who was elected in 1966. The Secretaries General have been M. M. F. F. A. de Nérée tot Babberich (1958–60) and Mr Hans Nord who was appointed in 1961.

regularly poll 20–25 per cent of the votes in the national elections in these countries, it can be seen that their exclusion weakens considerably the claim of the European Parliament to be—even indirectly—representative of the peoples of the European Community.[1] Until recently the Italian Socialist Party (PSI) was also excluded from the Parliament, but with the 'opening to the left' in Italy the representation of this party was, in theory at any rate, accepted. The party's demand that the Communists should also be admitted with them led to a national debate on the issue in Italy, though no change has so far been made.[2]

Although the Parliament is at present indirectly elected the Treaties provide for the eventual holding of direct elections.[3] The EEC Treaty states that 'The Assembly shall draw up proposals for elections by direct universal suffrage in accordance with a uniform procedure in all Member States. The Council shall unanimously decide on the provisions which it shall recommend to Member States for adoption in accordance with their respective constitutional requirements.'

In furtherance of this provision the European Parliament drew up a draft Convention on direct elections in May 1960 which it presented to the Council of Ministers. This Convention proposed a two-stage move to a fully elected Parliament, but fully defined only the first of these stages. During this first period, which was to last from the entry into force of the Convention until at least the completion of the third stage of the Common Market, the Parliament was to be enlarged to 426 members, of whom two thirds would be directly elected. The remaining third would continue to be nominated by the national parliaments.

The Convention did not provide for a uniform system of election for those members directly elected during the first stage. They were to be elected either according to the existing national electoral procedures for each state, or according to new procedures laid down by each state. A detailed and uniform electoral system for all its members was to be worked out by the Parliament during the first stage and to be implemented thereafter.

Despite repeated requests by the Parliament, the Convention has not been approved by the Council. The French Government has not

[1] There would have been a dozen Communist members in the Parliament in 1966 if a proportional system were used.

[2] The Italian delegation to the Parliament is still (1967) that designated before the Italian elections of 1963, many of whom have now either died or lost their seats at home.

[3] See *Direct Elections and the European Parliament*, PEP, 1960.

concealed its hostility to the whole idea, and few of the other governments have shown much enthusiasm, with the notable exception of the Dutch Government. There are of course many technical problems connected with direct elections, not least the fact that the Communist party is banned in the Federal Republic of Germany while it flourishes in France and Italy—but the main obstacle is clearly not technical, but political.

Although indirectly elected, the present Parliament possesses considerable independence. Its members are not bound by instructions from their national parliaments or governments. The Parliament's Secretariat in Luxembourg—some 550 strong—is responsible solely to the members of the Parliament and the Treaties give the Parliament full freedom to draw up its standing orders. In all these ways the Parliament can be said to be autonomous though, as will be shown, it does not control its own budget.

The Parliament holds about six or seven plenary sessions a year, each session lasting about five days; it also holds an annual joint meeting with the Consultative Assembly of the Council of Europe, lasting two days. The number of plenary sessions is only one indication, however, of the Parliament's activity, since much of its work is done by standing committees. The Parliament has twelve of these committees, each specialising in one aspect of the Communities' activities, and they meet very frequently both during the plenary sessions and between them, holding their meetings for the most part in Strasbourg, Brussels and Luxembourg. The committees are responsible for drafting the reports on which the general debates of the Parliament are based. In contrast to British practice but in line with the usual procedures of the European international assemblies, there is no debate before a matter has been referred to a committee.

The committees also perform the more general task of keeping the Parliament abreast of the Communities' activities. Members of the European executives (the Commissions, the High Authority) are frequently asked to attend committee meetings, and to expound and explain their policies before them. As the meetings are held *in camera* full and frank exchanges of views can take place.

Members of the Councils can also be asked to attend any committee meeting; in practice the Councils have agreed to attend meetings of the Budgetary Committee only.

Perhaps the most interesting aspect of the organisation of the European Parliament is the degree to which party affiliations and loyalties to international party groups have succeeded in replacing national affiliations. The emergence of the party groups started with their formal recognition in June 1953 in the former Common Assembly and the simultaneous decision to subsidise them from the Assembly's funds. The groups continue to receive official subsidies, an initial uniform sum being paid to all groups, and a further payment being made in proportion to the size of their membership.

The extent to which the party groups have tended to replace national alignments in the organisation and structure of the Parliament may be gauged from a number of indications. First and most obviously, the members of the Parliament sit according to party affiliation during plenary sessions. Secondly, membership of the standing committees is carefully arranged to mirror the balance of the parties, while a balance according to nationality is only approximate. Third, it is significant that spokesmen of the party groups are given official priority in the plenary debates, and that party considerations play a role in the election of the President and Bureau who direct the Parliament's activities. Finally, the chairmen of the party groups are officially authorised to assist the Bureau in drawing up the Parliament's agenda.

Of the three traditional party groups the Socialists are undoubtedly the most cohesive. The Group's members have, since 1961, been drawn exclusively from one party in each member country. The Group is linked to the constituent national parties by a liaison office in Luxembourg, and conferences between the national parties and the Group take place regularly. Through the *Courrier Socialiste Européen* the Group maintains a running commentary on the affairs of the Communities, and it establishes its own working groups to study and report on major European issues. The Socialists have never been the largest group in the Parliament but they have been consistently the most dynamic—acting as a catalyst for the others. They have gone furthest in hammering out a coherent European programme, have campaigned vigorously for closer integration and more powers for the Parliament, have exerted pressure on the executives to implement to the maximum the social provisions of the Treaties, and have taken a consistent minority stand against the fixing of high food prices in the Community.

It is more difficult to identify the Christian Democrat Group with a consistent European programme, but they are also well organised, and are certainly more than merely a loose amalgam of national parties. They have always been the largest Group in the Parliament (as they were in the Common Assembly), and have generally been drawn from eight or nine different national parties. Like the Socialists, the Christian Democrats organise various working groups to study particular European issues, and the group as a whole meets two or three times a year, in between sessions of the Parliament, to study specific problems. The Group also publishes the *Cahiers Européens* some three times a year, giving Christian Democrat views on the evolution of Europe and news about the activities of the Group.[1] The Group is in favour of closer integration, and on agricultural issues they support the fixing of high food prices in the Community though they are generally deserted by their Dutch members on this question.

The group of Liberals and associates is undoubtedly the most heterogeneous and loose-knit of the three, being drawn from fourteen or fifteen national parties, ranging from the Dutch liberals to the Italian neo-fascists. Since the secession of the UNR in 1962 it has been the third largest of the groups. It can rarely agree on a united policy, but some of its members are most effective speakers.

The newest and smallest group is the European Democratic Union, formed in 1965 when the minimum number required to form a group was reduced from seventeen to fourteen. Being composed of members of the French UNR it is a purely national group and differs from the others over the fundamental objectives of the Communities.

What powers does the European Parliament exercise within the Communities? The EEC Treaty defines them as 'advisory and supervisory'. In the first of these categories may be included the Parliament's right to be consulted over policies proposed in the EEC and Euratom, its right to be consulted on budgetary matters, and its right to recommend action or policies on its own initiative. In the second category must be included the Parliament's power to censure each of the executives, and force their resignation, its power to put questions to the executives and Councils, its right to discuss the executives' annual reports, and, more loosely, its practice of holding an annual joint debate or colloquy with the executives and Councils.

Looking first at the supervisory powers, the motion of censure is the most fundamental. It is true that it has only been threatened and never used, and that it has certain drawbacks. In particular, the Parliament has no right to nominate the successors of the censured body, and has therefore no guarantee that the new body will be more favourable to its views than the old. Some would also maintain that the motion of censure is also largely irrelevant in that the executives and the Parliament share the same 'European' viewpoint. There is an

[1] In 1967 the Secretariat of the Christian Democrat Group became the Secretariat of the European Union of Christian Democrats, thus linking the Group to the national parties in the same way as the Socialists.

element of truth in this, indeed and frequently the three main political groups often rally round the executives to bolster them *vis-à-vis* the Councils. But this identification of interests is not invariable. The EEC Commission is certainly interested in a European solution to the problems before it; but unlike the Parliament it is faced with the practical problem of tailoring its proposals to ensure their acceptance by the representatives of the six states in the Council. The Parliament and the Commission may, and often do, disagree on the amount of tailoring which should be done, and in these circumstances the Parliament's right to censure is by no means irrelevant. Apart from this the Parliament may simply disagree with the executives' policy. It expressed strong dissatisfaction with the High Authority's policy in 1963, for example, when the Socialist Group threatened to introduce a motion of censure. There is in effect no automatic harmony of interests between executives and Parliament.

It is also argued that the motion of censure is too drastic a weapon and that the Parliament needs subtler means of influencing the executives. This, however, overlooks the prime function of the weapon of censure, which is to serve as a solid underpinning for the other, less dramatic, weapons which the Parliament possesses. If the possibility of censure did not lurk in the background it is difficult to believe that the executives would either pay as much attention to the Parliament's questions as they do at the moment, or listen with such attentiveness to the Parliament's views.

Questions are undoubtedly the most effective means by which the Parliament supervises the day-to-day activity of the executives. There are three sorts of questions which the Parliament can put, either to the executives or to the Councils: written, oral, and oral with debate. By far the most use is made of written questions, the bulk of which are put to the executives.[1] Valuable questions are also put to members of the executives in the secrecy of the Parliament's committees.

A further instrument for supervising the executives is provided by the debate on their annual reports. This permits the Parliament to make a systematic survey of the executives' work as a whole. The ECSC Treaty states that only during this debate can the Parliament pass a motion of censure against the High Authority.

It will be apparent from this brief survey that the Parliament's supervisory powers relate almost exclusively to the executives, and not to the other major organ in the Communities' decision-making process, the Councils. Only the annual debates (colloquies) between

[1] In 1964, for example, the Parliament asked a total of 158 written questions, but only six of them were put to the Councils.

all the institutions—the Parliament, the executives and the Councils—enable the Parliament to enter into a regular dialogue with the Councils and at the colloquies the Councils are thinly represented.

The most important of the Parliament's advisory powers is undoubtedly its right to be consulted over major policy proposals in the EEC and Euratom. In practice, though not according to the letter of the two Treaties, this applies to all major policy proposals in these Communities. Only when it has been decided, within the framework of a given policy, to delegate implementing powers to the Commissions, is the Parliament no longer asked for its opinion.

This right of consultation provides the Parliament with the substance of most of its debates and committee work—though the substance is often highly technical. According to the EEC Treaty (the procedure in Euratom is similar), consultation is made by the Council after it has received a given proposal from the Commission. The Commission sometimes consults the Parliament while it is drafting its proposals, and has often sent its completed proposals to the relevant parliamentary committee at the same time as they were communicated to the Council. In 1965, however, the French Government accused Professor Hallstein of communicating the Commission's proposals on the delicate matter of agricultural finance before the governments had had time to consider them, and the timing of such communications was one of the points in the settlement of the Community's constitutional crisis of 1965–66.[1]

Once the Council has made its request for an opinion, the matter is submitted immediately to the relevant parliamentary committee, which presents a report containing a draft opinion to the Parliament. The debate takes place on the basis of this report, amendments are proposed and voted on, and the whole text is put to the vote.

The right of consultation, described here, is not a power of decision. The Council is not bound in any way by the opinion which the Parliament gives, and the Commission too may change its original proposals as it thinks fit, after the Parliament has been consulted. The most the EEC Treaty says is that 'the regulations, directives and decisions of the Council and of the Commission shall be fully reasoned and shall refer to any proposals or opinions' which the Treaty requires to be obtained.

How much influence does the Parliament's opinion have in practice on the final shape of EEC policies? In two particular instances—

[1] The EEC Protocol of January 1966 stated that the Commission's proposals should only be published after they had been placed in the hands of the governments.

the association agreements with Greece and Turkey—the Parliament's views had no influence at all, as it was consulted only after the agreements had been initialled. Apart from these two cases, the evidence would seem to suggest that the Parliament's influence varies considerably. On some issues, notably social policy, its influence has been quite extensive, on others, such as cartel policy, it has been moderate, and on others, such as agricultural policy, it has been negligible. The main factor which explains this variation in influence is undoubtedly the secret negotiation which takes place between the Commission and Council after the Parliament gives its opinion. The object of this negotiation is to find a solution acceptable to all or most of the member states. The greater the difference of view and the more prolonged the negotiations, the likelier it is that the Parliament's opinion will fall by the wayside. The prime example of this is provided by agricultural policy.[1]

The Parliament's advisory right in the budgetary field deserves separate consideration. In view of the decision on the fusion of the executives, the full complexities of the situation need not be explored. Suffice it to say that the Parliament derives a third of its funds from each of the Communities. The EEC and Euratom are financed entirely by contributions from the member states: in relation to the sums it receives from these Communities the Parliament has no concrete powers at all. It drafts its own estimates, it is allowed to discuss the two Community budgets as a whole, but the final, decisive power over both its own and the overall budgets lies with the Councils. In the ECSC, which has its own sources of revenue, the position is slightly different. Here the Parliament has virtually full power over its own budget and has in practice developed, though this is not specified in the Treaty, advisory rights over the Community budget as a whole.

According to the Treaty of April 1965, laying down the procedure for the fusion of the three executives, the Parliament will in future exercise in all three Communities the same budgetary rights which it possesses according to the EEC and Euratom Treaties.

Apart from its formal rights of consultation, the Parliament may make proposals and recommendations on its own initiative—though these have no binding power. In practice it has used its own initiative over a wide range of topics. Thus the joint conference between its own members and parliamentarians from the associated overseas territories, which took place on the Parliament's initiative in 1961,

[1] For further details on this and other points, see *The Parliament of the European Communities*, PEP, 1964.

influenced the final convention on association. But the Parliament has tended to be most vociferous in the political field, where it has pressed energetically for the fusion of the executives. The Parliament has, indeed, in all its work championed the 'European' point of view, and has frequently tried to strengthen the role of the Commission as well as its own, and to secure the widest interpretation and implementation of the provisions of the Treaties.

There has been steady pressure for increasing the powers of the Parliament, not only on the part of the Parliament itself but also from some other sources, notably the Dutch Government and Parliament. The possibilities of such a move were discussed amongst the Six during 1964 in connection with the merger of the Community executives but no action was taken. The EEC Commission's proposals on the financing of the common agricultural policy, made in April 1965, maintained that the Parliament should be given an effective voice in approving the Community budget, on the grounds that the direct revenues which it was proposed to raise should be subject to parliamentary control. During the debate in the Council, there was a consensus in favour of postponing the creation of direct revenues to 1970; but all the members except France continued to insist that a decision of principle on both that point and on the powers of the Parliament be taken at the same time as the definitive financial regulation was established. The issue was never fully debated before the start of the crisis, in which the proposal for increasing the Parliament's powers was one factor. When the same problems were taken up again in the first half of 1966, after the crisis was over, there was agreement to hold over their settlement until the end of the transitional period.

THE ECONOMIC AND SOCIAL COMMITTEE

The Economic and Social Committee is composed of 'representatives of the various categories of economic and social life'. It has 101 members, twenty-four from each of the three larger countries, twelve each from Belgium and the Netherlands and five from Luxembourg. They are appointed by the Council by unanimous vote for a four-year period and their mandate is renewable. Approximately one third of them are chosen to represent employers' organisations, one third the trade unions, and one third to defend 'the general interest'—experts in various matters covered by the Treaty. Members are, however, appointed in their personal capacity and the Treaty stipulates that they shall not be bound by any mandatory instructions. Of the three groups, the trade unionists usually achieve a high degree of internal consensus; the employers do so less frequently; the third group—which includes farmers' representatives—very rarely adopts a common position. Consumers' organisations, which are not firmly established in the Community countries, are not strongly represented in the Committee; but the defence of consumer interests is often taken up by the unions.

The Treaty is not clear as to whether the Economic and Social Committee is to be considered as an institution of the Community in a formal sense. Its standing is not the same as that of the Parliament, and its role is specifically defined as being consultative. As with the Parliament there are cases where the Council is bound to obtain the Committee's opinion on proposals from the Commission, and in cases where the consultation is optional the Council has increasingly tended in practice to seek its views. It is organised in eight 'specialised sections' on each of which all three groups are represented. These sections prepare draft opinions which are then debated and approved in the plenary sessions; these are held some six times a year, and are not open to the public.

Although the opinions of the Economic and Social Committee are not binding, they are taken seriously by the Commission, particularly since they reflect the views of qualified and influential groups; and the Commission has on a number of occasions amended its proposals to take account of them. The influence of the Committee on the general lines of Community policy is hard to assess. On most issues—with the notable exception of transport policy—it has supported the Commission's proposals; but the effort made to reach a large measure of agreement within the Committee has not infrequently meant that the opinions as adopted have been couched in very general terms. The relations of the Committee with the Council have been marked by a restrictive attitude on the part of the ministers about the role the Committee should play.

Mention must also be made of the wide range of bodies which have been established to represent organised economic and social interest groups at the Community level. The leading ones are the secretariats of the free trade unions and the Christian trade unions at community level; UNICE[1] which links the six national industrial federations; an organisation bringing together the national chambers of commerce; and COPA[2] which is the joint body established by the national farmers' organisations. In addition, most branches of industry have

[1] Union des Industries des Communautés Européennes.

[2] Comité des Organisations de Producteurs Agricoles.

established links at the Community level, as have agricultural and commercial interests, the liberal professions and such groups as banks, publicly-owned enterprises, and even the capital cities of the six member countries. In all more than three hundred such Community groups now exist and the majority of them have their headquarters in Brussels.

THE COURT OF JUSTICE

The Court of Justice is an essential element in the constitutional structure of the Communities. It was set up by the Treaty of Paris and its competence was extended by the Treaties of Rome to the two other Communities. It consists of seven judges and two advocates general, all appointed for six-year renewable terms by agreement between the member governments. The Court elects its own President. The position of the advocate general is without an equivalent in British or American terms: one of the advocates general must make an independent assessment of the issues in each case before judgement is passed: the assessment is read publicly and later published, but the Court is bound only to listen and need not follow the advocate's views. Since the Court was created in 1958 the two advocates general have been French and German: there has been one judge from each country, and a second judge from Italy (or, in the early years when there was an Italian president, a second judge from the Netherlands).

It is the task of the Court to ensure the observance of the rule of law in the Communities. Cases arising over non-observance of one of the Treaties, or over supposed infringements or other acts incompatible with the legal framework of the Communities, can be brought before it, subject to differing conditions, by the High Authority or the two Commissions, the member states, or firms and individuals in the Community. Individual suits may also be filed by the personnel of the Community institutions. The Court's ruling is binding upon all parties, including the governments, and is not subject to appeal. The Court may award damages and may also in certain circumstances impose sanctions for the non-execution of its decisions.

Cases may be conducted in any of the Community's four official languages. The first stage of procedure in any case is that of a written statement of claim, reply, memorandum in defence, and rejoinder. A 'judge *rapporteur*' is chosen to report to the Court on the written documents. There are then hearings at which the parties plead their cases and can be questioned by judges and the advocate.

Subsequently the advocate general reads publicly his conclusions to the Court, which then deliberates in secret before delivering its judgement in a public session.

There are few limitations on access to the Court for governments and for the High Authority and Commissions. Individuals and firms may not bring cases before the Court against other firms, but only against the executives or the Councils: a distinction is made between general decisions of the executives, appeal against which is limited to cases of abuse of power, and decisions affecting individuals, which deal with concrete specific situations, and can more freely be appealed against by the persons concerned.

The establishment of the rule of law in the Communities, implicitly intended to bring about change, clearly poses major legal problems. In the Coal and Steel Community the Court was generally restricted to legal considerations in its judgements, but chose to avail itself often of reference to the very general articles of the Treaty in taking the widest possible view of the Treaty objectives, whose attainment it was responsible for ensuring. In the EEC Treaty the same limitation was not imposed and the Court has invoked in its judgements the general economic aims of the Treaty rather than resorting to a narrow interpretation of legal texts.

There is not space here to consider the individual judgements of the Court nor the steady development of its activities. In the Coal and Steel Community framework it played an important part in holding the High Authority to strict standards of procedural correctness: numerous cases about the running of the scrap perequation scheme followed from the Court's severity on this count. It exerted a major influence when rejecting the so-called 'minor revision' with which it had been hoped to adapt the Treaty to changing conditions of competition.

In the early years of the Common Market the cases brought before the Court tended to concern infringements by the member states, particularly in customs matters. From 1962 onwards the Court began to play an important role in connection with the implementation of the Community anti-cartel policy: first through a series of requests from the national courts for preliminary rulings, and later through the Court's own rulings in cases brought against individual Commission decisions banning particular trade agreements. Of special significance was the ruling in July 1966 upholding the Commission's action in banning an exclusive dealing agreement between a German manufacturer (Grundig) and a French trader (Consten).

The role of the Court is concerned essentially with the observance of the Treaty and the correct implementation of all Community legislation. Given the dynamic nature of the Community operation, and the fact that the present Communities are seen as a stage in a longer and more far-reaching process, it is foreseeable that constitutional clashes involving member states may be so profound as to be incapable of solution by a judicial decision. This may be held to have been the case in the constitutional crisis of 1965–66, when French refusal to participate in the Council of Ministers or in work advancing the progress of the Community (see pp. 251–54) constituted an evident breach of Articles 5 and 169 of the Treaty. It was clear that appeal to the Court to confirm this would not have ended the crisis, and that it had to be solved by political means.

THE DEVELOPMENT OF COMMUNITY LAW

The decisions taken by the Council and by the Commission may take various forms. Thus both the Council and in certain cases the Commission can enact regulations which are binding upon member governments, and directives which are binding as to their ends, whilst allowing freedom as to the means to be adopted to achieve them; both can also have recourse to decisions applying directly to individuals. These various legal acts, together with the provisions of the Treaty, amount to a body of 'Community legislation'.

The task of ensuring the observance of this system is imposed upon both the Community and the national authorities. The Commission has to ensure that national governments conform to the Community's provisions and also has in certain fields (for instance, anti-trust legislation) the sole power to act *vis-à-vis* firms or individuals; in other cases the enforcement of regulations devolves on the governments.

Inevitably, problems have arisen about establishing the legal relationship between this Community system and the national systems. A satisfactory solution to this issue is particularly important since, whatever its political cohesion, the Community, having little administrative infrastructure, is largely a legal creation.

Three main problems have arisen, all of which continue to exercise the legal experts and judges of the Community. The first is the compatibility of the Treaties themselves with national constitutional provisions; the second is the primacy of Community law over subsequent national legislation; and the third the mechanics of the appeal from national judges to the Court of Justice for interpretation of Community law which is directly applicable.

The first of these problems arises in only two member countries. In France, Belgium, the Netherlands and Luxembourg there is no final legal body with the power to rule whether or not a treaty is constitutional. In Italy and Germany on the other hand a constitutional court has the final word on whether any legal act is in conformity with the constitution. In both countries the problem has arisen of whether the three Community Treaties and measures taken under them are constitutional: up to the middle of 1966 no direct conflict has arisen, but clearly if the courts were to rule that the Treaties were unconstitutional, a serious political problem would be created.

The second problem is that of ensuring that Community legislation takes priority over subsequent national legislation in case of conflict. Again no final solution has emerged. However, in creating the Communities the member states were clearly establishing a political and legal system which could work only if Community law does have precedence over national legislation. This practical view has been maintained by the Court of Justice of the Communities, which is the body competent in the last resort to rule on the meaning and effect of Community law.

If the primacy of Community law is admitted, there arises the third question, that of its enforcement. The Community has found the middle way in providing for preliminary rulings by the Court of Justice. This possibility is embodied in Article 41 of the ECSC Treaty, Article 177 of the EEC Treaty and Article 141 of the Euratom Treaty, all establishing the principle of appeal to Luxembourg for a preliminary ruling where Community legislation has to be interpreted. Recourse has increasingly been had to the European Court: by the end of 1965 it had examined nearly thirty cases. This approach has the advantage both of ensuring uniformity in the interpretation of Community law which has to be applied by the national courts. One problem in the early years was that national judges were unfamiliar with the implications of the Community system. However, with the steady rise in the number of Community measures directly applicable in the member states there is a growing appreciation of the problem and the system has been working satisfactorily.

In addition to the major political institutions referred to above, there exists a growing number of bodies with diverse legal status forming part of the Community system, some of them provided for in the Treaty, others established to meet institutional or consultative needs as they developed. They include the European Investment Bank, the European Social Fund, the European Development Fund and numerous Committees, particularly in the fields of economic and financial policy and the common agricultural policy. These bodies are discussed below.

FINANCIAL AND BUDGETARY PROVISIONS

The activities of the Community are financed by contributions from the member states, in the following proportions: France, the Federal Republic of Germany and Italy 28 per cent; Belgium and the Netherlands 7·9 per cent; Luxembourg 0·2 per cent. Contributions to cover the expenditure of the Social Fund are paid in the following proportions: France and Germany 32 per cent, Italy 20 per cent, Belgium 8·8 per cent, the Netherlands 7 per cent and Luxembourg 0·2 per cent. Either scale may be amended by the Council by means of a unanimous vote, but this has not been done. The financing of the common agricultural policy follows a more complex pattern which is explained below (pp. 208–17).

The total Community budget in 1966 amounted to just over $3 million for administrative purposes, excluding the financing of the Agricultural and Social Funds. The Community's financial year coincides with the calendar year. Each of the Community institutions is required to draw up provisional estimates, and these are combined by the Commission which submits a preliminary draft budget to the Council by 30 September each year. The Council adopts a draft budget by weighted majority vote and this is submitted to the European Parliament, which has the right to propose amendments by 31 October. After discussing any such amendments with the Commission and with the other institutions concerned, the Council takes its final decision by qualified majority vote. If the Parliament makes no comment and proposes no amendment, the budget is considered adopted. The Council is thus always the undisputed authority in fixing the budget. In the past the Council has generally cut the draft budget proposed to it by the Commission.

Article 201 of the Treaty provides that the Commission 'shall study the conditions under which the financial contributions of the member States . . . may be replaced by other resources of the Community itself, in particular by revenue accruing from the common customs tariff when the latter has been definitively introduced'. In addition, the decisions taken by the Council in January 1962 provided that the product of the levies on agricultural imports should accrue directly to the Community, when the final stage of the agricultural policy was reached, to help finance the farm policy.

As a result the Commission proposed to the Council in March 1965 that from 1 July 1967 onwards, when, according to its proposals, the common tariff would come into effect and the farm policy would be completed, all levies and a growing proportion of customs duties, rising to 100 per cent at the end of 1977, should be paid directly to the Community. In its memorandum of July 1965, which took account of the Council's debates in May and June, the Commission allowed for a postponement of the creation of direct revenues until the end of the transitional period, that is 1970. Views expressed in meetings of the Council had indicated that there would be pressure for the direct revenues, when decided, to be drawn not only from taxes on imports, but also from other sources of revenue, possibly a tax on firms in the Community along the lines of the ECSC levy. The issue is bound to recur by 1970, since the January 1962 decision should take effect at the end of the transitional period. The creation of direct revenues is, however, a move of considerable significance in a federal direction and if national positions have not radically changed this could occasion a new clash.

DIPLOMATIC REPRESENTATION

By 1966 there were over seventy diplomatic representatives of non-member countries accredited to the Community. The Communist countries are the only major group not to recognise the Community in this way. The application to accredit a representative requires the formal approval of the Commission and the Council, as does the person of the ambassador. Under the procedure which was used until 1966, each ambassador presented his letters of credence to the president of the EEC Commission and later paid a courtesy visit to the current chairman of the Council of Ministers. As an outcome of the 1966 crisis a new procedure was provisionally instituted whereby ambassadors present their credentials both to the president of the EEC Commission and to the current chairman of the Council of Ministers. Most representatives are also accredited to the two other Communities and present their credentials to them. Proposals made by the Commission in 1959 for the Community to be diplomatically represented in London and Washington met with the opposition of the French Government, and have not been revived.

The Implementation of the Treaty

In the preamble to the Treaty of Rome, the signatories of the Treaty declare that they have decided 'to ensure the economic and social progress of their countries by common action in eliminating the barriers which divide Europe', and will be 'directing their efforts to the essential purpose of constantly improving the living and working conditions of their peoples'. They recognise that the removal of barriers existing between economies results in a need for concerted action in order to guarantee steady expansion, balanced trade and fair competition. They commit themselves to smooth development so as to lessen the gaps between prosperous and backward areas within the Community. They also agree to adopt a common commercial policy which should contribute to the gradual removal of restrictions on international trade.

Article 2 of the Treaty states that the Community aims 'by establishing a common market and progressively approximating the economic policies of the member States, to promote throughout the Community a harmonious development of economic activities, a continuous and balanced expansion, increased stability, an accelerated raising of the standard of living and closer relations between its member States'.

Twelve years was set as the target for creating the common market, with the possibility of an extension to fifteen years at the most. The transitional period was divided into three four-year stages, the passage from the first to the second being subject to agreement that adequate and balanced progress had been achieved, that from the second to the third being automatic, unless postponed by unanimous agreement. The Treaty itself represents a careful balance of interests between the member states, and there is, in addition, an underlying assumption of the need for balanced progress in all areas covered by the Treaty, which has been adhered to by the Commission in its proposals and has frequently been invoked in the Council.

It is possible to distinguish two major aspects of the operations to be carried out under the Treaty, namely the creation of a 'customs union', by the removal of artificial barriers and forms of discrimination which make the member countries into separate economic units, and the more far-reaching creation of an 'economic union' by the establishment of common policies or the gradual co-ordination of national policies. These distinctions cannot be hard and fast: thus the removal of barriers to trade in agricultural produce, a sector where all member countries had managed markets, became possible only with the establishment of a common agricultural policy extending to the whole area.

FREE TRADE IN INDUSTRIAL GOODS

From 1 July 1968 onwards there will be no duties on trade in industrial goods anywhere within the Community, and a single rate of duty will apply to goods entering the area through its frontiers with the rest of the world. The Community will thus become an industrial customs union eighteen months ahead of the original schedule. The Treaty in fact laid down a timetable for the removal of customs duties on trade between the member states over the twelve years of the transitional period. Provision is also made for the elimination of taxes with equivalent effect to customs duties and other obstacles of a similar nature to trade between the member countries; the timing of this is left to the institutions. Finally, the removal of all quantitative restrictions on intra-Community trade is provided for, and was in fact achieved by January 1962. As restrictions on trade within the Community are removed, a common customs tariff on imports of goods into the EEC from the rest of the world replaces the previous national tariffs, and other trade policy instruments have to be harmonised.

The first 10 per cent cut in the tariffs on industrial goods traded between the member states took effect on 1 January 1959. In May 1960 and in May 1963 the timetable laid down by the Treaty was speeded up by decisions of the Council, acting on proposals of the Commission. The rate of tariff cuts during the third stage of the transitional period is left to the Council to decide, and in May 1966, 1 July 1968 was fixed as the date for the final tariff cut. Thus free trade in industrial goods, matching the free flow of farm produce under the common agricultural policy, will be achieved eighteen months ahead of the original schedule. Details of the cuts are given in the table on the facing page.

All customs duties on exports and charges with equivalent effect were removed in accordance with the Treaty by the end of the first stage, 31 December 1961.

The Treaty allows tariff cuts to be made ahead of schedule and the Federal Republic of Germany, France and Italy have all done this on occasions for reasons of internal economic policy. The Commission can also authorise member states to delay cuts on some products, but this procedure has seldom been invoked. Articles 30–35 of the Treaty laid down detailed provisions for the removal of quantitative restrictions on both imports and exports, and measures with equivalent effect. There was also an immediate ban on the introduction of any new measures of this kind. In practice it proved possible, as part of the Council's decision of May 1960, speeding up the creation of the customs union, to ensure the removal of almost all quota restrictions at the end of the first stage.

Several hundred measures with equivalent effect to customs duties have been removed as a result of the Commission's directives to the member states, of cases of infringement brought before the Court, or of the application of the common agricultural policy.

The Treaty provides for the progressive establishment of a single customs tariff on all imports into the Community from whatever source, to apply fully from the end of the transitional period: in fact it will come into effect on 1 July 1968. The four existing national tariffs—the three Benelux countries (Belgium, the Netherlands and Luxembourg) already had a common tariff and constitute for this

	Industrial Products		*Agricultural Products*	
	per-centage cut	percentage of original tariff remaining	per-centage cut	percentage of original tariff remaining
1 January 1959 (Treaty requirement)	10	90	10	90
1 July 1960 (Treaty requirement)	10	80	10	80
1 January 1961 ('accelerated' cut)	10	70	5	75
1 January 1962 (Treaty requirement)	10	60	10	65
1 July 1962 ('accelerated' cut)	10	50	5	60
1 July 1963 (Treaty requirement)	10	40	10	50
1 January 1965 (Treaty requirement)	10	30	10	40
1 January 1966 (Treaty requirement)	10	20	10	30
1 July 1967 (Council of Ministers decision 12 May 1966)	5	15	5	25
1 July 1968	15	0	25	0

purpose a single trading unit—were to be brought into line with the common tariff in three stages. The first move of 30 per cent towards the level of the comon tariff was made on 1 July 1961; at that time any tariff differing by less than 15 per cent from the duty in the common tariff was brought immediately into line. A second move of 30 per cent was made on 1 July 1963. The final alignment of 40 per cent will take place on 1 July 1968 when the last duties on trade between the member countries are removed.

The level of the common external tariff was fixed by decision of the Council of Ministers in 1960. The general rule was to take the arithmetical mean of the four existing tariffs; but the divergences between national tariff lists made necessary a vast operation of simplification, and the common tariff contains only some 2000 sub-headings as against several thousands in the four national tariffs. For about seventy products of particular importance to one or more member countries the level of the tariff was the object of negotiations, and lengthy debates in the Council of Ministers. There took place for the first time a clash between the member countries most concerned with protection against outside competition and those primarily concerned with the liberalisation of trade; such confrontations have since taken place on numerous other occasions. The tariff as it finally emerged had an overall average incidence of 8·2 per cent and it was submitted to the Contracting Parties of GATT as being less protective in its overall effect than the previous system—which had an average incidence of 9·3 per cent on the same basis—and therefore in conformity with the rules of GATT. In addition the Community decided, in anticipation of the outcome of the Dillon Round of tariff negotiations,[1] provisionally to reduce by 20 per cent the tariff as it had been established. The first and second alignments were in fact made towards this lower figure, save where a smaller cut had been negotiated and consolidated in the Dillon Round.

The Treaty provides for the granting of duty-free or reduced-duty quotas to meet the requirements either of the Community as a whole or of a given member state. These are not seen as permanent measures, but are intended to allow essential Community needs to be met. Some of them are subject to approval by the Commission, and others to decision, on the basis of a proposal of the Commission, by the Council of Ministers. It is also open to the Council, acting by unanimous vote, to modify or suspend the duties in the common tariff. After the end of the transitional period, such decisions may be taken by weighted majority vote but will be subject to renewal every six months.

In addition to customs duties and measures with equivalent effect there exist a wide range of customs formalities and technical restrictions which effectively hamper trade. In its proposals of November 1964 the Commission emphasised the need for such measures to be eliminated at the same time as the last customs duties between member states, and also for the wide range of different measures

[1] The name given to the fourth in the series of multilateral negotiations between the GATT contracting parties, aimed at reducing tariffs on industrial goods; the idea of the new round was first launched by the United States Under-Secretary of State, Douglas Dillon.

applied at the external frontiers of the Community to be fully and effectively harmonised by the time the common external tariff comes into effect.

FREE MOVEMENT OF WORKERS

The Treaty provides that the free movement of workers shall be ensured within the Community by the end of the transitional period at the latest. In practice the aim was not so much to make possible the movement of workers, which has long been a feature of the European economy owing to the combined pressures of unemployment and manpower needs, as to end all discrimination between workers on account of their nationality. Article 43 of the Treaty enumerates the rights of the worker to accept offers of employment, to move freely for this purpose, to reside in the country in order to work there, and to stay there after giving up a job.

A first basic directive drawn up by the Commission and adopted by the Council came into effect in June 1961. It ensured the fulfilment of the Treaty requirement that all periods of employment in member countries should be taken into account in the calculation of social security benefits to be paid to workers under national systems. This enables workers to move freely without any loss of benefits. The details of the necessary payments are settled on a bilateral basis between the member governments. Machinery was also set up to co-ordinate the clearance of vacancies between the employment agencies of the member countries. Further regulations extended the same equality of treatment in respect of social security arrangements to seasonal and frontier workers.

Regulation No. 17 also guarantees to workers from member countries the right to join, after a probationary period, trade unions in their country of work and the right to reside there and to bring their immediate dependants to live with them. In addition it gave them priority over workers from non-member countries in applying for work in the Community whilst maintaining for a limited period the prior claims of workers of the state in question (save in cases where a worker was offered the job by name). In 1964 a second major regulation abolished this priority of the national market except where exceptions are requested for particular sectors. It extended the right of residence to all members of a worker's family, and also extended to the workers the right to be elected to trade union office.

Freedom of movement for workers is of course closely linked with the wider need for a single social policy for the Community, covering such matters as vocational training and workers' housing.

Economic factors have in fact resulted in a steady decline in the number of workers moving between the countries of the Community: the main flow was from Italy to the other member countries, but this has fallen off as boom conditions resulted in a shortage of skilled and semi-skilled labour in the industrialised areas of northern Italy, and as the unemployed labour force of southern Italy began to be absorbed. The movement into the Community of workers from non-member countries has, on the contrary, increased. In addition to the hundreds of thousands of Algerians and Tunisians working in France, workers from Spain, Portugal, Greece, Turkey and more recently from as far afield as Africa and India have moved in to meet the labour shortage, especially in Germany and the Netherlands. This is a development which falls outside the immediate scope of the Treaty.

RIGHT OF ESTABLISHMENT AND RIGHT TO SUPPLY SERVICES

Freedom for business enterprises to treat the Community as a whole, and freedom to supply services of all kinds, were a necessary complement to the free movement of goods and workers. The Community has generally dealt with those two problems in parallel.

The Treaty lays down that 'restrictions on the freedom of establishment of nationals of a member state in the territory of another member state shall be progressively abolished in the course of the transitional period'. The definition of freedom of establishment is specifically extended to cover the setting up of agencies, branches and subsidiaries and also the right to engage in non-wage-earning activities.

As required by the Treaty, a general programme for the removal of restrictions on the right of establishment was drafted by the Commission and approved by the Council before the end of the first stage of the transitional period. It set time-limits for extending the right of establishment to the various sectors of economic activity during the period up to 1 January 1970.

The implementation of this programme requires the drawing up of detailed proposals by the Commission for each given activity, and their adoption as a directive by the Council. This work has proceeded steadily, although the complexity of the problems and the pressure of work on all the institutions, including the Parliament and the Economic and Social Committee whose opinions are sought in each case, has led to some delay in meeting the original schedule.

The pattern as regards the free supply of services—which is defined as covering industrial, commercial and artisanal activities as well as the liberal professions—has been very similar. The supply of services also includes the right to exercise an activity on a footing of equality with nationals of the member states in which the service is to be applied.

The freeing of both the right of establishment and, more particularly, the supply of services, is dependent upon mutual recognition between the member states of professional qualifications and diplomas, and the full implementation of the general programmes will partly be conditional upon progress in this direction during the third stage.

MOVEMENT OF CAPITAL

The Treaty provides that in the course of the transitional period, and 'to the extent necessary for the proper functioning of the Common Market', the member states shall progressively abolish restrictions on the movement of capital, as well as any discrimination concerning nationality or the place where the capital is invested. In this context restrictions on current payments were removed, as the Treaty required, by the end of the first stage. The first of three directives, adopted by the Council in May 1960, unconditionally freed some forms of capital movement (such as direct investment and dealings in securities quoted on stock exchange) linked to the free movement of goods, services and persons. It provided for the conditional freeing of a second group, including loans raised on capital markets, and dealings in securities not quoted on stock exchanges. Short-term capital movements were unaffected. A second directive took liberalisation considerably further. A third, proposed directive, aimed chiefly at freeing the floating of loans on capital markets.

RULES OF COMPETITION

'The establishment of a system ensuring that competition shall not be distorted in the Common Market' is required by Article 5 of the Treaty. Articles 85–90 set out the general rules to be applied to ensure fair competition between firms. Article 91 deals with dumping, and Articles 92–94 with the distortions which may arise through state aids.

The basic principle underlying the Community's action against cartels and restrictive practices is a ban on any practices which affect trade across frontiers and have as their object or result distortion of competition. The Treaty does not deal with practices affecting only the internal market of a member state. The practices referred to in

Article 85 are 'any agreement between enterprises, any decisions by associations of enterprises and any concerted practices'. Activities specifically condemned include price fixing, the limitation or control of production, market or supply-sharing, contracts imposing a competitive disadvantage, and contracts tied to the purchase of other materials. Similarly Article 86 is aimed at the abuse of a 'dominant position' by one or more firms within the whole or 'a substantial part of' the common market.

Thus the general effect of these provisions is to define what agreements are to be banned but the grounds on which agreements and activities may be exempted are indicated. Exempted measures are those which 'contribute to the improvement of production or distribution of goods or to the promotion of technical or economic progress whilst reserving to users an equitable share in the profit resulting therefrom'.

The Council of Ministers was required by the Treaty to adopt the necessary implementing measures within the first three years; if that limit was not met the measures could be adopted by a weighted majority vote. The basic regulation was not in fact adopted until November 1961, but in the end a majority vote was not used. The regulation, which came into effect in March 1962, was a compromise between the German and the French systems, the first assuming agreements to be illegal if not proved admissible, the second putting the onus of proving illegality on the authorities. The regulation required the registration of all agreements between firms in different member countries. It would then be the task of the Commission to determine which could benefit from the exemptions to be granted under Article 85 and which came under the ban and had to be dissolved. Some 36,000 agreements in all were registered. Since it was clear that it would take time to decide on them, it was indicated that agreements could be continued until those taking part were warned by the Commission that they might prove to be incompatible with the Treaty. The Commission is empowered to undertake enquiries into sectors of the economy where it has reason to suspect that cartels exist.

The large number of agreements registered made it impracticable to proceed by individual decisions on each case; some form of case law was clearly needed. Straight away the Commission had to give rulings on certain cases which had arisen in national courts, for the ban had force of law from the time the Treaty came into effect and was invoked before national jurisdictions. The Commission's first rulings were on cases specifically chosen to demonstrate that certain types of agreement could expect to benefit from the exemption; two cases involved foreign firms which had agreements with firms in the Community falling, potentially, under the terms of the Treaty. During 1964 and 1965 the Commission took a series of decisions which started to establish a body of case law. In addition to exemptions granted for certain agreements, participants in others were warned that they were no longer immune from fines; most of these cartels were consequently amended or dissolved by the parties to them. Action was taken against several exclusive-dealing cartels involving a large number of firms in several countries and covering whole sections of industry.

In 1965 the Council of Ministers, acting on a proposal made by the Commission, adopted a Regulation enabling a general exemption from the Treaty ban to be granted for categories of agreements.

The Commission's approach to concentrations (under Article 86 of the Treaty) has been one of caution, dictated by considerations about the need for larger productive units in the wider Common Market, the effect of competition from firms outside the Community, and the implications of technological progress for the size of the firm. No action has yet been undertaken under this article.

DUMPING

Article 91 of the Treaty relating to dumping has been applied rarely. It empowers the Commission to undertake investigations at the request of a member state or another interested party and where it finds dumping to exist to issue recommendations to those involved, calling on them to cease the practice. The second paragraph of the same article established the so-called 'boomerang' principle whereby any products originating in (or imported from outside the Community into) a member state, and exported to a second state, shall be completely free of customs duties and all other trade restrictions when re-imported. In the eight years to 1965 only twenty-four cases of dumping within the Community were reported, and ten of these reports proved unfounded. The Commission made recommendations in only three cases.

STATE AIDS

The Treaty lays down a general ban on any state aid (either direct or indirect) which distorts or threatens to distort competition by favouring certain firms or sectors of production, and in so doing adversely affects trade between member countries.

Exceptions are made for 'aids of a social character to individual consumers' provided there is no discrimination as to the origin of the products concerned; aids to meet 'natural calamities'; and 'aids granted to the economy of certain regions of the Federal Republic of Germany affected by the division of Germany'. Also excepted are: the institutions to allow aid to backward areas, aid intended to promote 'the execution of important projects of common European interest' or to 'remedy a serious disturbance in the economy of a member state'; and aid 'to facilitate the development of certain activities in certain economic regions'.

The Commission is given extensive powers to ensure the abolition of undesirable state aids. All systems of aid must be kept under constant examination. The Commission may call on member states to abolish or modify aid within given time limits, and in the case of failure to do so may refer the matter to the Court of Justice. A member state may ask the Council to find a particular case of aid compatible with the Treaty.

The Commission has acted in a large number of cases, authorising some forms of aid and having others amended or abolished. A major problem is posed by aids to shipbuilding: the Commission in a report in March 1966 emphasised the need for rapid adaptation to modern conditions and the possibility of authorising aid at the same level throughout the Community was envisaged. The Treaty further requires state trading monopolies to be adapted to ensure access for goods produced in the Community to the national markets for the goods affected. Acting in close consultation with the member states, the Community obtained the gradual application during the second stage of these provisions. The countries mainly involved are Italy (monopolies for tobacco, salt, matches, cigarette paper, quinine, etc.) and France (tobacco) but other trading monopolies in Germany and the Benelux countries are also gradually being adapted. In 1966 the Commission stepped up its pressure for changes in the remaining monopolies.

SAFEGUARD CLAUSES

Cases of escape clauses being applied under Article 226 have been very few. Safeguard measures were authorised to protect some uncompetitive basic industries, such as sulphur, lead, zinc and silk in Italy, but in all cases an effort was then made in the Community framework to promote a solution which would allow the special measures to be terminated.

HARMONISATION OF LAWS

There are clearly considerable disparities between different national laws which may result in the limitation of trade or in distortions of economic conditions in the wider area. Not all such cases could be covered specifically by the Treaty, and Articles 100–102 lay down the terms under which action can be taken to ensure the alignment of national legislation 'to the extent necessary', as Article 3 expresses it, 'for the functioning of the Common Market'. Article 100 provides that 'the Council, acting by means of a unanimous vote on a proposal from the Commission, shall issue directives for the alignment of such legislative and administrative provisions of the member states. . . .'

The Commission is required to enter into consultation with the member states concerned, where it considers this necessary, and if consultations do not lead to agreement the Council may settle the issue by a qualified majority vote.

Articles 100 and 101 have been employed with increasing frequency in a wide range of sectors and cases, notably: technical obstacles to trade, limitations on the right to employment and movement of capital, job safety, and taxation. Typical examples of their use are the harmonisation of legislation concerning the use of colouring additives in food products, the standardisation of lighting and traffic signals on farm tractors, and the harmonisation of safety regulations for tools used in mechanical riveting.

AGRICULTURE

By 1 July 1968 the Community will be operating a single agricultural policy applying directly to the whole area of the six countries and covering over 90 per cent of the total farm output. That this should be achieved eighteen months before the end of the statutory transitional period is a measure of the common market's success; moreover the common farm policy itself is one of the elements most closely binding the six countries, not only economically but politically, and it was established as the result of a series of decisions which were highly political in their implications.

Integration in the agricultural sector was crucial to the successful development of the common market. From the very beginning the Six had accepted that the balance of interests between members which was sought in the Community required the inclusion of agriculture in the process of integration. There could be no question, however, of simply removing barriers between the six farming economies. In each member country there existed a protected and managed farm market, and there were significant price and structural differences between them. Nevertheless, the basic pattern of protecting the farmer by managing the level of consumer prices was common to all member countries.

The Treaty of Rome did no more than rule that there should be a common agricultural policy, defining the products to which it would apply and laying down its objectives in very general terms. These were an increase in agricultural productivity, with higher farm wages; the stabilisation of markets; regular supplies; and reasonable prices for consumers. In pursuing these aims, allowance was to be made for the structural and social characteristics of agriculture, the need to make changes gradually, and the close links of the agricultural sector with the rest of the economy. The general principle was laid down that there should be common management of markets, at the Community level, by a system appropriate for each product and taking one of three forms: common rules concerning competition; compulsory co-ordination of the national market organisations; or the establishment of a Community market organisation. For the whole agricultural sector it is the third possibility that the Six have chosen.

The formulation of the 'guiding lines' of the common agricultural policy was left until after the Treaty came into force. It was laid down that the Commission should call a conference to compare the national farm policies, resources and needs of the Six. This conference took place in Stresa in July 1958. Subsequently, in a laborious two-year process of study, consultation and negotiation, the basic principles of the common agricultural policy were established.

The farm policy which has been developed provides in each sector for a uniform set of rules applying throughout the area, with the decisions taken in Brussels by the Council of Ministers or, in administrative matters, by the Commission. Farm policy expenditure falling within the common policy is gradually being taken over by a central fund, total expenditure being covered from 1 July 1967 for products already subject by then to a common policy. The basic pattern is one of price support in the Community market, a corresponding level of protection against imports, and measures to help make Community farming more efficient. For most products the determining factor is price, and the Council sets annually a common target price, from which is derived the level at which there is support buying. The price also determines the level of protection, which is ensured through a system of levies at the Community frontier: these bring the price of the imported produce up from the world market price to a 'threshold price' set a given percentage below the target price. Although this is the most common pattern, the details of the market organisation vary considerably from product to product: thus for animal products using feed grains (pigmeat, eggs, poultry) there is no target price but there is a levy and also the possibility of a supplementary levy to ensure adequate protection in a fluctuating market. For beef and veal the protection continues to be ensured partly by customs duties. More detailed indications about the various markets are given below. Table I shows the different elements in the policies for the various products.

The basic decisions necessary for establishing the common policy were taken between January 1962 and July 1966 and it is coming into force gradually over the period July 1962–July 1968. Both the extension to cover all major farm products, and the implementation of a single market organisation, destined in the end to allow complete free trade, had to be done by stages. The fundamental decisions were heavily political, both because of the economic and political implications of tying the financing of farm policy into a single Community system, and also because of the importance of agriculture on the internal political scene in all the member countries. The decisions were taken in a series of lengthy and difficult ministerial sessions which were landmarks in the progress of the Community.

Thus on 14 January 1962, after meetings which had gone on with little respite since before Christmas 1961 and had taken over 200 hours in all, the Council laid down the basic regulations for the wheat and feed grains sectors, for pigmeat, poultry and eggs, and partial regulations for fruit and vegetables and wine; it also established the rules for financing the common policy for the first three years. Decisions taken in December 1963 and formalised the following February extended a common market organisation to beef and veal, milk and dairy produce, and rice. A year later the Council took the momentous step of fixing the common price levels which would apply throughout the Community for wheat and feed grains from 1 July 1967. Finally, in May 1966 (after delay caused by the constitutional crisis of the previous year) the basic financial rules to apply from 1965 onwards were agreed; and in July 1966 a market organisation was laid down for fats and oils and sugar, and that for fruit and vegetables completed, whilst common prices were set for the remaining products, where the common system requires them. There remained a large number of implementing decisions to be taken during the period up to 1 July 1968. (See Table II for the timing of this process.)

(a) The transitional period

Both structural differences as between the member countries and the major differences between price levels mean that the common policies could not be brought in overnight. There was thus in most

TABLE I

Policy Measures in the Common Agricultural Policy

	Cereals	Durum wheat	Rice	Milk and milk products	Beef and veal	Pigmeat	Eggs, poultry	Sugar	Olive oil	Oil-seeds	Fruit and vegetables	Wine
Liberalisation of trade	x	x	x	x	x	x	x	x	x	x	x	(x)[1]
Quota arrangements between members states												(x)[1]
Unlimited price guarantee	x	x	x	x					x	x		
Limited price and marketing guarantee								x				
Reserve price											x	
Levies	x	x	x	x		x	x	x	x			
Customs duties					x					x[2]	x	x
Supplementary levy[3]					x	x	x				x	
Refunds[4]	x	x	x	x	x	x	x	x	x	x	x	
Measures in the case of shortage[5]								x	x			
Intervention on the market	x	x	x	x	x[6]	x[6]		x	x	x	x	
Direct Community aid to producers		x		x[7]					x	x		
Direct national aid to producers[8]				x				x				
Community compensatory measures[9]	x	x										
Consumer subsidies at national level	x[6]			x[10]								
Quality standards											x	x
Producers' organisations											x	

(1) Liberalised in Benelux.
(2) Exemption for raw materials.
(3) Calculated on the basis of: sluice-gate prices in the case of pigmeat, eggs and poultry; reference prices in the case of fruit and vegetables; guide prices in the case of beef and veal.
(4) At present the member states frequently refrain from paying refunds.
(5) Export levy; for sugar there is an import subsidy as well; in the case of olive oil, buffer stocks are provided for.
(6) Financed by the member states until the single market stage is reached.
(7) For skim milk for cattle feed, and a small number of products bound in GATT.
(8) Until the 1974–75 season, milk in Luxembourg; until the 1978–79 season, sugar in Italy.
(9) During the transition period, for Germany, Italy and Luxembourg.
(10) During the transition period, butter and cheese in Germany; butter in the Netherlands.

TABLE II

Timetable for Implementation of the Common Agricultural Policy

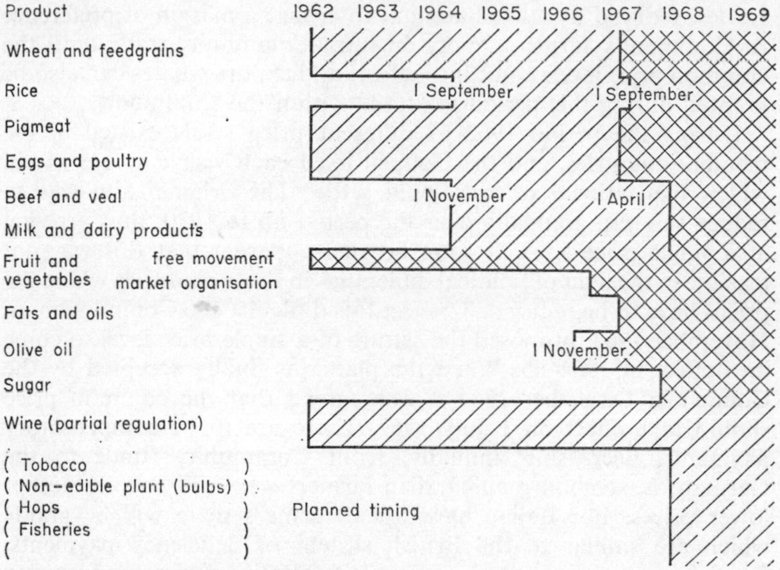

	1.7.62–1.7.63	1.7.63–1.7.64	1.7.64–1.7.65	1.7.65–1.7.67		1.7.67–1.7.69
FINANCING Art. 200 key	1 100%	2 90%	3 80%	4		5 90% levies to fund: rest shared
National contributions to Fund, proportionate to levies	0%	10%	20%	special Key		special Key
Expenditure covered by Fund (guarantee)	$\frac{1}{6}$	$\frac{1}{3}$	$\frac{1}{2}$	$\frac{6}{10}$	$\frac{7}{10}$	Fund pays all
Guidance:	$\frac{1}{3}$ total expenditure on guarantee			overall annual ceiling = $285 million		

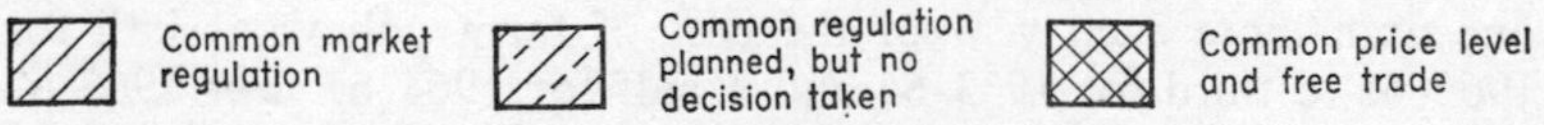

N.B. Some countries are also seeking market regulations for: potatoes, plant textiles, linen, mutton and lamb, hops, and cork.

cases a transitional period during which, although subject to the same system and financed partly from the central fund, the national markets remained separate and were protected against each other. Levies, reduced by a fixed amount to ensure a margin of preference to Community farmers, apply on intra-Community trade until the common price levels come into effect: and export rebates can also be granted during this period for trade within the Community.

During the period 1962–67 different price levels existed in the member countries, and the Council fixed each year a range within which the national prices should settle. The original aim was to reduce this gap gradually over the period up to 1970, thus arriving at a single price level. It soon became apparent that this was not feasible in the light of political difficulties in those countries where the prices have to be reduced. To meet this difficulty the Commission, in November 1963, proposed the setting of a single price level to come into effect in 1964–65. When the plan was finally accepted by the Council in December 1964 it was agreed that the common price should take effect on 1 July 1967. There are to be compensatory payments, decreasing annually, from Community funds to the German, Luxembourg and Italian farmers who will have to accept lower prices. For Italian hard-wheat farmers there will be grants which are similar to the British system of deficiency payments. Special arrangements were also made for Italian maize producers to enable them to accommodate to a much lower price. Common price levels for other products will take effect on appropriate dates in 1967 or 1968.

(*b*) *Financing*

The Agricultural Fund, which forms one part of the overall Community budget, will bear from 1 July 1967 the full cost of farm policy expenditure, within the framework of the common policy: that is to say, support buying on the Community market, export subsidies and grants for improving the efficiency of farming certain national subsidies outside the framework of the policy will continue to be allowed (see p. 211). The original financial decision taken in January 1962 covered a three-year period only (July 1962–June 1965); a second decision, taken finally in May 1966, covered the two years 1965–67 and also the period from July 1967 onwards when there is full Community financing. From 1962 to 1965 the Fund took over one sixth more each year of the cost of farm policy: a sixth for 1962–63, a third for 1963–64 and a half for 1964–65. For 1965–67 this rate of progression was not maintained, a progression by tenths being substituted (six tenths in 1965–66, seven tenths in 1966–67), to be followed by a jump to full financing. This slowing down took account of the concern of Italy and Belgium, which had been paying their full share of the Fund but had received relatively little from it since the farm products most important to their economies had not come under common market organisation on the dates originally set. During the first three years, most of the cost of the Fund was shared between the member states in the same ratio as the normal budget, with, however, a growing part (0–10 per cent to 20 per cent) shared instead in proportion to imports subject to levies—so that countries getting increased revenue from levies, as a result of buying non-Community produce, should bear a bigger share. A ceiling was, however, set for the various countries' contributions under this scheme (Germany 31 per cent, France and Italy 28 per cent, Netherlands 13 per cent, Belgium and Luxembourg 10·5 per cent). In December 1964 Italy (which through her rapid economic expansion had become a major food importer and had therefore been paying her full share although obtaining little from the fund) was granted a ceiling on her contribution of 18 per cent for 1965–66 and 22 per cent for 1966–67. Table III shows the amounts received from the Fund

TABLE III

Amounts Received from the Agricultural Fund, 1962–65

Receiving country	1962–3	1963–4	1964–5 (estimate)
	in millions of United States dollars (percentage of total in brackets)		
Belgium and Luxembourg	0·3 (1·0)	0·3 (0·6)	2·4 (1·4)
France	24·4 (86)	46·8 (85·2)	112 (67)
Germany	1·7 (6·3)	2·6 (4·7)	6·5 (4)
Italy	0·9 (3·2)	0·7 (1·3)	11 (6·6)
Netherlands	0·9 (3·3)	4·4 (7·9)	35·1 (21)
Total	28·4	54·9	167

by the various countries during the first three years it was operating. Under the second financial agreement, of May 1966, specific percentages were set for the national contributions for the two years 1965–66 and 1966–67, as follows:

	1965–66 per cent	1966–67 per cent
Belgium	7·95	7·95
France	32·58	29·26
Germany	31·67	30·83
Italy	18	22
Luxembourg	0·22	0·22
Netherlands	9·58	9·74

The principle of sharing out part of the cost in relation to imports was abandoned, although estimated income from levies on imports was taken into account in establishing the figures. For the period from July 1967 until the end of the official transitional period in December 1969, 90 per cent of national income from levies will be passed on to the Fund, covering in practice something less than half of total outgoings, the rest of the cost being shared out according to the ratio:

Belgium	8·1
France	32·0
Germany	31·2
Italy	20·3
Luxembourg	0·2
Netherlands	8·2

The change from the former system of paying a part only in proportion to levy incomes came as a result of the decision to give subsidies for gross exports rather than net exports (as was the case during the period 1962–67). Whilst there were barriers between countries, only the net exports of each were eligible for export subsidies; with no internal barriers, however, trade flows can change and a net system would be to the disadvantage of major importing countries (particularly Germany). Some of their producers would be obliged to seek export markets as their produce was displaced internally by that of other Community growers, but they would continue to have a net surplus of imports over exports.

In the original 1962 agreement it had been laid down that once the common market was complete the levies should go direct to the Community. It was on this that the Commission based its proposals of April 1965 for direct revenues. The postponement of direct revenues explains the decision to have only 90 per cent of levy incomes paid to the Fund in the period July 1967 to December 1969. A decision will have to be taken before 1970 on the implementation of the 1962 decision.

Total expenditure under the 'guarantee' part of the Fund rose steadily as a greater proportion of national outlays was taken over and as more products came under the system. According to estimates the figures are as follows, in millions of dollars per year:

1962–63	1963–64	1964–65	1965–66	1966–67	1967–68	1968–69
28·4	55·0	163	240	429	920	1216

Expenditure is expected to remain around the 1968–69 level. These figures do not take account of guarantees to be paid from the Community Fund to compensate German, Italian and Luxembourg farmers, during the period 1967–70, for the loss in income resulting from the application of the common grain price; nor do they allow for national subsidies which are still permitted in some cases until the end of the transitional period.

(*c*) *The Fund for 'structural improvements in agriculture'*

During the first three years (1962–65) the amount to be allotted under the second section of the Fund, for increasing the efficiency of the farm economy, was not to exceed a third of the expenditure on guarantees (that is a quarter of total expenditure). In the settlement of May 1966 an absolute ceiling of $285 million per annum was set on the 'guidance ' section. The money is granted by the EEC Commission, on an annual basis, towards the financing of projects submitted to it by the national governments. During the 1962–65 period the Fund could contribute up to a quarter of the planned expenditure; in 1966 the ceiling was set at 25 per cent but with the possibility of an increase to 40 per cent for particular cases. The rest is provided by the national governments or from other sources. The kind of projects financed are those which benefit the farming communities as a whole, not individual farmers. They include such things as fruit-packaging and processing plants, dairy plant, covered markets, slaughterhouses, etc. Submitted and approved individually during the first few years, such projects will in the future have to fit into the overall structural programmes which will be drawn up for the Community.

(*d*) *The machinery*

(i) *Grains*. The regulations which came into effect on 1 July 1962, setting in motion the gradual establishment of a common market organisation for wheat and the secondary cereals, were to some extent the prototype for the rest of the common farm policy.

From the start all existing national measures of protection, and in particular quota restrictions, were abolished, the sole remaining instrument of protection both at the external frontiers of the Community and between member states being the levies.

The determining factor of the system adopted for marketing cereals is the target, or indicator, price. In the organisation of the internal markets of member states, an intervention price is set, between 5 per cent and 7 per cent below the target price. If the wholesale prices drop to this level or below the state is bound to support measures by buying at that price. The target price also determines the level of protection against imports. A 'threshold price' is set, such that goods entering at that price can be sold at the target price in the area of greatest shortage. Variable levies are calculated on a daily basis to bring the prices of imported grain—the price taken is the 'most favourable purchase price' on the world market—up to the threshold price. To allow for the constant fluctuations of world prices and the fact that it takes about three weeks to transport grain from Canada or the United States, the advance setting of levies has been authorised to enable exporters to meet the 'levy risk'; the precise level of levies can thus be known between four and eight weeks in advance. In the case of trade between member countries a fixed sum is deducted from the levy in order to ensure a margin of preference to Community producers on the markets of other member countries.

Starting in the farm year 1967–68, there will be a single target price level for wheat and for each of the feed grains for the whole Community: these are set for Duisburg (area of greatest shortfall) and derived regional prices will apply for the rest of the Community. The result will be that grain can move freely within the Community without being subject to levies. The common price level will be set each year by the Council of Ministers on the basis of proposals made by the Commission.

(ii) *Rice.* The situation in the rice sector is a special one, since only two countries, France and Italy, are producers, whilst the others have a tradition of importing rice from abroad (the Netherlands from Indonesia and Germany from the United States and the Far East). The market organisation is modelled closely on that for grains, with a basic target price established for the non-producing areas and a derived target price for the producing areas. The intervention price is set each year for paddy rice (the variety produced in France and Italy) at a level 7 per cent below the derived target price for the area.

The intervention price for husked rice is set 4–7 per cent below the separate target price which is based on the paddy prices. As with grains, the threshold price in the two producing countries is set so that the imported product sells at the target price in the area of greatest shortage. For the non-producing countries there is a single threshold price set by the Council at the level of what is taken as being the most representative price on the world market during a given reference period. A common price level for rice will come into effect in the Community in 1967. In the intervening period (1964–67) there was a system of levies in intra-Community trade, the levy being equal to the difference between the free-at-frontier price and the threshold price of the importing country, less a fixed sum (not deducted in trade between producing and non-producing countries).

(iii) *Pigmeat*. The regulations which came into effect in September 1962 cover the whole range of pigmeat from the live animal through to sausages and various tinned products. The regulations at present in force make no provision for Community intervention on the market, but they are due to be extended to allow this.

Protection against imports from outside the Community is ensured by a levy system which is more complex than that applying for grain. Since coarse grains are the main 'raw material' for pigmeat, the levy involves a variable element which takes into account changes in coarse grain prices, and a fixed element which is calculated in relation to production costs. A further element of 'emergency' protection is provided in the case of imports from outside the Community by the setting of a 'sluice-gate price'; when the import price drops below this a supplementary levy is automatically applied to make up the difference. In the face of dumping by certain state trading countries, the Commission was obliged, in 1965, to obtain authorisation to discriminate in such a way that other countries were not unduly affected by the supplementary levy which this dumping provoked. The Community has already experienced the effects of the 'pig-cycle' of alternate surpluses and shortages of pigmeat with consequent low and high prices, and during surplus periods the Commission cut the levy for all Community countries to that of the lowest level being applied, thus helping to keep prices down.

There will be no common price level set for pigmeat, but from 1 July 1967 when the common price levels take effect for coarse grains there will be no levies on intra-Community trade.

(iv) *Eggs and poultry*. The general pattern for these products is identical with that for pigmeat. Again free circulation of eggs and poultry within the EEC comes into effect from July 1967 when the common grain prices are applied and Community financed support buying is due to be introduced on the same date.

(v) *Beef and veal*. The market organisation for beef and veal makes allowance for a situation of overall shortage in the Community and contains elements of both the grains and the pigmeat regulations. Thus on the internal market there is a support price and a 'guidance price'—which differs from the target price in being not the price which producers are guaranteed but the price which it is thought desirable to obtain, on the average, over the whole of a marketing season. The machinery is aimed at preventing market prices from diverging significantly from this 'guidance price'. The determining factor in its operation is the support prices: on these depend both the level of support buying authorised, and the application of levies. Customs duties continue to provide Community producers' basic protection against imports.

(vi) *Milk and dairy products*. The milk and dairy products regulations are closely linked with those for beef. They are the most important for Community farming in terms of the revenue they provide: 25 per cent of the total agricultural revenue comes from dairy produce, including milk, and a further 15 per cent comes from beef. The task of working out a common organisation for these products was made difficult by the major differences between the national systems, whilst the number of varying products derived from milk added to the complexity of the problem. Nevertheless, the regulations contain the same three basic elements: price setting, support intervention and protection by levies.

The single target price which will take effect on 1 April 1968 will be a price ensured to farmers for all their output over a year. In the interim period national prices are set within upper and lower limits determined by the Council and will be aligned gradually. The levies on imports cover the difference between the free-at-frontier price at the time of importation and the threshold price for thirteen groups of products (a representative product in each case being chosen for the price-fixing). At present there is a greater degree of government support of all kinds in the dairy sector than in any other agricultural sector: this amounts to £166 million a year, half of it in Germany. There are plans for the gradual removal of all aid linked directly to production, the aim being to guarantee prices which ensure farmers a living directly from the market.

(vii) *Wine*. The Community's aim in the wine sector is to stabilise markets and prices by adapting supply to demand and by quality control. The original regulations provide for the Commission to establish an annual table of Community output and requirements. To promote an increase in trade within the Community, annual quotas are set for the import of quality wines into France and Italy, and of all wine into Germany. A decision was pending in 1966 on the establishment of a Community regulation covering quality wines from a given area of the Community.

(viii) *Fruit and vegetables*. The regulations which came into effect in 1962 were different in structure and less complete than those covering the other products. The two main elements of the system for fruit and vegetables were the establishment of common quality standards and the gradual freeing of trade. Thus produce of 'extra' quality was freed from all restrictions on 1 July 1962, Grade 1 produce on 1 January 1964 and Grade II on 1 January 1966. An 'escape clause' mechanism is provided to prevent gluts from causing a disturbance on national markets, and this has been invoked on a few occasions. The escape clause may be applied at once, but is subject to the approval of the Commission, and appeal to the Council against its decision is possible.

The common policy for the fruit and vegetable sector was completed in July 1966 by a further regulation, coming into effect on 1 January 1967. This broke new ground in that no market organisation for the sector existed in any member country. Provision was made for encouraging the setting up of producer organisations, such as have long operated in the Netherlands, and for giving them a role in the market system. Buying-up of produce by these organisations to avoid gluts on the market will be allowed when the price drops a given percentage below a basic price set by the Council. Official support buying to be financed from the Community fund will be allowed at lower percentages of the basic price, also set by the Council. The intervention levels vary from product to product, and were set higher during an initial three-year trial period to give satisfaction to Italian claims. The long-term levels, set much lower, met the Dutch concern not to finance aid which would undermine the competitive position of their own growers on Community markets.

Export subsidies financed from the Community Fund will also be allowed for fruit and vegetables under certain conditions.

(ix) *Vegetable fats and oils.* Olive oil, for which France and Italy meet 70–80 per cent of Community requirements, is treated differently from other vegetable oils. A common price level took effect on 10 November 1966 (the first common price to become effective for the whole Community). The system provides for a market target price (to allow olive oil to compete with other products), backed up by intervention prices at which olive oil is bought by the authorities, and also a producer target price, intended to encourage the maintenance of an adequate level of production. It is equivalent in its function to a deficiency payment, producers receiving for the season the difference between the two target prices. Duties on intra-Community trade were removed in November 1966 and a complex levy system governs imports from outside the Community.

For other vegetable oils (mainly colza, navette and sunflower seeds) an annual target price and basic support price will be set, applying from 1 July 1967. Aid will be granted for oilseeds grown and processed within the Community. A tariff applies to imports from the rest of the world, and trade within the Community will be free from July 1967.

(x) *Sugar.* The general principles of a common policy for sugar were adopted in July 1966, and the basic regulation must be passed before the policy is due to take effect, on 1 July 1968. The starting-point for working out the policy was a situation where all Community countries except Italy meet their sugar requirements from home production, Belgium and France traditionally being net exporters. Whilst there will be a basic price set, as in other sectors, it proved necessary to put a ceiling on guaranteed marketing for a seven-year period. The system therefore involves, in addition to a basic intervention price and a threshold price, a series of basic quotas, with one minimum price applying for sales within the quota limits, and another for output up to a given level in excess of it. The basic quota is set for the Community as a whole and shared out between countries and between growers (or factories: the point remained to be settled). The marketing and price guarantees apply up to a ceiling of 135 per cent of the quota and output exceeding this can neither be sold inside the Community nor benefit from export rebates. Aid is allowed on a temporary basis to some Italian producers. Imports from the rest of the world will be governed by a levy system of the usual type. In the event of a sugar shortage there would be import grants and export levies.

(e) The administration of the agricultural policy

The day-to-day administration of the agricultural policy is the responsibility of the Commission, although major decisions on such matters as prices are taken by the Council. The Commission is assisted in its work by management committees, one for each product, with additional committees for the Fund and for structural policy. These management committees are made up of representatives of the national ministries of agriculture, and meet in Brussels as often as is needed, generally several times a month, under chairmanship provided by the Commission. Decisions which the Commission proposes to take are submitted to them for discussion. In the Committee there is weighted voting; if a proposal is rejected by less than the required total of twelve out of seventeen votes, the Commission may ignore the hostile vote. If the rejection is by a weighted majority and the Commission chooses to act despite this, the question may be taken to the Council which must give its ruling within a time-limit, and may reverse the Commission's decisions. In practice there have been only a very limited number of cases where a Commission proposal has met with an adverse vote and eighteen matters have been submitted to the Council. There are a number of decisions which the Commission is authorised to take: these include the daily calculation of the cost–insurance–freight prices on which the levies are based; the weekly setting of free-at-frontier prices for intra-Community trade; the setting as circumstances demand of the supplementary levies on pigmeat, eggs and poultry.

A COMMON TRANSPORT POLICY

Transport was one of the sectors in which the ECSC had already been confronted with the limitations of the sector approach to integration. Given the importance of transport in the economy of all the member states, in terms of its share both of the gross national product and of total employment, a single undistorted market for transport was necessary as one of the bases for economic union. The Rome Treaty, whilst laying down precise requirements about the elimination of discrimination in the transport sector, gives little guidance as to the nature of the common transport policy, which the institutions are to work out and apply. Article 74 states baldly 'the objectives of this Treaty shall be pursued by the member states within the framework of a common transport policy'. Articles 75–84, which follow, deal either with the removal of discrimination or with specific problems. Three aspects in the work of the Community concerning transport are to be clearly distinguished: discrimination; the development of a sound transport network; and the elaboration of a common policy with Community rules to meet the transport needs of the whole EEC area.

A regulation banning discrimination by a haulier on account of the country of origin or destination of the goods carried or the nationality of the customer was passed by the Council in 1960 and began to take effect on 1 July 1961. Discrimination of this kind was ended by 31 December 1963.

A ban on 'support tariffs'—special rates and conditions granted mainly by the railways, usually to favour a particular industry or region—came into effect in January 1962 with the move to the second stage. An indication of the complexity of the previous situation is given by the fact that by the end of 1964 forty-three special tariffs limited to transport within member states had been abolished, and a further seventy-four had been modified or extended to international transport within the Community: of rates applying only to exports or imports, thirty-nine had been abolished and ninety-five made compatible with the Treaty. Acting under Article 80 the Commission checked, during 1963 and 1964, in collaboration with the governments several hundreds of internal transport rate systems involving an element of support or protection for one or more firms or sectors of industry, and obtained the abolition of well over a hundred of them whilst some 350 were recognised as being economically justified.

Progress towards a system of steadily opening up access to national markets for hauliers from other member countries was slow, and it was not until March 1965 that the Council finally agreed on a plan for the introduction of a Community quota, to exist alongside the bilateral quotas which would be gradually widened.

Action is envisaged to ease procedures for frontier crossings, and to align national regulations about the maximum weights and dimensions of commercial vehicles—a vital element in ensuring fair competition.

The basic problem of achieving fair competition throughout the transport sector is, however, that of haulage rates and conditions. The Commission set out in April 1961 the basic lines of a common transport policy in a memorandum intended to serve as a basis for wide debate, and followed this in June 1962 with an 'action programme'. The principles laid down in both documents as being fundamental to a common policy were: equal treatment in terms of rates and conditions for all users; financial independence and freedom of action for haulage undertakings; free choice of means of transport for the user; and co-ordination of investments. A system along these lines would be a revolutionary break with the present complex situation, where nationalised railways co-exist with a mass of small firms in road and waterway haulage and many non-economic considerations dictate national transport policy. The basic method for achieving the first three was to be the application of 'fork rates'—upper and lower limits on the rate to be charged for any journey, and intended to ensure cheap transport whilst preventing cut-throat competition. It was not finally until June 1965 that the Council adopted a fork-rate plan and a timetable for its introduction. Opposition came mainly, as it had done in the ECSC, from the Netherlands, which wished to preserve its competitive position and defend an economy in which transport, including the supply of international transport services, played a far bigger part than in other member countries.

The solution adopted in June 1965 was for a two-stage move. For three years compulsory upper and lower limits are to be established for road and rail transport, except that under private contract, and rates charged must be published; for inland waterways—this was a concession to the Netherlands—the upper and lower limits would be for reference and only rates falling outside the brackets would have to be published. In the second stage, to finish on 31 December 1972, the rules would apply to hauls within countries as well as international transport. The reference tariff system will remain for international inland waterway transport, for certain types of bulk transport and for some other types of national transport; there will also be compulsory upper and lower limits for some national transport. This agreement fell far short of the Commission's original proposals but was the first serious commitment by the Council along the lines suggested.

Other problems which have arisen in the transport sector include that of Rhine transport, which is of particular importance since 11 per cent of intra-Community traffic is carried on the Rhine. International navigation was covered by the Mannheim Act of 1868, and the Commission's view expressed in April 1964 was that Community regulations are applicable so far as they do not conflict with the provisions of this Act.

Since the transport links between the member countries are not good, the Commission drew up, in 1961, a plan of the basic road, rail and inland waterway network which should be developed on a priority basis to serve the Community as a single economic region. In 1965 the Council's approval was obtained for an enquiry into infrastructure costs with a view to determining how they should be shared out between the different means of transport and how distortions could be avoided.

The Treaty leaves it to the Community institutions to determine whether and in what way the Treaty shall apply to air and sea transport. The view of the Commission, put forward to the Council in 1964, is that it must do so but no action has been taken. Plans for the creation of Airunion, a combination of the national airlines of the member countries to lessen costs and share routes and maintenance, are being considered outside the Community framework.

SOCIAL POLICY

Article 117 of the Treaty states the agreement of the member states on the need to 'promote improvement in the living and working conditions of labour so as to allow them to be harmonised in an upwards direction', and Article 118 charges the Commission with promoting 'close collaboration between the member states in the social field, particularly in matters relating to employment, labour legislation and working conditions, vocational and advancement, social security, protection against occupational accidents and diseases, industrial medicine, legislation on trade unions and collective bargaining between employers and workers'. In the social field the formula has been largely one of co-ordination of national activity rather than the elaboration of a single Community policy. The action of the Commission in the early years was limited largely to ensuring the implementation of the provisions of the Treaty relating to the free movement of workers and the transferability of social security benefits (see p. 197). During the second stage, from 1962 to 1966, the Commission took active steps to promote close co-operation between the member states in most of the fields referred to in the Treaty.

The Social Fund is the major instrument of Community social policy. The Fund is set up by Articles 123–128 of the Treaty, and is financed by the member countries according to a special ratio which allows for the differences in national income: France and Germany contribute 32 per cent each, Italy 20 per cent, Belgium 8·8 per cent, the Netherlands 7 per cent and Luxembourg 0·2 per cent. The task of the Fund is defined by the Treaty as being the promotion of employment opportunities within the Community and the mobility of workers, both geographically and between jobs. The Fund's method of operation is that of retroactive reimbursement by the Community of half the cost of schemes submitted by member governments (whether carried out by them or by private firms) or by recognised public undertakings. The operations which may be financed in this way are vocational re-training, re-settlement, and tide-over schemes for workers forced to work for lower wages whilst industrial reconversion is under way (this is based on the pioneer work of the ECSC in this field). Schemes must be submitted in advance and their financing can be authorised only when the workers have been employed in their new job or working in their new place of residence for at least six months. From the time when the Fund came into operation in September 1960 up to December 1965, grants had been made for schemes involving the retraining of some 175,000 workers, mostly in Italy, and the resettlement of a further 279,000, many of them Italians working in France. The sums paid out totalled $31·6 million, whilst applications involving a further $24 million were pending. In January 1965 the Commission submitted, for decision by the Council, proposals for extending the scope of the Fund's activities aimed at giving it a more active role in social policy and in regional policy by helping to increase the level of employment, and improving the standard of living of migrant workers. The amendments would make grants possible for the training of workers handicapped by their lack of professional qualifications; for tiding over workers during training schemes; for the creation of vocational training centres; and for the housing of migrant workers.

Vocational training is one of the fields in which the Commission has worked hardest to promote co-ordinated action by the member states. A Consultative Committee on Vocational Training was established in December 1963; in October 1964 a general draft programme was elaborated for vocational training, as was a special plan for agricultural workers; and in February 1965 a set of proposals was presented for the latter.

In May 1964 the Council adopted a first programme under the terms of Article 50 concerning the exchange of young workers.

Considerable efforts have been made to promote the harmonisation of social conditions in the member countries. Measures concerning workers' health and safe working conditions have already been taken and proposals were announced for 1965 concerning the alignment of national legislation on social security and the protection of young workers. It should perhaps be mentioned that the action of the Community in the social field has been frequently criticised by trade union representatives on the grounds that a more active policy could have been followed.

CO-ORDINATION OF ECONOMIC POLICIES

The progress made by the Community during its first nine years in co-ordinating the economic policies of the member states demonstrates the extent to which it is left to the institutions to exploit and develop the provisions of the Treaty as circumstances demand or allow. The part of the Treaty dealing with 'economic policy' is brief, consisting of one article (103) on cyclical policy (*politique conjoncturelle*) and five articles (104–109) on the 'balance of payments'. In fact, much of what has been done has been based implicitly on the general injunction in the first paragraph of Article 103: 'Member States shall consider their short-term economic policy as a matter of common interest. They shall consult with each other and with the Commission on measures to be taken in response to current circumstances.'

Article 104 provides that each member state shall pursue the economic policy necessary to ensure the equilibrium of its overall balance of payments and to maintain confidence in its currency, while ensuring a high level of employment and the stability of the level of prices. To help to achieve this aim 'the member states shall co-ordinate their economic policies. They shall for this purpose institute a collaboration between the competent services of their administrative departments and between their central banks' (Article 105). The establishment of a Monetary Committee to promote the co-ordination of national policies in monetary matters is also provided for.

In the event the Commission has chosen to promote collaboration on a pragmatic basis, giving it institutional form after the habit of joint meetings has been established. The result has been the emergence of a well-rooted Community tradition of consultation and debate, in which national economic problems are set against the wider context of the Community economy amongst those responsible for national economic policy. This development extends to ministerial level, the Finance Ministers of the Six having held informal two-day sessions on common market problems (though outside the EEC framework) every quarter since 1960. Thus the groundwork was laid for the first steps in active co-ordination which were taken in 1964 and 1965.

The Commission itself considered from the start that its responsibility was to watch over the economic situation of the Community as a whole and to encourage policies which took account of the interdependence of the national economies. Quarterly reports are produced on the situation and outlook for the economy of each of the member states and for the Community; although prepared in collaboration with the national civil services, these reflect the Commission's own independent judgement, and its recommendations on the policies which should be followed are in the best interest of the whole. The quarterly reports are supplemented by monthly publications called *Graphs and Brief Notes* giving basic economic data. The Communities' Statistical Office gradually built up a wide range of publications to provide a detailed overall picture of trade and production and other basic economic factors in the Community. Lastly, it became a tradition that at the January session of the European Parliament M. Robert Marjolin, the member of the Commission who was responsible for economic and financial questions, should present the Commission's assessment of the economic situation and prospects for the Community, this report being debated in full later in the year.

The Commission has not limited itself to the provision of data or to making recommendations. It has used its right of initiative gradually to develop an institutional framework in which the member countries could achieve economic co-operation. The background of this is a series of interlocking committees, which bring together the senior policy makers of the national administrations. Although they do not take decisions or accept commitments, they become involved in discussion of the problems arising in the wider framework of the Community. The model taken for these Committees was the Monetary Committee, the only one provided for in the Treaty.

THE MONETARY COMMITTEE

Article 105 of the Treaty states in fact that the Monetary Committee shall have the following tasks: 'to keep under review the monetary and financial situation of the member states and of the Community and also the general payments system of member states and to report regularly thereon to the Council and to the Commission; and to formulate opinions, at the request of the Council or of the Commission or on its own initiative, for submission to the said institutions.' The Committee consists of two members appointed by each member state and two appointed by the Commission. It meets in Brussels ten or twelve times a year. Sessions are devoted to a general examination of the overall economic and monetary situation and also to a detailed study of the situation in one member state, the formula being that of a 'cross-examination' by the representatives of another member country and of the Commission. The Committee has formulated frequent opinions, which are confidential, to the Commission and the Council. In 1964 the Council formally extended the functions of the Committee to include the co-ordination of the positions of the member states in the framework of international monetary bodies, where the Community has in recent years been in a strong position resulting from its sound monetary situation.

The member states have begun to co-ordinate their short-term economic policies. Steps were taken to ensure that the budgets of all member countries ran from January to December; and 'economic budgets' or estimates of budgetary income and expenditure during the following year are submitted to the Commission in time to form the basis of a report which is then debated.

In 1964 further action was taken to promote the co-ordination of policies. Responding to a German initiative, the Council of Ministers adopted, on the basis of a draft prepared by the EEC Commission, a series of recommendations to the member states about their economic policy for the succeeding twelve months in order to meet the threat of inflation in the Community. The recommendations set out general criteria and priorities to be observed. These recommendations were subsequently renewed.

SHORT-TERM ECONOMIC POLICY

The Monetary Committee provided a model for the creation of a committee of senior officials from the national ministries of economic affairs which, it was hoped, would play a similar role in the examination and co-ordination of short-term economic policy. A Budgetary Policy Committee, based on similar lines, bringing together officials of national treasuries, was set up in the spring of 1965 to examine, discuss and advise on the problems of co-ordinating the budgets of the member countries.

The governors of the five central banks (Luxembourg has no separate central bank) meet together regularly. They are all present for instance at the monthly meetings of governors of central banks held by the Bank for International Settlements in Basle. In April 1964 the Council institutionalised this co-operation by creating a Committee of Central Bank Governors with a similar advisory and consultative role.

The Treaty deals at some length with balance-of-payments problems. Article 108 establishes machinery for the provision of 'mutual assistance' by the member states in the event of balance-of-payments difficulties.

Article 108 has not yet been formally invoked. However, in May and June 1964, when Italy faced serious balance-of-payments difficulties, the EEC Commission acted in accordance with the first paragraph of Article 108, which gives it the responsibility, where serious national difficulties 'are likely to prejudice the functioning of the Common Market', of examining the situation and the action already taken, and indicating 'the measures which it recommends to the state concerned to adopt'. Although the Italian Government turned initially to the United States for help, the Commission followed the Italian situation closely, and, in unpublished correspondence, advised the Italian Government on the steps to be taken. In addition there were consultations between M. Marjolin, the member of the Commission responsible, and the Italian Government. The action of the Council concerning the co-ordination of national anti-inflationary policies was thus not formally a case of 'mutual assistance', but showed the readiness of member states to treat such problems as being genuinely 'a matter of common concern'.

THE MEDIUM-TERM ECONOMIC PROGRAMME

In April 1964 the Council of Ministers agreed upon a proposal from the Commission for instituting co-ordination of the economic policies of the member countries on a medium-term (five-year) basis. A Medium-term Policy Committee was set up along the same lines as the other committees mentioned above, with the specific task of preparing and submitting to the Council and Commission an economic programme for the Community for the five-year period, 1966–70. It met for the first time in December 1964. The chairman was the German Secretary of State for Economic Affairs; France is represented by the Commissaire au Plan. This Committee is assisted in its work by a committee of independent experts appointed by the Commission, their task being to draw up detailed estimates of the foreseeable trends in the economy of the Community over the same period. The draft of the first five-year programme was completed by the Committee at the end of March 1966 and adopted by the Commission, which sent it on to the Council with a number of suggested amendments: the most important of these concerned more effective action to co-ordinate regional policies and a greater emphasis on considerations of social policy. The Ministers of Economic Affairs debated the draft in the Council in December 1966 and it was to be approved early in 1967. Meanwhile work was proceeding on the second programme, thus ensuring the continuing contact and confrontation between those concerned with medium-term policy in many sectors of economic policy.

The main aim of the medium-term programme, which will be continually up-dated, and which is being extended in scope each year, is to provide a basis for recommendations about the kinds of policies the member governments should follow over the five-year period. Fields which are covered, in addition to general economic and financial policy, include the development of the economic infrastructure, teaching and vocational training, and scientific research, in all of which there is a need for the governments to coordinate their policies. The programme will also provide a framework within which well-directed efforts can be made to secure consistency between the various policies being worked out at Community level: the common agricultural policy in the first place, transport policy, industrial policy, energy policy, etc. The picture of the prospective medium-term economic trends in the Community provided by the programme should, moreover, be of use to small and medium-sized firms which lack the resources to make their own assessments and forecasts.

FISCAL HARMONISATION

Articles 95–99 of the Treaty provide for the elimination of forms of indirect taxation which are discriminatory as between domestic and other Community projects, or have an immediate distorting effect on trade. Certain internal charges and excise duties have been checked to ensure that the principle of non-discrimination was being complied with by member states. The major problem was that of the compensatory duties on imports and 'drawbacks'[1] on exports applied at national frontiers in connection with business turnover taxes. Article 99 specifically provides for the harmonisation of national legislation in this field. The Commission's examination of this problem led, in 1962, to a scheme for harmonising business turnover taxation in two stages. After further discussion, both by the finance ministers and by the competent secretaries of state, the Commission made new proposals in June 1964: a formal decision was not taken until 1967. In outline, it will mean the institution, in January 1970 at the latest, of a uniform system of business turnover taxation. Levied at all stages of production, it will tax only the value added (previous tax being subtracted) thus avoiding cumulative taxation. Governments are required to introduce legislation by 1970 in order to ensure that

[1] Rebates to compensate for internal taxation.

the change-over from their present divergent systems takes place by the end of 1971. This scheme is intended to achieve the double goal of eliminating the tax frontiers and removing a major cause of distortion.

Dutch agreement to the scheme was made subject to a commitment to remove all tax frontiers. The whole question of distortion resulting from differing levels of indirect taxation, as well as the potentially political problem of the relative levels of direct and indirect taxation, has been discussed but is bound to prove one of the most difficult fields in which to achieve equivalent competitive conditions within all the member countries.

REGIONAL POLICY

The preamble to the Rome Treaty states that the member states are 'anxious to strengthen the unity of their economies and to ensure their harmonious development by reducing the differences existing between the various regions and mitigating the backwardness of the less favoured'. The only specific measure relating to this aim laid down in the Treaty is the creation of the European Investment Bank, whose task is to contribute 'to the balanced and smooth development of the Common Market in the interests of the Community'. There is no reference to a regional development policy as such.

In 1961 the Commission convened a Conference on Regional Problems in which governments, local authorities and experts were represented. On the basis of the reports of three expert groups, set up at that time, the Commission presented a memorandum to the Council in 1965 setting out the general lines for a Community regional policy. It would be concerned with all regions, not just those considered as backward or as having specific problems, and would need to be carried out essentially by the regional authorities, though the Commission would co-ordinate the activities in the various regions. Progress is handicapped, however, by the lack of overall regional policies in some member states, and by the reluctance of others, particularly France, to envisage effective co-ordination.

THE EUROPEAN INVESTMENT BANK

The European Investment Bank is an independent institution with its own Statute. Article 130 of the Treaty lays down that its general task, as indicated above, shall be carried out 'by granting loans and guarantees on a non-profit-making basis to facilitate the financing of projects in all sectors of the economy'. Three kinds of projects are taken into account: (a) projects for the development of less developed areas of the Community; (b) projects for modernising or converting firms, or for setting up new activities, where the gradual establishment of the common market makes this necessary; and (c) projects of common interest to several member states. In the two latter cases the Bank's intervention is limited to projects which by their size and nature cannot be entirely financed by the means available in each of the member states.

The Bank was set up with a capital of 1,000 million units of account (equivalent to United States dollars) subscribed by the member states in the following way: Germany and France 300 million each, Italy 240 million, Belgium 86·5 million, the Netherlands 71·5 million and Luxembourg 2 million. A quarter of this sum is paid up. The Bank has also constituted a reserve fund of $100 million. The Bank is controlled by a Board of Governors consisting of the ministers of finance of the member countries. It is managed by a Management Committee of twelve and a three-man Board of Directors.

During the eight years up to the end of December 1966, the Bank granted 123 loans worth $420 million, for a wide range of projects. The Commission laid down that the first priority in the Bank's activities should be given to projects to aid the less developed areas. Examples of projects of this kind which have been financed are rural electrification in Brittany, the creation of local small industries in the south of Italy, and agricultural experiments in the Rhone estuary. The Bank has also contributed to the financing of major projects for the improvement of the transport infrastructure of the Community and has extended its activities to promote industrial development in areas of declining industry. Thus it collaborated with the High Authority in financing industrial schemes in the depressed mining areas of Belgium.

The Council of Ministers has extended the competence of the Bank by empowering it to handle the loans to Greece and Turkey which were granted within the framework of the agreements of Association signed with these countries.

The Bank obtains its funds primarily from loans floated on the capital markets. Loans have been floated within the Community and in the leading international financial centres.

ENERGY

No provision is made in the Treaty of Rome for the institution of a common energy policy. This is to be explained by the fact that coal was already regulated by the ECSC Treaty and research on the development of nuclear power was covered in the Euratom Treaty. Nevertheless, it was soon decided that there should be a general energy policy for the Community. A body was therefore set up consisting of representatives of the High Authority, the EEC Commission and the Euratom Commission, to draw up proposals on a common energy policy. These were to be submitted to the Council of Ministers of the ECSC (see p. 272). Although agreement was reached in the Council in 1964 on certain general principles, including rules applying to oil, it became clear that the elaboration of a detailed overall policy must await the merger of the executives of the three Communities.

The immediate responsibility of the EEC was for the oil, natural gas and electricity sectors. In 1964 the common external tariff for oil and oil products was finally agreed upon (at a very low duty) and was immediately applied, intra-Community trade being freed from all duties. French quota restrictions on oil imports were progressively relaxed as a result of the Commission's recommendations, but a special status was granted for Algerian oil.

External Relations

One of the basic aims of those who founded the European Economic Community was to restore Europe's position in the world. It was felt that a unit of equivalent size and economic power to the United States or Russia could play a major and constructive role in world economic affairs. Nevertheless the Treaty gives little indication about how the Community is to organise its external relations. Article 3 states that a common commercial policy is to be instituted, Articles 110–116 deal with the implementation of this policy. Article 3 also refers to the association of overseas countries, which came about through the association of the former colonies of the member states with the EEC, to which Part IV of the Treaty is devoted. Lastly, Article 237 provides the possibility of membership of the EEC for other European states, and Article 238 allows for the association with the Community of any non-member country.

The development of the external relations of the Community has been complicated by two factors: first, whilst in some domains the Community is competent to act as a whole, in others the member states retain full sovereignty; second, many of the problems of external economic policy, even when falling within the terms of the Treaty, have political implications such that progress towards genuine common action is very difficult whilst there is no agreement amongst the member states on a political union with a single community foreign policy.

This has tended to restrict the external policy of the Community to being a series of responses to initiatives from the outside. These have not been lacking. The commitment of the Six to the creation of economic union faced the Community's trading partners with the prospect of competition with a single economic and commercial unit of some 180 million people. Consequently there have been various moves by countries seeking to negotiate membership, association, trade agreements, or multilateral rounds of tariff cuts.

Most of these countries have been confronted with the extreme slowness of the Community in handling its external relations. The system is already cumbersome in dealing with internal matters where the concern for balanced progress or the need to meet deadlines imposed by the Treaty make for urgency; it can be almost unmanageable in the external field where there are no such pressures, and where national interests may diverge considerably. Procedurally any request from a third country will, after a preliminary debate in the Council, lead to exploratory talks with the Commission, which must then report back to the Council. A decision to open formal negotiations (which may well involve going over much of the ground already covered in the exploration) requires a negotiating mandate upon which it may take the Council months to reach agreement. At each stage in the negotiations the Commission will return to the Council with a report and will need a new mandate. Reluctance to use the majority-voting procedure is particularly marked in this field where it would seem most desirable in overriding the protectionist tendencies of individual member countries, and in generally speeding up the Community's negotiations with its trading partners.

THE ASSOCIATION WITH THE AFRICAN COUNTRIES AND MADAGASCAR

As a result of skilled and forceful negotiating by France, the Six agreed, in founding the Community, to take over a share of the responsibilities of certain member states towards their dependent countries and territories in the rest of the world. Part IV of the Treaty established an association, the purposes of which were 'to promote the economic and social development of the overseas countries and territories and to establish close economic relations between them and the Community as a whole'. The association involved three main elements: the freeing of trade with the associates at the same tempo as within the Community; the granting of direct aid in the form of investments by the Community as a whole; the establishment of joint institutions.

The countries involved were those in French West Africa, French Equatorial Africa, Togoland, the Cameroons under French Trusteeship, Madagascar and the whole range of French overseas settlements; the Belgian Congo and Ruanda-Urundi; Somaliland under Italian Trusteeship and Netherlands New Guinea. The original association was concluded for five years with the possibility of renewal. By 1960 most of the French colonies in Africa had attained political independence, as had the Belgian Congo. The Community consequently offered to renegotiate the association on a footing of equality with the newly independent African states and Madagascar. This offer was accepted by all the states concerned except Guinea, and a conference of Ministers from eighteen associated countries and the six member countries, at which the EEC Commission was present, met in 1961 and 1962.

The resulting Convention, which prolonged the Association for a further five years to 31 May 1969, was ratified by the States concerned, signed at Yaoundé on 20 July 1963 and came into effect on 1 June 1964. The eighteen associated states are: Burundi, Cameroon, the Central African Republic, Chad, Congo (Kinshasa), Congo (Brazzaville), Dahomey, Gabon, Upper Volta, the Ivory Coast, Madagascar, Mali, Mauretania, Niger, Rwanda, Senegal, Somalia and Togo. The Convention also extends to Surinam, the Netherlands Antilles and to the French overseas territories and departments. The new association followed the general lines set out in Part IV of the Rome Treaty. At the insistence of the Dutch and German delegations, and with a view to meeting criticisms of the association made by other primary producing countries, the relative preference accorded to the association was reduced, by a lowering of the common external tariff of the Community on a number of tropical products, whilst the amount of economic aid contributed by the Community was raised from $580 million in the first five years, to $730 million in the five years of the new Convention together with a further $70 million to be granted from the European Investment Bank.

(*a*) *Provisions of the Convention: free trade*

Under the terms of the Association, products of the associated countries will benefit from a steady reduction of duties and they will have free entry into the EEC area from July 1968 onwards. They enjoy preference over products imported from other non-member countries to the extent that these are subject to the common external tariff. From the start the associated countries applied the same treatment to imports from member countries as to those from the countries with which they were linked; and the duties applied are abolished according to the same timetable as duties on trade between the member countries. However, associated countries are permitted to apply those customs duties considered necessary for their development, and for the protection of developing industries. They may also impose fiscal duties needed as a source of revenue. These must also be reduced to the level of the duties on imports from the state with which the associated country had special relations. Countries already applying a non-discriminatory customs duty at the time the Treaty came into force were not required to implement the gradual abolition of duties.

The first convention included, and the Yaoundé Convention confirmed, the free right of establishment in the associated countries for firms from member countries, and the free movement of capital.

(*b*) *Provisions of the Convention: economic aid*

The economic aid provided by the Community to the associated countries within the framework of the association is channelled through a European Development Fund. The $581·25 million of aid allotted for the first five years was paid by the member countries in the following proportions: France and Germany $200 million each, Belgium and the Netherlands $70 million, Italy $40 million and Luxembourg $1·25 million. Of the payments from the Fund $511·25 million went to areas linked with France, $35 million to the Dutch areas, $30 to the Belgian and $5 million to Italian Somaliland. Contributions to the Fund and grants from it were spread in mounting amounts over the five-year period.

Under the Yaoundé Convention the $730 million are paid according to an amended scale: Germany and France $246·5 million each, Italy $100 million, Belgium $69 million, Netherlands $66 million and Luxembourg $2 million. The amounts available to each associated country are laid down in the Convention.

Two kinds of project may receive money from the Fund: social projects, involving the provision of hospitals, teaching or technical research establishments and institutes for vocational training; and economic projects 'of general interest directly connected with a programme of productive or direct investment projects'. In practice this has meant road-building, the provision of harbour facilities, water supplies, etc. The Fund is administered by the EEC Commission, which is responsible for allocating the funds available. On the basis of projects submitted, the Commission draws up a programme which in turn is submitted to the Council and is considered approved if within a month no member state has requested that the proposals be considered by the Council. Where the Council does intervene it must decide by weighted majority vote, within two months.

Once a project has been approved, it is announced in the Official Gazette of the Communities as being open for tender, and all firms established in the Community or in the associated countries can compete.[1] The contracts are allotted by the authorities of the associated state in question, but their execution is supervised by the representatives of the Commission on the staff of the Fund, which is part of the Commission.

(*c*) *Provisions of the Convention: institutions*

The Yaoundé Convention established a Council of Ministers which is responsible for taking major decisions on the policy of the association. It meets at least once a year, under the alternate chairmanship of a minister from the associated countries and the chairman of the Council of the Community. In 1965 a Secretariat was established in Brussels with a joint African and European staff. During the life of the first association a series of meetings of members of the European Parliament and the members of parliaments of the associated countries were organised, at the initiative of the European Parliament. In the Yaoundé Convention a Joint Parliamentary Committee is established to meet alternately in Africa and in Europe. It is made up of thirty-six members of the European Parliament and two representatives of each of the parliaments of the eighteen associated states.

(*d*) *Other applications for association: Nigeria*

At the time of the signature of the Yaoundé Convention the governments of the Six, mainly at the instigation of the Dutch and German Governments, issued a statement of intent indicating that the Community would give favourable consideration to requests made by states in a similar economic situation to those already associated, for an arrangement which could take one of three forms: joining the

[1] In the autumn of 1963 an experiment was made in opening two projects to tender by firms from third countries, but there was little response and the Commission did not follow this up by proposing that the Council should make the practice general.

existing Association under the terms of the Yaoundé Convention; an association *sui generis* along similar lines; a non-discriminatory trade agreement. This declaration had its origins in the negotiations concerning possible British membership of the EEC, when it had been agreed that association with the Community should be open to Commonwealth countries in Africa and the West Indies, and, when this offer was refused by Ghana and Nigeria, that special trade agreements should be concluded with these two countries.

In 1963 the Nigerian Government applied to open negotiations under the second of the three formulae. Exploratory talks were held between the Commission and a Nigerian delegation in the autumn of 1963 and in June 1964 the Council gave the Commission a mandate to open formal negotiations. Five rounds of negotiations took place, leading to agreement on an association between Nigeria and the Community. The main element is entry to the Community market for Nigerian exports on the same terms as those applying to exports from the associated countries, except for the four major Nigerian export products which compete with exports from the associated countries: cocoa, palm oil, ground-nut oil and plywood. For these products import quotas, increasing annually, were agreed, imports above that amount being subject to the common external tariff. Nigeria will grant duty-free entry for Community exports. However, she will avoid discrimination against other countries by changing her customs duties to fiscal duties. Community exports will continue to pay these, but in the case of twenty-six products an additional small customs duty is levied which is paid by other countries and not by the Community. Thus the association involves reciprocity and conforms with the GATT rules defining a free trade area.[1] Nigeria's association does not provide for access to the European Development Fund.

The Association Treaty was signed in Lagos in July 1966, to come into effect after ratification in certain Community countries. It will expire on the same date as the Yaoundé Convention on 30 May 1969, thus providing the possibility of renegotiating the two arrangements in parallel.

(*e*) *Other applications for association: East Africa*

In 1963 the three East African countries, Kenya, Tanganyika and

[1] It has however been criticised as going against the general policy established during the United Nations Conference on World Trade and Development of 1964, that industrial countries should not require preferential treatment from developing countries.

Uganda, applied to negotiate an association with the common market. Exploratory talks took place in late 1963 and early 1964. By this time Tanganyika had been replaced by Tanzania, following its merger with Zanzibar. In June 1965 the Council of Ministers granted the Commission a mandate to open formal negotiations, and a first round took place; after a suspension talks were resumed in November 1966.

A COMMON COMMERCIAL POLICY: TARIFFS

Articles 18–24 of the Treaty, as we have seen, provide for the institution of a customs tariff towards the rest of the world. The existence of this tariff and the removal of barriers to trade within the Community made necessary the establishment of a common commercial policy. Article 110 lays down the basic attitude on which this policy is to be based.

By establishing a customs union between themselves the member states intend to contribute, in conformity with the common interest, to the harmonious development of world trade, the progressive abolition of restrictions on international exchanges and the lowering of customs barriers.

The common commercial policy is to take into account the favourable incidence which the abolition of customs duties between member states may have on the increase of the competitive strength of the enterprises in those states.

The Treaty confers upon the Commission the specific responsibility of conducting tariff negotiations with third countries—the opening of which the Council has authorised on the basis of recommendations of the Commission—'in consultation with a special Committee appointed by the Council to assist the Commission in this task and within the framework of such directives as the Council may issue to it' (Article 111). Thus the Community is represented in negotiations within the framework of the General Agreement on Tariffs and Trade by a delegation from the Commission acting according to directives laid down by the Council, and working closely with 'the 111 Committee' made up of national officials; observers from the member states are present at the negotiations but play no active part in them.

In 1960 the Community had to present to its partners in GATT the common external tariff which was to replace the four pre-existing tariffs,[1] and to defend it under the terms of the General Agreement,

[1] The French, German, Italian and Benelux tariffs.

which requires that the average incidence of tariffs in a customs union should not be greater than that of the individual tariffs it replaces. Most of the Contracting Parties to GATT declared themselves satisfied that the common external tariff met these conditions: the Community undertook commitments to others about consultation (in particular towards the United States concerning certain agricultural products for which the national tariffs would be replaced by the provisions of the common farm policy).

The Community took part in the Dillon Round (see p. 196) of multilateral tariff negotiations in GATT held between 1960 and 1962. The aim of these talks was a 10 per cent cut in industrial tariffs and in anticipation of the reductions to be made the Community announced that the first alignment of national tariffs on the common tariff should be made on a common tariff reduced by 20 per cent. In some cases the cuts thus provisionally assumed in the common external tariff were partially or totally confirmed as a result of the negotiation. In other cases alignments continued to be made on the tariff less 20 per cent in anticipation of the outcome of the Kennedy Round (see p. 143) negotiations in GATT.

In May 1963, following President Kennedy's initiative, the Council, on the proposal of the Commission, had formally agreed to take part in the Kennedy Round of tariff and trade negotiations. The negotiations proper opened in Geneva in May 1964 after a year of preparatory work in which attention was concentrated mainly on the problem of 'disparities' between the Community and United States tariffs. This was the name given to cases where the United States tariff was much higher than that of the EEC, so that a linear cut would leave the former highly protective whilst rendering the latter ineffective.

In December 1963 the Council approved general negotiating directives for the Commission for both the industrial and agricultural sectors of the forthcoming negotiations. On the industrial side a common approach was agreed on the 'disparities' problem and a commitment was undertaken to give special attention to the interests of the Community's major European trading partners. On the agricultural side the Council agreed that the Community should propose a new system of discipline in international agricultural trade, similar to that existing for industrial goods. The effect of all national agricultural policy measures in terms of support for their farmers would be determined by measuring the difference between a world reference price and the income ensured to the farmer. This gap would be 'bound' and any increase in support would have to be negotiated against concessions in other fields. Every three years there would be a general negotiation covering the whole agricultural sector and intended to reduce the obstacles to trade. This plan was of course linked internally to progress with the Community's own agricultural policy, since, without the setting of common price levels, the Community would have no policy on which to negotiate.

In the autumn of 1964 the Council issued a further directive to the Commission containing the list of 'exceptions' from tariff cutting which the Community would seek at the Geneva negotiations. The preparation of this list was a good instance of the Community method. The EEC Commission first consulted the representatives of all sectors of industry through their organisations at the European level, refusing to consult with purely national organisations. It then ascertained the wishes of the governments. Finally it drew up its own list of exceptions in the light of these consultations. To meet the deadline set for the presentation of the exceptions list in GATT the Council sat until 7.20 a.m. The original list proposed by the Commission was considerably lengthened, though it still fell short of the list that would have resulted from the straight addition of national demands. Following the adoption of the Mansholt Plan[1] for common grain prices the Community was able, in May 1966, to table proposals for a world grain agreement, and in July 1966 after internal decisions on price levels, offers were made in most of the rest of the agricultural sector.[2]

TRADE AGREEMENTS

The requirements for a common commercial policy go beyond the field of tariffs. Article 112 of the Treaty requires the gradual harmonisation of export aids by the end of the transitional period, to the extent needed to ensure that competition between firms in the Community is not distorted. The Council, acting on proposals from

[1] So named after the Dutch member of the Commission principally responsible for agriculture.

[2] The negotiations were successfully concluded in May 1967 and cuts in duties on industrial trade averaging nearly 35 per cent were agreed upon. During the closing months the Council of Ministers gave the EEC Commission greater discretion in the conduct of the negotiations, and on the eve of the final round of bargaining in Geneva empowered it to conclude an agreement. The outcome of the Kennedy Round cannot be assessed here. It should be noted however that the Community's plan for a world agreement on agriculture was turned down by the United States; the Contracting Parties accepted only a limited scheme for food aid to the developing countries.

the Commission, is empowered to issue directives to this end by majority vote after the beginning of the third stage.

The full implementation of the common policy is not required until after the end of the transitional period, when 'the common commercial policy shall be based on uniform principles, particularly in regard to tariff amendments, the conclusion of tariff or trade agreements, the alignment of measures of liberalisation, export policy and protective commercial measures to be taken in cases of dumping or subsidies.' It is laid down that 'where agreements with third countries require to be negotiated, the Commission shall make recommendations to the Council which will authorise the Commission to open the negotiations'. The Commission is also charged with the conduct of the negotiations. After the end of the transitional period all the necessary decisions involved in this procedure can be taken by a weighted majority. In addition, Article 114 lays down that during the third stage of the transitional period the Council, in concluding both trade and tariff agreements on behalf of the Community, may apply the majority rule.

The interim steps towards a common commercial policy, which clearly cannot be brought into being overnight at the end of the transitional period, have proved difficult to take. This is the area of policy where the requirements of an economic union overlap most clearly with questions of foreign policy, which remain the prerogative of the national governments, and the lack of progress towards a political union has not helped in creating a willingness to work towards a genuine common policy in trade matters, particularly where relations with Eastern Europe are concerned. In October 1960, the Council adopted a regulation requiring member states to engage in prior consultations with their partners and the Commission before concluding or renewing a trade agreement. In addition, no new agreement could outrun the end of the transitional period, and any agreement extending beyond the end of 1965 should contain either a 'Community clause' permitting any revision made necessary to conform to Community policy, or an annual revision clause. The obligation to consult has been largely, though not entirely, respected, but some member countries have been obliged to seek derogations from the 'Community clause' requirement.

In April 1964 the Commission submitted a series of proposals to the Council for moves towards the common commercial policy: these covered common measures of defence against dumping by state-trading countries; a strengthening of the machinery of prior consultation; the negotiation of a Community commercial treaty with Japan; and the establishment of a timetable for the remaining moves to a common commercial policy. Little progress has been made with these proposals in the Council.

It was foreseen that until commercial policies were harmonised, divergences between national policies might lead to the diversion of trade or economic difficulties. Article 115 of the Treaty calls on the Commission to 'recommend the measures where the other member states shall provide the necessary co-operation'. It also allows the Commission to authorise the member states to take 'the necessary protective measures', the details of which the Commission is left to determine. This clause of Article 115 has in fact been regularly used by member states to counter the trade deflection resulting from differences in commercial policies towards state-trading and low-cost countries. In 1966 Article 115 was being invoked for some hundred products. Each request for its application must be renewed periodically.

Until the application of the common commercial policy the Treaty requires only that 'member states consult with each other with a view to concerting their action and as far as possible adopting a uniform attitude'. Progress along these lines has been checked by the reluctance of the member states to accept any limitation of their freedom in fields not specifically covered by the Treaty—in particular technical and financial assistance. Thus in the United Nations Conference on Trade and Development in 1964, the member states were separately represented, whilst the Community as such had only observer status. The Commission proposed the establishment of a common line of action to the Council but discussions in this body failed to yield agreement. In the work of the permanent bodies created by the Conference the positions of the member countries have, however, been partly co-ordinated.

There is a formal requirement in Article 116 that, after the end of the transitional period, the 'member states shall in respect of all matters of particular interest in regard to the Common Market, within the framework of any international organisations of an economic character only proceed by way of common action'.

The Commission has taken part from the start in the work of OECD, where it has the status of observer, and it has a permanent liaison office with the OECD Secretariat in Paris. Co-ordinating meetings are held by the delegations of the Six, together with representatives of the Commission, on the eve of most OECD meetings.

MEMBERSHIP: NEGOTIATIONS WITH BRITAIN, DENMARK, NORWAY AND IRELAND

In the preamble to the Treaty the member states call upon the peoples of Europe who share their ideal to join in their efforts. Article 237 of the Treaty states that: 'Any European state may apply to become a member of the Community', and rules that the decision to admit a new member shall be taken by the Council by unanimous vote after obtaining the opinion of the Commission. At the time of the negotiations on the Rome Treaty, as of the earlier ones on the Treaty of Paris establishing the ECSC, the Six had envisaged other European countries joining them: in 1957 British observers were withdrawn from the preparatory talks when it became clear that a prior commitment was required to a supranational form of co-operation. The German Bundestag, in ratifying the Treaty, insisted on the need for the Community to remain open to new members.

The first application for membership came from Britain, and was made in August 1961. It followed a period of exploratory diplomatic contacts in the latter part of 1960, which confirmed that the way was open. Britain informed her EFTA partners at a meeting of the EFTA Council in Geneva in July 1961. An application for membership by Denmark followed the British one in August and Norway followed suit after a full and vigorous debate in the country and in the Storting. The Republic of Ireland applied almost simultaneously with Britain. The EFTA Council having stated that no member of EFTA would agree to an arrangement with the Community unless a satisfactory solution was found for all its partners, the three neutral members, Austria, Sweden and Switzerland, after concerting their attitudes, made separate applications for association under Article 238 in September 1961.

The British application was considered by the Council of Ministers and was formally accepted in September. The Council debated at length the method of negotiation to be adopted. The idea of entrusting the Commission with the conduct of the negotiations was rejected, as was that of appointing a single supervisory chairman to preside over them. Instead, the formula adopted, mainly at French insistence, was that of a separate intergovernmental conference at which all seven countries took part, the Commission also being present. The negotiations were formally opened in Paris in October 1961, Mr Edward Heath, then Lord Privy Seal, leading the British delegation.

Whilst Britain was prepared to accept the Rome Treaty, and also to subscribe to the political aims of the Community, three main problems had to be solved: the fate of Britain's relations with the Commonwealth; the means of phasing the British agricultural system into that of the Community; and a solution for Britain's EFTA partners. Constitutional problems were left to be settled at the end.

Before negotiations proper could begin, some five months were spent in detailed work defining and grouping the problems to be solved, particularly those concerning relations with the Commonwealth. The length of this period of pre-negotiation had been justified on the grounds that it led to improved understanding on both sides: by the British side of the motives underlying the Six's refusal to accept certain demands for exceptions to Community rules, such as the permanent maintenance of preferential treatment to countries outside; and by the Six of the nature and significance of the Commonwealth. The start of work on the agricultural part of the negotiations was delayed until February 1962 since the Six wished to agree first on the basic elements of their own common agricultural policy.

Major progress in the negotiations was made in May 1962 when it became clear that Britain could accept the provisions of the Treaty relating to economic union and the texts approved up to that time by the Council. In June the conference agreed—all agreements being provisional and subject to the overall success of the negotiations —on arrangements for the Commonwealth: the gradual phasing out of the 'Commonwealth preference' accorded by Britain to Australia, Canada and New Zealand on industrial products; an offer to Commonwealth countries in Africa and the West Indies of association with the enlarged Community on terms corresponding to those outlined in the Yaoundé Convention which was being negotiated at that time; and the offer of an overall trade and aid agreement to be concluded between the enlarged Community and India, Pakistan and Ceylon. The problem of imports of temperate foodstuffs from the Commonwealth countries was a key one. At the outset Britain wished to obtain assured outlets for these products, and on their side the Six refuted any possibility of granting quantitative guarantees, on the grounds that this was not possible under the machinery of the common agricultural policy. The bases of an agreement were found at the beginning of August, in terms of a commitment that the enlarged Community would take the initiative in negotiating world agreements, but its significance was marred by a dispute amongst the Six over the commitment that levies on imports would be paid to the Community at the end of the transitional period. No solution was found to the special problem of guarantees about export markets for New Zealand butter. In June a first step had been made towards agreement over agricultural policy with the acceptance by the Six of the notion of an annual farm review.

Negotiations were resumed in October, following the Commonwealth Conference and the Conservative Party Conference, both of which approved the policy of the British Government (after hotly contested debates and only after the Government, especially in the Commonwealth Conference, had exerted strong pressure). The negotiations hung fire in the agricultural sector, though progress was made on minor aspects of the Commonwealth problem. Britain had already accepted the basic principles of the Community's common agricultural policy, and the negotiations concerned the timing and methods for the transfer from the British system of deficiency payments to farmers to the Community system of prices set to ensure the farmer a fair income.

At the end of the year a full study of the agricultural problem was prepared and the ministers were starting a two-week session intended to solve the major outstanding problems, particularly agricultural ones, when, on 14 January 1963, President de Gaulle in a press conference indicated that in his view Britain was not yet ready for membership of the EEC. The negotiations continued until 16 January when the French Foreign Minister, M. Maurice Couve de Murville, called for them to be suspended on the grounds that they could not succeed. This view was disputed by France's partners and by the EEC Commission, but a final session of the Six failed to yield any concession from France, and since unanimity was required to complete the negotiations, they were formally suspended on 29 January 1963. Negotiations on British membership of the ECSC, which had opened in the meantime, were suspended, as were those for membership of Euratom.

Negotiations on the Danish application for membership had started and rapid progress had been made, so that they had reached a stage when the final problems could be quickly solved once the outcome of the negotiations with Britain was assured. No formal decision was taken but the Danish negotiations were considered as suspended after January 1963. The same applied to the negotiations with Norway, which had also progressed rapidly. Formal talks had hardly begun on the Irish application for membership, which was also suspended. The same applied to the three applications for association. In all of them a first round of talks to ascertain the problems to be solved had taken place between the EEC Commission and a delegation from the country concerned, and on this basis the Commission had reported to the Council, but no formal negotiations had opened. Applications had also been received from Portugal—though with no clear indication of what arrangement was sought—and from Spain.

No commentary is required here on the real or alleged motives for the French refusal to continue the talks with Britain.[1] The following quotation concerning the stage reached in the negotiations is taken from the speech made by Professor Hallstein, President of the EEC Commission, to the European Parliament in March 1963: 'It is not possible to say of the negotiations at the moment when they were interrupted that they had in practice failed, or to say that it had been proved that they could succeed.' In general, however, it was felt by all those taking part, with the exception of the French delegation, that there was every chance of reaching a successful conclusion if the negotiations were to be pursued.[2]

ASSOCIATION WITH EUROPEAN AND NEIGHBOURING COUNTRIES

Article 238 of the Rome Treaty offers the possibility of association with the Community for a non-member country (or a union of states or an international organisation). It is not restricted, as is membership, to European countries. Such associations, which are to embody 'reciprocal rights and obligations, joint actions and special procedures' are to be concluded by the Council by unanimous vote, after consulting the European Parliament. It is accepted that all such associations are to be negotiated by the Commission under a mandate from the Council. No indication at all is given concerning the nature of association.

(*a*) *Austria*

In July 1963 Austria, with the consent of its EFTA partners, renewed her application for association with the Community.

[1] Various theories on this subject can be studied in Nora Beloff, *The General Says No*, Penguin, 1963; Robert Kleiman, *Atlantic Crisis*, New York, W. W. Norton & Co., 1964; Miriam Camps, *Britain and the European Community, 1955–1963*, Princeton, Princeton University Press, 1964.

[2] A renewed British approach to join the Community was made in May 1967. It differed from the 1961 approach in being a formal application for membership under Article 237 rather than a request for negotiations to see whether membership was possible. On the same day a new Danish application was made and the Irish application renewed. Norway applied again for membership in July 1967, and the Swedish government asked for an arrangement compatible with Swedish neutrality.

Exploratory talks were held in the autumn of that year between Austria and the Commission. The principle of negotiating with Austria was approved by the Council in June 1964 but no agreement proved possible on the terms of a negotiating mandate to the Commission until March 1965. Formal negotiations began on the basis of a partial mandate in May 1965 and five rounds of negotiations were held in the period up to February 1966. An extension of the Commission's mandate was granted at the end of 1966.

The main problems to be solved are those posed by Article 4 of the State Treaty of 1955, which lays down that Austria must not enter into any form of economic union ('*Anschluss*') with the Federal Republic of Germany,[1] and by Austria's status of neutrality. This was unilaterally declared but constituted a condition of the withdrawal of Soviet forces from Austria in 1955 and was guaranteed in the State Treaty of that year. The Austrian Government considers that Austria's neutrality precludes it from accepting the political commitments and the degree of supranationality involved in full membership of the EEC. Austria expressed its willingness to accept as far as possible the provisions of economic union with the Community whilst keeping a measure of independence in the field of commercial policy. It is also necessary to find a solution in the agricultural sector, where the supranational character of the common agricultural policy rules out direct Austrian participation. There appear to be no major objections to Austrian association on the part of the member countries.[2]

(*b*) *Greece*

Greece was the first non-member country to apply for association under the terms of Article 238 in June 1959, on finding itself excluded not only from the EEC but also from the European Free Trade Association which was being formed at that time. After exploratory talks and negotiations which were protracted and difficult, a Treaty of Association was concluded in July 1961 and came into effect in November 1962. It provides for the establishment of a customs union with the Community over an extended transitional period of twenty-two years, although Community tariffs are to be cut towards Greece at the same rate as intra-Community trade. Economic policies are to be gradually harmonised over this longer

[1] A difficulty which has been aggravated by Soviet hints that links with the EEC would constitute a 'union' with the separate members of the community.

[2] Although the vexed problems of the South Tyrol still bedevils Austria's relations with Italy.

period, and the prospect of eventual full membership is specifically held out, Greece having emphasised its complete readiness to accept the political implications. The Community agreed to grant $125 million over a five-year period towards the development of a Greek economy, and this money is being made available through the European Investment Bank. The Treaty sets up a Council of Association at ministerial level, which meets at least once a year; there is also a Parliamentary Committee of Association.

The reduction of customs duties on Greek exports to the EEC has been to some extent reflected in the trade figures. The major problem of the association has proved to be the harmonisation of agricultural policies. This is provided for in the Treaty of Association, although without any time limits, and Greece sought an immediate move. The Community refused, however, to envisage Greek participation in the complex decision-making procedure of the common agricultural policy and proposed, instead, a gradual increase in preferential treatment for Greek agriculture as Greek policy became autonomously aligned on that of the Community.

(*c*) *Turkey*

The Turkish application for association followed that of Greece, in July 1959. Exploratory talks were temporarily suspended in 1960 owing to the military coup in Turkey. The agreement which was concluded in 1963 and came into effect in 1965 reflects a more cautious approach on the part of the Community, in the light of its experience in the Greek case. The Treaty provides that during a preparatory period lasting five years (with the possibility of extension to nine years or even longer) Turkey shall be assisted by the Community to reach a position where it can accept the responsibilities of a customs union. The Community grants Turkey tariff quotas at reduced rates of participation in duty for four of her key products (raw tobacco, raisins, dried figs and nuts) amounting to nearly 40 per cent of her exports to the Six, and makes available $175 million in loans through the European Investment Bank. The 'transitional period', similar to that provided for in the Greek association and involving both a customs union and measures of economic union (the details of which are to be worked out later), will start only when the preparatory period is complete, and will last for twelve years. The possibility of eventual membership is left open.

(*d*) *Algeria, Morocco and Tunisia*

At the time of the signature of the Treaty of Rome, Algeria was legally a part of metropolitan France, and most of the Treaty provisions applied to it (free movement of workers being a major exception). Morocco and Tunisia, former colonies, had special arrangements with France, and a protocol annexed to the Treaty conferred on them the right to apply to negotiate an association with the Community. This right was finally taken up in 1964 when Morocco and Tunisia both applied to negotiate an association and Algeria followed suit. Exploratory talks took place with all three Maghreb countries during the latter part of 1964. In June 1965 the Council agreed on a partial mandate to the Commission, enabling formal negotiations to be begun with Morocco and Tunisia. A full mandate awaited the completion of the common market regulation for fruit and vegetables.

It has become evident that the Community's relations with the different Mediterranean countries cannot be dealt with in isolation. An Italian memorandum presented at the Council in 1964 stressed that the products of these countries are competitive with those of Italy, and that concessions made to them in the framework of associations or other trading arrangements could undermine the advantages which had been counted on by Italy in agreeing to join the common market. Italy called for an overall policy on external relations under which association would be open only to those countries which were potential full members, nothing more than trade agreements being possible with other countries.

Association has, however, been represented as being the most effective framework within which to aid the Community's southern neighbours—and in the case of Morocco and Tunisia there is a prior commitment. It seems likely that the solution will take the form of a free trade area.

NON-DISCRIMINATORY TRADE AGREEMENTS: IRAN, ISRAEL, LEBANON

Other Mediterranean countries have also sought to solve the special problems of their trade relations with the Community, and where the association formula was not sought or was not practicable, non-discriminatory trade agreements have been concluded. These have been in each case negotiated by a Community delegation consisting of representatives of the Commission and of the member states, and since they covered some matters within the domain of the Community and others within the competence of the member states, have been concluded with both the Community and its individual member states.

The agreement with Iran, which came into force in 1963, provides for the granting by the Community of tariff quotas at reduced duty for a number of goods produced in Iran.

These quotas are non-discriminatory, in other words they are open to all countries enjoying most-favoured-nation treatment from the Community, but they will primarily benefit Iran. A Joint Committee set up under the agreement watches over trends in trade between Iran and the Community and takes any necessary decisions on the application of the agreement.

Israel was one of the first countries to seek an arrangement with the Community. As a country with a widely diversified economy dependent on agriculture and on light industry, Israel saw its exports threatened by the development of free trade within the Community. Lengthy and difficult negotiations led to the signing of a trade agreement in 1964. This fell far short of Israel's hopes and has been criticised as unsatisfactory by members of the Israel Government and the Knesset. It provided for various measures (partial suspension of the common external tariff, or speeding up of alignment on the tariff by countries with national tariff levels above it, or both) to cover a very limited list of tariff headings selected to benefit Israel. A protocol ensured Israel's right to consultation in the event of an association agreement between the Community and other major producers of oranges. The Agreement established a Joint Committee with similar tasks to that set up by the Iran agreement. Israel made it clear that it wished to consider this agreement as only a beginning and that the long-run solution it seeks is association with the Community. In October 1966 a formal application was made for association under Article 238.

The agreement signed with the Lebanon in 1965 constituted a new departure for the Community in that it covers technical assistance as well as trade. In fact there was little scope for aiding the Lebanon by trade concessions, although the agreement does ensure that this country, which is not a member of GATT, will receive most-favoured-nation treatment from the Community in the future. The important element in the agreement is a commitment by the Community to co-ordinate technical assistance by member countries and to increase its overall volume. A Joint Committee is set up to supervise the working of the agreement.

THE CASE OF SPAIN

During the course of the negotiations with Britain, Spain made an application for association with the Community. In February 1964, it reminded the Council of this application and stressed its desire to pursue it. After a debate in the Council in which institutional links of any kind were opposed by some member countries on account of the non-democratic nature of the present Spanish regime, the Commission was instructed to open talks with Spain and did so on the understanding that the arrangement to be made could not in the present circumstances go beyond a non-discriminatory trade agreement. A first round of talks in December 1964 was followed by an exchange of memoranda and factual information during 1965, and in July 1966 the Council asked for a report from the Commission on possible solutions. By the end of 1966 it had been agreed, however, to give the Commission a partial mandate to begin negotiations for a preferential agreement.

LATIN AMERICA

In general the Latin American countries were critical of the Community in its early years, and, particularly within the framework of GATT, maintained that the preferences accorded to the associated African countries by the EEC would be harmful to their own trade with the member countries. The Community defended its policies by claiming that the rapid expansion of the Community economy, due in part to the creation of the Common Market, was resulting in a marked increase in imports from the Latin American countries.

In the summer and autumn of 1963, in response to an initiative of the Latin American countries, a series of consultations were held between the Commission and the diplomatic representatives of the Latin American countries to the Community. The Commission made proposals to the Council about the possible general lines of an overall policy towards Latin America but the Council took no action on this. In 1965 and 1966 a second round of consultations with the Latin American ambassadors took place with the aim of isolating any trade problems.

ASIAN COUNTRIES

The Community has not developed formal relations with Asian countries. Following the breakdown of the negotiations for British membership the Commission proposed to the Council that the Community should conclude with India and Pakistan the kind of overall agreements which had been envisaged within the framework of an enlarged Community. This did not meet with the agreement of the Council. In 1964, in response to Indian requests, a number of minor tariff measures were undertaken unilaterally for products which had been scheduled for cuts in the negotiations with Britain. In 1963 Britain and the Community mutually agreed to suspend their tariffs on tea and tropical hardwoods from third countries.

RELATIONS WITH THE UNITED STATES

The United States has given the Communities its fullest support and approval from the start. President Kennedy's championship of the idea of partnership was widely welcomed in the EEC, and the President of the EEC Commission, Professor Hallstein, was one of the leading exponents of the concept. The original assumption had been that Britain and several other countries were to become members of the Community, whilst others would be associated with it. The breakdown of the negotiations on British membership and the continuing basic differences of opinion between the member countries both about the creation of a political union and the relations between Europe and the United States have prevented any concrete development of the partnership theme.

Historical Summary

During the first nine years of the existence of the European Economic Community, the ambitious aim of merging the economies of the six member countries into an economic union has progressed rapidly and successfully. This progress has tended to take place on two planes.

Gradual implementation of the provisions of the Rome Treaty has gone forward on a wide front: in some cases it has proved possible to move ahead of the Treaty schedule, in others—on the whole less significant—there has been delay because of the extreme technicality of the problems involved or of fundamental political problems. This process has involved a growing number of national civil servants, businessmen and experts in the elaboration or the application of the necessary measures, and there has been an increasing readiness to admit the need for a change in divergent national practices to fit them into a harmonised Community framework.

The positive climate in which the Treaty has been applied is reflected on the one hand in the fact that there have been very few infringements resulting from active attempts to evade its obligations, and on the other by the lack of organised opposition to the implications of the common market from any sector of economic opinion.

The second plane on which progress has occurred is that of

periodical leaps forward, with difficult and long-drawn-out negotiations leading to the acceptance by member governments of important new commitments to the Community system. Such negotiations have always had a positive outcome, not possible without an overall commitment to the Community undertaking. The crisis which came to a head on 30 June 1965, and delayed the work of the EEC until the beginning of February 1966, arose over divergences of a political nature, rather than from a fundamental inability to agree on the particular economic issues under debate; the economic issues were to be resolved little over a year later.

The detailed account of the Community given above can perhaps best be set in perspective by recalling briefly the major steps of the first nine years. The first of these was the decision taken in May 1959, less than a year and a half after the first tariff cuts, to speed up the rate at which the customs union would be achieved. It was at the end of 1961 that the method of a 'package deal', in which a series of politically difficult decisions came to be grouped, first emerged. On that occasion the bases of the common agricultural policy had to be agreed by the end of 1962 in order to ensure the 'balanced progress' that was required as a condition of moving from the first to the second stage. The 'stopping of the clock' at midnight on 31 December, to enable the decision to be formally taken by the end of the year, symbolised the will of the member governments to succeed in their negotiations. Another major success of the Community in 1962 was the re-negotiation of the Convention of Association with the independent African countries.

It was during 1961 that the applications for membership from Britain and other countries showed the extent to which the success and permanence of the Community had already been accepted by the outside world. Nevertheless, the talks on political union which took place during the autumn and spring of 1961 to 1962 ended in deadlock, a reminder that whilst economic union was progressing a fundamental divergence existed about eventual political union.

The shock of the French veto on British membership, an act contrary to the newly established tradition of mutual consultation and joint action, briefly threatened to hold up the progress of the Community. In the event the mutual interest of all six partners in its progress was such that work was rapidly resumed and a second 'marathon' session in December 1963 yielded agreement on a major extension of the common agricultural policy machinery. At the same time a compromise on the Community's basic policy in the Kennedy Round of tariff negotiations at Geneva emphasised that outside demands and pressures were obliging the Six to act as a unit. There followed, within months, a series of decisions laying some of the foundations for the co-ordination of short-term economic policies and the development of a medium-term economic programme.

The agreement on the 'Mansholt Plan' for common grain prices, achieved at the end of 1964, represented a joint commitment, requiring political courage from several governments, to major economic changes even though these were to take effect at a point well in the future. It was an important step towards the creation of an economic union.

With that goal in sight it was perhaps inevitable that the latent political clash about the future of the Community in terms of its democratic and political structure should come into the open. For the crisis which occurred in the Community in 1965 and the early part of 1966 was of a different nature from the difficulties which had arisen on earlier occasions over the bigger steps towards economic union. It can best be characterised as a constitutional crisis, since what was directly at stake was the functioning of the Community decision-making machinery as laid down in the Treaty. It was a first round in the basic conflict, latent for many years, between the advocates of integration and a federal union on the one hand and the defenders of national sovereignty and an intergovernmental or confederal political solution on the other. The imminence of two vital and irrevocable steps made an open clash hard to avoid. On the one hand the decision on the financing of the common agricultural policy, due to be taken by 30 June 1965, would imply an open-ended commitment to pay into the common fund, whose major beneficiary for the foreseeable future would be France, sums amounting to over $2,000 million a year. In addition, the Council's 1962 decision provided that, with the completion of the agricultural policy, the income from levies should go directly into the fund, and the Treaty provided for customs duties also to form direct revenues from the time the common external tariff came fully into effect. Thus there would be the beginnings of a federal budget, in other words revenues not contributed by the member governments would accrue directly to the Community, and the Community decision-making procedure would extend to sums controlled neither by the national parliaments (although subtracted from national revenues) nor, effectively, by the European Parliament. There was a natural desire on the part of many of the Community's supporters to obtain at that time at least the first guarantees of a move to a federal Community with an effective voice for the European Parliament in the budgetary procedure. This was the requirement which the Dutch Parliament, in December 1964, imposed for any agreement by the Dutch Government to the financing system.

The second major move would come with the passage (automatic unless the Commission should propose and the Council unanimously decide otherwise) into the third stage. This would mean the generalised application (except concerning a limited number of reserved issues) of the rule allowing majority voting which is fundamental to the Treaty. It was predictable that this formal surrender of the national right of veto would meet with opposition from General de Gaulle.

When the French boycott of Community institutions began, it was ostensibly in protest against the failure of the Council to agree by the deadline of 30 June on the new financial provisions. This failure was itself the result partly of a lack of time but also of the French refusal to accept the link between the three elements of the Commission's proposals: the financing of agricultural policy, the creation of direct revenue, and a stronger voice for the Parliament. Not content with obtaining the postponement of the latter issues to 1970, the French delegation wished no reference to be made to them, whilst the other countries backed the Commission in insisting that decisions on the three matters be linked.

It emerged subsequently from the press conference given on 9 September by the French President, that he was in fact seeking as a condition of further French co-operation in the forward progress of the Community[1] a revision of the Treaty which would perpetuate the national veto on matters which member governments considered to be of vital interest. In addition, provoked by the action of the Commission in linking matters of political significance with the financial settlement, he was seeking to have the powers of the Commission reduced in an undefined way.

Throughout the crisis, and in the final settlement, France's partners refused to accept the re-introduction of the national veto. They maintained that in the Community there was in practice no danger of a country being put in a minority on a matter of vital national interest: majority voting was on the other hand an essential instrument for the effective functioning of the decision-making machinery. Political and economic pressures inside France combined to rule out an indefinite maintenance of the boycott (faced with which the five might have made use of their right to take decisions in

[1] The boycott did not extend to the day-to-day management of already existing Community regulations or politics.

the absence of France), and France was obliged to return to the Council table. The formula finally worked out in Luxembourg amounted to 'an agreement to disagree': a re-statement of their position by the five countries and a unilateral declaration by France to the effect that majority decisions should not be taken on matters of vital national interest. The issue of the role of the Commission proved to be largely a hollow one, the five refusing any substantial limitation of the Commission's powers as defined in the Treaty. Agreement was reached on a list of seven points, to be discussed between the Council and the Commission, where relations between the two bodies might be improved.

In retrospect, a number of points in the way the crisis developed are revealing as to the nature of the Community. A major turning point was clearly the decision of the five countries to ensure that the Community institutional machinery continued to function. The Community is essentially a legal creation, dependent on respect for obligations, and the feeling was shared that the other countries must not themselves be drawn into infringing the Treaty. Had meetings of the Council been suspended, a settlement would have had to be sought by traditional diplomatic means outside the Community framework, as was the French aim until the eve of the Luxembourg meetings. The fact that the Council continued to meet enabled the ministers of the 'five' to address themselves to France through the Council and to insist that problems concerning the operation of the Treaties be solved within the Community framework. The success of this tactic was vital to the survival of the Community.

Secondly, the crisis revealed the extent of commitment to the Community system on the part of political and economic groups of all kinds, not least within France. Thus interest groups, including the trade unions, the employers' organisations and the farmers' unions, at the level of the Six, all called for an end to the crisis and respect for the Treaty. Strong pressures were exerted on the French Government both by the farmers and by industrial and financial groups, thus emphasising the vested interest of the French economy in the pursuance of economic integration, and the realisation that the maintenance of the existing Community system was a guarantee of this. Equally significant was the emergence of the European problem as a major issue in the French presidential elections, with the leading opposition candidates challenging not only the French boycott but also the French President's opposition to moves towards a federal solution for Europe.

Thus a crisis which threatened the structure of the Community had the effect both of revealing the degree of commitment to that structure on all sides, and also of confirming both the economic and the legal ties binding the six countries. The clashes over which the crisis arose—about the federal goal and the need for effective democratic control at the European level—have not been solved but postponed. There is an acceptance of the general interest of all concerned in pushing on with economic union.

With the constitutional crisis postponed, if not resolved, the implementation of the Treaty continues. In the six months following the settlement of January 1966, the Council succeeded in taking not only the decisions which had been postponed by the crisis, but others which were linked to them. So far-reaching and complex were the decisions to be taken that they required two successive 'marathon' sessions, one in May and the second in July, with a special additional meeting to settle part of the Commission's mandate for the Kennedy Round negotiations. Only when agreement on the last point was achieved were the solutions worked out at the other two sessions confirmed. The outcome of the decisions was to set 1 July 1968 as a firm deadline on which the Community would achieve not only a full industrial customs union, with no duties on intra-Community trade and the application of the common external tariff, but also free trade in agricultural goods and the application of a common policy, centrally financed, for over 90 per cent of the total agricultural output.

With the customs union fully established and the virtual completion of the farm policy in sight, emphasis can be expected to shift, as it has already begun to do, to the problems of full economic union. The Community medium-term economic programme, annually revised, will provide a framework not only for co-ordinating national economic policies to a growing extent, but also for tackling the problems of industrial policy, research and development, vocational training, regional planning and energy policy at the Community level. With no rules or requirements laid down in the Treaty, the approach and methods will foreseeably follow the pattern developed to date in the co-ordination of national monetary and economic policies.

Conclusions

An operation of the scope and implications of that undertaken by the Six over the past decade could not have been entered upon without a firm political will on the part of all partners. Political commitment to a long-term aim is a necessary condition for the solution of the major problems of economic integration, which will inevitably demand political risks or sacrifices on the part of all the governments.

It may be argued that once the operation is launched the absence of political will to implement the treaties fully on the part of one partner will not reverse the process or even block it for long. The question is an open one. For a certain degree of economic integration a total commitment to federal solutions going beyond the legally binding commitments of the Treaty has not so far proved to be essential. In so far as far-reaching economic integration does have political and federal implications, however, it may be blocked by a country strongly opposed to such developments.

Without the special institutional machinery of the Community, even very considerable political goodwill would not have sufficed. The dialogue between the Commission and the Council is the vital and original element. Other elements (the Parliament and the Court) have so far been less important for the development of the system, though they may take on greater significance in the future.

To charge an independent and essentially political body with defending the interests of the Community as a whole, and ensuring that the aims set out in the Treaty were carried through, was a major development of the institutional method pioneered in the ECSC. Among the main attributes that have enabled the Commission to fulfil this central role have been its right to participate fully in the decision-making process and to defend its proposals in the Council, combined with what amounts in practice to the exclusive right of initiative in the formulation of policies.

It has also been found that the Community's advance often depends on balanced progress as between major sectors of policy; thus agricultural policy had to keep step with the industrial customs union, and commitments about trade policy have been made concurrently with decisions on the internal development of the Community. The EEC has repeatedly shown that movement on one front stimulates demands for progress on another; amongst the most striking examples have been the pressure for co-ordinated anti-inflationary measures that followed the removal of barriers between the national economies, and the effect of the common foodstuff prices (set in a single currency unit) in placing an obstacle in the way of changes in exchange rates which has thus brought monetary union nearer. Other significant examples are to be found where harmonisation of national legislation has proved necessary if the freeing of trade was not to be ineffective.

It is not only in relation to different aspects of economic policy that it has been shown that progress in one sector leads to progress in another, by what has been called the 'spillover' effect. Many 'Europeans' believe that the Economic Community—whose competences cover such a large part of the area of government that the Community may already be said to constitute part of, rather than a step towards, a broad political union—will have to be complemented by the development of Community institutions to ensure common foreign and defence policies. It has even been claimed that this was an automatic process, but the difficulties in securing agreement between General de Gaulle and the governments of the other five countries, together with the 1965–66 crisis in the EEC over the functions of the Parliament and the Commission, have shown that this is an illusion, at least in the short or medium term. The establishment of a union in the foreign policy and defence domains will require a consensus on the part of all member governments not only on the need to take such a step, but also on the form of the new institutions to be set up and in particular on the extent to which the union has federal characteristics.

Meanwhile the steady progress of economic integration is laying the basis of the '*de facto* solidarity' to which Robert Schuman referred in May 1952 as being the first step towards a united Europe. The economic destinies of the member countries have become very closely, perhaps inextricably, linked. Internal and external incentives to create an effective political union are strong and getting stronger. So is the attraction of the Community, even in its present incomplete form, to other European countries. There are strong grounds for thinking that the Community does represent a valid starting point and first stage towards a more complete European union.

Chapter Seven

THE EUROPEAN COAL AND STEEL COMMUNITY

The Origins

The French Government's proposal to pool the resources of the German and French coal and steel industries under a single authority was announced on 9 May 1950 by M. Robert Schuman, then Foreign Minister, though the plan had been drawn up by M. Jean Monnet. The plan for the coal and steel pool was intended to give a new impetus to the movement to European unity. If accepted it would be open to other European countries.

The motives of those who launched this scheme were avowedly political. As Schuman said in his declaration, 'Europe will not be built all at once, or according to a single general plan. It will be built through concrete achievements, which first create a *de facto* solidarity. The gathering together of the nations of Europe requires the elimination of the age-old opposition of France and Germany. The first concern in any action undertaken must be those two countries.' The ultimate aim was the creation of that 'European federation which is indispensable to peace'. The coal and steel sectors were chosen for a first experiment in '*de facto* solidarity' for both political and economic reasons. They were the two industries basic to any war effort—and basic to the modern industrialised economy. As Schuman said in his statement: 'The solidarity in production thus established will make it plain that any war between France and Germany becomes not merely unthinkable but materially impossible.' At the same time, for geographical reasons, the sector lent itself to such an exercise: a very high percentage of Western Europe's coal and steel output was concentrated in a triangle of land covering northern and eastern France, southern Belgium and Holland, the Ruhr, Luxembourg and the Saar.

This desire to build Europe on the basis of a Franco-German

rapprochement was backed on the French side by considerations of national interest. There was considerable fear of an uncontrolled revival of the Ruhr heavy industries, which might in the future once again serve aggressive national policies. Germany shorn of its agricultural lands in the East and flooded with refugees would need an expanding industry. But the Western powers would not continue indefinitely to impose control on the industry of a democratic Western Germany. France was therefore offering to give up full control of her own industries in return for a measure of European control over German industry. It was also felt on the French side that the Saar question, which was becoming once again a cause of tension in Franco–German relations, could best be permanently settled within the framework of an international solution. For Germany, the plan had the obvious immediate advantage of offering a more favourable situation and better prospects for the coal and steel industries than the system of Allied control.

The favourable reaction to the Schuman–Monnet proposals from Belgium, the Federal Republic of Germany, Italy, Luxembourg and the Netherlands reflected above all the climate of readiness for an experiment in European federation which existed at that time, particularly in the Christian Democrat parties of Germany, Italy and France, but also amongst many in other political parties. Italy and the Benelux countries also saw economic advantages, though Belgium required an assurance about special consideration for its backward coal industry.

Negotiations for the Treaty to establish the European Coal and Steel Community were begun in June 1950 by a group under the chairmanship of M. Jean Monnet, and concluded in April 1951. Ratification was completed in July 1952 and the High Authority, the executive body of the new organisation, began its work in the following month.

Both M. Schuman and M. Monnet had wanted Britain to take part in the plan, but the British Government refused the formal invitation which was extended to it to take part in the negotiations, on the grounds that acceptance of a supranational authority was a pre-condition of entering the negotiations. Mr Clement Attlee, the Prime Minister, told the House of Commons:

'We on this side are not prepared to accept the principle that the most vital economic forces of this country should be handed over to an authority that is utterly undemocratic and is responsible to nobody.'

The fact that the ECSC covered only a sector of the economy necessarily imposed limitations, and the experience of the first thirteen years has made it possible to evaluate these clearly. At the beginning two kinds of basic delimitations had to be made: on the one hand the sector to be covered had to be defined, as did the powers to be exercised within this sector. The exact definition of the products constituting the coal and steel sector raised no great difficulty, and a certain flexibility was maintained by the possibility of the Council being able to add others to the list; nevertheless the overall result was a distinction, with no economic justification, between products subject to the Treaty rules and those left under the existing regime. The real problem arose for products competing with coal and steel, and this became acute with the creation of the other two Communities. Thus although coal came under one system, other energy products came under another, yet structural changes occurring only a few years after the ECSC was created made it necessary to formulate policy for the energy sector as a whole.

The other delimitation needed was between the powers allotted to the supranational organisation within the coal and steel sectors and the powers remaining to the governments. The Treaty banned the national governments from imposing any measures which would distort competition (trade barriers, subsidies or discrimination) and in particular laid on them an obligation to facilitate the working of the Community. The institutions of the Community were given certain powers of direct action covering the following fields: guidance of investment decisions; aid to research and the re-adaptation of workers; the authorisation and institution of joint financing machinery for firms; a Community system of production quotas in the event of a manifest crisis; a Community price system based on non-discrimination and the publication of price schedules; prior authorisation of cartels and concentrations and control of 'dominant market positions'. In three major fields few such direct powers were allotted: social policy, where the High Authority nevertheless later initiated much activity; transport policy where it was obliged to rely mainly on persuading the governments to act; and policy on foreign trade in coal and steel where the Community had virtually no powers. Two areas of some importance to the coal and steel sector were not mentioned: the right of mining concessions, and property and establishment rights.

The essential innovation of the ECSC lay not only in the far-reaching nature of the powers transferred to a non-national authority, but also in the nature of the institutions established to carry out its tasks. The fact that only one sector of the economy was concerned, together with the favourable political climate in which the Community was created, accounted for a willingness to grant direct powers of considerable significance and concerning a wide range of matters to a supranational body.

The basic institutional pattern established in the ECSC was reproduced in the EEC and Euratom: an independent executive, the High Authority, representing the interest of the Community as a whole; a Council of Ministers in which the interests of the member countries were represented and defended, and decisions taken on issues of a general or political nature; a parliamentary assembly with mainly consultative status which could, however, in theory, overturn the executive; an advisory body enabling major economic interests to be consulted; and a Court of Justice with final jurisdiction. The six agreed in 1965, in order rationalise the structure of the three Communities, to an institutional merger as well as a merger of the three Treaties (see p. 168).[1]

The Institutions

THE HIGH AUTHORITY

The High Authority has nine members, eight of whom are appointed by a conference of representatives of the member countries, whilst the ninth is co-opted by the existing members. The appointments are for six years, three members being re-appointed every two years. The renewals are made alternately by decision of the Council and by co-option by the High Authority. The appointments of President and Vice-President are made for a two-year period. All members are bound by the Treaty to 'exercise their functions in complete independence, in the general interest of the Community'. There are two members each from Germany and France, and one each from Italy and the three Benelux countries. In practice the power to co-opt has been used to ensure the presence of a member coming from a trade union background. The post of President was occupied first by M. Monnet who, once the operation was launched—and also because he was disillusioned by the slowness of progress towards further integration—handed over to M. René Mayer, who was in turn followed by M. Paul Finet (a co-opted member and an ex-trade

[1] The merger of the High Authority into the combined European Commission took place on 1 July 1967.

unionist), Signor Piero Malvestiti and Signor Dino Del Bo (formerly Italian Minister of Trade).

It is the responsibility of the High Authority, either by direct action or in collaboration with the Council of Ministers, to ensure the implementation of the Treaty. Since the end of the transitional period early in 1958, this has taken the form mainly of policy decisions to respond to new circumstances or to ensure the balanced development of the coal and steel industries. The High Authority can act by means of *decisions*, which indicate both the end to be achieved and the detailed means, and are binding in all respects; by *recommendations*, which are binding as regards the aim but not the means for achieving it; or *opinions*, which are in no way binding.

Fields where the High Authority acts directly are: the Community tax, loans, opinions on investment projects, prices, *ententes* and concentrations, and re-adaptation aid. In order to act in other domains it needs either a 'consenting opinion' or approval from the Council, in some cases by a majority vote, in some cases by unanimous decision. In a few areas the Council can act alone: for instance over the setting of maximum and minimum levels of customs duties.

The High Authority can enforce its decisions by imposing fines for failure to carry them out; it can also fine firms for infringing the rules of the Treaty. Fines have been imposed in a number of cases: for infringement of the price publication rules; for offences against the rules on the Community tax; in connection with the working of the scrap 'perequation' scheme (see p. 274); and for carrying through a concentration without prior approval. Fines may amount to up to 1 per cent of a firm's daily turnover for a limited period; initial fines are light but they are increased in the case of continued infringements. The decisions of the High Authority are prepared by working groups, each composed of three members, but decisions of the High Authority are always collegiate; they may be taken by a straight majority of at least five members. In preparing its decisions the High Authority has traditionally consulted the competent government departments and the organisations representing employers and trade unions at the European level.

THE COUNCIL OF MINISTERS

The Council of Ministers did not figure in the original plans for the Community established by M. Schuman and M. Monnet, but was added to the institutional structure during the negotiations at the request of the Benelux countries. It is composed of one representative of each member country, and meets several times a year in Luxembourg; normally it has been the Ministers for Industry, for Economic Affairs or for Trade who have attended its meetings, but the Foreign Ministers have also been present for major decisions. The Council has its own administrative Secretariat, which since 1958 has been merged with that of the Councils of the EEC and Euratom, and its decisions are prepared by a Co-ordinating Committee (known as COCOR) composed of senior officials from the member countries.

The Council of Ministers developed, particularly in the years before 1958, a 'Community character' of its own, and ministers meeting regularly in the Council framework were prepared to accept measures which they were then hard pressed to defend at home. This phenomenon has been more marked in the ECSC than in the EEC, since in the coal and steel sectors ministers were involved in the operation of a method which was entirely foreign to their cabinet colleagues. The Council thus came to serve as a link between supranational and national policies. The High Authority is represented at Council meetings and is able to present and defend the policies for which it is seeking approval from the Council.

The Council was conceived as a check on the powers of the High Authority in fields where the member governments were not prepared for a complete surrender of their right to influence decisions. In the early years the High Authority was able to dominate the affairs of the Community, partly because of the personalities of M. Monnet and his successor, partly because no major problems arose in which member countries were jealous of their national interests. The balance changed with the emergence of the major crisis on the coal market, when the High Authority failed to obtain the agreement of the Council to Community measures. Also, as the Community has developed, the High Authority has extended its action in fields such as social policy, where it had few direct powers conferred upon it by the Treaty, and had to seek approval from the Council, whilst serious problems have arisen in fields such as commercial policy, where only the Council could take decisions. Progress then became dependent upon the unanimous agreement of the Council and hence on the political will of each member government and their readiness to compromise. Some Council decisions may be taken by a weighted majority, in which case the votes are weighted to take account of national coal and steel output, and a certain percentage of total Community output must be represented for a measure to be adopted. But this procedure has been little used.

The lack of effective majority voting system in those domains which were covered by the Treaty but where the High Authority needed the approval of the Council was a major handicap which has made it difficult for the ECSC to deal with the critical weaknesses that have arisen during recent years in the coal and steel markets. In retrospect there is an irony in the fact that the authors of a Treaty granting effective supranational powers should at the same time have been so chary of the majority voting system in the sectors they had reserved to be decided by their national representatives in the Council.

THE EUROPEAN PARLIAMENT

The Treaty creating the Coal and Steel Community provided for the establishment of a 'Common Assembly' with seventy-eight members (eighteen each from France, Germany and Italy, ten from Belgium and the Netherlands and four from Luxembourg). Members were chosen from the national parliaments, though the Treaty provided for the eventual holding of direct elections. In 1958 the Common Assembly doubled its membership and became the joint assembly of the three Communities: the European Parliament, whose present functioning and role are described above (pp. 177–85).

Both before and after its transformation into the European Parliament, the ECSC's Assembly has had an essentially consultative role: its only direct power over the High Authority is to pass a vote of censure on the annual general report, which can force the High Authority to resign. It also has an indirect voice, through its President's participation in the Committee of Four Presidents (of the High Authority, the Council, the Parliament and the Court), in deciding the Community budget; and in the 'little revision' procedure—which permits limited changes in the Treaty with the agreement of High Authority, Council and Assembly and the approval of the Court—it can be said to play a genuine, if limited, legislative role. From the start, the Assembly tended to be critical of the High Authority more for what it was failing to do than for what it was doing. It has always given the High Authority its full support in interpreting its powers under the Treaty as broadly as possible, and has urged it, on many occasions, to extend its action, particularly in the field of social policy.

THE CONSULTATIVE COMMITTEE

The Consultative Committee does not have the official status of a Community institution but the High Authority is obliged to obtain its opinion on most matters and often does so on other questions where the consultation is not compulsory. The Committee consists of up to fifty-one members, appointed by the Council of Ministers, and chosen to represent producers', users' and workers' organisations in the different sectors coming under the Treaty. Its deliberations are prepared by a series of sub-committees. The ready direct access to the High Authority enjoyed by interest groups has necessarily diminished the importance of the Committee in determining policy: within the Committee only the trade union members have tended to act as a coherent group.

THE COURT OF JUSTICE

The Court of Justice set up under the ECSC Treaty became, in 1958, the Court of Justice of the three Communities (see p. 187). Its structure of seven judges and two advocates general was not changed.

The Court has played an extremely important role in the history of the ECSC. It provides a necessary juridical check upon the action of the High Authority, governments and individual firms, and its judgements are binding on all firms coming under the Treaty, as well as upon the High Authority and upon governments. They can be enforced by penalties in the same way as the decisions of the High Authority. The role of the Court was bound to be considerable under a Treaty setting out detailed rules, and its decisions on the interpretation of these rules could not fail to have considerable economic consequences. From the start the Court interpreted its responsibilities broadly. Its rulings took into account the general economic aims and principles of the Treaty as set out in the early Articles of the Treaty, as well as the exact texts of the particular clauses invoked in any particular case.

The most striking illustration of the power and authority of the Court was the case of the proposed revision of Article 69 of the Treaty, to allow a more flexible approach to cartels in the coal-mining industry in response to the fundamentally changed competitive situation in that sector. (The case is explained in greater detail on p. 227.) The High Authority and the Council of Ministers were agreed upon a revised text of Article 69 which they hoped to have adopted by the procedure of the 'little revision'. Despite the arguments presented by the High Authority and the Council, and the favourable vote in the Assembly, the Court felt obliged to rule that the proposed changes were too great to be considered as a 'little revision'. The search had then to begin again for a method of adapting the Treaty rules to the changed situation.

A number of the Court's judgements have upheld decisions of the High Authority against appeals from firms or member governments. Thus in March 1955 the Court rejected the Dutch Government's appeal against three decisions, the effect of which was to maintain the system of keeping a ceiling on prices for coal from the Ruhr and from the Nord-Pas de Calais fields sold within the common market. On other occasions, the High Authority has been obliged by a Court ruling to reverse its decisions: thus the Court upheld appeals by the Italian steel manufacturers' associations backed by the Italian and French Governments, against a High Authority decision to relax the enforcement of its 'fair trading code' requiring the sale of steel at published rates. Many court cases arose over the scrap 'perequation' system, and whilst appeals against the principle failed, the High Authority's delegation of powers of execution to private bodies for the running of the system was ruled to be incompatible with the Treaty.

FINANCE

The activities of the Coal and Steel Community are financed from a direct levy on the business turnover of firms producing coal and steel. The levy is set by the High Authority after consulting the Parliament and the Council, whose assenting opinion by a two-thirds majority is required if it is to exceed 1 per cent. In fact the levy was set at the beginning at 0·9 per cent and has fallen steadily, standing during 1965 at 0·25 per cent. The possession of its own independent financial resources was an important element in assuring the High Authority's political independence and freedom of action. It became of considerable importance when, to meet the coal crisis, the High Authority was obliged to exploit general Treaty provisions and could then use its own funds to make its action effective: grants to Belgian miners and grants for the holding of stocks at the pitheads came from the proceeds of the levy. Much of the proceeds of the levy were devoted by the High Authority in the early years of the Community to the creation of a reserve fund of $100 million which then served as security enabling the Community to establish adequate credit to borrow on the international money markets as well as within the Community. In 1965 the Community budget totalled some $36 million.

The Work of ECSC

THE TRANSITIONAL PERIOD

The fundamental and immediate economic aim of the ECSC was the creation of a single market for coal, coke, iron ore, scrap iron, pig-iron and steel throughout the territory of the member states. This meant not only the removal of trade barriers—both customs and quotas—and the elimination of all forms of price discrimination, in transport as well as in the basic products, but also ensuring fair and undistorted competition under strict rules, by removing both private and governmental restrictions, so that the common market led to increased supplies and lower prices.

This was a formidable task, in a sector of the economy where firms had long enjoyed the whole range of protection offered by tariffs, quotas, exchange controls and discriminatory pricing on freight rates, as well as the advantages to be obtained from cartels and concentrations controlling production and distribution. Clearly it was not to be rapidly achieved. The Paris Treaty set out the rules by which the common market is to be regulated and maintained, whilst Article 85 indicated that the ways and means of implementing the common market were to be established in an annexed Convention.

This Convention lays down the conditions for 'ensuring the gradual adaptation of the units of production to the new conditions' thus created, 'whilst at the same time facilitating the disappearance of the disequilibria resulting from former conditions'. It covered both a six-month preparatory period, when the institutions were set up, and a transitional period of five years. The preparatory period ran from 10 August 1952 to 10 February 1953, and the transitional period for the subsequent five years. The Convention laid down a precise timetable, which in most sectors was kept without difficulty.

Tariffs and quota restrictions on trade within the Community were abolished for coal and iron ore on 10 February 1953, for scrap on 15 March and for steel on 1 May of the same year. There had in fact been no import duties in force for coal, iron ore or scrap, but all member countries imposed duties on crude and finished steel. Quota restrictions, however, were numerous for both coal and steel products. The two exceptions to liberalisation were the authorisation granted to Italy to maintain its customs duties on coke and steel products, reducing them annually by fixed percentages during the transitional period, and the partial isolation, also for the transitional period (subsequently extended to 31 December 1962), of the Belgian coal market. Together with the compensatory levies (see p. 267) these measures were accepted in order to allow the high-cost sectors of the Community industries to adapt themselves to the common market.

The transition to a single market involved complex problems resulting from the numerous national subsidies to producers, since their removal had potentially serious consequences for both producers and consumers. Whilst it was reckoned that the need for subsidies would disappear with the development of the common market, the Convention allowed for the introduction of temporary schemes of compensation, based on equalisation of returns amongst producers, to ease the adaptation of certain sectors or regions. The two major schemes involved the Belgian coalfields and the Italian mines at Sulcis in Sardinia. A compensation fund was established, financed in part by a levy (starting at 1·5 per cent of receipts per ton sold, and steadily reduced) on the output of German and Dutch fields (where costs were lowest) and in part by the Belgian and Italian Governments. This was used to provide a progressively diminishing subsidy. Payments to the Sulcis field ended in March 1955, whilst the measures of aid to some of the Belgian pits had to be replaced by other action as a result of the structural crisis of the coal market which later developed. Provision had been made in the Convention for steps to assist French coal producers, but these proved unnecessary. In the steel sector the only special treatment needed was the temporary maintenance of protection which was granted to the Italian steel industry; a similar possibility for the Luxembourg steel industry was not taken up.

Thus the establishment of the common market turned out to be, as the High Authority later concluded in retrospect, 'relatively easier than the authors of the Treaty had foreseen'.[1] The changed situation had positive effects on output, productivity, trade and workers' incomes so that 'it could be concluded, at the end of the transitional period, that the setting up of the common market very largely responded to what its creators expected. Interpenetration of markets and the ban on discrimination were establishing that '*de facto* solidarity' envisaged by the preamble to the Treaty. In the social field this was taking concrete form in re-adaptation operations. Expanding production was accompanied by rising living standards. The financial credit of the Community was solidly established. Trade with non-member countries was developing in parallel with intra-Community trade. An association agreement had been concluded with the United Kingdom.

The fact that the transition to a single market was carried out

[1] *ECSC 1952–62, Results, Limitations, Prospects*, Luxembourg, 1963, p. XII.

so smoothly was undoubtedly due in part to the general shortage prevailing at that time in both industries. This provided favourable conditions for rapid expansion. The real test of the Community, and the main problems, emerged after the common market had been completed. The situation of both the coal and steel industries has undergone basic change since then and the record of the Community has been less successful.

Of the two main elements of change in the steel industry, the first, in the form of rapid technical developments necessitating a high level of investment and research, was one which the Community proved well-equipped to meet, by its guidance of investments and its action to stimulate research. The second element, which came to the fore only in the early sixties, was the pressure of outside competition. During the initial years, Community steel output almost doubled, but from 1960 onwards it levelled off despite the continued rise in demand. The pressure of competition from cheap imports brought out the need for the Community to develop what had hitherto been lacking, a common commercial policy (see p. 235).[1]

The main problems for coal, since the establishment of the common market, have been that it has had to meet, first, a temporary crisis resulting from a flood of cheap imports and then a structural crisis resulting from the steady competition of other sources of energy, in particular oil, which have brought to an end its dominant, and finally even its major position in the energy market.

The way the crisis in the coal industry has been met has tested the possibilities and limitations of the Community. Many provisions of the Treaty, in particular those connected with the re-adaptation of workers, more than proved their worth. On the other hand the rules about competition were inadequate, and the measures specifically provided for meeting a crisis failed to function. In 1959, when the coal crisis was at its height, with over-production, excessive stocks and widespread short-time working, the necessary majority could not be obtained in the Council of Ministers for the application of Article 58 of the Treaty which provides for the establishment of production quotas and quantitative restrictions on imports. The Community was deprived of any means of direct action to solve the problems of the coal market, although, as the High Authority wrote in its report on the first ten years of the Community, 'in retrospect, no one will doubt any more that the Community was in fact in 1959

[1] The resulting problems are considered in *Steel Pricing Policies*, PEP, December 1964.

in the first phase of a structural crisis in the coal-mining industry.'[1]

Since it was the lack of flexibility in Article 58, making it impossible to differentiate the forms of intervention, which caused certain governments to refuse to permit its application, the High Authority felt that the question arose of whether the Treaty was really adapted to the facts of the changing situation and recalled that at the time it was drafted the authors were thinking more in terms of a possible cyclical crisis of over-production or shortage rather than of long-term structural problems. Following the failure to use Article 58 on 'manifest crisis' in the Community, action to help the coal industry was taken under an article in the chapter on 'the institutions of the Community' devoted primarily to the Court. Article 37 states that 'if a member state considers that, in a given case, an action or failure to act by the High Authority is such as to provide fundamental or persistent disturbances in its economy, it may seize the High Authority. The latter, after consulting the Council, shall recognise, if this is the case, the existence of such a situation and decide the steps to be taken on the conditions provided for in the present Treaty, to end this situation whilst safeguarding the essential interests of the Community.'

The role of the Court in this case is to rule on any appeal either against the High Authority's decision or against a possible refusal to recognise the existence of the claimed emergency.

It was under the terms of this article that steps were taken to meet the crisis which threatened to become insoluble once the provisions of the transitional period had run out. Belgium was authorised by the High Authority to isolate, temporarily, its coal market from the rest of the Community, the conditions for this being the application of a programme intended to solve the major structural problems of the area, in particular by the phased closing down of uneconomic mines.

The other Treaty clauses which have been invoked in meeting the general coal crisis have also been procedural ones. Thus unemployment grants were made to Belgian miners (in conjunction with the Belgian scheme mentioned above) under the terms of Article 93 which states that 'a decision or recommendation of the High Authority' may be taken with the unanimous agreement of the Council 'in all cases not expressly provided for in this Treaty' if it 'appears necessary to fulfil, in the operation of the common market for coal and steel . . . one of the objectives of the Community'. The financing

[1] ECSC, *op. cit.*, p. XV.

of coal stocks was also decided under the same Article concerning 'cases not provided for'. The High Authority allocated Community funds to cover the cost of stocks of coal held at the pit-head by mines in France, the Federal Republic of Germany, Belgium and the Netherlands, thus enabling them to maintain a certain level of production in order to avoid unemployment. Lastly, amendment of Article 56 to extend the possibilities for intervention for readaptation, retraining and industrial redevelopment was also carried through under the terms of Article 93. These various measures taken together represented an effort by the High Authority to exploit to the full the scope afforded by the Treaty, and by the political willingness of the member governments, to meet the coal crisis. A failure to do so would have resulted in a return to purely national policies.

None of these steps was, however, more than a palliative, leaving the basic structural problem of the coal industry intact. Having ceased, in 1962, to supply more than half of the Community's energy needs, coal continued to decline to the point of ceding its position as the major source of energy to oil. Despite this relative decline, the absolute level of coal output has been maintained in recent years at a fairly stable level: but this was due largely to a wide range of measures taken by the Community and national authorities. Proposals made by the High Authority, under Article 95, led to a decision taken on 17 February 1965 with a unanimous *avis conforme* by the Council, authorising a Community system of financial intervention by member governments to help the coal-mining industry. The mining companies are relieved of some of the extremely heavy burden of social security contributions which has been placed on them as a result of the steady reduction of the number of workers. Member governments are able to obtain the authorisation of the High Authority, according to commonly accepted criteria, for state aid intended to facilitate the closing-down of marginal mines and the modernisation of those still economically viable, and also to regulate the rate at which adaptation takes place in order to avoid economic and social upheaval in the areas most affected. The agreement also led to consultation by the German and French Governments with a view to achieving co-ordination of the steps they plan to take to aid the coal industry. Thus after a period in which the failure to work within the Treaty framework had led to separate and unco-ordinated national policies, a return was made to a Community system. It remained evident, however, that this could be of only limited value unless worked out and applied, in the long run, in the framework of an overall Community energy policy.

A COMMON ENERGY POLICY

The growing competition provided by oil products, and the resultant structural crisis of the coal-mining industry, were the elements which led the governments of the Six to accept the need for a common energy policy. As the High Authority wrote in the introduction to its report on the first ten years of the ECSC, 'Only five years after the start of the common market for coal, it had effectively become necessary for all sources of energy to be placed together under a common set of rules . . . coal policy, if it is to be effective, can no longer be conceived of except as an integral part of energy policy.'[1] With the creation of the new Communities, oil, natural gas and electricity came under the rules of the Rome Treaty, and research on atomic energy as a source of power came under Euratom, whilst coal remained under the ECSC, and there were no specific Treaty requirements or indications about a common energy policy.

A Protocol adopted in October 1957 made the Council of Ministers of the ECSC formally responsible, however, for elaborating such a policy, and extended the competence of the Joint Council–High Authority Committee, which had been set up in 1953, to the whole energy field. The High Authority with the two executive Commissions of the EEC and Euratom set up a joint Inter-executive Committee to work on energy problems.

The following years were to be rich in debates but to yield few effective decisions on energy policy as a whole. From 1960 onwards annual forecasts were produced of demand and consumption for energy in the Community. 1959 saw the presentation by the Inter-executive Committee of a first report on the co-ordination of national policies, and in 1960 an interim report set out the objectives of a common policy: energy supply on the best economic terms to maintain the competitiveness of the Community economy on the world market; a certain co-ordination of investments in order to ensure the smooth development of the energy market; a constant energy supply; and certain minimum conditions to assure the security of supply. The objective criterion by which these potentially conflicting goals were to be judged was to be the setting of a guide-price reflecting, on the one hand, long-term supply and demand prospects and, on the other, a choice between the exigencies of competitiveness and political considerations connected with social or regional policy.

The outcome of the discussions on these principles in 1960 and 1961 was inconclusive. In 1962 the ministers of the Six, at a meeting

[1] ECSC, *op. cit.*, p. IX.

in Rome, called on the executives of the three Communities to produce proposals for the creation of a common market for energy, allowing for competition between sources of energy and adapted to overall economic policy: its aims were to be relatively low energy prices (allowing for the security of supply and social considerations); the free movement of sources of energy; and the flexibility of energy production.

The proposals presented in June 1962 by the three executives set out the basic principles of a common energy policy: cheap supplies, security of supply, the gradual substitution of one source for another, long-term supply stability, a free choice for users and the unity of the market.

The memorandum containing the proposals of the three executives was examined by the Council, which requested a further report from them on the legal modifications required to put the proposed policy into effect. A draft agreement on modifications to the ECSC Treaty was subsequently submitted to the Council in April 1963.

Agreement on this basis was, however, not yet ripe. The Council turned back to the memorandum and a special committee of national experts under the High Authority's chairmanship was formed to report on this. By the end of 1963 its report had been submitted but agreement was still not quite within reach. It was only after extensive diplomatic contacts by the members of the three executives that an acceptable draft was produced and finally signed by the governments on 30 April 1964.

The Protocol of Agreement on Energy, as this document was known, was much less than a complete set of rules for a common energy market. Its most specific clauses applied to coal and in particular set out the procedure for introducing a system of subsidies. In other fields the Protocol was primarily a declaration of intentions. Its chief novelty was that, in addition to committing themselves for the first time to introducing a common energy policy, the governments accepted a tentative timetable for this step. It was agreed that, since the principle of merging the three Community Treaties had already been accepted, full provision for a common energy policy could best be made as an integral part of the new treaty.

It is not only the divergences between the three Treaty systems which have complicated the situation. There is also the fact of the rapidly changing relations between the forms of energy, oil successfully challenging the position of coal, and finds of natural gas within the Community establishing an important supply position for this source of energy. Added to this is the political difficulty arising from divergent national interests: two member countries have no significant coal-mining industry, whereas in three others mining remains an important factor in the economy. In the oil sector also the interests of the member countries diverge, Italy having practised a cheap energy supply policy based on imported oil, whereas member countries with coal industries to defend have imposed heavy taxes on oil.

PRICING SYSTEMS

When the High Authority was established it was faced with an extremely complex range both of government-imposed price systems (different from systems resulting from competition in a single market) and of systems adopted by the steel industries themselves to discriminate in favour of certain sectors of industry or certain consumers. Its general policy was to seek to bring about a gradual elimination of all discriminatory pricing systems.

The first step was the immediate abolition, with respect to intra-Community trade, of double-pricing, by which firms in most member countries had consistently charged higher prices for exports than for sales within the Community. In some cases the differences had been as much as 30 per cent (for Belgian steel, for instance), whilst in others sales had simply been made at the prices prevailing on the export market (for example, French steel exports to the Federal Republic of Germany).

During the transitional period, the High Authority concentrated its attention on securing the implementation of the rules laid down in the Treaty about the publication of price lists. The High Authority has no powers to fix prices for coal or steel, except to set maximum or minimum prices during crises of shortage or of glut, but has, from the beginning, exercised strict control over the pricing system, ensuring that firms keep to their own published schedules and do not depart from the rules of non-discrimination. The control is backed by the right to inspect the accounts of all firms subject to the Treaty. The system adopted was that of 'basing points': each firm must file publicly with the High Authority a list of prices for all its products for a given base point; apart from adding the cost of transport, the firm can depart from the list price only to meet the lower price of a Community firm using a different basing point or that of a non-Community producer, through 'aligning' with the prices of firms outside the Community, subject to High Authority approval. An attempt by the High Authority to allow greater price flexibility for steel with a variation of up to 2·5 per cent from the published rate (this came to be known as the 'Monnet rebate' after the then President of the High Authority) was overruled by the Court of Justice in December 1954.

The High Authority concluded in 1963 that this Community system had had a positive effect, maintaining greater price stability than had prevailed in the past and exercising a moderating effect on price levels despite the boom prevailing during most of the period, and in addition reducing the use of discriminatory pricing. Since 1958, however, a major problem has arisen from the fact that the forms of energy competing directly with coal are not subject to the price publication rules, thus putting coal, restricted in the methods it can use in price competition, at a distinct disadvantage: this can be solved only by the merger of the Treaties yielding a uniform system. It has begun to appear in recent years that steel too may face a similar problem, with substitute products (such as plastics) coming under the Rome Treaty. A further weakness of the ECSC price system is that it does not apply to independent traders, who are subject to no discipline. Imported coal and steel products also escape Community rules.

'PEREQUATION' FOR SCRAP

The High Authority dealt effectively in the early years of the Community with a particular price problem arising in the scrap sector. The Community was subject to a structural shortage of scrap and was dependent on imports from the world market, where prices were consistently high, for a large part of its supplies. The system instituted was intended to share out between all steel firms the cost of importing scrap, and also to prevent import requirements from forcing prices up. By a scheme known as 'perequation', a levy was imposed on all scrap sales within the Community, creating a fund from which a subsidy was paid on all imports of scrap purchased on the world market. Although it ran into administrative difficulties—and the High Authority was obliged by a Court ruling to take into its own direct control the administration of the scheme—the results were positive. Scrap prices in the ECSC remained stable at a level well below that on the world market, and major harmful effects of the Community shortage were avoided. The scheme was ended in December 1958, but litigation before the Court resulting from the winding-up arrangements continued until 1965. Mention should also be made of a case which became notorious for several years in connection with large-scale fraud by Dutch firms which passed off scrap from ship-breaking as imported scrap to obtain the subsidy.

One of the results of the High Authority's action in guiding and assisting investment was to bring about a major change in the ratio of scrap to pig-iron in steel works, thus making the Community steel industry less dependent upon imported scrap.

CARTEL POLICY

Article 4 of the Treaty lays down a general ban on 'restrictive practices tending towards the division or exploitation of the market', whilst Articles 65 and 66 set out in detail the terms under which this ban is to be applied by the High Authority to agreements and to concentrations respectively. There is a basic difference in the orientation of the two articles: whereas cartels, price-rings and other similar practices are seen to be harmful to free competition, and are subject to strict regulations—a reflection of American experience as well as of European experience of cartels during the inter-war period—concentrations are seen as being economically desirable, unless carried to excess, in so far as they fulfil the basic aim of rational production and reduced costs which underlies the creation of the wider market.

The major problem which faced the High Authority in implementing the Treaty provisions on cartels was that of the selling arrangements existing for coal. Most member states had large selling organisations which effectively eliminated competition. The policy followed in the early years was to obtain either the elimination or the adaptation of these cartels in order to initiate a degree of competition. With the changing structural situation of the coal industry, however, it became evident that a realistic judgement could be made only in the light of the position of coal on the overall energy market. This led to attempts to modify the Treaty so that the High Authority could be more flexible in allowing the existence of coal-sales cartels, but this proved impossible without a full-scale revision of the Treaty.

In May 1954 the High Authority informed two national coal-trading agencies that they could not be maintained in their existing form, as they prevented competition on the market. One was OKU (Oberrheinische Kohlenunion) which was the sole selling agency for the south of Germany for coal from the Ruhr, Aachen, Lorraine and Saar fields, which together accounted for more than two thirds of the Community's coal output. Following major changes in the nature of its activities, so that it became essentially a joint wholesalers' buying agency, also making arrangements for the shipping and stocking of the fuel handled by its members, OKU was recognised by the High Authority in July 1957 as being compatible with the Treaty.

ATIC (Association Technique de l'Importation Charbonnière) was the French national coal import agency, handling all imports, which it subsequently resold through authorised trade channels to French consumers, no consumer or dealer being allowed to negotiate directly with suppliers outside France. The internal selling system was also restrictive and highly centralised. Since ATIC was a state organisation, the High Authority had to deal with the French Government, which resisted strongly any attempt to change the system to bring it into line with the Treaty. A decision of the High Authority in 1956 ruling ATIC incompatible with the Treaty was challenged before the Court of Justice. The appeal was withdrawn and negotiations took place followed by a High Authority decision in December 1957 giving France two years in which to ensure direct access to the French market for other Community suppliers and two years to end ATIC's monopoly position as general supervisory agency. Again the French Government appealed to the Court, but the suit was withdrawn and in 1961 a settlement was reached allowing French buyers to place orders direct with non-French dealers, whilst the High Authority exercised supervision of the activities of ATIC.

A third major coal cartel was GEORG (Gemeinschaftsorganisation Ruhrkohle) which controlled six nominally separate selling agencies disposing of all the coal—some eighty million tons a year—produced in the Ruhr. It not only fixed prices but allocated orders and directed deliveries. It was defended by both the mine-owners and the miners' trade unions as being the only effective method of ensuring stable employment by the sharing out of orders. The High Authority, in seeking to bring about a degree of competition, made allowance for this consideration. The plan applied in April 1956 after negotiations with mine-owners, unions, dealers and the Government of the Federal Republic of Germany, replaced GEORG's six agencies by three separate marketing agencies, subject to High Authority supervision to ensure that they compete with each other, and each disposing of the production of a group of from fourteen to nineteen firms. A separate organisation was established to handle exports. The authorisation to the three agencies was revised and renewed in March 1959, when a number of other joint bodies were authorised allowing the agencies and the mining companies to co-operate to a certain extent.

In 1960, faced with the continued difficulties of the German coal market and the demands of the producers for changes to allow them to meet the steadily increasing pressure of market competition from oil, the High Authority proposed to the Council the setting up of a Joint Committee to study the possibility of amending the Treaty. The ensuing report, dealing essentially with the problem of the coal market, proposed a revision of Article 65 on cartels. On a German initiative, the Council of Ministers, in agreement with the High Authority, decided in June 1961 by a five-sixths majority on proposals for a 'little revision' of the Treaty under Article 95. The essential element in the changes proposed would have been the addition of a clause to the effect that 'in the event of a fundamental and persisting change in marketing conditions for the coalmining and/or the iron and steel industry', the High Authority could authorise joint-buying or joint-selling agreements, waiving the requirements of the existing version of the Article provided the agreements 'are such as to aid the achievement of adjustment objectives recognised as appropriate by it and are calculated to help ensure that the changes in marketing conditions will not result in serious economic and social disturbances'. The new kind of authorisations would be 'subject to a time-limit and checks upon their application by the High Authority, with the possibility of laying down prices, conditions of sale and delivery schedules should the authorisation be abused'. The High Authority and the Council defended their text at length, but the Court finally ruled that a 'little revision' was not possible; the main grounds were that such a revision could not be used to replace a system of prior examination for joint buying and selling arrangements by a system of subsequent checking and direct intervention; and that Article 65 contained an objective criterion, 'a substantial part of the products in question within the Common Market', which constituted an entrenched principle determining the application of the general ban laid down in Article 4.

In May 1962 a Court ruling rejected an appeal against a High Authority decision of June 1960 refusing to authorise a single coal selling agency in the Ruhr; following the refusal of the little revision no such authorisation was possible without a major revision of the Treaty. By a decision of March 1963 the High Authority allowed the establishment of two Ruhr selling agencies to replace the three previous ones, at the same time requiring that all organisational links between the agencies be dissolved, and laying down a series of conditions to ensure that the two new agencies remained independent of each other.

The iron and steel industry was already fairly competitive when the Treaty came into effect, with some 250 competing firms as against eighty-five in the much larger United States market. The scrap 'perequation' scheme set up in 1953 replaced certain organisations which had been established by private interests to set scrap prices and allocate scrap. In the steel sector the High Authority has taken no specific action against cartels but it authorised a joint selling agency set up by a group of Belgian iron and steel firms which accounted for just over 3 per cent of ECSC steel output and which were, in any case, virtually merged.

CONCENTRATIONS

The basic philosophy underlying Article 66 of the Treaty of Paris, on dominant positions in the coal and steel markets, was that mergers and concentrations tending to serve the same ends as the common market—more rational production and lower costs—should be encouraged. Article 66 requires the High Authority to authorise a merger if it will not give the firms concerned the power 'to determine prices, to control or restrict production or distribution or to prevent the maintenance of effective competition in a substantial part of the market' for the products in question. The High Authority must also take into account the size of the existing firms in the sector and has in practice been influenced by considerations about the attitudes of the firms.

There had already been, before the creation of the Community, a marked trend towards mergers in Belgium, France, Italy and Luxembourg. But even the largest Community firms were of only moderate size if judged against American standards. Throughout the life of the Community the High Authority has continued fairly steadily to authorise mergers and concentrations both vertical and horizontal,[1] the greatest number being in Germany. The High Authority was influenced in its policy by the consideration that the technological advances in the steel industry and the capital expenditure required were liable to encourage mergers, but that on the other hand the need to keep such installations working nearer full capacity would be a stimulus to competition.

In 1962 the High Authority gave a ruling on the creation by a group of Belgian, Luxembourg and French companies of a new steel firm, to be known as Sidmar, and in so doing broadened the principles already established in its earlier decisions. It took the view that where one of the controlling firms produces the same or much the same

[1] 'Vertical' concentrations are those between firms and their suppliers; 'horizontal' ones are between one coal, or steel, firm and another.

products as the newly created firm, there must be a 'group effect' on all the firms involved. The principle was also established of taking into consideration the potential competition in the whole common market. Lastly, the authorisation was specifically limited to the lines of production planned and submitted for approval.

In recent years, with steel facing far keener competition from efficient producers on the world market, the High Authority's attitude has changed radically and it has become an advocate of larger groupings in the European steel industry. Thus it has authorised the merger of two major German firms (August Thyssen Hütte and Phoenix Rheinrohr) to create a 7-million ton concern, which it had refused to allow in 1958.

TRANSPORT

One fifth of the selling price of steel, and up to 35 per cent for coal, is accounted for by transport costs; moreover, freight rates being easier to manipulate than basic prices, disparities in these rates resulting from discriminatory or merely divergent national policies were considerable. Article 70 of the ECSC Treaty laid down clearly that 'the establishment of the common market requires the application of such transport rates for coal and steel as will make possible comparable price conditions for consumers in comparable positions', and set out a number of detailed requirements. The High Authority enforced the Treaty provisions in this sector vigorously, in particular by the introduction of international through rates for rail haulage, and by publishing for almost all transport rates, but in the areas where it had no direct competence and had to proceed by obtaining the agreement of the member states—essentially for the harmonisation of national freight rate structures—progress proved slow and laborious.

More than thirty cases of 'discriminations in transport rates and conditions of any kind which are based on the country of origin or of destination' were declared incompatible with the Treaty. For example, the French railways were charging Belgian steel firms more than French for the transport of Lorraine ore, whilst Belgian railways penalised French firms as against Belgian for the carriage of steel for export through the Belgian sea-ports.

Between May 1955 and May 1956 the High Authority obtained the abolition of the practice of 'breaks in rates' whereby a consignment crossing a frontier by rail was held to start a new haul and lost the benefit of proportionately lower rates for the longer haul. The resultant international through rates not only meant that internal and international hauls of coal and steel were put on the same footing, but also resulted in decreased costs for international coal and steel haulage. In 1956 and 1957 agreements were signed by the Community extending the through rates system to hauls between member states through Switzerland and Austria respectively, a measure of great importance for Italian trade with the rest of the Community.

The harmonisation of the transport rates charged in the different member countries proved a far more intractable problem. Not only has the High Authority no power to enforce harmonisation of freight rates, but there is no requirement for a single uniform rate structure, which Article 70 specifically states is to remain subject to the legislative or administrative provisions of the member states. Certain steps have nevertheless been taken to eliminate distortions: thus in January 1955 the Council agreed, for a great part of coal and steel haulage in the Community, on a uniform rate of 'tapering' for freight rates decreasing with distance. Extra charges for carriage in covered trucks and rates for large indivisible loads have also been harmonised.

The Treaty requires the publication (or communication to the High Authority) of freight rates being charged for coal and steel but the High Authority ran into stiff resistance in two member countries in trying to obtain the implementation of this. Publication of freight rates for rail transport between countries raised the least difficulties, but it proved impossible at first to enforce the application of published rates for transport within member states. The major object of dispute was the road haulage sector: in February 1959 a High Authority decision made publication of rates for road transport of coal and steel compulsory, but this was ruled null and void by the Court of Justice in July 1960 on formal legal grounds. As a result the High Authority issued, in January 1961, a recommendation requiring the publication of freight rates for all forms of transport of coal and steel products, and in its ruling of July 1962 rejecting an appeal against this measure by the Netherlands Government, the Court of Justice finally settled disputes on this point. The recommendation, whilst leaving governments entirely free as to the means they select, binds them to ensure that rates and conditions are so published as to make possible, first, the elimination of discriminations, the introduction of international through rates and the harmonisation of rates and conditions of carriage, and secondly, the published knowledge of these rates and conditions which is necessary to the proper functioning of the common market.

A sector where the High Authority was more successful, largely because the Treaty did give it direct powers, was the elimination of discriminatory rates in transport within a country. It ruled in a decision of February 1958 that special rates granted for reasons of competition with another form of transport were permissible; on the other hand 'support rates' granted to benefit a particular firm or sector, unless expressly approved by the High Authority for exceptional social and economic reasons, were banned by the same decision, varying periods being granted for their removal: this ruling was confirmed by the Court of Justice in 1960. This led the German State Railways to replace the former discriminatory advantages granted through support rates by an overall non-discriminatory measure: special rates for whole trains for both domestic and international hauls.

A completely different and extremely complex set of problems faced the High Authority in connection with transport by inland waterway. The existence of both very large and very small firms, the combination of basic freight rates for transport within a country and free rates for international haulage and the special status of navigation on the Rhine, all combined to make the implementation of some of the Treaty requirements difficult.

The problem concerning which little progress has proved possible is that of the harmonisation of the ratios between freight rates—that between coals and coke being particularly important in the ECSC. It seems very difficult to take this basic step within the framework of the Coal and Steel Community before the implementation of a common transport policy for the whole Community economy, containing an overall principle applying to freight rates. The argument of principle is backed here by the hard economic fact that ECSC products account for almost half the volume of rail traffic within the Community whereas for other forms of transport the proportion is lower. Harmonisation of rail rates is therefore inconceivable without harmonisation of other transport rates, and that is possible only in the EEC framework. Thus this is a case where the limits imposed by partial integration have clearly been reached.

ECONOMIC POLICY: GENERAL OBJECTIVES, INVESTMENT, RESEARCH

The role of the Community is not limited to the creation of the common market by eliminating barriers and discrimination. The Treaty obliges the institutions to 'promote the regular expansion and modernisation of production as well as the improvement of quality' (Article 3(g)). The mission is to be carried out by 'limited intervention' and measures indicated include placing 'financial means at the disposal of enterprises for their investments and [participating] in the expenses of re-adaptation'.

The High Authority has developed steadily its role in both guiding and stimulating the development of the economy of the coal-mining and iron and steel industries, the main instruments for this being the establishment of general objectives, opinions on investment projects, financial aid to investment, and the financing of research.

Article 46(3) of the Paris Treaty lays down that the High Authority is to define from time to time 'general objectives' concerning 'modernisation, the long-term planning of production and the expansion of productive capacity'. The Treaty gives no clear indication of the relationship between these 'objectives' and the general economic policy to be followed by the High Authority in all the fields covered by the Treaty. In its Fifth Annual Report, published in 1957, the High Authority laid down that the general objectives would be of 'an indicative nature and would be intended to enlighten the action of all those involved (producers, users and workers)'. Four main aims were established: to guide firms as to their investments and output; to provide a criterion for assessing possible financial aid to investments; to provide a basis for High Authority proposals to governments on taxation, price-fixing and financing; and, lastly, to constitute the basis for the High Authority's coal and steel policy.

In the early years this last, more general, aim was of little significance since in the circumstances of the time, the general policy in both sectors was one of seeking maximum output to meet Europe's expanding needs. Later the High Authority arrived at the concept that the most desirable lines of development must be determined in the light of the position of the two industries in the overall economic context of the Community. In the case of coal it was realised that 'general objectives' would be of little use except in the framework of an overall energy policy. In the iron and steel sector, however, the High Authority's concern came to be first the balanced development of the industry and, later, the maintenance of its competitive position in the face of rapid technical development and increasing world competition. The most striking example of this was the emphasis put on the need to change the scrap to pig-iron ratio of the Community's blast furnace consumption, both to escape the consequences of the relative scrap shortage and to assist the pig-iron industry. Two other successes of the 'general objectives' were the development of markets for the low-grade output of the coal-mines (through the development of power stations using low-grade fuel) and, in general terms, the balanced development of the steel industry in the light of forecast needs.

The influence of the general objectives on the course of investments and of industrial development is backed by the wide range of information which the High Authority provides. An annual enquiry yields a clear picture of current and planned investment by sector. In addition the total sums involved in investment programmes and their expected incidence on the level of output are published periodically by the ECSC. A certain number of special enquiries are also undertaken into the structure of production, the level of technical equipment and the growth of capacity.

The first direct instrument available to the High Authority in shaping the development of the coal and steel sectors lies in the obligation imposed on firms to declare major investment projects, and the opinions which the High Authority is called to give on them. All new investments exceeding $0·5 million must be registered. In the coal-mining industry this covers only some 40 per cent of total current investment but in steel it covers almost all projects. The opinions which the High Authority gives on all projects may be positive or negative or may express reservations: they are given in the light of the current general objectives. In the first ten years of the ECSC alone some 1,150 projects were declared. A negative opinion does not amount to a ban on the project, which is possible only if it is found to require subsidies or discrimination incompatible with the Treaty. But the influence of the High Authority's opinions, though hard to estimate, has been considerable. Apart from the cases of projects abandoned following a negative opinion, the High Authority considers it has been successful in promoting the construction of pithead power stations and, in recent years, putting a brake on the too rapid expansion of electric furnace steel production and wide-strip hot and cold rolling mills.

The third possibility for the High Authority is to contribute directly to the financing of investment projects. It may make loans or guarantee them. The early years of the ECSC were devoted to a study of investment trends, revealing a disturbing situation where, as the Second Annual Report noted, '75 per cent of the funds obtained by firms outside their own resources . . . came from sources which cannot be considered as normal since they come from either short-term bank loans or American aid and public funds'. Some loans were even obtained at rates of interest up to 8 per cent. Of the contributions made by the High Authority to financing since it entered this field, some 70 per cent has gone to industrial projects, the rest mainly to workers' housing and research. Schemes favoured in this way are normally those involving modernisation or mechanisation, and in 1961 the High Authority established a scale of priorities, which was renewed in 1964. The financial aid given to the Belgian steel industry is of interest since it was partly dictated by considerations of regional development and of reconversion to prevent social hardship.

The High Authority's action in this domain has been made possible largely by its financial autonomy based on the ECSC levy. An indenture negotiated with the Bank for International Settlements in Basle in 1954 and known as the 'common pledge' strengthens the Community's credit by ensuring that all ECSC securities are held in common for the *pro rata* benefit of all lenders to the Community. During the early years a large part of the proceeds of the levy was devoted to establishing a Guarantee Fund which by 1956 had reached the target of $100 million, and which gave the High Authority the necessary confidence for large-scale borrowing not only within the Community but on the international money market, and also enabled it to guarantee loans obtained by coal and steel firms from third parties; thus capital resources previously out of reach were opened to the industries of the Community.

Lastly, Article 55 of the Treaty states that the High Authority 'must encourage technical and economic research concerning the production and the development of consumption of coal and steel as well as workers' safety in these industries'. The High Authority has carried out this obligation both by financial aid for research projects, and by the suggestion of themes for research; it has from the start considered this an essential element in its policy. In the early years it limited itself to providing aid for research projects already planned. From 1957 onwards, however, it began to lay down the lines along which research in the coal and steel industries should be developed. It provides loans or grants drawn mainly from the proceeds of the levy (research projects are not suitable for financing by loans since they do not yield a direct return). In the coal-mining sector the policy has been to favour research which will enable coal to hold its own against other forms of energy on the market. In the iron and steel sector priority has been given to research aimed at increasing productivity, and also to the search for iron ore deposits, in the rest of the world as well as in the Community. Research on safety and on industrial medicine has also been financed (see p. 285).

SOCIAL POLICY

Article 2 of the Treaty includes in its definition of the tasks of the Community, to be achieved through the creation of the common market, 'the development of employment and the improvement of the standard of living in the participating countries', and Article 3 imposes on the institutions an obligation to 'promote the improvement of the living and working conditions of the labour force in each of the industries under its jurisdiction so as to harmonise those conditions in an upward direction'.

Social policy is held by the High Authority to be the field in which the Coal and Steel Community has made its most original contribution. The introduction to the High Authority's report on the first ten years of the Community[1] states: 'it can even be said that, in the field of re-adaptation and re-conversion, ECSC has contributed an extremely constructive innovation to economic and social policy. The basic idea of re-adaptation is that technical progress must not be achieved at the cost of the workers, the public authorities having the duty to facilitate their finding a new line of work if economic developments should make this necessary. This new philosophy has come a long way since the Treaty of Paris was drafted. It is to be found in the Treaty of Rome, in the recent legislation of some member countries and even in that of third countries'.

The High Authority's success in this field is particularly significant since the Treaty is relatively vague in its indications on the subject: it is dealt with, as far as the text of the Treaty itself is concerned, only in Article 56. It was particularly significant that the sole successful use of the procedure of the 'little revision', extending the scope for action under the Treaty, should have been made to allow the steps taken in the transitional period to be extended.

The High Authority has made all aspects of social policy a major concern, and its action has fallen under three main headings: information; protection of workers; promotion of workers' interests, covering in practice, in addition to re-adaptation and industrial redevelopment, free movement of workers, workers' training schemes, housing and research on safety and industrial medicine. The Community's social policy has been carried out against the background of considerable migration of unskilled workers, and full employment in the steel industry, while in coal-mining there have been a constantly declining labour force and major problems of under-employment.

[1] ECSC, *op. cit.*, p. IX.

RE-ADAPTATION

Paragraph 23 of the Convention on the transitional period was the basic text for the development of the policy of Community responsibility for re-adaptation, and for its implementation, from 1954 to 1960. During that period some 115,000 workers benefited from aid: the greater part from 1958 onwards, when the deterioration of the market situation revealed more cases where redevelopment was needed. As early as 1957 work was begun on ensuring that the re-adaptation policy could be maintained when the transitional arrangements expired in 1960, and this was obtained by a revision of Article 56, proposed by the High Authority and the Council, backed by the European Parliament, by the unions throughout the Community, and approved by the Court as compatible with the Treaty. During the period from 1960 onwards the amount of aid given to steel workers fell off, whereas the aid to workers in the iron ore mines rose, the proportion going to the coal-mining industry remaining stable. Taking into account the transitional period, aid provided by the High Authority up to mid-1965 totalled nearly $21 million (matched by an equivalent sum from the governments), benefiting directly nearly 200,000 workers.

Re-adaptation aid granted by the Community consists either of 'tide-over' payments to workers who have been either temporarily laid off or obliged to seek new employment, or of a temporary sliding-scale grant, intended to enable a worker to accept employment which is initially or even permanently less well paid than his former job. Re-settlement grants are also made if a worker has to move house in order to take up another job, and in this case transport costs for his family and for his belongings are also paid.

The re-adaptation aid is financed half by the High Authority from Community funds, and half by the government of the country in question, which organises and controls the schemes. The scale of the aid is negotiated by the High Authority with the governments on an *ad hoc* basis and varies from case to case. Except in Italy and in certain depressed areas elsewhere, workers enjoying re-adaptation aid have found new jobs, whilst attempts have been made to find a solution for those whom age or physical handicaps prevented from taking a new job. The High Authority, the European Parliament and the unions have devoted considerable energy over a number of years to establishing a 'miners' charter' dealing with working and living conditions, but political difficulties have prevented its being adopted by the governments.

FREE MOVEMENT OF WORKERS

Article 69 of the Treaty laid down the principle of free movement of workers, as a necessary complement to free movement of the other factors of production: this was limited, however, to skilled or semi-skilled workers, and in practice it was found that these men were the least likely to move. Both miners and steel-workers affected by the closing down of firms proved reluctant to move, with the result that the re-adaptation and industrial redevelopment provisions of the Treaty proved more important than those on free movement. The fact that large numbers of unskilled workers were employed in the ECSC industries in countries other than their own—especially Italians in the other member countries—was not the direct result of Treaty provisions.

INDUSTRIAL REDEVELOPMENT

The aim of the Community's reconversion schemes was to enable workers to remain in areas where their original employment had ceased as a result of structural changes, whether provoked or not by the erection of the common market. The basic policy, which began with the revision of Article 56, has been to prepare industrial redevelopment projects well in advance, before the firms in question had to close down: thus the High Authority has always taken into account potential unemployment as well as actual unemployment in determining its support for such projects. It should be pointed out that this is an area where the member governments retain the initiative in submitting projects, and where the financial contributions of the Community are intended to match an existing national effort. In this domain the High Authority has worked closely with the EEC Commission and the European Investment Bank since 1958.

The High Authority's assistance to Community firms in improving the training schemes for their personnel falls under the general heading of measures intended to raise the living standards of workers. In 1955 and 1956 the High Authority concentrated on a detailed study of methods and needs for apprentice and training schemes; from 1957 to 1960 attention was concentrated on skilled workers, and since 1961 the accent has been placed on the requirements which result from rapid technical progress. National schemes have been co-ordinated and far-reaching discussions organised as a basis for harmonisation. Since 1964 the High Authority has given financial assistance to the development of occupational training centres. Workers' housing has been an important subject of co-operation in this field.

At the time the Treaty came into effect most of the coal-mining and steel manufacturing areas of the Community faced an acute housing shortage. A High Authority enquiry in 1958 revealed, for instance, that 16,000 workers living with their families were housed in huts or temporary structures. A first experimental housing scheme was launched in 1954, followed by a major programme covering the next five years. Altogether two experimental programmes and five major programmes have been organised at a cost of $623 million: of this the High Authority provided $46 million as a direct grant and $25 million in the form of loans. The total number of dwellings partially financed by the High Authority under the Community programmes up to 31 January 1966 was 95,296. Although this is less than 10 per cent of total coal and steel workers' housing, the stimulus provided has meant that the High Authority has not only been able to help meet some of the worst gaps but also to encourage greater standardisation and industrialisation in building.

COMMERCIAL POLICY

The Treaty of Paris specifically states that 'the responsibilities of the governments of the member states for commercial policy shall not be affected by the application of this Treaty'. Governments were left free to set their tariffs, though the High Authority might take the initiative in proposing changes in national tariffs. The High Authority was granted only the limited powers to make recommendations to the governments if there was dumping by non-member countries, in the event of low-price external competition due to different competitive conditions, and of imports seriously threatening Community production. It was also empowered to put forward methods for the member states to co-operate on commercial policy. This limitation of the role of the Community was a clear case of the limitations of sector integration, commercial policy on coal and steel being considered an inseparable part of a country's overall trade policy.

The first effect of co-operation between member states in this field was the introduction, at the end of the transitional period in 1958, of a harmonised tariff for steel products. This differed from a common tariff in so far as the external tariffs of each country were not the same but were sufficiently close to prevent trade diversion through the low tariff countries: thus the Italian tariff of 9 per cent average was the highest and the Benelux tariff of 5 per cent the lowest. The system of co-operation on commercial policy also led to the High Authority being given a mandate to negotiate for the Community in the Dillon Round and to seek agreement on a common position to be adopted in the Kennedy Round of negotiations in GATT where the High Authority also represented the Community.

The need for a common or harmonised commercial policy became more marked as a result of changed structural conditions. In the fifties both imported coal and steel had been thought of essentially as being available to make up total requirements. From 1958 on, imported coal became a determining element—and during the crisis the High Authority authorised increases in national protection including a charge of 20 German marks per ton on coal imports into Germany. In recent years the pressure of steel imports has likewise increased. The High Authority consequently pressed for more coherent action in this field, particularly in view of the contrast with the unified tariff policy of the EEC. In 1963 the High Authority sought from the Council agreement to align all national tariffs on the Italian level. Failing agreement on this it addressed a recommendation to the member states requiring them to ensure a level of temporary protection for steel not lower than that of Italy. In 1963 agreement was reached on a system for limiting imports from state-trading countries, and this was prolonged through 1966. Nevertheless the limitations of the Treaty system remain, and are likely to be removed only when the Treaties of the three Communities are merged.

EXTERNAL RELATIONS

The Convention on the Transitional Period bound the High Authority, immediately upon taking up its duties, to 'enter into negotiations with the governments of third countries, and particularly with the British Government, on general and commercial relations concerning coal and steel between the Community and such countries'. Negotiations in the autumn of 1954 led to the signing of an 'Agreement of Association' establishing a Standing Council of Association, with four High Authority and four British representatives; the High Authority also appointed a representative with ambassadorial rank in London. The essential aim of the agreement is consultation and 'where appropriate' co-ordination of action on a wide range of measures. It reflected the cautious British approach of the time by leaving it entirely open how close the association would be in practice.

Committees on Trade Relations, Coal and Steel were set up by the Council and these have tackled various problems arising in relations between the United Kingdom and the Community: thus, in 1956 the Coal Committee intervened to prevent hardship to traditional users in the Community as the result of the restrictions on British coal exports. The British Government has also closely followed the work of the Community in the social sphere.

The existence of the Association led to the signature, on 25 November 1957, of an agreement on commercial relations between Britain and the ECSC within the context of the Association. Under the agreement mutual tariff cuts on iron and steel products were made, in the case of the Community to the level of the harmonised tariff, and these concessions were extended to the other members of GATT through the most favoured nation clause. The agreement also laid down the obligation of prior consultation before the imposition of new restrictions on trade between the two partners. The imposition of the British 15 per cent surcharge on imports in November 1964 was followed by a formal protest from the High Authority, since the obligation to consult had been ignored.

Apart from the association with Britain, two agreements on transport facilities have been negotiated with Austria and Switzerland. Over thirty countries have diplomatic representatives accredited to the High Authority.

Conclusions

The European Coal and Steel Community was the first experiment in the 'Community method' of carrying through economic integration. The immediate aim of a common market in coal and steel products was achieved without any great difficulty and brought valuable results in terms of increased trade, lower costs and price stability. In subsequent years major weaknesses in the markets for coal and steel created problems which the provisions of the Treaty were not strong enough to solve satisfactorily, particularly because the national governments, whether in their own right or as represented in the Council with its insufficiently decisive voting procedures, retained the power to prevent the formation of Community policies in various key questions such as tariff or quota action against dumping from abroad or the setting of minimum prices during a period of market crisis. Community action was thus entirely dependent on the political readiness of the governments. Some aspects of the Treaty nevertheless met the challenge of the lean years, notably those concerned with investments, research and the readaptation of workers: in this latter domain the action of the Community constituted a new departure in social policy. The experience of the early years of the ECSC, moreover, had demonstrated the effectiveness of the Community method of integration as compared with other forms of international co-operation, and without it the subsequent creation of the EEC would not have been possible.

The first fourteen years, taken as a whole, show both the possibilities and limitations of the sector approach to integration. The limitations are encountered in areas such as commercial policy or taxation, where it is hard to draw a separate line down the middle of national policy to meet the needs of sector integration, and, secondly, in cases where economically competing sectors of the economy are not subject to the same rules and restrictions. The creation of the industrial and agricultural common market from 1958 onwards did nothing to resolve this second difficulty, whilst in cases like commercial policy the anomaly remained because the coal and steel sectors were subject to a lesser degree of integration than the rest of the economy. These were among the considerations which made it clear that the time had come for the pilot Community to be merged, under a single Treaty, with the two other Communities for which it had forged the way.

Chapter Eight

THE EUROPEAN ATOMIC ENERGY COMMUNITY

The Origins

The Treaty establishing the European Atomic Energy Community (Euratom) was negotiated in parallel with the EEC Treaty by the same countries, was also signed at Rome on 25 March 1957 and came into force on 1 January 1958. The idea that the civil uses of atomic energy should be one of the sectors for further integration among the six member countries of the ECSC emerged at the meeting of the ministerial conference at Messina in June 1955. Besides basing the *relance européenne* on a general common market, the Ministers proposed 'vertical' integration in a number of specific sectors, the peaceful uses of atomic energy being one. However, the study group, presided over by M. Paul-Henri Spaak (see p. 33), quickly came to the conclusion that atomic energy was the only sector where integration would give rise to special problems falling outside the scope of measures for economic integration in general.[1] From September 1955 the study group worked out proposals for the two treaties. These were presented in a final report at the Venice conference of May 1956, at which they were accepted by the governments as a basis for the detailed drafting of the treaties by an intergovernmental conference.

The peaceful uses of atomic energy seemed a good example of a sector in which integration could quickly yield great benefits to the participants while interfering with few, if any, established commercial interests. The interest of Community industrial undertakings in nuclear energy was still very limited. Apart from France, where an ambitious national programme was already under way, nuclear research and development in the Community countries was at an

[1] See statement by M. Spaak at Noordwijk, September 1955.

early stage and was dispersed between a number of public and private bodies. In the Federal Republic of Germany, nuclear research and development had scarcely begun owing to the ban on civilian nuclear activities imposed by the Allies until Germany became fully independent in 1955. Apart from this dispersal of efforts the total expenditure on nuclear research and development was still low: probably well below British expenditure alone (the total budget of the Atomic Energy Authority was over $200 million for 1956–57) and certainly far lower than the American $400–500 million per year. Public concern about the Community's nuclear backwardness increased with the realisation that the share of imported oil in satisfying the energy needs of the Six was rising very rapidly. The report, *A Target for Euratom*, drawn up by three experts at the request of the six governments and issued in May 1957, shortly after the Suez crisis, called into question 'the whole future of Europe's economic growth' in the absence of a massive recourse to atomic energy. It foresaw a capacity of 15,000 megawatts of nuclear capacity installed by 1967 and the stabilisation of energy imports at the 1963 level, and assumed that nuclear power would be competitive with conventional sources in the near future. As will be seen later, fears of energy shortage soon gave way to the problems of surplus, and these estimates were drastically reduced.

Article 1 of the Euratom Treaty gives the Community the task of creating 'conditions necessary for the speedy establishment and growth of nuclear industries'. The Euratom Treaty, like the Treaty establishing the EEC, aims to strike a balance between national interests and Community action, but it is a different type of integration that is involved. The first substantive chapter of the Treaty and an annex deal with research but it is difficult to set out in legal provisions the mechanism by which integration—here mainly co-ordinating and complementing the national research programmes—should be achieved. Integration in this major sector of Euratom's operations has a new dimension in that its subject is scientific endeavour and it is difficult to do more in a treaty than to lay down a number of principles and rules. The basic method envisaged was the confrontation of programmes rather than the central direction of national policies, on the grounds that a knowledge of projects in progress elsewhere in the Community, and the pooling of information on the results of research undertaken by Euratom or in which it shared, would usually suffice to dissuade public or private research bodies from embarking on research that would duplicate work being done elsewhere. In this and other ways (such as the association contract formula developed later) Euratom acts as a co-ordinating body. Its complementary role is to undertake work on its own account at its research establishments or under contract. The aim is thus to place as much as possible of the research in the six countries on a mutually agreed basis.

While, under the Treaty, research is to be carried out on a joint basis by Euratom and its individual member countries, the atomic industry, whether power production or the manufacture of equipment, normally remains within national competence. However, the Treaty vests a large number of legal responsibilities and powers of regulation in the Community. These powers were considered necessary to enable Euratom to overcome obstacles to the Community's development of atomic power. The Treaty also gives Euratom a legal and supervisory role in the domains of supplies and security control as well as in that of establishing links with third countries. Dealing as they were with an industry that was still in its early stage, the negotiators included in the Treaty provisions covering a number of situations and problems which have not in fact so far arisen and some of which are now unlikely to arise. Since this chapter deals largely with Euratom's activities and achievements, the sections of the Treaty which have not been implemented will be mentioned only briefly.

As has already been explained in the chapters on the EEC and the ECSC, the Six agreed in 1965 to merge the Treaties and institutions of the three Communities (see p. 168).[1]

The Institutions

The two main organs of Euratom are the Commission, which has five members, and the Council of Ministers. The Commission represents the corporate interest of the member states, the Council (apart from having a certain corporate nature as a Community body) their individual interests. While the Commission is independent of the governments and may exercise certain powers independently, its chief role is to initiate policy proposals on which the Council decides and to implement Council decisions.

THE COMMISSION

The Commission has far-reaching administrative tasks including the organisation of the work of a large research staff in the four estab-

[1] The merger of Euratom's Commission into the combined executive took place on 1 July 1967.

lishments of the Joint Research Centre and elsewhere, the control of a research budget of around $90 million a year, the conclusion of research contracts and the operation of the security control system.

The members of the Commission are appointed by the governments, acting in agreement, for a four-year period. They are chosen for their 'general competence' and 'undisputed independence', are collectively responsible to the European Parliament and may be removed by the Court. The Commission which took office in 1958 consisted of M. Louis Armand, a leading French administrator, scientist and engineer and member of the Académie Française, as President, Signor Enrico Medi, an Italian physics professor, as Vice-President; M. Paul De Groote, a Belgian university economist and former minister; Mr Emanuel Sassen, formerly Dutch Minister for Overseas Territories and a prominent member of the European Parliament; and Dr Heinz Krekeler, formerly director of a chemical firm and German Ambassador to Washington. In January 1959 M. Armand retired and was replaced by M. Etienne Hirsch, formerly Commissaire Général au Plan; he was not renominated by the French Government when his term of service ended in December 1961, and was replaced by M. Pierre Chatenet, who had been Minister of the Interior in the Government of M. Debré. M. Hirsch had attracted the resentment of the French Government for having piloted through the Council, against strong French opposition, the Power Reactor Participation Programme, and for his generally 'European' stance, federalist sympathies and 'maximalist' view of the role of the Euratom Commission. Dr Krekeler retired in 1964 and was replaced by Herr Robert Margulies, a German FDP (Free Democratic Party) politician and a prominent member of the European Parliament. Signor Medi resigned in 1964, his place as Vice-President being taken by Signor Antonio Carrelli, also an Italian university physics teacher. By the end of 1966 the Commission had recruited a research staff of some 2,700 working at the four Joint Research Centre establishments as well as at thirty-five other places within the Community and outside (in the United States, the United Kingdom and Canada). In addition, it was served by an administrative staff of about 800.

THE COUNCIL OF MINISTERS

The Council of Ministers, as in the EEC, is composed of representatives of the member states: the ministers responsible for scientific affairs, the finance ministers or the foreign ministers, depending on the business to be discussed at any one meeting. As far as decisions are concerned, although the Treaty provides for qualified majority voting in thirty-four cases, and simple majority in fifteen cases, compared with thirty-five cases requiring unanimity, in practice unanimity is usually sought and reached. Weighted majority decisions have, however, been taken on a number of occasions: the three most important were in July 1961 when France was outvoted on the issue of the Power Reactor Participation Programme (Amendment to Research Programme, Article 215 and Annex V of the Treaty), and on the 1964 and 1965 research budgets, France and Italy respectively being overruled. Unanimous votes are required for many of the more important decisions, such as the adoption of Research Programmes. There are no provisions, as there are under the EEC Treaty, for majority voting to be extended by stages to other subjects. A modification of the present balance between weighted and unanimous votes would require modifications to the Treaty.

THE SCIENTIFIC AND TECHNICAL COMMITTEE

Attached to the Commission is a consultative Scientific and Technical Committee (CST) of twenty experts appointed by the Council. It must be consulted by the Commission on all research proposals, health protection legislation and on other scientific and technical activities of the Commission. It may also be consulted where the Commission considers it desirable. The advice of this Committee, which includes some of the leading nuclear experts of the Community, has frequently been of great value to the Commission, particularly in the preparation of the Research Programmes. In January 1961 the Council and the Commission set up a second consultative committee, the Consultative Committee for Nuclear Research (CCRN), composed of officials responsible for the national programmes, which tries to make easier the dovetailing of the national and Community research programmes. It meets under the Chairmanship of the President of the Commission.

THE ECONOMIC AND SOCIAL COMMITTEE

The Economic and Social Committee (see p. 185) is common to the EEC and Euratom. Although, as in the EEC, both the Commission and Council may consult it, only the Commission is required to do so, and in only relatively few cases. In fact, it has been consulted by the Commission on a number of issues, such as health protection legislation, nuclear insurance, free movement of qualified labour, economic forecasts, energy policy and patent policy. This Committee certainly carries much less weight on Euratom matters than does the Scientific and Technical Committee.

THE EUROPEAN PARLIAMENT AND COURT OF JUSTICE

The European Parliament and the Court of Justice are common to all three Communities, and both are described elsewhere.[1] Because of the highly specialised and technical nature of nearly all Euratom's work, the plenary sessions of the Parliament on Euratom affairs are seldom well attended and the debates tend to be limited to the more political aspects. The parliamentary committees, on the other hand, do get to grips with atomic technicalities: the Research and Culture, the Health Protection and the Energy Committees devote most attention to Euratom. Other committees, however, may examine particular aspects of the Community's affairs: early in 1965, the Internal Market Committee examined and commented on the Commission's proposals for the revision of the Treaty regulations on nuclear supplies. In accordance with the Treaty, annual reports are submitted to Parliament, as are budgetary proposals. The Parliament has usually supported the Commission in conflicts with the Council, such as those that have often arisen over the research budgets. It strongly condemned the Council's dilatoriness over the revision of the Second Five-Year Research Programme; and, as regards the annual budgets under the Programme, it has always defended the Commission's budgetary proposals and opposed reductions made by the Council. In general, the Parliament has supported a 'maximalist' interpretation of the Treaty and has urged the Commission to exert its authority to the full.

The Court of Justice has not been resorted to on questions of interpretation of the Treaty, though a number of minor cases concerning Euratom staff, such as allegations of wrongful dismissal, have been put before it.

FINANCING AND COUNCIL VOTING

Euratom is financed by two budgets, one 'operational' and the other for 'research and investment'. Member countries contribute to both on a percentage basis. France, Germany and Italy each contribute 28 per cent to the total of the operational budget, Belgium and Holland 7·9 per cent each and Luxembourg 0·2 per cent. The corresponding votes in weighted majority voting in the Council of Ministers are four, two and one votes respectively, twelve votes constituting a majority. To the research budget, France and Germany

[1] See pp. 177 and 185.

each contribute 30 per cent, Italy 23 per cent, Belgium 9·9 per cent, Holland 6·9 per cent and Luxembourg 0·2 per cent. Weighted majority voting on research issues (the budget, for instance) operates on a percentage basis corresponding with the budget contributions, namely 30, 30, 23, 9, 7 and 1 per cent; sixty-seven votes constitute a majority. Weighted majorities are required for the adoption of both budgets.

The Work of Euratom

The chapter of the Treaty entitled 'Development of Research' (Articles 4–11) is quite short. It sets out a number of lines of action for the Commission and the Council and the obligations of those engaged in nuclear research in the member countries, while Annex I lists the fields of research falling within Euratom's competence. The Community is charged with promoting and facilitating nuclear research and with supplementing national programmes with Euratom's own programme. To promote co-ordination the Commission is to invite all undertakings engaged in research in subjects listed in Annex I to communicate details of their programmes but it has no power to compel them to do so. The Commission may thereupon formulate a reasoned opinion and is bound to do so when the undertaking requests it. Such opinions are intended to discourage unnecessary duplication and to direct research towards sectors in which studies have been insufficient. The Commission may encourage the communication of research programmes by such measures as furnishing financial assistance through granting research contracts, supplying basic or raw materials, by making available facilities, equipment or expert assistance and by initiating joint financing arrangements.

The Community's own research programmes are to be laid down by the Council by unanimous agreement and are to run for up to five years, and will be financed from the Community's research and investment budget. Lastly, the Commission is to set up a Joint Research Centre, which may be divided into separate establishments.

The provisions have in fact represented little more than a legal framework for Euratom research. As regards the subjects to be selected, Annex I to the Treaty encompasses a very wide range of activities relating to the practical exploitation of nuclear energy, so wide that it has not been and is unlikely to be amended. The practical character of this research stands in direct contrast to that of CERN (the European Nuclear Research Centre), which is concerned with fundamental research; this accounts for there being no formal link between the two organisations.

It is probable that Euratom's role in Community research has not developed exactly along the lines foreseen by those who drafted the Treaty, which is, for instance, somewhat imprecise about respective Community and national competence. Public and private undertakings have indeed communicated their programmes, but the value of this has been more as guidance in the preparation of the Community's own programme (i.e. financed by Euratom research funds) than as a means of discouraging duplication or directing research to other fields. The Commission has, in general, been less concerned to resort to the various means provided to encourage implementation of the programme communicated (Article 6 of the Treaty) than to tie certain promising national projects into the Community programme. In short, the Treaty has provided a framework within which parts at least of national research programmes could be welded together with the Community programme.

ORGANISATION OF EURATOM RESEARCH

Euratom research programmes have hitherto run for periods of five years. Activities for the First Programme (1958–62) to which $215 million was allocated were set out in Annex V to the Treaty. While going into some detail about the laboratories of the Joint Research Centre, the exchange of information and the construction of materials' testing reactors, Annex V left the details of experimental reactor programmes to be decided later. Expenditure under this initial programme was in the event devoted mainly to equipping the establishments of the Centre, to a large-scale programme of contractual work on light water reactors under the US–Euratom Research and Development Programme, to the Power Reactor Participation Programme and to various smaller projects. In fact the sum allocated proved more than adequate and there was a small financial carry-over to later years. During this initial period, in addition to the farming out of work under contract, the association contract formula was devised (see p. 301).

It was only under the Second Five-Year Research Programme (1963–67) that Community research took real shape. The survey of activities under national programmes, begun in 1958 but kept constantly up-to-date, provided the basic data necessary for the preparation of the Community programme. In 1961, the Commission started to prepare a first draft, which was subsequently discussed with the two scientific committees (CST and CCRN) and at technical meetings with national experts at many levels. The final draft was put before the Ministers in June 1962 with a request for an allocation of $480 million. The Council gave its unanimous approval to the Commission's proposals and granted $425 million—to which should be added $24·4 million from the First Programme and an additional $5·6 million awarded in 1965 with the revision of the Programme. The total sum available is thus an average of $90 million a year. This sum compares with total national expenditure on civil uses in 1966[1] of the order of $600–650 million (it is impossible to arrive at a precise figure).

In general the Community is entrusted with large-scale projects which, while not necessarily beyond the means of certain at least of the countries, can by general agreement be carried out more effectively on a Community basis. Along with this go certain central services such as information and the standardisation of measurements. A little over half of Community research (in terms of expenditure) is taking place at the four establishments of the Joint Research Centre: at Ispra (near Varese in northern Italy) with a staff of 1,700; at Petten (Holland) with a staff of 140; at Geel (Belgium) with a staff of 130; and at Karlsruhe (the Federal Republic of Germany) with a staff of 300. Ispra and Petten are 'general competence' centres. Ispra was formerly an Italian research centre, and its transfer to Euratom was completed in February 1961; at Petten, a materials testing reactor and certain laboratories were transferred to Euratom by the Dutch authorities. Geel and Karlsruhe are specialist establishments built alongside national centres; the former is the Central Nuclear Measurements Bureau, charged with preparing or perfecting measurements relevant to nuclear energy; the latter, the Transuranian Elements Institute, is concerned mainly with developing plutonium-based fuel elements for nuclear reactors.

[1] Since 1965 the published CEA (France) civilian nuclear budgets have all been in excess of $400 million. No satisfactory breakdown of expenditure has however been published in these years, but these figures cover heavy expenditure on mining and production operations, stocks etc. A realistic estimate of the CEA's research outgoings would be of the order of $250–300 million. As for Germany, expenditure by the Federal Government and the *Länder* (no recent figures are available for the latter) certainly tops $200 million. Taking into account the fact that in Germany major and expensive reactor development programmes have been mounted by private industry, it may be estimated that the Federal Republic is at least as heavily committed in civilian nuclear research and development as France. Public expenditure on nuclear programmes in Italy and the Benelux countries is very much smaller and added together it certainly does not equal the amount spent under either the French or the German programme.

The rest, about half, of Euratom's research in terms of the Commission's expenditure is carried out under various types of contract. Article 10 gives the Commission the power to 'entrust Member States, persons or enterprises or also third countries or international organisations or nationals of third countries with the implementation of the Community's research programme'. This article has been very fully implemented. More than 700 research assignments have been farmed out to national research authorities, private undertakings and universities. Research has been performed by third countries in only a few instances, notably where no satisfactory tenders are received from within the Community. The United States–Euratom Joint Research and Development Programme forms a special category (see p. 315) in that the results of research contracts performed in the Community and the United States under this joint Programme flow automatically to the two sides; hence work is being carried out in the United States for Euratom and vice versa.

About thirty of Euratom's research contracts, representing one-third or so of total expenditure, have taken the form of 'association contracts'. These provide for a partnership between Euratom and an undertaking in a member country for the joint direction, financing and staffing of a large-scale research project, usually one already under way. Euratom participation enables the scope and scale of the work to be widened. It is also a means of bringing the minds of scientists of a variety of different scientific formations and backgrounds to bear on the problems in question. The results of the research are shared. In some sectors Euratom has concluded a series of such contracts covering most if not all of the research under way in the Community in the field in question. The Commission is thus enabled to exercise a co-ordinating role between the projects and to weld them into a single coherent programme. Euratom is participating in all the thermonuclear fusion research in the Community under six such contracts. Five large-scale association contracts cover all the fast reactor work in the member countries. Other fields where this formula is employed include nuclear ship propulsion, advanced gas reactors, the Community's largest materials' testing reactor (at Mol in Belgium) and biology and health protection. Euratom usually contributes between one third and a half of the cost of the project, often 40 per cent. This in fact gives a multiplier effect to Euratom's own outlay. For instance, the $82·5 million available for fast reactor research will generate, with the contribution of the partners, about $235 million worth of work from which the Community will benefit.

Euratom's participation in projects of the OECD's European Nuclear Energy Agency resembles the association contract formula. Euratom accepted an invitation to take part in ENEA's work, being represented on the Steering Committee as well as taking part in the Agency's technical work. The Community participated for some years in the Agency's Halden project (in Norway) for research on heavy boiling water reactors and has been a partner from the outset in the 'Dragon' high temperature gas-cooled reactor project at Winfrith (in the United Kingdom). Euratom is not only participating in the direction of the project and contributing 46 per cent of the total cost on behalf of the member countries to reactor construction and associated research over an eight-year period; it has also detached to the project some thirty engineers from its staff and they are integrated into the multi-national research teams. The Community has full access to the results of the research.

AIMS OF THE RESEARCH PROGRAMME

Roughly 80 per cent of Euratom's research expenditure under the Second Programme is devoted to nuclear power production (reactor development and closely associated fields—operation of materials' testing reactors, re-processing of irradiated fuel and radioactive waste); another 7 per cent is spent on the long-term quest for power from thermonuclear fusion; the remainder goes to such ancillary sectors as health protection and the biological uses of atomic energy, the use of radioisotopes in industry, nuclear measurements, the dissemination of information, and training.

Euratom's first commitments were in the field of proven-type (first generation) reactors under the United States–Euratom Joint Programme. The aim here was to improve the performance of light-water (enriched uranium fuelled) reactors, the types being installed under the United States–Euratom Joint Power Programme (see p. 315); by the end of 1966 total approved expenditure by the two sides had reached some $56 million. Along with the work on the other main proven-type reactor string, gas-graphite natural uranium reactors, this work is being phased out and is unlikely to have any place in a third programme. Reactors of both these 'conventional' types are being installed for the commercial generation of electricity on a large scale, notably in the USA and Europe.

'Advanced converters' are a much bigger sector of Euratom reactor research. This 'second generation' of reactors should produce ('convert') much more plutonium and holds promise of reaching the stage of industrial scale construction in the early 1970s. One, the Orgel (organic-cooled, heavy-water-moderated) reactor, was selected in 1959 as a specifically Euratom research project and is being developed almost exclusively under the Community programme, at Ispra, where 80 per cent of the centre's work is devoted to it. (Ispra's equipment includes a critical assembly and a large test reactor (ESSOR) operating on the Orgel system. 'Dragon' and the BBC-Krupp 'pebble-bed reactor' are the two high temperature gas-cooled types of advanced converters which Euratom is developing.

'Fast breeder' reactors represent a third step in Euratom reactor research and Euratom devotes a larger sum to this sector than to any other. It is expected that they will be ready for installation on an industrial scale in the early 1980s. Close co-operation with the United States Atomic Energy Commission in the form of information exchanges was instituted for fast breeder reactor research in May 1964. This research is being performed under two major association contracts (the French CEA and the German GfK), two minor association contracts with Belgian and Dutch concerns, and an *ad hoc* arrangement with the Italian CNEN (the association contract, which expired in July 1966, not having been renewed). Euratom is thus contributing to and, with the exception of the Italian contract, directly participating in all fast reactor developmental work in the Community. Disagreements arising over the coverage of Euratom's share of additional costs incurred in this work escalated in 1966 into a major crisis, which was not resolved before 1967. It remains uncertain whether the whole of fast breeder reactor research in the Community will continue as part of the Euratom programme after the end of the 1963–67 Programme, particularly as regards a French and two German fast breeder prototypes, the construction of which is due to begin in 1969–70.

The fourth stage of nuclear power research is thermonuclear fusion. Scientists everywhere seem to agree that the expensive and laborious work on harnessing this untapped source of power is unlikely to be completed much before the end of the century.

Though most of the research projects in which Euratom is involved fall under the heading mentioned above, this survey is not comprehensive. One sector not mentioned is nuclear ship propulsion: Euratom is taking part in the building of Europe's first nuclear ship, the *Otto Hahn*, under construction at Kiel and due for completion in 1967.

Only a proportion of Euratom's research consists of Community projects wholly independent of national programmes: the Orgel project at Ispra is one example and most of the work at Geel and

Karlsruhe are others. Most of Euratom's research is closely linked with activities in the member countries. Not surprisingly, then, the spread of Euratom's research activities is wide—some critics have said too wide—for the funds available. But it could be said that this wide involvement is necessary if Euratom is to fulfil its function of co-ordinating the Community's nuclear research.

REVISION OF THE SECOND FIVE-YEAR RESEARCH PROGRAMME

The main criticism of the widespread nature of Euratom research activities came from France, and the decision to review the Second Five-Year Research Programme provided the opportunity not only to voice it but also to make a general stocktaking of national attitudes on the subject. This review was decided on by the Council of Euratom in October 1963. One pressing reason for this, from the Commission's standpoint, was the effect of inflation which during 1962–63 had resulted in an average rise in equipment, building and labour costs of about 10 per cent (one of the places where inflation was greatest was Ispra where roughly one third of Euratom expenditure is concentrated). Moreover, appropriations in 1963 and 1964 were well above the rate laid down by the Programme. If the Programme was to be fully implemented, expenditure would have to rise still higher, hence the initial request of the Commission for over $100 million for 1965.

But the Council had a more fundamental reason for a review: the progress made in nuclear technology during the previous two and a half years. One example was the remarkable cost reductions effected in the light-water reactor technology. Could the greater part of the $29·5 million allocated to reactors of a proven type continue to be devoted to this category? The French were emphatically of the opinion that this research (the subject of the United States–Euratom Agreement) should be phased out as soon as practicable. Most of the other governments, except the Italian, agreed to at least a reduction of the effort here.

The French Government's view was expressed in May 1964 in a memorandum to the Council. This document suggested a positive and logical view of Euratom's role in nuclear research. The memorandum criticised, among other things, the focusing of Euratom research on light-water reactors, asserting that there was little scope for the expansion of European industry in this sector and pointing out that these reactors depend on the United States for their fuel supplies. It went on to offer to put the information and experience of France's own natural uranium reactors at the disposal of the Community (this was the first time that such an offer had been made and doubt has been expressed by some observers as to whether it was meant seriously) and to name the three sectors of priority action: Orgel (likely to be fuelled with natural uranium), fast breeder reactors and thermonuclear fusion. There was, however, fairly general agreement about these as priority sectors; indeed the Commission had itself only a month previously, in its Seventh Annual Report, distinguished four stages for Community power production research: 'proven-type' reactors, advanced converters (including Orgel), fast reactors and thermonuclear fusion.

Three other governments submitted memoranda. It is impossible to go into the details of all the national positions here, but the debate was centred on the question of the sectors in which, and to what extent, Euratom research should be cut back. The French view was that industry in the Community had developed to such an extent in certain sectors, including waste disposal and fuel reprocessing, that it no longer required additional help from Euratom. But by how much should Euratom research be reduced in these sectors to the profit of the 'priority' ones? The debate lasted nearly a year and seven meetings of the Council were required before a compromise was reached in May 1965. Under the revision then agreed, the programme received an additional \$5·6 million (compared with the \$38 million extra originally requested by the Commission). The allocations for the priority sectors were increased, while a number of sectors suffered quite substantial cuts. Research on proven-type reactors was cut by slightly over 20 per cent. A notable feature of the revision was the shifting of the emphasis of research away from contracted work and towards research at the Joint Research Centre or under association contract, in other words towards research performed wholly or partly by Euratom staff. The Joint Research Centre as a whole received an extra 5 per cent and Orgel an extra 13 per cent. Virtually all the work for the other two 'priority' sectors, fast reactors and fusion, which received increases of 13 per cent and 10 per cent respectively, is being performed under association contracts.

By the end of 1966 a second revision had become essential in order to find financial coverage for deficits that had arisen in the fast reactor programme and to agree on the scope of the programme during the period remaining. Were it not for the expected merger of the Commission and the reinforcement of Community action that appeared likely to follow, the prospect of agreement on such a revision would have been faint.

DISSEMINATION OF INFORMATION

The sections of the Treaty (Articles 12–29) dealing with the dissemination of information are intended to reconcile the need to maintain the incentive of a patent system with the need to make available important new information as widely as possible within the Community. The Commission has a responsbility, under Articles 12–13 of the Treaty, to disseminate information resulting from its own or contractual research. The Commission has set out its interpretation of the Treaty's requirements in a series of declarations to the Ministers. The first, in 1961, deals with patented information resulting from research contracts and establishes a system for awarding non-exclusive licences while maintaining a balance between the interests of the Commission and its contractor. The second, in April 1963, deals with the dissemination of non-patented information resulting from research financed by Euratom, the conditions of publication of scientific data and the selective dissemination of information within the Community by a system of national correspondents. The third, in April 1963, covers the issue of patented licences to states and firms outside the Community: here the aim is to ensure for the Community's industry priority of rights in exploiting information arising from the research programme. The fourth, in May 1963, deals with the basic patents held by contractors and provides for cases when it is impossible to use the results of research without infringing contractors' patent rights; the Commission's contractors must therefore notify the Commission of the existence of patents held in the field in question. The last, in 1964, institutes a regime for patents resulting from association contracts and is an extension of the 1961 regime for ordinary contracts.

By the end of 1965, over 250 enterprises and individuals had requested access to restricted information resulting from Community research or communicated to the Commission about the right to make free use of it. By the end of 1966 some 1,075 inventions were the subject of applications for patents and had been examined by the Community's patents office. Although many patented inventions resulting from Euratom research are being used in its own laboratories, by the end of 1966, twenty four non-exclusive licences and licences had been awarded. Evidently the fact that the licences are non-exclusive diminishes the interest of enterprises in obtaining them.

A second section of the chapter deals with 'other information', of a kind which neither results from Community research nor is made available to it. Each member state must notify the Commission when applications for patents are filed (including patents filed by third countries) and must request the applicant for permission to inform the Commission of the contents of the application. The applicant has the power to delay communication of this information for eighteen months; after this time the member state is required to inform the Commission. This system has worked effectively with the full co-operation of member states. By the end of 1966, the existence of 13,907 patent applications had been notified to the Commission, while the contents of 10,116 patent applications had been communicated.

Articles 17–23 of the Treaty setting out the procedure for arbitration or *ex-officio* intervention by the Commission where a patent owner objects to the communication of information to the Commission have not as yet been invoked. The provisions concerning Security (Articles 24–27), under which information communicated to the Commission the 'disclosure of which might be harmful to the defence interests of one or more Member States shall be treated as classified information', have been resorted to in a few cases. While it is for the state in which the information originates to assess its possible military value, the Commission undertakes that other member states apply the same security grading as that applied by the state in question.

INFORMATION AND DOCUMENTATION CENTRE

Euratom's Information and Documentation Centre (CID) has been set up to distribute restricted information arising from Community research as well as information relevant to nuclear activities, from whatever source it might come. Apart from Community research, sources of information include the United States Atomic Energy Commission's *Nuclear Science Abstracts*, all of which have been made available to Euratom, and periodicals from many countries, including those from Eastern Europe. The information which has been collected together is coded and stored in a computer (some 500,000 documents and other 'items' are stored in this way) which came into operation in 1966 to undertake semi-automatic documentary research for inquirers in the Community and later outside it. The CID publishes a series of periodicals such as *Transatom Bulletin* (information on translations) and *Euratom Information* (summaries of Euratom research reports) as well as some 600–700 reports a year dealing with non-patented research items. The Centre has also organised libraries at Euratom headquarters and at the research establishments.

HEALTH PROTECTION

Articles 30–33 of the Treaty require the Commission to draw up basic standards for the protection of the health of workers in nuclear establishments and of the general public. These standards indicate the maximum doses of ionising radiation which workers and the public should be allowed to absorb. Member governments must incorporate these standards in national legislation. The Commission's proposals for the basic health standards were approved by the Council in February 1959 and are now in force virtually in their entirety in all the Community countries. The Community is therefore now a single area as regards nuclear health protection standards.

The members of Euratom are required to set up measuring facilities for the control of radioactivity levels in the atmosphere, water and soil, and reports must be made to the Commission on the controls established by the Six under Articles 35–36 of the Treaty, and the Commission, which regularly publishes the results of the radioactivity measurements, has reported itself satisfied with the network. It is, however, working out a programme for the standardisation of methods of measuring and of presenting the results of such measurements. Article 37 requires member states to submit data on their plans for radioactive waste disposal to enable the Commission to determine whether a plan will affect another member state. Opinions on projects in all member countries are given regularly, after detailed analyses from the standpoint of health protection.

EURATOM'S INDUSTRIAL ROLE

Although Euratom has no direct responsibility for the construction of nuclear power plants it has various functions designed to promote the speedy growth of a Community nuclear industry. The ways in which it intervenes include the indication of production targets, direct means of promoting certain projects which are considered desirable, regulatory functions (concerning supplies and security control), and the establishment of regimes for the free movement of nuclear products and specialised labour, and insurance.

(*a*) *Production targets*

Firms operating in branches of the industry specified in Annex II to the Treaty must inform the Commission about details of investment projects (see Article 41). The declarations, along with other information made available, have assisted the Commission in drawing up programmes (see Article 40) indicating production targets for nuclear energy and the types of investment needed for their attainment.

In 1960, the Commission published a preliminary assessment of the nuclear power needs of the Community: an installed capacity of 40,000 megawatts in 1980 was the forecast and this has been reiterated on a number of occasions. The Commission has also participated in the work of the Inter-Executive Energy Group and assisted in drafting the Memorandum on Energy Policy submitted to the Council of Ministers of the ECSC in June 1962. The most thorough forecasts were published in July 1965 in an 'indicative programme for the nuclear power industry. Holding to the forecast of an installed capacity of 40,000 megawatts for 1980, projections were made to the year 2000 for which a 'minimal' forecast of 370,000 megawatts of nuclear capacity is made, namely two thirds of total electricity-producing capacity. The implications for the various branches of the industry are dealt with in detail. The 1980 forecast has recently been raised to a minimum of 60,000 megawatts. This forecast is based on indications published by authorities in the member countries. As in the United States (where the official forecast of nuclear power capacity in 1980 has been raised from 40,000 to 150,000 megawatts over only a few years) the changeover to nuclear power for new electricity generating capacity is going ahead more rapidly than foreseen during the first half of the decade.

The Community's reliance on energy imports has risen far more rapidly than foreseen in *A Target for Euratom* in which the forecast was an increase of 33 per cent in 1967 and of 40 per cent in 1977. In fact, over 50 per cent of the Community's energy needs were imported in 1966 and the Commission's current forecast is that imports will not be stabilised until 1975 when half to two thirds of the total will be imported; even by the end of the century it is expected that imports will furnish nearly 50 per cent of total needs.

Nuclear power plants in operation, under construction or planned should represent over 4,000 megawatts of capacity in 1970.

(*b*) *Power plant*

There are a number of ways in which the Commission can promote the construction of a number of power plants which could not be justified by economic considerations alone. One such means is through bilateral agreements; another is provided by the terms of Annex V to the Treaty which defines Reactor Prototypes as a research sector under the initial research programme; the last is the granting of Joint Enterprise status.

The Commission has been concerned with two overlapping power reactor programmes. The first to be launched was the United States–Euratom Joint Programme for the installation in the Community of up to 1,000 megawatts of nuclear capacity on which research and development in the USA was well advanced, namely light-water reactors using enriched uranium. The cost of the programme was put at $350 million. Its aim was to make Community electricity producers familiar with these reactors and a number of incentives were provided such as the availability of $135 million in long-term American credits to Euratom to be re-lent to enterprises and the sale or lease of thirty tons of enriched uranium. A Joint Reactor Board of United States and Euratom representatives was set up to consider the suitability of projects for the programme. Owing to the decline in interest in nuclear power which began in 1959, only three plants with a total capacity of about 700 megawatts were included. This programme has been reasonably successful under the economic circumstances and has done much to gain for light-water reactors the firm footing they now enjoy in the Community, particularly in Germany.

The second means of action is the Community Power Reactor Participation Programme approved by the Ministers in July 1961. This is strictly speaking a research operation in that $32 million of research funds have been allocated to it from the First Five-Year Research Programme. The aim is to encourage the construction of a number of industrial-scale plants and to disseminate the resulting information. The Commission has made grants ranging from $5 to $8 million to five projects (the three United States–Euratom Joint Programme projects and two others), as a contribution towards the cost of fuel element manufacture (if this takes place in the Community), reactor parts (in two cases) and towards underwriting supplementary start-up costs (in three cases). In return engineers from Euratom, working on power and constructional undertakings in the Community may be assigned to the project to take an active part in the work in both the construction and start-up phases (sixty-eight were assigned to the projects during 1966). Information on problems arising during the construction and start-up phase may be made available to all interested parties through reports submitted to the Commission.

Another means of encouragement is to grant the status of Joint Enterprise (Articles 45–51) to 'undertakings of outstanding importance to the development of nuclear industry in the Community'. Those who drafted the Treaty had in mind large installations such as a Community isotopic separation or fuel reprocessing plant. The offer of adequate supplies of American enriched uranium removed, temporarily at least, the incentive to undertake the first of these projects as a Community venture, though the Commission stated that 'the advisability of a Community initiative in the field of isotopic separation should from now on be studied' (Eighth Annual Report). This status confers on the undertaking any or all of a number of special advantages including exemptions from certain taxes, duties and charges on the acquisition of immovable property, customs duties, etc. (see Annex III to the Treaty). In the cases where this status has been granted (three nuclear power plants in Germany and one in the specially constituted Franco-Belgian SENA project) the concerns are required to make available to the Commission information gained concerning the construction and operation of the plant; all non-patented information communicated to the Commission may be disseminated by it. The status is conferred for varying periods, but the Council has the power to annul the benefits which accrue from it if and when the economic situation of the undertaking permits.

(*c*) *Supplies*

Articles 53–76 of the Treaty set up a Supply Agency under the control, and subject to the direction, of the Commission, but with legal and financial autonomy. It must ensure that all consumers have equal access to nuclear materials. It has a right of option on all ores, source and fissile materials produced in the Community, and an exclusive right to conclude contracts for the supply of both raw (ores and source) and fissile materials, whether originating in the Community or imported from third countries. The Agency must ensure that the principle of equal access to materials be applied (thus preventing discriminatory pricing). Prices must follow the normal law of supply and demand except when the Commission proposes and the Council authorises price fixing by the Agency. To ensure that mineral deposits are adequately worked the Commission may give financial assistance to prospection and member states must make annual reports to the Commission on the development of prospection and production, on probable reserves and on mining investment in their territories; the Commission must submit the reports to the Council accompanied by its opinion as laid down by Article 70 of the

Treaty. The whole chapter of the Treaty dealing with the Agency's functions is subject to review at the end of seven years; on the proposal of the Commission, the Council may decide either to confirm or to amend the provisions.

A glut of uranium on the world market, adequate resources in France for the French programme, and the absence of fissile materials produced in the Community for civil use have made it unnecessary for the Agency, which was set up in June 1960, to exercise all its functions under the Treaty. For the supply of ores the Agency introduced, in December 1960, a simplified system permitting direct negotiations between consumers and producers, though the contracts must be submitted to the Agency which thus exercises a control and retains the exclusive legal right to make contracts. The Agency has, however, exercised a full role in negotiating the supply of fissile materials from outside the Community: it has negotiated the supply of 24 tons of enriched uranium for the Community's seven light-water power reactors so far in operation (including the three included in the Euratom–US Joint Power Programme), as well as numerous contracts for the supply of small quantities of fissile materials for research projects in the Community.

No action has been necessary to maintain the principle of equal access to materials. The reports in respect of Article 70 of the Treaty have been made regularly up to 1966. The Agency and its Consultative Committee's own market surveys have provided striking evidence that within a decade the present ore glut will most likely be replaced by a shortage unless prospection is stepped up by the member countries. In 1964 the Commission addressed an opinion to the governments setting out this view.

In 1965 the Commission decided in favour of the revision of certain articles of the chapter on the Supply Agency. A new text was submitted to the Council and the European Parliament but the Council failed to reach agreement on the matter and the issue has been shelved, for the time being at least. While five member countries consider that until a decision is taken one way or another the Agency's statute remains in force, this is contested by France. The main changes proposed were the substitution of the principle of 'non-discrimination' for that of 'equality of access' to nuclear materials; a confirmation of the procedure permitting direct negotiation between consumer and producer for ores; and a strengthening of Article 70 of the Treaty so as to make the Agency directly responsible for the execution of a common supply policy. The rules governing the Agency's operations would be made generally more flexible.

(*d*) *Nuclear common market*

A common market for nuclear materials and equipment was set up on 1 January 1959 by Articles 92–95 of the Treaty. All intra-Community barriers to trade in raw materials including fuel elements (list A1), and reactors and other equipment (list A2) were abolished. A common external tariff was established: this was nil for virtually all items on list A1 and the range of 0–12 per cent (in effect mainly 10 per cent), was fixed for list A2. The application of the A2 tariff was, however, suspended until the end of 1961. In March 1962 the Ministers accepted the transfer of fuel elements from the A1 to the A2 list and confirmed the 10 per cent duty on A2 items though with certain temporary reductions or suspensions. With the exception of the reduced duty on natural uranium fuel elements. the full 10 per cent tariff came into operation at the end of 1966. On a further list (list B) consisting of chemical products, together with equipment relevant to the nuclear industry, Euratom has taken no action. List B items are subject to the reductions on intra-EEC trade in industrial products.

Increasing pressure for tariff protection for industry in the Community has accompanied rising industrial interest in the nuclear sector. The Commission has succeeded in establishing a liberal regime, for the 10 per cent rate duty is low compared with other nuclear tariffs such as the American, British and Canadian ones.

In March 1962 the Council issued, in accordance with Article 96 of the Treaty, directives on free access to specialised employment in the nuclear field. Qualified workers will be granted automatic permits to work in the nuclear industry of another member country on presentation of a work contract. No accurate assessment of the results of either of these measures can be made at present. Statistics are not available, but so far it is believed that they have had little impact, potentially important though they may be.

(*e*) *Insurance*

The Euratom countries are parties to the OECD Convention on Third Party Liability in the event of an accident resulting from nuclear activities. Euratom took the initiative in negotiating a Supplementary Convention with most of the OECD countries (including the United Kingdom) which was signed in January 1963. It obliges the government concerned to take responsibility for third party liabilities for a nuclear accident occurring on its territory for damages up to a maximum of $70 million; should this prove insufficient the parties to the Supplementary Convention will intervene jointly to provide additional sums above $70 million and up to a maximum of $120 million. The two Conventions, along with the International Atomic Energy Agency's (IAEA) Convention in the same field, have not yet been ratified by all the parliaments.

SECURITY CONTROL

The Commission is given the twofold task of ensuring that nuclear materials are used for the purposes stated by the users and that the control provisions of any agreements with third countries are observed, notably with the United States which normally insists on inspection rights by its own staff or, now, by IAEA inspectors (see Articles 77–85 of the Treaty).

The Commission system operates in two ways. All plants using source or fissile materials are obliged to make a declaration to the Commission about the basic technical characteristics of their plant. Further, operating records must be made available, which permit accountability for stocks and transfers of all nuclear materials. By the end of 1966, 185 and 216 installations were co-operating with the two sections of the system respectively. Secondly, inspectors on the Commission's staff carry out checks to ensure that the declarations have been made accurately; by the end of 1966, 294 inspections had taken place in all member countries. Although a system of sanctions is provided for by the Treaty, none has yet had to be imposed, for no serious discrepancies have been detected and member governments have co-operated fully in assisting the inspections. One exception to this has been the French CEA's plutonium-producing reactors at Marcoule which were constructed to supply plutonium for France's military programme. The United States Government, which supplies practically all the Community's imports of fissile materials, accepts the Euratom control system and its experts are kept regularly informed about the operation of the system.

Although it operates in a comparatively small territorial area this is the first and only international atomic control system binding on and accepted by a group of states. It is thus more advanced than the International Atomic Energy Agency's system, which relies on control by national governments. The clause on security control in the draft Non-Proliferation Treaty, being worked out by the United States, the USSR and Britain at the end of 1966, was to run into opposition for failing to make allowance for the Euratom system.

External Relations

Under Article 101 of the Treaty, Euratom may make agreements with third countries and international organisations. These are to be negotiated by the Commission in accordance with directives laid down by the Council, which finally approves them. But agreements which do not require new funds or Council action to implement them may be negotiated and concluded by the Commission provided the Council is kept informed.

Article 206 of the Treaty also provides for 'agreements creating an association with a third country, grouping or international organisation'. The five agreements that have been concluded up to now are in the 'co-operation' category. This word may be inadequate to describe the first in the series, the agreement with the United States, signed on 8 November 1958. The aspects of this agreement relating to the Joint Power Research and Development programme have been mentioned on pp. 302–303. The section of the agreement which covers the supply of materials has been amended in several ways. Initially thirty tons of U235 was to have been available for projects under the joint programme. An additional agreement of June 1960 released part of this material for Euratom research projects. Two amendments to the Agreement signed in May 1962 made more flexible arrangements for the supply of materials: the thirty tons of U235 became available for all Euratom or national power projects, together with highly enriched uranium for certain research projects. It also permitted the leasing of the materials as an alternative to a deferred payments system. Following the United States Government's decision to release larger quantities of fissile materials for export, a further amendment was signed in August 1963 removing the thirty-ton limit on quantities of U235 available for Euratom.

United States–Euratom co-operation was taken a stage further by a ten-year agreement for exchanging information on any results of the research on fast reactors in which the two sides are engaged. This more informal agreement, which is neither a Treaty nor a modification of the existing one, marked an important change in the relationship between the two partners. In 1958 co-operation had begun on a basis of American support for a new facet of European integration through assistance to the Community's development of atomic power. The new agreement, by virtue of the roughly equivalent progress of the two partners in developing this advanced technology, is described in the joint communiqué as 'a concrete example of Atlantic Partnership . . . in this advanced field of nuclear technology'. The development of Orgel-type reactors may become the subject of similar co-operation.

In Euratom circles there had been hopes of achieving similar arrangements for close co-operation with the United Kingdom. These hopes had their basis in the strong political interest shown in Britain during 1957–58 in forming a close link with Euratom, the strong commercial interest in obtaining an assured market for British reactors of the Calder Hall type in the Community and in securing some sort of counterweight to American influence. In fact, the co-operation agreement that was signed on 4 February 1959 merely provided a framework for various *ad hoc* co-operation arrangements rather than for joint research or a joint power programme. The co-operation includes the exchange of information and training facilities and the two sides undertake to assist nuclear enterprises to obtain research and power reactors from the other side and to obtain appropriate materials and equipment. The United Kingdom Atomic Energy Authority undertakes to supply, on commercial terms, fuel for research and power reactors supplied by Britain or, in special cases, for other reactors. Two committees have been set up: a Continuing Committee made up of the President and a member of the Euratom Commission, and a member of the British Government and the Chairman of the United Kingdom Atomic Energy Authority; the other a joint working group of officials and scientists. These committees have met regularly. Exchanges of information have taken place as have temporary secondments of staff. An informal agreement is in operation for a regular exchange of information on certain aspects of fast reactor development. Small quantities of fissile materials have been supplied by the United Kingdom and a 90-kilogram delivery of plutonium has been made to Euratom for research purposes. Although this co-operation is not as intimate as had been hoped, United Kingdom–Euratom relations are reasonably close as a result of the agreement.

Two agreements between Euratom and Canada were signed on 6 October 1959: one with the Canadian Government, the other with Atomic Energy of Canada Limited. The main outcome of the agreements has been the establishment of research cooperation on heavy water moderated reactors (Euratom's contribution being the Orgel programme). This co-operation has led to the development of an informal three-way exchange of information with the United States.

Agreements with Brazil and the Argentine were signed in June 1961 and September 1961 respectively. They provide for co-operation in a large number of fields, including that of ore prospection.

Euratom plays an important part in the work of the European Nuclear Energy Agency (see p. 454). It has links with ENEA and with many of the UN specialised agencies, though full participation in the work of the International Atomic Energy Agency, to whose meetings Euratom sends observers, has been vetoed by the Soviet bloc.

Conclusions

Euratom was set up to deal with problems which were essentially those of an industry of the future. Thus there was inevitably an element of speculation in the Treaty which, in some ways, has not been the ideal instrument for the tasks that have confronted Euratom in practice. Nevertheless, nearly all Euratom's work involving legislation or regulations has been carried out as required by the Treaty. The section of the Treaty dealing with research was sufficiently vague to permit the development of an empirical approach.

It is extremely difficult to assess Euratom's impact in economic terms. It is probable that integration has brought benefits, although it is not possible to measure them quantitatively. Some of the benefits can be expressed negatively, for instance savings in technical and financial resources due to the avoidance of duplication. Others can be expressed positively: the impulse given to research and development in both the private and public sectors, especially the former, through the awarding of Euratom research contracts; the more rational expenditure of public funds resulting from the confrontation of programmes; the partnership of the United States which would have been almost inconceivable between the Americans and an individual European country or a looser grouping of countries. Euratom has, moreover, gone some way towards taking this costly field of scientific endeavour out of a purely national framework, though the large initial discrepancy between the scale of the efforts of France and those of its partners in 1958, as well as between their stages of progress in developing a nuclear energy industry, has constituted a formidable obstacle to the formation of a real Community programme. This obstacle will not necessarily be removed by the fact that the Federal Republic of Germany now rivals France in the growth of its reactor programme and the progress made in developing second and third generation reactor technologies. Until now, France has been ahead of its partners in developing a nuclear industry, in the scope of its research programme, in its drive to harness atomic power and in the number of its nuclear scientists and engineers. To these factors must be added the desire to isolate any activities relating to France's military programme from Euratom's purview and the French Government's open opposition to Euratom's political objectives. Yet the fact remains that France has played a full part in Euratom's work, which is evident by the large-scale association contracts being executed in French centres and the fact that French fast reactor and fusion research is (until the end of 1967 at least) entirely integrated into the Euratom programme.

Many uncertainties surround Euratom's future. The merger of the Executives and Councils of the three Communities may well be a step towards the solution of such problems as a common energy policy, which has hitherto fallen under three separate authorities. Should the Community be given responsibilities in new areas of advanced technology, it will likewise be more logical for one authority to supervise all such activities including nuclear work, much of which is in any case relevant to research in other fields.

These institutional changes are, therefore, likely to have positive results. The same cannot be said with any confidence, however, about the uncertainties surrounding the prolongation beyond 1967 of the work in which Euratom is at present involved. At the end of 1966 the Commission had as yet put no proposals before the Council for research after the period of the Second Research Programme expires at the end of 1967; nor did it seem likely that the member Governments would be able to agree quickly on any proposals that came from the Commission.

Whether or not the member Governments can eventually reach some consensus remains to be seen. Certainly the new, merged Commission will wield far greater authority than the old. There are, moreover, good prospects that the minor disagreements that have impeded Euratom's progress, for example the delay in deciding on the 1967 budget, will be much more easily settled as an element in package deals concerning mainly other areas of the Communities' operations. Doubts nevertheless remain as to the willingness of at least certain countries to put key or commercially promising areas of research into the Community pool. If these doubts prove justified, the emphasis of Euratom's operations may well be on long-term and more fundamental work rather than on reactor development.

A final uncertainty is that of the size of the Community. British membership would have a big and probably a favourable impact on Euratom.

Part 5

BRITAIN AND EUROPE

Chapter Nine

WESTERN EUROPEAN UNION

The two organisations dealt with in this Part of the book resulted from Britain's refusal, during the 1950s, to join the Six in their efforts to establish supranational communities. Chapter One has shown how the attempt to set up a European Defence Community failed partly because of French hesitancies and partly because Britain would not accept the supranational principle. After the failure of the proposed EDC, Western European Union was set up by Britain and the Six in the form of an intergovernmental organisation, as a means of enabling the Federal Republic of Germany to contribute German forces to the defence of Western Europe. It succeeded the Brussels Treaty Organisation, the first postwar body to organise collective defence and to promote economic, social and cultural collaboration in Western Europe. The Brussels Treaty Organisation was established under the Brussels Treaty of March 1948 by the Governments of Belgium, France, Luxembourg, the Netherlands and the United Kingdom. The essential aims of the Treaty were to organise a system of automatic mutual assistance in the event of 'an armed attack in Europe', and to promote economic, social and cultural co-operation among the member countries. New provisions were added in 1954 when the Brussels Treaty Organisation was transformed into Western European Union with the accession of Italy and the Federal Republic of Germany, following the refusal of the French National Assembly to ratify the European Defence Community Treaty in August. These included the promotion of European integration as an aim of WEU and the creation of a parliamentary assembly as a new organ.

The original Brussels Treaty was an extension to the Benelux countries of the Anglo-French Treaty of Alliance and Mutual Assistance signed at Dunkirk in 1947. This bound the two countries to join in resisting any revival of German aggression, and also pledged them to consult regularly on matters concerning their mutual economic relations in order to promote prosperity and economic security. The establishment of the Brussels Treaty Organisation was an important step towards the consolidation of Western Europe. In common with OEEC it had its origin in the wider conception of Western organisation, both European and Atlantic, which became the core of Anglo-American policy under the leadership of successive Secretaries of State, General Marshall and Mr Dean Acheson, and their British equivalents, Ernest Bevin and Sir Anthony Eden,[1] after the Soviet Government had proved unwilling to assist its wartime allies in the establishment of political stability and economic prosperity in Europe.

The Brussels Treaty Organisation

A brief account of the structure and activities of the Brussels Treaty Organisation are an essential for any study of WEU. The signatory governments set up permanent machinery for consultation on all matters dealt with in the Brussels Treaty. This consisted of: a Consultative Council of Foreign Ministers as the supreme organ; a Permanent Commission (in practice a committee of the ambassadors of the member states in London) to act on the Council's behalf when it was not in session; a defence organisation; and committees of experts on economic, social and cultural questions. The defence organisation established under the Treaty was under the general direction of the Consultative Council. It was headed by a Defence Committee composed of the Defence Ministers who were assisted in their strategic and operational planning by a Chiefs of Staff Committee and a Military Supply Board. On the strictly military side a Western Union Command Organisation, headed by a Commanders-in-Chief Committee (Field-Marshal Lord Montgomery and General de Lattre de Tassigny), was created at Fontainebleau to study the tactical and technical problems of Western European defence. A Finance and Economic Committee was also set up to consider problems of production and the financing of supplies of military equipment. During the first year of its existence the Brussels Treaty Organisation drew up and agreed a comprehensive plan for the common defence of Western Europe, which included an integrated plan of air defence based on the use of radar. It also made arrangements for the production of arms and equipment on the basis of mutual aid, set up the nucleus of a joint command organisation, agreed on measures for the standardisation of arms (which have not

[1] Later Lord Avon.

been implemented) and military training programmes, and held a number of combined exercises involving the land, sea and air forces of member countries. The work of the Brussels Treaty Organisation in devising an appropriate organisational structure and drawing up defence plans undoubtedly helped to mould the eventual shape of the defence organisation created under the North Atlantic Treaty a year later.

With the establishment of NATO the Brussels Treaty Organisation lost most of its military functions, and owing to the concurrent development of the Organisation for European Economic Co-operation, formally established only one month after the signing of the Brussels Treaty, its responsibilities in the economic field have not been pursued. In the social and cultural field, however, the Brussels Treaty Organisation acted as a central co-ordinating body for collaboration between the five countries. Four social committees and a cultural committee were set up by the Brussels Treaty Consultative Council in August 1948 to implement Articles II and III of the Treaty (providing for co-operation in social and cultural matters). The regular consultations and joint activities in the social and cultural spheres started by the Brussels Treaty Organisation were continued by Western European Union until their transfer to the Council of Europe in 1960.

THE LONDON CONFERENCE

After the failure of the French National Assembly to ratify the EDC on 30 August 1954, the Western European Powers, including France, were anxious to find some form of European military and political co-operation to replace it. The Bonn Convention signed in 1952 had anticipated that the EDC would provide the framework within which a restored Germany would simultaneously make her contributions to Western defence. Now these interlocking arrangements collapsed, and an alternative means had to be found for rearming the West Germans and securing their admission to NATO on a basis acceptable to France. This, in fact, meant that Britain must also participate in any new moves to Western European military co-operation since one of the reasons which led the French National Assembly to reject the EDC Treaty was the feeling that while the former enemy of two world wars would contribute military forces to the EDC the ally of two world wars would not. Had the EDC Treaty been ratified, German soldiers would have been placed in a supranational European army. The defeat of the EDC project, largely because of the refusal of Britain to take part in such a

European Army, but also because of opposition in some French political parties to the rearmament of Germany on any terms and to the supranational elements in EDC, meant that under the arrangements which were made in WEU German soldiers were placed in a German army.[1] Because the British were also taking part this arrangement was acceptable to the French. Largely on the initiative of Sir Anthony Eden, a series of discussions were held with the governments of the six EDC countries which led to the London Conference attended by these countries, together with Britain, the United States and Canada, to discuss new proposals for a German contribution to Western defence. The aim of the EDC Treaty had been to set up a supranational defence community with common institutions, common armed forces and a common budget. An Assembly of eighty-seven members, drawn from the national parliaments of the member states, was to study the constitution of a directly elected body that would function as part of the federal or confederal political structure. This was the basis of the draft constitution of a European Political Community (EPC) which was drawn up by the *Ad Hoc* Assembly (see p. 31). The 'common institutions' proposed for the EDC were modelled broadly on those of the European Coal and Steel Community. The Board of Commissioners was to have broad executive and supervisory powers particularly over the production of armaments. The assembly of the proposed EDC was allotted the task of exercising parliamentary control over the activities of the Board of Commissioners. An adaptation of this proposal led to the establishment of the Assembly of Western European Union.

The agreements reached by the nine countries at the London Conference were drawn up in the form of a series of Protocols which were signed in Paris by the foreign ministers of the countries concerned on 23 October 1954. These documents were incorporated together into the Final Act, often referred to as the Paris Agreements.

They provided for:

(*a*) the termination of the occupation regime in Western Germany;

(*b*) the revision and extension of the Brussels Treaty, to include the Federal Republic of Germany and Italy, under a new name: Western European Union;

(*c*) the admission of the Federal Republic of Germany to NATO;

(*d*) a Franco–German Agreement on the Saar, providing for a referendum to be held, under the auspices of WEU, on a future 'European Statute' for the territory.

[1] Even if this was 'assigned' in its totality to NATO.

The Protocols

The original Brussels Treaty of 1948 was revised and extended by four Protocols. The first Protocol amended the Treaty itself by providing for the accession of the Federal Republic of Germany and Italy. All references to the possibility of German aggression were deleted from the preamble, which was given extra weight by the statement that one of the aims of the revised Brussels Treaty should be 'to promote the unity and to encourage the progressive integration of Europe'. Continental member countries of WEU attached great importance to this addition, and to a similar insertion in Article 8; they did not wish to create an organisation devoted only to defence matters, but to invest WEU with a duty to promote political unification as well. In addition, provision was made for a new body known as the Council of Western European Union to be responsible for implementing the Treaty, and a new article was inserted providing for co-operation between the Council and NATO. Its terms were:

'recognising the undesirability of duplicating the military staffs of NATO, the Council and its Agency will rely on the appropriate military authorities of NATO for information and advice on military matters'.

The second Protocol dealt with the level of armed forces within WEU and specifically determined the maximum total strength and number of formations of land and air forces which each member state could station on the European mainland in peacetime. The maximum strengths for Belgium, France, Germany, Italy and the Netherlands were fixed at those laid down in the secret Special Agreement annexed to the old EDC Treaty; in the case of Germany, this was stated to be twelve divisions, which would be placed under the control of the Supreme Allied Commander, Europe. The Luxembourg contribution was fixed at one regimental combat team. The maximum strength laid down by the second Protocol could be increased at the request of NATO, but only with the unanimous agreement of the member states of Western European Union. The level of military and police forces required for internal security was to be the subject of a further agreement, which was eventually signed on 14 December 1957.

Article VI of this Protocol contained a British undertaking, first given by Sir Anthony Eden on the second day of the London Conference, that for the duration of the Treaty (i.e. until 1998) the United Kingdom:

'will continue to maintain on the mainland of Europe, including Germany, the effective strength of the United Kingdom forces which are now assigned to the Supreme Allied Commander, Europe, that is to say, four divisions and the Second Tactical Air Force or such other forces as the Supreme Allied Commander, Europe, regards as having equivalent fighting capacity'.

There were, however, two riders to this commitment. Although the United Kingdom agreed: 'not to withdraw those forces against the wishes of the majority of the High Contracting Parties, who should take their decisions in the knowledge of the views of the Supreme Allied Commander, Europe', the undertaking was not to be binding on it in the event of 'acute overseas emergency'. There was another qualification stating that:

'If the maintenance of the United Kingdom forces on the mainland of Europe throws at any time too great a strain on the external finances of the United Kingdom, Her Majesty will . . . invite the North Atlantic Council to review the financial conditions on which the United Kingdom forces are maintained.'

From the purely military point of view, the commitment was not new and this pledge did not involve any increase in the number of British formations stationed on the European mainland. Britain already maintained forces of that order on the European mainland and military planning had been based on their remaining there under the Supreme Allied Commander. But, as the British Government emphasised, it was an important step for an island people to take, particularly in view of its other responsibilities in Africa, Asia, the West Indies and elsewhere, and one that marked a significant change in British foreign policy. It certainly helped to reassure French opinion regarding the German contribution towards Western defence. In practice the British Government has acted against the spirit of its commitments by reducing the number of its forces in Germany from 77,000 to 55,000 in 1957, threatening to do this unilaterally if necessary though receiving the grudging agreement of the Council. Since 1959 British forces have been consistently several thousand below the new level, and in 1966 the issue of further withdrawals was raised again (see p. 407).

The third Protocol provided for the control of all types of major armaments (including atomic weapons) of WEU members on the mainland of Europe. It also recorded the agreement of the other members of WEU with the undertaking given by the Federal Republic of Germany not to manufacture on its territory any atomic, biological or chemical weapons; and not to produce long-range and guided missiles, large warships and submarines, or strategic bomber aircraft without a specific request from SACEUR and the consent of a two-thirds majority of the Council of WEU. No other member of WEU gave similar assurances. Between 1958 and 1964 six amendments to this Protocol were voted by the Council of WEU allowing the Germans to manufacture larger warships and certain types of small submarine and guided missile.

This Protocol also provides that, when effective production of atomic, biological or chemical weapons is started in the territory of any of the members of WEU (apart from Germany, which had voluntarily renounced the manufacture of such weapons), the Council of WEU would decide by a majority vote what level of stocks could be held by the country concerned. Thus France has a legal obligation to submit its atomic weapons to control by WEU, but General de Gaulle's government has consistently refused to honour this undertaking. Among the arguments put forward to defend this breach is that the Treaty is discriminatory because it applies only to the stocks held by the WEU members on the mainland of Europe and this excludes both the British nuclear weapons in the United Kingdom and the American nuclear weapons on the mainland of Europe. The French Government has declined to agree to a request by the Armaments Control Agency to be allowed to recruit atomic experts on its staff, and all attempts by the Assembly of WEU to persuade France to submit to nuclear controls have failed to move the French Government from its opposition to these measures.

The fourth Protocol provided for the establishment of an Agency for the Control of Armaments which was to be responsible to the Council of WEU for controlling the levels of major armaments of all WEU members on the mainland of Europe, and also for ensuring that the German undertakings not to manufacture certain types of armaments were observed. The Agency was empowered to examine statistics and budgetary information of member governments and to carry out inspections of, and test checks and visits to, production plants, depots and military units. Regulations approved by the

Council of WEU on 3 May 1956 authorised officials of the Agency to carry out inspections and test checks in both government and privately owned establishments. However, a further convention signed on 14 December 1957, which sought to establish a tribunal to enable the Agency to enforce access to establishments for control purposes and to determine claims for compensation arising out of actions by officials of the Agency, has not yet come into force as it still awaits ratification by France and Italy.

There are thus a number of elements of discrimination in the Protocols. The Federal Republic of Germany is the only member which has undertaken not to manufacture atomic, biological or chemical weapons on its own soil, and the United Kingdom is the only member not subject to arms inspection in its own territory by the Armaments Control Agency (although Gibraltar is subject to such inspection). On the other hand, the German undertaking not to manufacture certain type of weapons was given voluntarily, and reflected the 'strategic zone' concept of the EDC Treaty; and Britain was the only member that voluntarily undertook to maintain a minimum level of forces on the mainland of Europe.

The transformation of the Brussels Treaty Organisation into WEU enlarged, in the first place, the competences of its governmental body, the Council. Secondly, it led to the establishment of subordinate organs to deal with WEU's new concern, namely the control of levels of forces and of stocks of armaments which the several countries were allowed to manufacture; co-operation between its members in the field of armaments production, including the standardisation of weapons and components; and the settlement of the Saar problem. Finally, it entailed the creation of a parliamentary assembly which, once established, soon assumed that its purpose was to exercise parliamentary supervision of the Treaty's implementation.

The Institutions

THE COUNCIL

The Council is the decision-making organ of WEU. Since July 1963 it has met quarterly at the level of Foreign Ministers and otherwise generally meets at ambassadorial level in London, when it is composed of ambassadors of the six continental member countries in the United Kingdom—which are also the same six states that form the EEC—and a representative of equivalent rank from the British Foreign Office. The composition of the Council ensures governmental control of the organisation's policies. At ministerial level the chairmanship is held in turn for three months by each member country in alphabetical rotation. At ambassadorial level the Secretary General of WEU is the permanent chairman.

The Council uses different voting procedures depending on the kind of decision it is required to make. Questions for which no special voting procedure has been agreed must be decided by unanimous vote, including any increase in the level of forces of a member state above the agreed levels. Questions submitted to the Council by the Agency for the Control of Armaments, and the level of stocks of atomic, biological and chemical weapons which can be held by member states (other than Germany), are decided by simple majority vote. The Council also used this procedure in making decisions over the Saar Statute. Finally a two-thirds majority is required for any decisions regarding the amendment of the list of armaments (other than atomic, biological and chemical weapons) which the Federal Republic of Germany is forbidden to produce. The taking of majority decisions in the Council of WEU has a special procedural interest: the Council is the only governing body in the intergovernmental organisations studied in this report, where this procedure is used in taking major policy decisions binding on all members, though the Committee of Ministers of the Council of Europe may take majority decisions by a simple or two-thirds majority concerning violations of the European Convention of Human Rights and on all matters not specifically listed as 'important'.

Thus the member states have delegated real powers of decision to the Council as regards the military provisions of the revised Treaty, but it should be remembered that the Paris Agreements included a resolution of the North Atlantic Council accepting WEU as part of the NATO defence system. The Council of WEU has, indeed, consistently taken the view that so long as existing arrangements apply, the North Atlantic Council is the proper forum in which to discuss strategic planning and defence policies.

THE ASSEMBLY

As a result of the modification of the Brussels Treaty a consultative assembly of parliamentarians was added to the structure of the old Brussels Treaty Organisation. Article 9 of the amended Treaty states that the Council 'shall make an annual report on its activities, and in particular concerning the control of armaments, to an Assembly composed of the representatives of the Brussels Treaty

Powers to the Consultative Assembly of the Council of Europe'. Owing to the wording of the single article of the amended Treaty by which the Assembly was created (which was seized upon by a handful of 'European' parliamentarians and international civil servants as an opportunity to try to bring about a rapprochement between Britain and the Six), the Assembly of WEU was able to lay down its own rules of procedure, define its own nature and composition, establish its budgetary powers and choose its seat, thus completing the Treaty by a 'Charter of the Assembly' which is unique in the annals of international law, especially in view of the fact that this 'Charter' has never been approved by the Council. The Assembly, like that of the Council of Europe, is purely consultative in its powers which are limited to addressing recommendations to the ministerial Council. The reply of the Assembly to the Council's Annual Report is by no means a mere formality. The Assembly's Charter specifically provides for a 'motion of disapproval' which requires an absolute majority of the members of the Assembly. Such a motion was tabled in 1957, concerning the reduction in British troop levels required under Protocol II. It failed to gain the necessary number of votes, but another motion criticising the inadequacy of the Council's Report was adopted in June 1967.

The Assembly consists of eighty-nine members, eighteen each from France, the Federal Republic of Germany, Italy and the United Kingdom, seven each from Belgium and the Netherlands, and three from Luxembourg. The members of the Assembly are normally the same parliamentarians who represent the seven member countries of WEU in the Consultative Assembly of the Council of Europe.

The President of the Assembly[1] and six vice-presidents form the Bureau of the Assembly which is elected annually; with the addition of the chairmen of the Assembly's five permanent committees they also form the Presidential Committee. The Bureau of the Assembly prepares the agenda for Assembly meetings and is concerned with the administrative running of the Assembly. The Presidential Committee approves the agenda and plans the work of the Assembly and its committees. The five permanent committees are the Committee on Defence Questions and Armaments, the General Affairs Committee, the Committee on Space Questions, the Committee on

[1] The Presidents of the Assembly have been: Mr John Maclay, later Viscount Muirshiel, (1955–56), Sir James Hutchison (1957–59), Signor Vittorio Badini Confalonieri (1959–61), M. Arthur Conte (1961–62), Herr Carlo Schmid (1963–66) and Signor Badini Confalonieri again in 1966.

Budgetary Affairs and Administration and the Committee on Rules of Procedure and Privileges. There is also a Working Party for Liaison with National Parliaments. Since December 1957 the Presidential Committee and the Defence and General Affairs Committees have held *ad hoc* joint meetings with the Council to discuss matters of mutual concern or to promote closer co-operation between the two bodies. Speakers at meetings of the Assembly and of its committees may use the official language of their country. Speeches, which are usually made from a rostrum, are simultaneously interpreted from and into English, French, German and Italian.

The Assembly has three party political groups to which most of its members belong. The Liberal Group was the first group to be established, in January 1956, and it was quickly followed by the Socialist and Christian Democrat Groups which were set up in April 1956. British Conservatives and members of the French UNR are not affiliated to party groups.

The Assembly of WEU has certain distinctive constitutional features, notably its separate budget and independent secretariat. The Assembly's budget is prepared by two of the Assembly's committees, the Committee on Budgetary Affairs and the Presidential Committee, and, on the responsibility of the President of the Assembly, is submitted first to the Assembly and secondly to the Council for approval.

President Carlo Schmid has complained, and in this is supported by members of the Assembly, that the Council is not adequately represented at meetings of the Assembly and that the Council pays little attention either to the Assembly's recommendations or to the questions put to the Council by members of the Assembly.[1] In a report dated May 1964,[2] Freiherr von Mühlen, *rapporteur* of the General Affairs Committee, stated:

'The practice of written questions was included in the Charter so that parliamentarians, in addition to obtaining the political views of their own governments through the means provided under constitutional law in their own countries, could enrich the knowledge of European parliamentarians by comparing this national point of view with the political views of the ministerial body of the European institution they wished to develop. These goals have been reduced by the Council to a purely formal procedure which consists of acknowledging the receipt of the question, complimenting the parliamentarian

[1] Under arrangements made in December 1957.
[2] Assembly Document 342.

on the interest of the matter and giving assurances that the Council will not fail to draw the attention of member governments to this problem. Finally, in many cases, the Council states that it is not competent to study the problem raised even if its competence is clearly defined in the text of the modified Brussels Treaty.'

The Assembly of WEU meets twice a year. At first it met in Strasbourg immediately before or after sessions of the Consultative Assembly of the Council of Europe, but since 1960 it has met in Paris at the Palais Iéna. In June 1961 the Assembly met in London and in June 1964 in Rome. A new wing of the Palais Iéna houses the Office of the Clerk of the Assembly and the two divisions of the WEU Council Secretariat in Paris: the Agency for the Control of Armaments and the Standing Armaments Committee.

THE SECRETARIAT

The Secretariat of WEU is divided into two separate parts. The WEU Council Secretariat is headed by a Secretary General[1] who is assisted by a Deputy Secretary General and two Assistant Secretaries General. The Secretariat of the ministerial organisation consists of about fifty at the London headquarters of the Organisation together with a further fifty at the Agency for the Control of Armaments and thirty at the Standing Armaments Committee, both in Paris. The staff of the Agency for the Control of Armaments, though otherwise a distinct body working under a Director appointed by the Council, is 'subject to the general administrative control of the Secretary General'. The Secretariat of WEU is an international staff drawn from all the member countries.

The Assembly has an independent staff, which is responsible only to the Assembly and is in no way answerable to the Secretary General. It is headed by the part-time Clerk of the Assembly,[2] who is appointed by the Assembly, and a permanent Clerk Assistant.[3] There are also a number of committee secretaries and a small administrative staff amounting to a total of twenty-six. These officials are paid out of the Assembly's budget and are responsible

[1] The Secretary General of WEU was M. Louis Goffin from 1955 until 1962 when he was succeeded by M. Iweins d'Eckhoutte.

[2] The Clerk of the Assembly, since the establishment of the WEU Assembly, has been M. Francis Humblet, who is also the Clerk of the Belgian Senate.

[3] The Clerks Assistant have been Mr Noël Salter (1955–63), M. Jean-Marie Le Breton (1963–65) and M. Georges Moulias, who was appointed in 1965.

for the administrative running of the Assembly. About 160 additional temporary staff are engaged to assist the permanent Secretariat during Assembly meetings.

THE AGENCY FOR THE CONTROL OF ARMAMENTS

The main tasks of this Agency are to ensure that the undertaking given by the Federal Republic of Germany not to manufacture on its own soil atomic, biological, chemical and certain heavy weapons is observed, and also to control the level of stocks of those weapons held by each member of WEU on the mainland of Europe. To enable the Agency to carry out these tasks each member is required to provide it with an annual statement, in reply to a detailed questionnaire, of the total quantities of armaments required for its forces stationed on the continent under NATO authority and the current stocks of such arms. The statement also declares the method by which the total quantities will be achieved, by manufacture, purchase from other countries or military aid. In addition, each member must supply information concerning the strength of its internal security and police forces and on its forces under national control on the European mainland. The Agency verifies these statements by comparison, cross-checking and co-ordination of all data supplied by member states in reply to its annual questionnaire and information from any other available sources, and refers to national defence budgets and information supplied to NATO. The Agency is required to report to the Council immediately if inspection or information from any other source reveals that forbidden armaments are being manufactured or if stocks of armaments are found to be in excess of those reported by member States.

The Agency began its control activities in 1956 and has continued, each year, to carry out inspections of units under national command, quantitative control activities at military depots and units, shipyards and factories, and non-production exercises (ensuring that production not allowed under the Treaty is not taking place). Inspections are carried out by teams usually composed of three officials: the group leader, an expert on the type of armament in question, and a national of the country concerned. Inspection teams are generally accompanied by an officer from SHAPE in the case of joint inspections carried out by the Agency together with SHAPE. The Agency has studied and carried out control exercises concerning the development of new weapons, such as guided and self-propelled missiles. It has also carried out non-production control exercises concerning chemical and biological weapons and nuclear weapons. About sixty-five field control operations are carried out annually. The Agency has established a central documents office which has a comprehensive collection of books, documents, reports, press and magazine articles, together with its own documentation, concerning weapons and the armaments industry.

As has been pointed out, the French Government has never notified WEU of its nuclear production, and it has fixed the level of its stocks of nuclear weapons without reference to the WEU Council, despite the provisions of Protocol III. Moreover, the Armaments Control Agency has been unable to carry out its controls in accordance with Protocol IV. The detailed experience of arms inspection and control by the Agency since 1956 could, however, possibly be of use in providing a starting point for measures of international inspection and control to be applied on a wider scale under any future general disarmament treaty.

THE STANDING ARMAMENTS COMMITTEE

The attempts that have been made to rationalise the production of armaments and to standardise military weapons in WEU were due to two distinct causes: France's original fear of German rearmament and the generally felt need for standardisation of arms research and production as a desirable objective in itself. The French Government urged that there should be more than *ex post facto* control of the German level of forces, certification of armaments stocks and of non-manufacture of prohibited weapons. France wanted to organise a specific Western European arms production programme which would link the arms production of the member states inextricably together. The principle of encouraging co-operation in armaments production was adopted by the Nine Power Conference at Paris in October 1954, but it was only at the first meeting of the Council of WEU in May 1955 that proposals were given definite shape and a Standing Armaments Committee was set up within WEU. The Committee consists of representatives of all seven member governments and is served by an international staff. The Committee works in close liaison with NATO.

In WEU as in NATO the need for arms standardisation has stimulated talk rather than action. The Committee has, however, attempted to develop its activities in four ways: the exchange of information on existing equipment; the production and development of new equipment; bilateral and trilateral co-operation; and the exchange of technical and scientific data. As early as 1958 the Committee found, however, that 'there is little chance of aiming at efficacious joint production of existing equipment. The producer countries, and even the purchasing countries, are generally too far committed for any attempt at a bringing together of the present decisions of the different countries to have a reasonable chance of success.'[1] Working in close liaison with NATO the *ad hoc* Group, composed of representatives of the War Offices and Chiefs of Staff of the six continental member countries, has carried out a considerable amount of work on the specification and development of new equipment. During 1959 and 1960 seven agreements were approved by the War Offices and Chiefs of Staff of the six continental member states. These laid down the military characteristics of certain weapons which were to be developed. Work of this kind has continued and during 1963 progress was made on the study of a 'family of wheeled vehicles to be used between 1970 and 1980'. Practical results of this work have, however, been slow to emerge; and national traditions of arms production, industrial interests and the predominance of American influence in NATO have constituted considerable obstacles to far-reaching arms integration in Western Europe.

Apart from its contacts with NATO, the Standing Armaments Committee also maintains close relations with FINABEL.[2] FINABEL, which was set up following an initiative taken by the French Chief of Staff in 1953, consists of the Chiefs of Staff of the military forces of the six member countries of the EEC.[3] It holds regular meetings to discuss the strategic basis governing the joint production of armaments by its member countries. FINABEL is non-governmental in character. It has no juridical existence or autonomous secretariat and is not officially recognised by the governments. Its character is thus purely military. Although it is institutionally ill-defined, FINABEL has been effective in harmonising strategic thinking in its different member countries and its work on the joint production of armaments has led to the development of a series of armoured carrier vehicles.

[1] *Third Report of the Council to the Assembly*, Assembly Document 79, February 1958.

[2] The word FINABEL derives from the initial letters of its members: France, Italy, the Netherlands, the Federal Republic of Germany (Allemagne), Belgium and Luxembourg.

[3] Germany joined FINABEL in 1956. Up to that time the organisation had been known as FINBEL.

The Work of WEU

THE MILITARY WORK OF WEU

The Assembly of WEU is a useful forum for the discussion of military affairs, particularly the defence of Western Europe. It is, indeed, the only formally established Assembly competent to discuss the military aspects of European defence problems. In order to avoid duplication between the Assembly of WEU and the Consultative Assembly of the Council of Europe in the defence field, the Bureaux of the two Assemblies agreed, at a joint meeting on 5 June 1956, that the Assembly of WEU should limit its activity to the discussion of the military aspects of defence—leaving the Consultative Assembly to discuss the political aspects—with the reserve that its discussions could be extended to political questions which had a direct link with military ones. In practice this decision has not restricted the WEU Assembly from the discussion of the political as well as the military aspects of defence. Although not all the member countries of NATO are represented in the Assembly its most valuable work has been its discussions of the effectiveness of the NATO defence system. The reports presented to the Assembly on behalf of the Defence Committee by its *rapporteurs* have regularly provided searching evaluations of NATO defence and have also dealt with proposals of a political as well as a military nature, such as the American Government's proposal to establish a Multilateral Nuclear Force (MLF) and the British suggestion of an Atlantic Nuclear Force. The MLF debates in 1963 and 1964 were of a high order, and the American Government sent Mr Walt Rostow to give its official view to the Rome meeting of the Assembly. The Council of WEU has, in general, been reluctant to provide the Assembly with military information other than that already available to the parliaments of the member states on the grounds that the revised Brussels Treaty transferred the Council's responsibilities for the supervision of international defence arrangements to the North Atlantic Council. There has been continual friction between the two organs of WEU concerning this situation which was aggravated by a decision of the NATO Council in 1958 that only 'unclassified' information could be given to parliamentarians. This position has been partly mitigated by the development of joint meetings between committees of the Assembly and the Council of WEU. This development has enabled the Assembly's Committee on Defence Questions and Armaments to obtain more information from the member governments than previously. Since 1958 joint meetings have been held every year between the Council and the Committees on Defence Questions and Armaments and General Affairs. These meetings resemble the efforts made by the Consultative Assembly of the Council of Europe and the European Parliament to achieve a closer dialogue with their respective ministerial bodies. In all three cases a freer flow of information about the views and policies of the member governments seems to have been achieved, but in no case have the results led to a spectacular improvement in the relations between the parliamentary and ministerial bodies.

The Defence Committee has taken the initiative in supplementing the information given to it by the member governments by visiting NATO forces and military installations. In the period between 1956–61, for instance, the Defence Committee made fifty-two visits of this kind to places such as Vernon, the French ballistic studies centre; the headquarters of the Central European Command at Fontainebleau; and Holy Loch in Scotland to inspect the Polaris submarine squadron. The Committee has also made two extensive official visits to NATO installations in the United States. The information obtained by the Defence Committee from these visits enables the Assembly to make informed and useful criticisms and recommendations concerning European defence problems. Apart from the technical points made in these recommendations the Assembly has continued to underline the need for Western governments to reject, in the words of its Recommendation 69 of December 1961, 'nationalistic concepts of defence in favour of common defence'.

THE NATO CRISIS AND WEU

The crisis in NATO resulting from the French Government's memoranda of 11 and 29 March 1966 and its decision to withdraw its forces from the military structure of the organisation as from 1 July 1966[1] inevitably involved WEU, since NATO is responsible for taking the military steps necessary for the defence of the area of the members of the modified Brussels Treaty. The *rapporteur* of the Defence Committee of the Assembly, Mr Duncan Sandys, in his report[2] to the Assembly in June 1966, raised the question of whether the French Government still considered itself bound by the automatic mutual defence commitment of Article 5 of the revised Brussels Treaty. In the debate on this report representatives of the French government party reaffirmed France's loyalty to its obligations under

[1] See p. 402.

[2] *State of European Security*, Assembly Document 375, June 1966.

the NATO and WEU Treaties, and this was subsequently confirmed by other spokesmen of the French Government.[1] Hopes expressed by some members of the Assembly that France would be prepared to go further in co-operating over defence matters with its six partners in WEU than with its other allies in NATO proved unfounded when M. Jaques Baumel, Secretary General of the UNR, told the WEU Assembly that France rejected the principle of integration whether in NATO or in WEU.

The political work of WEU

Although the military aspects of the work of the WEU Assembly have been consistently important throughout the history of WEU, the political work of the organisation has come to the fore in recent years. In particular, the WEU Assembly played an interesting, if marginal, role in the period leading up to Britain's application for membership of the EEC in July 1961, and since the breaking off of the negotiations the Council and the Assembly of WEU have provided a useful meeting place for Britain and the Six.

In June 1960, a report submitted by M. Arthur Conte, *rapporteur* of the General Affairs Committee, invited the Council of WEU to examine the possibility of full British membership of Euratom. During the Assembly debate on this report Mr John Profumo, Minister of State for Foreign Affairs, stated that Britain would accept an invitation to join Euratom and the ECSC. In November 1960, Mr Molter, in another report submitted to the Assembly by the General Affairs Committee, urged the British Government to join all three Communities of the Six and to take part in the meetings of the Heads of Government of the Six due to take place in December of that year. In June 1961 the Assembly, meeting in London, adopted Recommendation 65 in which it invited the Council to 'initiate general discussions between representatives of the seven member States and of the Commission of the EEC with a view to proposing an agreement providing for the accession of the United Kingdom to the European Economic Community without weakening the political content of the Treaty of Rome'. These discussions and moves should be placed in the context of the debate being held at that time in European circles on the possibility of British accession to the EEC. Mr Macmillan's statement concerning Britain's application for

[1] Though further doubts concerning the French commitment arose from the statement made by M. Maurice Couve de Murville in the French National Assembly on 3 November 1966 (see p. 407).

membership of the EEC followed shortly afterwards at the end of July. The General Affairs Committee, whose *rapporteur* on this subject was M. Leynen, followed the negotiations between Britain and the members of the EEC between 1961 and 1963 with close attention and in two reports prepared by Mr Robert Mathew and M. Sourbet proffered its advice to the negotiators on the agricultural problems involved. Since the breaking off of the negotiations in January 1963, the Assembly of WEU has been used as a forum where British parliamentarians can discuss with their colleagues from the Six Britain's relations with the EEC.

Until 1963 there was little consultation on political or economic matters in the Council of WEU, although the Council met quarterly at ministerial level from March 1960 to mid 1962. The breaking off of the Brussels negotiations led, however, to a reappraisal of the potentialities of the Council as a political meeting place by those governments which considered it desirable to maintain the greatest possible degree of contact between Britain and the members of the EEC. At its meeting of 10–11 July 1963, the EEC Council decided, following initiatives by the German Government, to make the following proposal to the British Government:

'The Council proposes to the British Government to organise quarterly contacts in the framework of WEU designed to permit the seven countries, in the course of these discussions, to take stock of the political and economic situation in Europe. It proposes to inscribe on the agenda of the Ministerial meetings every three months, in addition to political questions, an item to be added as follows: "Exchange of views on the European Economic Situation". Discussions will take place in principle at Ministerial level. When economic problems are to be discussed the Commission of the EEC will be invited by the Ministers of the Six to participate in the meeting.'

The British Government accepted this invitation and the first of the new series of quarterly meetings was held at The Hague on 25–26 October 1963. At this meeting an interesting precedent was created by the participation of members of the EEC Commission in the discussions of the ministers concerning the forthcoming tariff negotiations in GATT, relations between Britain and the EEC, the work of EFTA and agricultural problems. Discussing the prospects of economic co-operation between Britain and the EEC the Ministers expressed their determination to work closely together to obtain progress. But although these quarterly meetings have enabled the foreign ministers of Britain and the members of the EEC to hold formal discussions of such political questions as East–West relations and relations between Western Europe and Latin America, and, further, although the EEC Commission has been represented at those meetings where European economic problems have been discussed, no concrete proposals for specific measures of co-operation between Britain and the EEC have emerged from them.

The Assembly has followed the quarterly meetings of the Council at ministerial level with great attention and it has advocated the establishment by the Council of 'a special permanent body responsible for following economic relations between the member states'.[1]

WEU has also followed with close attention the changing fortunes of the plans for establishing a European political union of the Six and Britain's possible role in any talks on European political unity. As early as April 1962 Mr Edward Heath first expressed the British Government's support for the idea of a European political union at a meeting of the Council of WEU. In June of the same year he went further, in stating to the Assembly, 'Naturally, we shall want to play our part in shaping a political structure for the Community which we hope to join, and we have assurances that we shall have full opportunity for this when the time comes'.

After the long interval which followed the breakdown of the Fouchet/Cattani Committee's discussions concerning a treaty of European political union in April 1962[2] the Assembly of WEU played a prominent part in the *relance* of discussions among the Six on this subject. Thus, of the three plans which were put forward in 1964 for the construction of a European political union the one which attracted most comment and support from the 'Europeans' was that launched in September by M. Paul-Henri Spaak at a special meeting of the General Affairs Committee of the WEU Assembly to which the chairmen of the foreign affairs committees of the national parliaments were invited. The Assembly has held a series of debates on the issue of political union.

THE SAAR REFERENDUM

The attempt to settle the Saar problem has been one of the main tasks so far undertaken by WEU. The Franco-German agreement on the Saar, of October 1954, which was based on the Statute elaborated by the General Affairs Committee of the Assembly of the Council of Europe in 1952 and 1953, provided that (subject to approval by a referendum of the Saarlanders) the Saar was to have a

[1] Recommendation 113, December 1946. [2] See pp. 36–37.

'European Statute' within the framework of WEU. The Council of WEU was given the responsibility for supervising the referendum and making the necessary arrangements in the event of the Statute being accepted. Elaborate provisions were made in a Franco-German agreement for the implementation of the Statute. A European Commissioner, appointed by a majority vote of the Council (including favourable votes by France and Germany and the assent of the Saar), was to represent the Saar over foreign affairs and defence matters and ensure that the Statute was observed. He was to be responsible to the Council and make an annual report to it, which was then to be transmitted to the Assembly. He was also to attend meetings of the Council in an advisory capacity. The Saar was to continue to send representatives to the Council of Europe and they were also to sit in the Assembly of WEU. Provision was to be made for the participation of the Saar in Western European defence arrangements and for its representation in the European Coal and Steel Community. All these arrangements came to nothing. When the referendum was held on 23 October 1955 the Saar people rejected the proposed European Statute by a vote of 423,000 to 200,000. The voters showed a marked preference for the incorporation of the Saar into the Federal Republic of Germany, and following this expression of their will the Saar became part of the Federal Republic politically in January 1957. Economic integration followed after a transitional period.

SOCIAL AND CULTURAL ACTIVITIES

Article 2 of the Brussels Treaty stated that the signatory governments should co-operate in social matters 'to promote the attaining of a higher standard of living by their peoples and to develop on corresponding lines the social and other related services of their countries'. Three social committees were established by the Brussels Treaty Consultative Council in August 1948 to implement this Article. These Committees, made up of civil servants representing the ministries and departments concerned with social affairs in the member countries, were: the Social Committee; the Public Health Committee; and the War Pensions Committee. A fourth body, the Joint Social–Public Health–War Pensions Committee, charged with making a separate study of the rehabilitation and resettlement of the disabled, was set up shortly afterwards. These committees prepared recommendations for the Brussels Treaty Permanent Commission in London which transmitted them to the member governments for action and reported to the Consultative Council on the working of the committees. In some cases proposals were implemented by multilateral conventions between the member governments, in others by agreements between the appropriate technical departments.

When WEU succeeded the Brussels Treaty Organisation in May 1954 and was joined by the Federal Republic of Germany and Italy, the amount of work that the new organisation undertook in the social field expanded considerably. Under WEU the social committees established by the Brussels Treaty Organisation were retained and a number of new committees dealing with social affairs were set up.

The Brussels Treaty Organisation concluded a number of multilateral social security conventions. These conventions established the principle that member states should treat nationals of the other members in the same way as their own citizens when resident in their territory. Nationals of the member states, it was agreed, should be treated alike under social security schemes. The conventions provided: (a) for contributions under different national schemes to be considered on aggregate for benefit purposes; (b) for certain specific benefits to be paid to people moving from one of the member states to another; (c) for money to be paid and other benefits given to dependants in one member country of persons employed in another. Other conventions were drawn up covering the exchange of student employees and facilitating the free movement of frontier workers.

In public health matters the Brussels Treaty Powers decided to form a single area for the health control of air and sea communications. The Public Health Committee in conjunction with the Social Committee carried out work which led to the signing, in November 1954, of a multilateral Social and Medical Assistance Convention by which member countries were required to give both financial and medical assistance to nationals of any of the other member states on the same basis as to their own citizens. Under WEU the Public Health Committee extended its arrangements on health control over air and sea traffic. The seven member states now form an 'excepted area': aircraft and ships starting their journeys within this area and not breaking outside it are not normally subject to health control when arriving at destinations within the area.

Under WEU the other committees carried out useful work on the harmonisation of war pensions schemes, rehabilitation resettlement of the disabled and the establishment of rehabilitation centres.

Article 3 of the Brussels Treaty stated that:

'The High Contracting Parties will make every effort in common to lead their people towards a better understanding of the principles which form the basis of their common civilisation and to promote cultural exchanges by conventions between themselves or by other means.'

The Brussels Treaty Organisation accordingly established a Cultural Committee in August 1948 to act as the co-ordinating body for cultural collaboration between the member states.

In 1950 the Brussels Treaty Organisation introduced a cultural identity card to encourage foreign travel for teachers, research workers, scientists, students, youth leaders and others. Certain advantages and facilities were given to holders of these cards when travelling in the member countries, such as free or reduced entrance prices to museums, exhibitions and theatres and reduced transport rates. After a transitional period this card was replaced in 1954 by another valid in all the member countries of the Council of Europe.

When the Brussels Treaty Organisation was first set up the member governments concentrated their joint cultural activities mainly on education and the free movement of persons and cultural material. Later, under the Brussels Treaty Organisation and WEU, they dealt with more specialised questions, such as: public administration, on which annual courses for government officials have been held; university and school education, on which various conferences and courses have been held; youth activities which have included the sponsoring of exchanges; cinema, radio and television.

In the early years of the WEU Assembly there was a considerable degree of duplication between it and the Consultative Assembly of the Council of Europe, particularly concerning social and cultural questions.

While at first a temporary solution was found by the practice of the two Assemblies consulting each other on overlapping subject-matter, there was little long-term success in avoiding duplication between the two Assemblies. In October 1956 Mr Nigel Nicholson, *rapporteur* of the Cultural Committee of the Consultative Assembly, proposed that cultural affairs should be removed from the competence of WEU and transferred to that of the Council of Europe. In its Resolution 128 of May 1957 the Consultative Assembly of the Council of Europe noted that of the seven social questions on the agenda of WEU, six had already been the object of study and of decisions by the Council of Europe and other international organisations. The Assembly held that duplication 'would gradually lead to a state of confusion and thus not merely impede progress, but bar the way to European unification'.

In 1959, following the submission of a memorandum on the rationalisation of the work of European organisations by M. Wigny, the Belgian Foreign Minister, to the Committee of Ministers of the Council of Europe, the Foreign Ministers of the countries concerned agreed that the cultural and social activities of WEU should be transferred to the Council of Europe, and the expert committees of WEU were transformed into committees of the Council of Europe in the spring of 1960.

Conclusions

WEU was set up primarily as a means to allow the rearming of the Federal Republic of Germany and the creation of a separate German army. This followed the defeat of the EDC (due to fears of German military resurgence), in which German soldiers would have been integrated in a European army, but in which Britain refused to join. WEU was also set up to promote European political and economic integration on the basis of its seven members. Although it is a regional defence organisation, WEU has no separate command system outside the NATO structure. Since the rearmament of the Federal Republic of Germany and the assumption by NATO of the task of implementing the military responsibilities of WEU, the organisation has tried to ensure the effectiveness of the automatic military defence arrangements by which its members are linked under the terms of the Brussels Treaty. It is important to note that these provisions, contained in Article 5 of the Brussels Treaty, being completely automatic, go further than the equivalent provisions of the North Atlantic Treaty, and are more binding. At the time the French Government withdrew its forces from the integrated military structure of NATO on 1 July 1966 its representatives emphasised that France continued to accept its NATO and WEU commitments, including those set out in Article 5 of the modified Brussels Treaty, though a statement made by the French Foreign Minister towards the end of 1966 was more ambiguous (see p. 407). The work of NATO in defending the geographical area of the WEU states is subject to the scrutiny of the different organs of WEU, and in particular, that of its Assembly. The reports of the Assembly's Defence Committee have in fact provided, over the years, a useful annual critique of NATO's strategy and its defence preparedness, and the Assembly's debates on defence matters have provided a certain degree of parliamentary supervision over the work of NATO and Western European defence policy in general.

The Agency for the Control of Armaments has continued to carry out the tasks originally assigned to it of controlling the levels of weapons held by the members of WEU on the continental mainland, but has been unable to control the level of stocks of nuclear weapons produced by the French Government. As early as December 1958, however, Mr Frederick Mulley, *rapporteur* of the Assembly's Committee on Defence Questions and Armaments, held that there was a need 'to put more emphasis on keeping the contributions of all member States to NATO above a prescribed minimum, although, of course, the maximum would remain'. The Committee expressed its view that 'this should be done by the conclusion of a new Protocol to the modified Brussels Treaty, laying down the minimum levels for the forces which member states will maintain in a full state of preparedness on the continent, and place at the disposal of the Supreme Commander'. This interesting suggestion has not been implemented, though WEU's unsuccessful attempts to persuade the British Government to maintain its promised numbers of troops on the Continental mainland show how difficult it is to obtain wholehearted governmental co-operation over such matters in changing political circumstances. The performance of the Standing Armaments Committee in laying down the criteria according to which new weapons should be developed has been disappointing. WEU has not so far attempted to create an armaments production pool between the member states. If this is to be achieved member states will have to show a very much greater willingness to co-operate from the very earliest stages in research on and production of new weapons.

The social and cultural competences which were conferred on WEU by the Brussels Treaty led to useful pioneer work in these two domains which the Council of Europe took over and extended, on the basis of its wider membership, in 1960.

Politically, WEU's membership has provided a framework in which contacts between the six members of the European Communities and Britain are being developed, especially since the breakdown of negotiations between Britain and the members of the EEC in January 1963 after which the Six agreed, on the proposal of the German Government, that quarterly meetings of the Council should be held at ministerial level in order to provide for contacts between Britain and the Six. But although the quarterly ministerial meetings began promisingly no concrete results have yet emerged from them. The Assembly, on its side, had already played a small but significant role in preparing the way for the British Government's application for membership of the EEC in July 1961.

WEU's most useful function, which will probably continue, is to provide a form of parliamentary supervision over the Western European defence system through the work of its Defence Committee and the debates of its Assembly. Further, the methods of weapons control devised by the Agency for the Control of Armaments may be helpful, in the future, in implementing a general disarmament treaty, especially a zonal disarmament agreement in Europe. Finally, the Council of WEU provides a convenient meeting place for the discussion of some of the common problems of its members—a meeting place which is smaller and more appropriate for this purpose than NATO, some of whose members have little concern with the regional problems of the 'Seven'.

Chapter Ten

THE EUROPEAN FREE TRADE ASSOCIATION

Chapter Five has shown how the EEC was established as a result of the *relance européenne* in the mid-fifties, which followed the rejection of the European Defence Community by the French National Assembly in August 1954. EFTA was set up as an indirect consequence of the establishment of the EEC, and was consciously conceived as an interim arrangement that would come to an end as soon as its primary objective—the formation of a single market embracing the whole of Western Europe—was achieved. While it remains in existence, however, Western Europe is divided into two economic groupings, with Britain and its EFTA partners separated from the Community of the Six.

The Origins

For a considerable time after the Messina Conference, Britain and some other OEEC member countries outside the Six failed to recognise that the Six were determined to go ahead in and succeed in establishing a customs and economic union among themselves. It is difficult to understand why this should have been so in view of the fact that British representatives were present at the meetings and participated in the discussions of the Spaak Committee from its inception until they were withdrawn five months later. During the spring and early summer of 1956, however, the British Government began to take more seriously the prospect of a successful conclusion of the Spaak Committee negotiations, and proposals for a European Free Trade Area began to be advanced at that time. A major policy reappraisal with respect to the projected common market was under way in Whitehall and it soon emerged that the possibility of linking the United Kingdom and other OEEC countries to the common market by means of a free trade area was being closely examined. The arguments for a free trade area had been outlined to the Spaak Committee by the British representatives and the Spaak Report itself suggested that some kind of link between the Six and the rest of OEEC Europe along free trade area lines would be a feasible and perhaps even desirable arrangement. The idea of establishing a free trade area covering the whole of Western Europe was not of interest to Britain alone. The prospect of tariff discrimination in intra-European trade resulting from the creation of a customs union of the size and potential of the common market not unnaturally gave rise to concern in the OEEC countries outside the Six and stimulated keen interest in the free trade area project.

The first step towards negotiating such a free trade area was taken at the July 1956 meeting of the OEEC Council of Ministers which decided to establish a special working party to study possible forms and methods of association between the proposed customs union of the Six and the other OEEC countries and, specifically, the possibility of creating a free trade area which would include the customs union of the Six as one element. The objective of this proposal, which was strongly supported by the British Government and probably inspired by it, was to complement the Rome Treaty by a Free Trade Area Convention, both these international instruments to come into force simultaneously in order to maintain wider European co-operation and avoid division in the trade and economic fields. The working party soon reported that a free trade area incorporating the common market as one unit was technically feasible and detailed negotiations on the terms of a treaty to achieve this end were started in March 1957. They continued—from October 1957 onwards in an intergovernmental committee at ministerial level with Mr Reginald Maudling, the British Paymaster-General, as chairman—until November 1958, when they came to an end because no measure of common agreement on the fundamentals of the scheme could be reached.

The negotiations failed after discussions lasting more than two years because France, and to some extent the other Community countries as well, had come to the conclusion that they were fundamentally opposed to linking the common market with a free trade area that would give comparable trade benefits without requiring commitment to a common external tariff, common commercial policies and a substantial harmonisation of economic and social policies. 'Europeans' felt that this would thus place Britain, and no other country, profitably at the cross-roads of European free trade and Commonwealth preference.

In these circumstances, and with the prospect of tariff discrimination as soon as the tariff and quota provisions of the Rome Treaty became operative on 1 January 1959, the next step to be taken by the other OEEC members outside the Community, particularly the six countries with the most clearly defined common position (Austria, Britain, Denmark, Norway, Sweden and Switzerland), was quite easily conceived. As the large, OEEC-wide free trade area with the common market as one component could not be established, the 'Other Six', as they had become known during the Maudling Committee negotiations, would go ahead with the formation of a limited free trade association among themselves. In OEEC, and especially during the long negotiations just ended, these countries were generally in agreement on key issues and as a result a habit of close consultation developed among them. It was against this background that the governments of the 'Other Six' plus Portugal,[1] with the very active encouragement of the industrial federations in their countries, particularly in Sweden, proceeded during the early months of 1959 with the plan for an industrial free trade area in which the members would dismantle the barriers to trade in industrial goods among themselves, but maintain their own tariffs and their own independent commercial policies towards the rest of the world. From the very beginning, although for somewhat different reasons in each case, all seven countries were agreed on the form and scope of the association they wanted to create. The ground had already been covered during the Maudling Committee deliberations and most of the problems and the possible solutions to them had been identified and thoroughly examined. For some years also the three Scandinavian countries had closely studied the problems inherent in freeing trade in the context of the proposed Nordic Customs Union. With this extensive preparatory experience behind them and with a large measure of agreement already reached, the senior officials engaged in drawing up the draft plan for a European Free Trade Association were able to complete the task in the short space of two weeks during June 1959. Ministers approved the draft plan at a meeting in Stockholm on 21 July and at the same time instructed their officials to prepare the text of the Convention establishing the Association, which was signed on 4 January 1960 and came into force on 3 May of the same year.

[1] Portugal joined the group in February 1959.

ASSOCIATION AGREEMENT WITH FINLAND

At the same time as the seven governments were drawing up the Stockholm Draft Plan, the negotiations for a Nordic Customs Union, to which Finland as a full member of the Nordic Group was a party, had reached an advanced stage. The creation of EFTA and the consequent decision to shelve the plan for a Nordic Customs Union posed problems of special importance to Finland. For basic foreign policy reasons determined by her position as a neighbour of the Soviet Union, Finland, whilst anxious to preserve the closest links with the other Scandinavian countries, considered that she could make agreements on tariffs and trade only if they were consistent with her traditional trade relations with Russia and in particular the most-favoured-nation clause of the postwar Russo-Finnish trade agreement. In view of these considerations and in order to add emphasis to the country's policy of neutrality, Finland preferred an association agreement with EFTA to full membership of the organisation. After several months of intricate negotiations an association agreement between the member states of EFTA and Finland was signed in Helsinki on 27 March 1961. The agreement established a new free trade area between Finland and EFTA on the basis that Finland was granted the same rights and assumed the same obligations towards the members of EFTA as these states had among themselves. A similar timetable of tariff reductions to that contained in the Stockholm Convention was laid down in the FINEFTA Agreement, but in view of some especially difficult problems of adaptation in a number of Finnish industries, a slower rate of tariff reductions was allowed for a few items. On balance-of-payments grounds Finland was also permitted to maintain quantitative restrictions on certain goods. The Agreement is supervised by a Joint Council consisting of representatives of each EFTA country and Finland. The Joint Council has the same powers and functions in respect of the FINEFTA Association as the Council of EFTA has under the EFTA Convention. The two bodies are distinct entities and meet separately.

During the past year or two Finnish participation in EFTA activities has grown considerably. This is a direct consequence of the intensification of work in connection with the internal development of EFTA itself. As the great majority of policy issues involved concern Finland equally, substantive discussion of these matters has, for the first time, been concentrated in the Joint Council rather than in the EFTA governing body.

The Stockholm Convention

The Stockholm Convention is a carefully negotiated document. It states the guiding principles and establishes the basic framework of economic relationships for the EFTA group, and also sets out what its framers considered to be the necessary detailed rules of operation and procedure, though these were deliberately kept to a minimum. The Convention relies heavily on a readiness to find satisfactory solutions to problems as they arise. The seven EFTA governments hoped to demonstrate that trade can be freed and all the economic advantages of an enlarged home market secured, with only a minimum of common rules and limited institutional arrangements, and in particular that a system of origin certification could work smoothly in a free trade area and deflections of trade would be found in practice to be few. There were also other considerations. One was to show that this method would prove to be especially advantageous to European countries with substantial trading interests outside Europe. Another was to put pressure on Germany, through competition in its Scandinavian markets, to press for a wider free trade area. And finally it was an essential part of the strategy of the Seven to establish an organisation that could stand on its own feet and be of real value to its members while they continued to work for the wider European association that all of them wanted and still seek.

To understand fully the scope and character of the EFTA free trade area system it is necessary to consider the structure of the Convention as a whole and to bear in mind that there were three fundamental matters on which the other members of OEEC failed to reach agreement with the Six during the OEEC-wide free trade area negotiations: external tariffs and external commercial policy; the harmonisation and co-ordination of internal economic and social policies; and the institutional arrangements.

The Stockholm Convention includes among its basic economic objectives the establishment of a market free of all artificial barriers to trade and the strengthening of the economies of the member states by promoting expansion of economic activity, full employment, increased productivity and the rational use of resources, financial stability and a rising standard of living. A point worth noting in this connection is that the Stockholm Convention speaks of promoting all these things 'in the Area of the Association and in each Member State', emphasising by this form of words the need to ensure that a satisfactory balance of advantages is maintained between the member states and the different economic interests of special concern to them.[1]

The British Government's original concept of a free trade area, it is true, was confined to the removal of barriers to trade in industrial goods alone, but this policy proved unrealistic and had to be abandoned very quickly to meet the views of Britain's OEEC partners in the Maudling negotiations. By common consent agriculture could not be left out of the provisions of the proposed OEEC-wide free trade area, but there was never any question of including agricultural products on the same footing as industrial goods. Establishing a single market for industrial products is one thing, but in view of the distinct social, economic and political factors which have given a special structure and character to the agricultural and fishing industries in all countries, to do the same for agricultural and marine products is quite another and would involve integration of policies, not just freeing of trade. For reasons that have to do with the pattern of domestic production and consumption as well as the supply of foodstuffs from traditional sources overseas, a common agricultural policy has never been one of the objectives of EFTA. The policy objective of the Association in the agricultural sector is more modest and generally less liberal than that governing the freeing of trade in industrial products. Its aim is to promote an expansion of trade in agricultural goods (the same applies to fish and fish products) in order to give reasonable reciprocity to the food-exporting countries in EFTA and provide them with adequate opportunities to increase their exports of these products.

Although, in general, agricultural and fish products are outside the scope of the EFTA programme of tariff cuts, a few such products of very substantial interest to some member countries are treated as 'industrial goods' so that the normal EFTA tariff reductions can be automatically applied to them. This technique is one of the two direct methods employed by EFTA to expand trade in agricultural products. In addition to the items originally classified in this way,

[1] The most difficult part of the negotiations for the European Free Trade Association was that devoted to finding a way of making the plan acceptable to the Danish farmers and the Danish Government. A free trade area limited to industrial goods had little to offer to the Danes, who insisted that the abolition of quotas and tariffs on these products must be matched by appropriate measures to allow food-exporting members adequate opportunities not only to maintain competitive exports of agricultural products, but to increase such exports. In the end the Danes agreed to come in only because the British Government had made substantial tariff concessions on bacon, blue-veined cheese and canned cream, and the Norwegians did so only after the British agreed to treat frozen fish fillets as an industrial product.

another dozen products have been transferred from the agricultural list to the industrial sector since the free trade area came into operation. The other method of dealing with the problem of increasing trade in farm products is through concessions agreed in bilateral agreements under which specific agricultural exports from one EFTA country enjoy duty-free entry or special facilities in another member state. So far nine of these agreements have been concluded. They form an integral part of the Convention and the tariff provisions in them are extended equally to all EFTA suppliers of the goods concerned. In addition to this, the EFTA Council, the organisation's governing body, now carries out an annual review of the development of trade in agricultural products within the Association. This is a detailed review in the course of which the Council can deal with any aspect of this trade and consider whether additional measures need to be taken to further its growth in order to achieve a sufficient degree of reciprocity for those member states whose major exports are agricultural.

The structure of the Convention reflects both the different policy objectives of the Association in respect of trade between the members in the products of the main sectors of their economies (industrial, agricultural and fisheries), and the overall balance of benefits negotiated between them. It is clear that the need to maintain such a balance is a fundamental condition for the development of the Association. What the organisation does and the speed at which it is doing it are largely determined by this. This is exemplified by the series of Council decisions taken at the Lisbon ministerial meeting in May 1963, four months after the breaking off of the negotiations for British entry into the Community. The new situation called for a vigorous move forward. The best way to stimulate intra-EFTA trade and strengthen the Association was to shorten the transitional stage leading to the full establishment of the free market in manufactured goods.

Advance on one front, however, had to be compensated on another. After hard bargaining an acceptable balance was achieved consisting of the final shortened timetable of tariff reductions in which Britain, Sweden and Switzerland as the major manufacturing countries in EFTA were primarily interested, and a number of decisions of direct interest to the exporters of farm and fisheries products in the Association—Denmark and Portugal. The most important of these were the agreement to begin annual reviews of agricultural trade and the decision to delete a number of items from the list of agricultural goods (Annex D to the Convention) thereby making them eligible for full free trade area treatment. Also forming part of the package was the decision to set up the Economic Development Committee to deal with the technical problems of economic development in the member countries and Finland. It is a step specifically designed to assist the less advanced industries and regions in EFTA with the object of promoting the balanced expansion of trade and economic activity generally.

As far as industrial products are concerned the provisions of the Convention can be grouped together under two broad headings: the rules for the freeing of trade and the rules of competition. The first covers the abolition of tariffs and quantitative restrictions, including the elimination of any protective element in revenue duties, drawback[1] in respect of duties on materials or components in goods which benefit from EFTA tariff treatment, and export duties. The rules of competition are intended to deal with the indirect barriers to the free movement of goods so as to ensure that the effects of the removal of customs duties and quotas are not nullified by government aids to domestic producers, discriminatory purchasing practices of public undertakings, restrictive business practices in the private sector and laws and regulations discriminating against nationals of other EFTA countries who wish to establish business enterprises in the territory of a member state. These practices can hamper trade as much as tariffs and quotas and interfere with the proper working of the free trade area by distorting competition among EFTA producers. Following the abolition of tariffs and quotas on 1 January 1967, the Association has begun to pay much more attention to the removal of indirect barriers to trade and also to the question of closer European co-operation over patents and industrial standards.

Apart from the provisions dealing with agriculture and fish referred to earlier, the remaining substantive provisions of the Convention are concerned with the circumstances in which 'escape clauses' and safeguarding action may be invoked (i.e. security exceptions, balance-of-payments difficulties and cases of hardship to a particular industry or region resulting directly from EFTA tariff and quota disarmament), the consultation and complaints procedure and the institutional arrangements of the Association.

THE ELIMINATION OF TARIFFS AND QUOTAS

The central feature of the EFTA regime for trade is the progressive

[1] 'Drawback' is the reimbursement of customs duty paid on an import which is then exported in a processed form.

reduction and final abolition of tariffs and quantitative restrictions on all industrial products and some others that have been classified as such for EFTA purposes, produced in and exported from one member country to another. The original timetable for the removal of import duties allowed nine and a half years for the completion of the process. Starting with a reduction of 20 per cent on 1 July 1960 followed by eight cuts each of 10 per cent, the process was to be completed not later than 1 January 1970. In line with the Association's objective of working for a wider European agreement the dates and percentage reductions of EFTA tariff cuts follow closely those set out in the Rome Treaty for the EEC. With an eye on a possible future accommodation between the two groups the Seven wanted to keep in step with the tariff cuts inside the common market. In the favourable economic conditions of the early 1960s changes in the original timetables were soon made by both organisations. EFTA at first adopted a piecemeal approach. Two separate acceleration decisions were taken in 1961, bringing forward the second and third steps in its tariff cutting programme, but leaving the remainder of the timetable unchanged. As a result of these decisions EFTA tariff rates were brought down to half their original level by the end of 1962, two years ahead of the date laid down in the Stockholm Convention. Earlier fears expressed in some EFTA countries that they would not be able to face competition without tariff protection and that they would suffer from diversion of trade and unemployment have proved to be groundless. That this would prove to be the case was already apparent at the halfway point in the tariff cutting programme.

After the Brussels setback in January 1963 the desire to move forward to the full establishment of the free trade area as quickly as possible grew very much stronger in most of the EFTA countries, and particularly so in the three most highly industrialised members: Sweden, Switzerland and Britain. This led to the decision, taken at the Lisbon ministerial meeting in May 1963, to shorten the transitional period and finally to agree on a new timetable of tariff cuts. The remaining reductions were accelerated and the date for the completion of the process was brought forward by three years to 31 December 1966.

Finnish tariffs in trade with its EFTA partners have been reduced broadly in accordance with the original and revised EFTA timetables. But because Finland became a party to the EFTA arrangements a year after the start of the free trade area, the final tariff cut in its case need not be completed until 31 December 1967.

Special, and in the nature of the case complex, arrangements have been made to encourage industrial development in Portugal so as to enable the Portuguese economy to adapt itself progressively to the competitive conditions of the free trade area. So far as the elimination of import duties and quotas is concerned, Portugal is allowed to work to a much slower timetable which sanctions a transitional period for the elimination of these barriers in respect of some industrial products that could extend until the end of 1979 at the latest.

Simultaneously with each round of tariff reductions the remaining quantitative import restrictions have been dismantled.[1] The liberalisation of quotas is being carried out in almost all cases on a global basis. Few restrictions now remain and with the exception of some Finnish and Portuguese quotas the rest were lifted at the end of 1966.

In principle quantitative restrictions no less than tariffs are outlawed in the fully established free trade area, but, following the GATT rule in this matter, quotas may be re-introduced temporarily in case of balance-of-payments difficulties. As was made very clear to the British Government when it imposed the 15 per cent import surcharge in October 1964, there is no mention in the EFTA Convention of any other kind of emergency measure to safeguard a member country's external payments position. The surcharge, therefore, was certainly contrary to the letter of the Convention: whether it was contrary to the spirit was less clear. No reference is made to anything but quantitative restrictions in Article 19 of the Convention. It is also clear that Article 3 dealing with import duties and other charges with equivalent effect, of which the surcharge was obviously one, is written in a way which precludes the possibility of the re-establishment of import duties once they have been abolished. On the other hand, the Convention does not specifically exclude all measures of control other than quantitative restrictions. For example Article 10, dealing with quantitative restrictions, says that the member state may propose to the Council such alternative arrangements, and the Council may authorise a member to adopt them. Similarly Article 20, dealing with difficulties in particular sectors, states that a member state may take such measures instead of or in addition to quantitative restrictions as the Council may authorise by majority decision. The measures referred to in Articles 10 and 20 could be held to include measures such as the surcharge.

[1] Most quota restrictions imposed by the EFTA countries had already been removed in the 1950s under the OEEC trade liberalisation programme.

THE EFTA ORIGIN SYSTEM

The essential difference between a customs union and a free trade area lies not in their techniques of dismantling internal trade barriers, but in their external relations with non-member nations. As mentioned earlier, the most important of the substantive issues on which agreement could not be reached between the Six and the rest during the OEEC free trade area negotiations was their fundamental difference of view on the need for a common external tariff and a common commercial policy. The French delegation in particular challenged the validity of the concept of a free trade area and considered that an effective system of origin controls was not feasible. If nothing else EFTA has certainly demonstrated that its free market, which is not surrounded by a common tariff wall, works perfectly well and that an effective origin system can be devised and operated smoothly without administrative difficulties: though some economists have argued that this may have been made easier by the scattered location of the EFTA countries, which makes transport a more important factor than in the EEC, whose members are adjacent and contiguous.

The need for an origin system arises because EFTA, unlike the customs union of the Six, has no common external tariff. Each member country of the Association retains control over its own tariffs on imports from countries outside the EFTA area. It follows that without adequate safeguards in the form of a set of origin rules there would be a constant danger that goods from outside the Area would first be imported into the EFTA country with the lowest external tariff and then passed on from there, at EFTA tariff rates duty free after 31 December 1966, to member countries with higher external tariffs. With widely varying national tariff rates towards non-member countries and bearing in mind that extra freight and handling charges would not in many cases be sufficient wholly to offset the difference between the tariffs of the member states concerned, the result might well be that deflections of trade would occur and national tariff structures would be undermined. It was, therefore, essential to have a set of origin rules and customs procedures to determine which goods traded between member countries were entitled to benefit from EFTA tariff reductions.

Briefly, goods are regarded as eligible for EFTA tariff treatment if they have been consigned to the importing EFTA country from another member state and if they satisfy one of three origin criteria: if they have been wholly produced within EFTA; if they have been produced within the EFTA area by one of the specified processes of production ('process criterion'); or if the value of any materials used in their production imported from outside the EFTA area does not exceed 50 per cent of the export price of the goods ('percentage rule'). In general importers can choose for themselves under which of these rules they will claim the EFTA tariff preference.[1]

Also forming part of the EFTA origin system is a list of raw materials and semi-manufactured goods known as the Basic Materials List. It covers a very wide range of essential materials used by industry which in most cases are either not available from EFTA sources or are available only in insufficient quantities. The significance of the list is that wherever any of the materials included in it are used in the production of goods in the EFTA area, they are counted as being of EFTA origin whatever their actual origin may be. This means, in particular, that where the percentage criterion is used, goods will often qualify for Area origin, even though they have an actual non-Area content of well over 50 per cent of their value.

Described briefly in this way, the system may appear much simpler than it is. To operate it successfully is in fact a highly technical operation which depends on carefully drawn up administrative regulations and speedy customs procedures. In its simplest form documentary evidence of EFTA origin consists of a signed declaration on the ordinary invoice where a manufacturer is exporting directly. An exporter who is not himself the producer of the goods must obtain a declaration from the manufacturer, or a certificate of origin from a government department or a Chamber of Commerce, which has satisfied itself that the origin requirements have been fulfilled. Enforcement is by sample checks, which are constantly being made by the various customs administrations, and the ultimate sanction is prosecution for false declarations with the usual penalties (mostly fines) for this type of offence. There have been several successful prosecutions, but the number is not large. Responsibility for taking judicial proceedings rests with the authorities of the country in which the fraudulent declaration of origin was made. The system as a whole is kept under constant review by the EFTA Customs Committee, which is one of the organisation's standing committees. As a result of its work, a number of minor modifications have been made to the

[1] The basic EFTA origin rule is the 50 per cent rule. The process rule as an alternative to the percentage rule greatly simplifies the origin procedure. For most textiles and clothing, however, the alternative of establishing EFTA origin under the 50 per cent rule is not available. For these goods the process criterion only applies and in general two processes must be carried out in the Area, e.g. spinning and weaving or weaving and making up.

origin rules and the process and basic materials lists have been extended.[1]

REVENUE DUTIES, INTERNAL TAXES AND DRAWBACK

Generally customs duties are levied primarily to give protection to domestic producers rather than to raise revenue. The essential purpose of the EFTA tariff provisions is to eliminate this form of protection within the Association. For some countries, however, the revenue derived from customs duties is an important element in their budget for which they were not prepared to find alternative sources of revenue. The signatories of the Stockholm Convention, therefore, decided that the right to levy duties for revenue purposes should not be impaired by the rules of the free trade area.

In contrast to the method adopted by the EEC, where revenue duties are abolished in the same way as tariffs and replaced, if desired, by internal taxes which must bear no more heavily on imports than on equivalent goods produced at home, the EFTA arrangement imposes no restrictions on revenue duties, provided any protective element in them has been eliminated. Not unexpectedly, perhaps, it has been found that the determination of this element is often extremely difficult in practice. Nevertheless several revenue duties have been reduced on imports from EFTA countries to bring them into line with excise duties charged on similar home-produced products. The Customs Committee, moreover, is currectly carrying out an examination of member countries' revenue duty lists to see how they are interpreting and fulfilling their obligations in this matter.

In connection with the problem of revenue duties, an interesting case, which has become a bone of contention between the British and Swedish motor-car manufacturers and the Norwegian Government, is the latter's retention of a 20–30 per cent *ad valorem* import duty on motor vehicles. This is undoubtedly legal. Norway neither produces nor assembles cars and therefore has no home industry to protect. The duty is applied for revenue-raising purposes and for general economic policy reasons. But the effect of the duty is that EFTA car manufacturers are denied a competitive advantage over rival non-EFTA producers in the Norwegian market. They want Norway to remove it for EFTA vehicles in the same way as other tariffs, making up for the loss of revenue by an internal tax bearing evenly on

[1] A comprehensive guide to the EFTA origin system has been published by the EFTA Secretariat: see S. A. Green and K. W. B. Gabriel, *The Rules of Origin*, Geneva, European Free Trade Association, revised ed. 1967.

imports from all sources. Switzerland, which has a car assembly plant, has eliminated what she considered to be the protective element in the duty on passenger cars, i.e. 50 per cent of the full rate, leaving half the tariff as a pure revenue duty.

Harmonising national systems of taxation and working towards a common fiscal policy is not one of EFTA's objectives. As with revenue duties, the extent of the common concern within the Association, as far as internal taxes generally are concerned, is limited to ensuring that any protective element in them is eliminated. Goods imported from other member countries must not be subject to internal taxation exceeding that levied on the domestic output of those goods.

For the reason that they distort competition by giving protection to the home market and a subsidy to exports, neither a customs union nor a free trade area can allow member states to continue to operate 'drawback' schemes. Drawback can take various forms, but essentially it means any arrangement for a refund of all or part of the duty on imported materials which are used in the production of goods for export. Over a period of nearly four years until the autumn of 1965, the EFTA Committee of Trade Experts and the Customs Committee of the organisation spent an inordinate amount of time on all aspects of the drawback problem. There was a deep division of opinion among member governments as to whether the provision of the Convention abolishing drawback should in fact be implemented. The solution that has been adopted is that goods traded within EFTA may not benefit both from EFTA tariff treatment and from drawback. Exporters have the alternative of foregoing either the drawback refund or the EFTA tariff advantage. This decision, taken by the EFTA Council in Copenhagen in October 1965, is noteworthy also from a constitutional point of view. It was the first Council decision taken by simple majority vote. A decision, in similar terms, dealing with export rebates in intra-EFTA trade was taken on the same occasion.

The Institutions

EFTA is an intergovernmental organisation under the direct control of its member governments. Its organisational structure and working methods are closely modelled on those of the old OEEC, now OECD. Its institutional machinery is simple and flexible. It consists of a permanent Council representing all the member governments, each having one vote, a number of standing specialist committees set up by the Council to assist it in its work, and a small Secretariat to serve both the Council and its committees.

In fact as well as in name the governing body of the Association is the Council, which alone has full powers of decision in all matters arising in connection with the implementation of the Convention. It is responsible not only for general supervision and broad questions of policy, but also for the day-to-day running of the Association. Following the OEEC pattern, the Council meets either at ministerial level (three or four times a year) or at approximately weekly intervals at the level of senior officials—the heads of member states' permanent delegations resident in Geneva, the seat of the Association's headquarters. To speed up the conduct of the Council's business, an informal committee, the group of deputies, made up of officials belonging to the EFTA delegations in Geneva, has been formed. Its task is to draw up the agenda for each meeting and to prepare the ground for subsequent agreement in and decision by the Council. By this means continuous contact between the delegations and between them and the EFTA Secretariat is maintained. The Council, moreover, is always available to take decisions at a few days' notice.

Meetings of the Council in ministerial session take place at regular intervals of three to four months. On these occasions member governments are usually represented by two of their ministers. The meetings are necessary so that the ministers most directly concerned with EFTA affairs can exchange views and discuss longer-range issues or resolve matters with a more than usual political content. They give a sense of occasion and not a few have had their moments of drama. The chairmanship of the Council is held by each member country in turn for a period of six months. Ministerial meetings are usually held in the EFTA country currently occupying the Chair, but sometimes a gathering in Geneva is preferred.[1]

Much of the essential work of the organisation is, of course, done in the various specialist committees. There are now six of these and in addition there is the Consultative Committee, which is intended to serve as a link between the Association and economic interest groups, including labour, in each country. The members of the Consultative Committee (up to five persons from each member country may attend meetings) are appointed by governments and

[1] Until the middle of 1967 there were twenty-four meetings at ministerial level, including the special summit meeting of EFTA Prime Ministers in London in December 1966. As mentioned earlier, meetings at the level of officials are much more frequent; for example, between the middle of 1965 and the same date a year later, the Council met fifty times altogether.

serve in their personal capacities and not as mandated delegates or authorised representatives of the organisations to which they belong. The Committee is strictly an advisory body serving two main purposes: to put forward suggestions to the EFTA Council for developing and deepening co-operation within the Association and to assist in the creation of informed opinion on the work of the organisation among the people most directly affected by its activities. As an advisory group the Committee has not been very effective because the representation of interests and the desired consultations between them and the governments concerned necessarily continue to take place at the national rather than the international level. Despite this experience or perhaps because of it, the Committee has recently extended its activities. Following agreement on a proposal of the British Trades Union Congress, a Social and Economic Sub-Committee was established in the summer of 1966. Its structure is tripartite along the lines of the International Labour Organisation (ILO), with members drawn from unions, employers' organisations and officials from the appropriate government departments in each country. The civil servants, however, while taking part in the deliberations of the sub-committee, do not share responsibility for any decisions it may make. Its terms of reference are to examine and make recommendations on economic and social problems resulting from 'structural or other changes brought about by the process of integration in the EFTA market, in the economy of individual countries and of EFTA as a whole.' The first investigation being carried out by the new body is looking into the need for and the methods of improving mobility of labour, both between sectors of industry and geographically.

The six specialist or technical committees, all of which have been established by the Council and make their recommendations to it, are: (a) the Customs Committee which brings together officials from the national customs administrations and is concerned with everything that has to do with Area Customs rules and procedures; (b) the Committee of Trade Experts which deals with the technical problems of operating the trade provisions of the Convention and is responsible, in particular, for keeping the origin rules under review; (c) the Agricultural Review Committee which, since 1964, has carried out the annual review of EFTA trade in farm products and in connection with this exercise examines the effect of national agricultural policies on that trade; (d) the Economic Development Committee which was created in 1963 and which represents an extension into an area of activity not originally intended to be covered by the Association, to stimulate economic growth in parts of EFTA which, in comparison with the rest, are economically less developed; (e) the Economic Committee which was set up as a direct result of the situation produced by the British balance-of-payments crisis in the autumn of 1964 and has been given the responsibility of keeping a watchful eye on the economic and financial policies of member states, much on the lines of the Economic Policy Committee of OECD; (f) and finally the Budget Committee, which for the financial year 1966–67 has established the Association's budget at nearly 7 million Swiss francs, about £560,000, of which Britain contributes 30 per cent.

Although the size of the EFTA Secretariat has doubled in the first six years it still numbers less than 100 people, including clerical and general service staff, with just over forty in the professional grades. In the beginning almost all, and now about half, of the officials in the professional grades were seconded by their national administrations for periods of two to three years. EFTA's first Secretary General was Mr Frank E. Figgures, a senior civil servant in the British Treasury who, on his return there in November 1965, was succeeded by Sir John Coulson of the Foreign Office. Internally the Secretariat is organised into six departments.[1]

Informal meetings of parliamentarians from the EFTA countries are held at the Council of Europe in Strasbourg immediately before or after sessions of the Consultative Assembly. The parliamentarians attending these meetings, which are open to the press, are the members of the delegations of the EFTA countries to the Assembly of the Council of Europe. At these meetings frank discussions are held of the main problems confronting EFTA.

The Development of EFTA, 1960–66

In forming EFTA the governments concerned had primarily two aims in mind: to establish an industrial free trade area among themselves, while simultaneously continuing to seek agreement with the Six on the creation of a single European market. Whereas the way in which the first of these objectives is to be achieved was clearly laid down in the Stockholm Convention, the means by which the second might be reached could, of necessity, not be determined in advance.

[1] They are the Trade Policy, General and Legal, Economic, Co-ordination and Development, Press and Information, and Administration and Finance Departments.

The founders of EFTA certainly did not envisage a long life for their Association. On the contrary, they regarded it principally as an important and definite step towards a wider European grouping—as an interim and second-best, but none the less valuable, solution to what they hoped would be a short-lived problem. But to set up EFTA mainly in order to bring about the creation of another, wider organisation, was to make it from the start an instrument of policies external to it and to deprive it of much of the internal *raison d'être* that it needed if it was to live its own life fully and satisfactorily for even a short period. Recognition of this innate conflict between EFTA's different objectives is basic to the understanding of the Association's role and progress so far.

There have been three distinct phases in the development of the Association from the time of its formation in 1960 to the abolition of all tariffs and quotas on industrial goods in EFTA at the end of 1966. During the first phase the emphasis as far as EFTA's relations with the EEC were concerned was on finding a way to prevent the economic gap between the two groups from widening as each cut its internal tariffs. To this end the EFTA countries proposed that each group should extend to the other, and generalise to the other members of the GATT, the tariff cuts they were due to make on 1 July 1960. For most of this period the dominant assumption in EFTA thinking was still that, in time, 'bridge-building' (establishing some kind of free trade area link between the two groups and possibly including other European countries as well) was not only the most desirable but also a genuinely negotiable solution to the European trade problem.

Internally, apart from setting the institutional machinery of the free trade area in motion and devising its customs procedures, the Organisation's greatest achievement during this first phase was the close association of Finland with EFTA.

The second and most trying period in the Association's development began with the decision of the British Government, taken some time during the spring of 1961, to seek full membership of the Community. Although most of the EFTA Governments supported the change of course in British policy there was, not unnaturally, considerable uneasiness lest the new bilateral approach might mean that the interests of the neutral members of EFTA in particular would suffer because they did not accept any of the political implications of the Rome Treaty. Clarification of British intentions and reassurance on those aspects of the integration problem that caused concern among the other partners were obtained at a series of meetings, including two at ministerial level (London, 27–28 June 1961 and Geneva, 28 July 1961), held before the British and Danish Governments on 31 July announced their decision to make formal applications to join the Community as full members. In an important policy statement which has become known as the 'London Communiqué', the members of EFTA agreed to co-ordinate their actions and remain united throughout the proposed negotiations and, most far-reaching of all, pledged themselves in words that have been much quoted and analysed, to maintain 'the obligations created by the Convention . . ., and the momentum towards integration within the Association. . ., at least until satisfactory arrangements have been worked out in negotiations to meet the various legitimate interests of all members of EFTA, and thus enable them all to participate from the same date in an integrated European market.'

In another statement, known as the 'Geneva Declaration', issued a month after the 'London Communiqué', the EFTA Governments reaffirmed their earlier decisions and expressed the view that the British and Danish applications provided 'an opportunity to find an appropriate solution for all EFTA countries.' Accordingly, all of them applied to open negotiations with the EEC either for full or, in the case of Austria, Sweden and Switzerland,[1] associate membership. As agreed between them, the pledge not to abandon EFTA, and to enter the larger market together, did not in any way establish a right by one member country to veto an agreement with the EEC made by another. It amounted rather to an undertaking given by Britain to use its influence and bargaining strength also on behalf of its EFTA partners.

Broadly this remains the situation in the British Government's renewed approach to the EEC. It has been made clear in a number of ministerial statements that Britain will again keep in close touch with the other EFTA countries as the exploratory talks and any future negotiations proceed, and that it will consult them fully before an agreement is reached.

Inevitably, though to a lesser extent than might have been expected, the internal development of the Association slowed down during the period of the British negotiations at Brussels in 1961–63. But as far as the timetable of tariff reductions was concerned the members stuck firmly to their policy of keeping in step with the Community. Accordingly the EFTA Council twice accelerated the original tariff-cutting programme during this period, bringing EFTA

[1] These three countries considered that their status of neutrality precluded full membership of the EEC.

customs duties down to half of what they were when the Association started and doing so more than two years ahead of the date originally stipulated in the Convention.

At the same time, while the accession negotiations were in progress, the member countries were understandably reluctant to enter into new contractual obligations limited to their own number or even to implement some they had already accepted, if this meant forfeiting the greater part of their individual bargaining strength in the negotiations with the Six. Clearly it would not have been prudent at that juncture to have agreed on mutual concessions only within EFTA in return for limited benefits in view of the overall size of the market, if the same concessions could be made with much greater advantage in the bargaining for the larger European market.

The main turning point in the development of EFTA—the begining of its third phase—came with the breaking off of the Brussels negotiations in January 1963. The inhibiting uncertainty of the previous eighteen months concerning EFTA's immediate future having been removed by General de Gaulle's action, the overriding fact now was that EFTA would continue in business on its own for a period of three to five years at least and probably longer. There were now no compelling reasons for not making EFTA co-operation a reality and at the Geneva (February 1963) and Lisbon (May of the same year) ministerial meetings the member governments showed a new-found determination to implement the Stockholm Convention fully. Indeed they added a new field of activity to the Association's work. They set up an institutional framework, the Economic Development Committee, for dealing with specific technical and economic development problems in the member countries. The new Economic Committee came into being after the imposition of the 15 per cent import surcharge by the British Government in October 1964, in order to keep the economic and financial policies of the EFTA countries under review.

Since the Lisbon meeting EFTA has paid much more attention to the problem of how to deal with non-tariff barriers to trade, which became relatively important when the remaining customs duties were removed at the end of 1966.[1] The expansion of trade in agricul-

[1] A number of working parties have been active since the middle of 1964 examining the purchasing policies of public undertakings, restrictive business practices, national provisions governing the right of establishment, double taxation, industrial standards and patent law, and the Council has taken several decisions on the further implementation of some of these provisions in the Convention.

tural products is another matter which has recently been more vigorously pursued.

EFTA's rekindled sense of purpose and energy was severely shaken by the British import surcharge, especially by the manner in which it was imposed with no prior consultation. It produced a crisis of confidence in the Association which was overcome only with much difficulty. There can be no doubt that the powerful reaction in EFTA and the direct pressure which the other member governments brought to bear on the British authorities had a major influence on the reduction of the surcharge from 15 to 10 per cent after six months and its final removal after two years.

In external affairs a renewed attempt by EFTA to seek the collaboration of the EEC in building functional and technical 'bridges' between the two organisations was made on the initiative of the British Prime Minister at the Vienna ministerial meeting in May 1965. The proposal to establish contacts between the two groups included the suggestion that a permanent standing consultative council, representing the governments of EFTA and the EEC, should be set up. This proposal met with no response from the Community, and was superseded in 1966 by the decision of the British Government to explore whether the conditions were ripe for a renewed application for membership of the EEC.

Part 6

EUROPE AND AMERICA

Chapter Eleven

THE NORTH ATLANTIC TREATY ORGANISATION

The Origins

In 1947, the Dunkirk Treaty had bound Britain and France to resist any revival of German aggression. This fear was soon replaced by distrust of the Soviet Union. Soviet expansion in Europe had begun during the war with the annexation of Estonia, Latvia and Lithuania together with parts of Finland, Poland, Rumania, Germany and Czechoslovakia. It continued after the war with the establishment of political control over Albania, Bulgaria, Rumania, East Germany, Poland, Hungary and Czechoslovakia. Soviet policy was thus a political and military threat to the West and some form of concerted defence system was clearly indicated.

The Brussels Treaty of 17 March 1948 (signed by Belgium, France, Luxembourg, the Netherlands and the United Kingdom) pledged its members to establish a joint defence system and also to strengthen their economic and cultural ties. The Treaty provided that should any of the member countries be the object of 'an armed attack in Europe' the others would afford 'all the military and other aid and assistance in their power'. Although Article 7 of the Treaty referred to the possibility of the renewal of German aggression, the real preoccupation of the signatories was the possibility of a Soviet attack on Western Europe.

The events of 1948, which included the subjugation of Czechoslovakia, the threat to Greece, the blockade of Berlin and the pressure placed on Yugoslavia, underlined the need for Western political and military solidarity. In September 1948, the Brussels Treaty powers decided to create a military agency, the Western Union Defence Organisation.

The Brussels Treaty Organisation was primarily a recognition that a purely national response to the Soviet threat was inadequate, but it was soon realised on both sides of the Atlantic that a limited regional response was also inadequate. In April 1948 Mr St Laurent, the Canadian Prime Minister, suggested that there should be a single mutual defence system embracing the countries of North America and Western Europe, which would include and enlarge the Brussels system. In the same month discussions were begun in the United States by the Secretary of State, General Marshall, and an Under-Secretary, Robert Lovett, with two Senators, Arthur Vandenberg and Tom Connally, on the security problems of the North Atlantic area. These discussions culminated in the Vandenberg Resolution of 11 June 1948, which showed the readiness of the United States to enter an Atlantic Alliance. The Vandenberg Resolution and the resulting North Atlantic Treaty were striking proof of the reversal of the isolationism of prewar United States policy.

The North Atlantic Treaty

The preliminary negotiations leading to the North Atlantic Treaty began in July 1948 in Washington. The negotiators' recommendations were approved by the governments of the Brussels Treaty powers and of Canada and the United States. Work on drafting the Treaty, which was modelled on the 1947 Treaty of Rio de Janeiro, through which the United States underpinned the security of the western hemisphere, began in September. The North Atlantic Treaty was signed by the foreign ministers of Belgium, Canada, Denmark, France, Iceland, Italy, Luxembourg, the Netherlands, Norway, Portugal, the United Kingdom and the United States on 4 April 1949. Greece and Turkey joined the Alliance in February 1952, as did the Federal Republic of Germany in May 1955.

The preamble to the Treaty states that the signatories 'are determined to safeguard the freedom, common heritage and civilisation of their peoples, founded on the principles of democracy, individual liberty and the rule of law'. The Treaty binds the signatories to a multilateral political alliance involving mutual defence obligations and economic co-operation. Article 5, which is the core of the Treaty, states:

'The Parties agree that an armed attack against one or more of them in Europe or North America shall be considered an attack against them all; and consequently they agree that, if such an armed attack occurs, each of them in exercise of the right of individual or collective self-defence recognised by Article 51 of the Charter of the United Nations, will assist the Party or Parties so attacked by taking forthwith, individually and in concert with the other Parties, such action as it deems necessary, including the use of armed force to restore and maintain the security of the North Atlantic area. Any such attack and all measures taken as a result thereof shall be terminated when the Security Council has taken the measures necessary to restore and maintain international peace and security.'

It was originally intended by those who drafted the Treaty that Article 5 should have more force, and in the draft Treaty each signatory was pledged to take action against attack without qualification. But the United States Senate Foreign Relations Committee, in conjunction with the Secretary of State, Mr Dean Acheson, reviewed the draft and insisted, for constitutional reasons, upon inserting the words 'as it deems necessary'.[1] Senator Vandenberg has commented: 'This left to the individual signatories complete discretion in determining individual action; each was pledged to act, but the type of action was left to each sovereign nation.'[2] There is a significant difference between the non-automatic clause of the North Atlantic Treaty and the fully binding automatic clause which was the form used in the Brussels Treaty. Some anxiety was felt at the time of signature that the addition of this phrase weakened the Treaty. After 1969, moreover, members of NATO can withdraw from the Organisation at a year's notice, whereas the modified Brussels Treaty under which WEU was set up in 1954 is effective until 1998.

Article 5 applied to the area (as amended by the Greece–Turkey Protocol of October 1951) defined as being the territory of any of the member countries in Europe, North America, Greece and Turkey and those islands under the rule of any of the member countries in the North Atlantic area north of the Tropic of Cancer.[3] In the case of an attack on North America, the European member countries are committed to take action in the same way as the North American powers are committed to the defence of Western Europe. Defence obligations in NATO are, therefore, reciprocal.

The deterrent aspect of the Treaty is expressed in Article 3 by which the signatories undertake 'by means of continuous and

[1] By the Constitution of the United States a declaration of war requires a specific decision of Congress.

[2] *The Private Papers of Senator Vandenberg*, Boston, Houghton Mifflin, 1952, p. 476.

[3] The Algerian Departments of France were originally included in the area, but ceased to constitute part of it when Algeria became independent in 1962.

effective self-help and mutual aid, to maintain and develop their individual and collective capacity to resist armed attack'. Articles 3 and 5 are complementary.

In April 1948, Mr St Laurent had suggested that the purpose of a North Atlantic association would be to 'create the dynamic counter-attraction to Communism—the dynamic attraction of a free, prosperous and progressive society, as opposed to the totalitarian and reactionary society of the Communist world'.

Although the Treaty primarily constitutes a military and political Alliance, Article 2 of the Treaty states: 'The Parties will contribute towards the further development of peaceful and friendly international relations by strengthening their free institutions, by bringing about a better understanding of the principles upon which these institutions are founded and by promoting conditions of stability and well-being. They will seek to eliminate conflict in their international economic policies and will encourage economic collaboration between any or all of them.' This Article was included partly because the Brussels Treaty contained a similar clause, and partly because the signatories did not want NATO to be considered as a purely military Alliance, since the future of OEEC as a continuing organisation dealing with economic affairs had not yet been assured.

Article 4 of the Treaty also stipulates that the signatories 'will consult . . . whenever, in the opinion of any of them, the territorial integrity, political independence or security of any of the Parties is threatened'. The nature and extent of the political consultation carried out in NATO is described below (pp. 383–85).

In 1950 the Korean war led the Alliance to develop into a more effective defence system with a considerable degree of political consultation, but following the development of greater European prosperity, strength and unity, more peaceful relations between Eastern European Communist and Western powers and the developing tension between the Soviet Union and the Chinese People's Republic, the sense of danger in Western Europe has receded. The feeling that the Soviet threat had diminished was reinforced when the Russians backed down, following the firm stand taken by President Kennedy over the Berlin and Cuba crises. In the years since the North Atlantic Treaty was signed the Soviet Union has, however, developed intercontinental missiles which are capable of reaching the United States. These political and strategic developments have completely changed the basis of the political and defence postures of the members of the Alliance. Nevertheless, it is clear that a strong and alert North Atlantic defence system is likely to be maintained while Germany remains divided and Russian divisions remain in the countries of Eastern Europe.

The Institutions

THE NORTH ATLANTIC COUNCIL

The highest authority in NATO and the only institution directly established by terms of the Treaty is the Council. Article 9 of the Treaty states: 'The parties hereby establish a Council, on which each of them shall be represented, to consider matters concerning the implementation of this treaty. The Council shall be so organised as to be able to meet promptly at any time. The Council shall set up subsidiary bodies as may be necessary; in particular it shall establish immediately a defence committee which shall recommend measures for the implementation of Articles 3 and 5.' If a distinction is to be drawn, as it has been by the French Government, between the Alliance and NATO, it could be said that the structure of integrated headquarters represents the military organisation, of which the Council is the supreme authority, and that the Alliance is represented by the Treaty commitments of the member countries together with the political and other activities conducted under the aegis of the Council, which is also the supreme political authority. The Council thus plays a double role.

Originally the 'normal' composition of the Council was the foreign ministers of the member countries. It was decided at the first session that the Council should meet annually in ordinary session, and also 'at such other times as may be deemed desirable'. The 'extraordinary' sessions provided for by Articles 4 and 5 of the Treaty could be called at the request of any Party invoking one of these articles. Mr Dean Acheson, the United States Secretary of State, became the first Chairman of the Council and it was agreed that the chairmanship should be held by each member country in turn for a year. The North Atlantic Council now usually meets at ministerial level twice a year and once or twice a week at the level of permanent representatives who are senior national civil servants acting for the governments.

At the December ministerial meetings it is normal for foreign defence and finance ministers to represent their governments: the spring ministerial meetings are usually attended by the foreign and defence ministers. Member countries may also be represented by Heads of Government.[1] Decisions of the Council are taken by unani-

[1] The Council met at the level of Heads of Government in December 1957.

mity and, as the members of the Council are representatives of their national governments, the character of the North Atlantic Council is intergovernmental. Although national obligations in NATO, apart from the general obligation to join in the defence of the North Atlantic area in the event of any external attack, do not theoretically entail any ceding of sovereignty, the transfer in time of emergency or war of the command of 'assigned' national forces to NATO Supreme Commanders would represent a very great concession of national powers.[2] The powers of the NATO Supreme Commanders are, however, limited in peacetime to making recommendations to member governments, which are responsible for making the decisions concerning their national forces. The main concession made by member governments, which is at the same time the main strength of the Alliance, lies in joint planning: the plans, strengths and capabilities of national forces assigned to NATO are worked out jointly and known throughout the Alliance.

SUBSIDIARY BODIES

The Council carried out its obligations to establish the necessary subsidiary bodies by setting up a Defence Committee composed of defence ministers, whose main task was to draw up comprehensive defence plans for the North Atlantic area. A Military Committee consisting of the chiefs of staff of the member states, with an executive body, the Standing Group, composed of representatives of Britain, France and the United States, was also established. The Military Committee was to be responsible for providing advice on military policy.

Five Regional Planning Groups were established: these Regional Planning Groups were 'to develop and recommend to the Military Committee, through the Standing Group, plans for the defence of the Region'. The permanent Standing Group provided policy guidance to the Groups and was to co-ordinate their defence plans.

The Council also set up, in November 1949, a Defence Financial and Economic Committee of Finance Ministers. The Council gave the Committee a long-term programme to carry out but it was not

[2] 'Integration' in NATO is that achieved in the working out of the military plans established by the military headquarters of the Alliance which are internationally staffed by officers from the different countries of the Alliance. National forces 'assigned' to the Supreme Commander remain under national command, but in time of war or emergency they receive their orders from the integrated NATO headquarters under the overall command of the Supreme Allied Commander, Europe (SACEUR).

until the Korean war broke out in June 1950 that a stimulus was provided for its implementation.

In November 1949 the Council also decided that the permanent NATO secretariat should be in London, and approved the establishment of the Military Production and Supply Board by the Defence Committee. This body was to review the military supply situation and to encourage the more efficient production of military equipment. It was responsible to the Defence Committee. In practice it did not work effectively. The national delegations did not succeed in making entirely objective collective recommendations and as the Board did not sit in permanent session there was a lack of continuity in its work. In December 1950, so as to deal more effectively with the problems raised by the Korean war, the Board was replaced by the Defence Production Board. Under the Board nine international 'task forces' (teams of production specialists) visited and examined production facilities in the member countries and drew up a series of reports recommending specific means of increasing production. These proposals were placed before the Financial and Economic Board which decided that such questions, involving large expenditure, could not be considered in isolation.[1]

THE COUNCIL OF DEPUTIES

At the fourth meeting of the North Atlantic Council in London in May 1950 it was realised that the military and civilian institutions of NATO were not adequately co-ordinated. The foreign ministers met only every three or four months, with a consequent lack of continuity in the direction of NATO's affairs. A communiqué of the North Atlantic Council stated: 'A year's experience has shown that, on the political side, the meetings of the Council have been too infrequent to permit a sufficient exchange on matters of common interest within the scope of the Treaty'. The Council accordingly decided to create a permanent civilian body to be responsible for implementing the policies of NATO governments between meetings of the North Atlantic Council. This body, the Council of Deputies, was to sit in permanent session in London. Each government was represented by a Deputy in the North Atlantic Council. The Council of Deputies was to work on behalf of, and in the name of, the North Atlantic Council. It was to see that the decisions of the Council were carried out and to formulate policies for the Council's approval. The Council decided that the Deputies should study the problems of maintaining

[1] See the section on 'The 1951 reorganisation', pp. 378–80.

adequate military forces and their financial costs as one problem, not separately.

The first Chairman of the Council of Deputies was Mr Charles Spofford, the American Deputy. The threefold role of national deputy, international chairman and head of the Secretariat soon proved unsatisfactory, and Mr Spofford himself advocated that a 'NATO Chairman' be appointed. The Council of Deputies played a specially important part in the political development of NATO. As in OEEC a technique was developed by which the deputies sought to reach unanimous recommendations, without a formal vote, through a process of negotiation involving their fellow deputies and their home governments.

THE 1951 REORGANISATION

In 1951 the structure of NATO was simplified. With the additional strains imposed by the Korean war it had become increasingly obvious that political, military and financial problems were inextricably linked and could not be considered by separate ministerial committees. They had also become so important that they could be resolved only at the highest level and by continuous co-ordination at that level. It was therefore announced by the Deputies in May 1951 that the North Atlantic Council would incorporate the Defence Committee and the Defence Financial and Economic Committee and so become 'the sole ministerial body in the Organisation' with 'the responsibility of considering all matters concerning the implementation of the provisions of the Treaty'. The Council could be made up of foreign, defence or finance ministers, according to the agenda. Heads of Governments might also attend the meetings of the Council. The Deputies now represented all ministers in their governments concerned with NATO affairs: they became the permanent working organisation of the North Atlantic Council.

At the same time the Financial and Economic Board (FEB), responsible to the Council of Deputies, was set up in Paris to take advantage of the facilities provided by OEEC. The establishment of FEB marked the determination of NATO to deal with the growing defence burden caused by large-scale Western rearmament. FEB studied the ways in which the economic effects of defence obligations would be felt. At the Ottawa Conference, in September 1951, FEB presented an interim report which contained the first comprehensive and objective analysis of the financial and economic problems raised by the national defence programmes. The report emphasised that no simple formula for the 'equitable' sharing of the defence burden could be provided. FEB recommended that any final decision about the size of the NATO defence programme should follow a careful appraisal of both the economic dangers of making increases and the military risks of not making them. Despite the useful work carried out by FEB 'it soon became evident that the procedure under which . . . [it] reviewed individual national submissions with the aim of blending them into an overall programme was failing because of the absence of agreed standards and an agreed approach.'[1]

At the meeting of the Council at Ottawa in 1951 the Temporary Council Committee (TCC) was established to carry out the tasks, which lay outside the scope of FEB, of making progress in the sphere of defence production and of reconciling the requirements of 'fulfilling a militarily acceptable NATO Plan for the defence of Western Europe and the realistic political–economic capabilities of the member countries'. TCC was given powers to ask for information, advice and help from member governments. TCC in turn delegated this task to a sub-committee of three: Mr Averell Harriman, M. Jean Monnet and Sir Edwin Plowden.[1] The members of the sub-committee were to act not as representatives of their governments but as a corporate NATO body. The sub-committee obtained the information it required through questionnaires sent to the member governments, which it then submitted to searching cross-examinations. In this way it obtained far more military information from these governments than had previously been thought possible. In December 1951 TCC presented its final report to the Council, in which it emphasised the need for the further strengthening and co-ordination of the agencies of NATO. This report was of outstanding value in providing the first assessment of the defence effort of member states to NATO definition and shown as a percentage of the gross national product at factor cost. It recommended that there should be regular appraisals of NATO's defence programmes. This recommendation was the origin of the 'Annual Review'.

The task of reconciling defence needs and available funds has always been one of the crucial problems of NATO. There has been, and still is, a wide gap between the demands of the military authorities and the willingness or ability of governments to meet the cost. In making their recommendations the NATO military authorities consider the capacity of each NATO country to contribute to the total effort. A government may accept NATO requirements but may reserve its position as to when and how it can meet them. The

[1] Ronald S. Ritchie, *NATO, The Economics of an Alliance*, Toronto, Ryerson, 1956, p. 41.

[2] Later Lord Plowden.

politicians have constantly pressed the military planners to reduce their requirements, and in practice force levels are fitted to the amount of money available.

THE LISBON REORGANISATION

At the Lisbon meeting of the North Atlantic Council in February 1952 it was decided by the Council, acting on a report by the Council Deputies and recommendations by TCC, that there should be a radical reorganisation of the civilian agencies of NATO. These decisions were:

(*a*) The terms of reference of the North Atlantic Council should continue to be the North Atlantic Treaty.

(*b*) The Council should continue to be a Council of governments, represented by ministers for foreign affairs and/or ministers of defence and/or other competent ministers, especially those responsible for financial and economic affairs, as required by the agenda of each meeting. When appropriate, member countries could be represented by heads of government.

(*c*) Ministerial meetings should be held at least three times a year.

(*d*) The chairmanship of the Council should continue to rotate annually, as it had done hitherto. The Secretary General (see (*f*) below) should serve as Vice-Chairman of the Council and preside in the absence of the Chairman.

(*e*) In order to enable the Council to function in permanent session with effective powers of decision each government should appoint a permanent representative to represent his government on the Council when ministers were not present. Permanent representatives could be of ministerial rank or senior officials according to the practice of the state concerned. In any case, they should be sufficiently close to their governments and entrusted with adequate authority to enable the Council to discharge its collective tasks and to reach prompt decisions. Each permanent representative should head a national delegation, consisting of those advisers and experts necessary to assist him in all phases of the Council's work.

(*f*) A Secretary General should be appointed by, and be responsible to, the Council. He should not be a member of any national delegation. He should be responsible for organising the work of the Council and directing the work of the International Secretariat (see (*g*) below). He should initiate and prepare matters for Council action and ensure that appropriate steps are taken to follow up Council decisions. He should have direct access to all NATO agencies and to governments.

(*g*) The International Secretariat should be unified and strengthened so as to play an effective role in the initial preparation and follow up of action in all matters for which the Council is responsible. It should perform analytical and planning functions at the request of the Council, including preparatory work for the annual TCC-type review.

(*h*) The Council should assume responsibility for the tasks hitherto performed by the Council Deputies, the Defence Production Board, and the Financial and Economic Board, as well as those initiated by the Temporary Council Committee.

(*i*) The Permanent Headquarters of the Council should be located in the general area of Paris.

(*j*) The position of the North Atlantic Council in relation to the military agencies of NATO should continue unchanged. Liaison arrangements between the Council and those agencies should be strengthened.

(*k*) The new arrangements should become effective and the new Treaty agencies should assume their functions at a date to be fixed by the Council Deputies. On that date the Council Deputies, the Defence Production Board, and the Financial and Economic Board should cease to exist.

On 12 March 1952 the Council Deputies appointed Lord Ismay, at that time a member of the British Government, to be Secretary General of NATO and Vice-Chairman of the Council.

The implementation of these decisions meant that the peripatetic Council and the Council Deputies were replaced by a new Council with a permanent Secretariat at one headquarters in Paris. In April 1952 the new Council and Secretariat moved to the Palais de Chaillot.[1] At the same time the permanent representatives and their delegations also assembled in Paris. The new Council held its first meeting in Paris on 28 April. In its new shape the Council again exists in two forms: one when it meets at ministerial level, and, more usually, when it sits at the level of permanent representatives.

THE NEW COUNCIL

At the Lisbon meeting the Council agreed on the lines along which

[1] Later the NATO Secretariat moved to a new building at the Place du Maréchal de Lattre de Tassigny. In October 1966 the North Atlantic Council decided that its seat should be moved to Brussels.

it should transact its business. Meetings of the Council were to be held weekly on Wednesdays, though there have in practice very often been additional meetings, sometimes at short notice. At 'normal' sessions of the Council the members can attend with four advisers and on occasion more. At 'restricted' sessions when business of a confidential nature is considered one or two advisers may attend from each delegation. At the strictly private 'informal' sessions only the permanent representatives themselves attend. Lord Ismay has written:

'These informal meetings, at which there is no agenda, no record, no commitments—and therefore no formal discussions—are characterised by the utmost frankness. They enable Permanent Representatives to inform their governments of the climate of opinion in the Council, and in particular to report the preliminary views of their colleagues on important questions which are destined to come up later for Council decision. Governments are thus able to take those views into account in their own instructions to their Permanent Representatives.'[1]

There are no written procedural rules for the Council, and no need for any such rules has yet been felt. Council business is carried out in English and French, which are the official languages of NATO. Some NATO committees often conduct their business in both languages without interpretation.

Decisions of the Council are unanimous and there is no voting. If views clash, negotiations are continued until unanimous agreement is reached. If one or two states disagree with the majority the pressure of the other powers and the Secretary General is brought to bear on them. In general a situation of this kind does not arise since decisions are usually discussed informally and agreed on before they are raised for official approval.

From the time the Council began to sit in permanent session with powers of decision it has not been found necessary for ministers to meet three times a year, as laid down at Lisbon, but periodic meetings of ministers have continued. Ministerial meetings enable ministers to keep in touch with developments in each other's national policies and to give guidance concerning political developments affecting NATO. Foreign, defence and finance ministers meet to make the decisions concerning overall military policy and to approve the Annual Review. Only once, in December 1957, has the Council met at the level of Heads of Government.

[1] *NATO—The First Five Years*, Paris, NATO, 1954, p. 58.

The Council has established various Standing Committees which carry out work in specialised fields. The Chairman of each Committee is appointed by the Council and membership of the Committees, which varies, is open to all member countries. The principal Committees set up by the Council are: the Committee of Political Advisers, the Committee of Economic Advisers, the Annual Review Committee, the Committee on Information and Cultural Relations, the Civilian Budget Committee, the Military Budget Committee, the Armaments Committee (at first the Defence Production Committee), the Security Committee, the Committee of European Air Space Coordination, the Science Committee, the Committee of Defence Research Directors, the Infrastructure Committee, the Infrastructure Payments and Progress Committee, the Senior Civil Emergency Planning Committee, the Civil Communications Planning Committee, the Civil Defence Committee, the Planning Board for Ocean Shipping, the Industrial Planning Committee, the Civil Emergency Co-ordination Committee, the Food and Agricultural Planning Committee, the Planning Board for European Inland Surface Transport, the Manpower Planning Committee, the Medical Committee, the Civil Aviation Planning Committee and the Petroleum Planning Committee. Temporary working groups on various subjects have also been set up by the Council. From time to time the Council in Permanent Session constitutes itself as a Defence Planning Committee to consider defence planning questions.

POLITICAL CONSULTATION IN THE COUNCIL

Because NATO has been very important to the security of its members, its main policies have required decisions at the highest political level. With fifteen members involved, therefore, the planning of the uses of military forces at the disposal of the Alliance clearly required much political activity and consultation.

The Committee on Non-military Co-operation, which was accordingly set up in May 1956, reported to the North Atlantic Council in December 1956 and recommended the development of political co-operation and consultation in the Council. The Committee of Three[1] suggested certain guidelines for the future development of political consultation in the Council. These proposals, which were approved by the Council, aimed to make the Council a major forum in which members of the Alliance would inform each other of important developments affecting NATO, consult together concerning the development of major policies or pronouncements, and try to

[1] Signor Gaetano Martino, Mr Halvard Lange and Mr Lester B. Pearson.

reconcile their own national policies with those of their allies. A Committee of Political Advisers was set up in January 1957 under the Assistant Secretary General for Political Affairs to prepare the political discussions of the Council and to advise the permanent representatives of the member countries on political questions.

In practice while consultation in NATO has helped its members to reach agreement over such matters as the Icelandic fisheries dispute and the initial settlement of the Cyprus affair, the North Atlantic Council has in general failed to develop common policies on most of the major political problems confronting the Alliance.

Paradoxically, the success of the Alliance in fulfilling its initial purpose has served only to increase these political problems. When the North Atlantic Treaty was signed the aims of the Alliance were clear. The North Atlantic area, and the mainland of Western Europe in particular, had to be defended from the possibility of Soviet aggression. The success of the Alliance in taking collective measures to resist this threat was largely instrumental in creating a new situation in which, following the Cuban confrontation, Western statesmen and peoples have come to believe less and less in the likelihood of an East–West military conflict. This has resulted in a more complex pattern of aims and interests emerging among the members of the Alliance and has caused them to pay greater attention to the problems of the internal balance and structure of NATO.

The American Government considers that it does not receive the support that it should have from its European allies over its policies, outside the North Atlantic area, in Vietnam and elsewhere. European members of NATO have been worried on their side about the implications of the American strategic doctrine of graduated response. They also consider that they are expected to back policies adopted by the United States with regard to questions in which they do not feel a direct interest, without prior consultation, and this has caused resentment. Likewise the policies of the former colonial powers concerning regions outside the North Atlantic area meet with indifference or criticism on the part of the other countries. At present there is no agreement about the relationship between the defence of the North Atlantic area and the co-ordination of their policies outside it. President Kennedy's proposal for an Atlantic partnership, made in 1962, the main military consequence of which was the abortive project for a multilateral nuclear force, failed to reduce these differences and to provide an impulse towards greater political cohesion.

In recent years there has, however, been a remarkable increase in the extent to which information about developments in East–West relations is exchanged in the weekly meetings of the North Atlantic Council at the level of ambassadors. Practically every official contact between the NATO governments and those of Eastern Europe is fully described by the representatives of the Western countries concerned and assessments of Eastern European policies are increasingly correlated, so that the attitude of each Eastern European country on a wide range of specific issues is carefully charted.

THE SECRETARIAT

The NATO Secretariat is headed by the Secretary General who is appointed by the Council. Whereas at Lisbon it was decided that the Secretary General should also hold the office of Vice-Chairman of the Council, in 1957 it was decided, as advocated by Lord Ismay, that he should be the Chairman (though he does not combine this office with that of President of the Council, which rotates). Since this change the Chairmanship of the Council has assumed much greater importance. The Secretary General may initiate policy and is responsible for implementing the Council's decisions. He has, however, no executive power except such as is specially given to him by the Council.

From 1952 the Secretary General took the chair at meetings of the Council at the level of permament representatives, and since 1957 he has presided at all Council and ministerial meetings. The authority of the Secretary General has been greatly increased by this change: there is a marked difference between the power of a Secretary General who merely initiates and one who both initiates and presides. He may mediate in disputes between member countries if invited to do so by the states involved. He has direct access to all NATO agencies and to all member governments. Although the powers of the Secretary General were increased in 1957 (following the report of the Committee of Three of December 1956), the extent to which he can use these powers depends partly on his personality. The Secretary General is helped by the Deputy Secretary General who presides over Council meetings in the absence of the Secretary General, and by four Assistant Secretaries General and an Executive Secretary. The Assistant Secretary General for Political Affairs is responsible for the Political Affairs Division, the Information Service and the Press Service. The Assistant Secretary General for Economic Affairs and Finance is responsible for the Economic Affairs and Finance Division. The other Assistant Secretaries General are responsible, respectively, for the Division of Production, Logistics and Infrastructure and the Division of Scientific Affairs. The Executive Secretary acts as Secretary to the Council and is responsible for co-ordinating the activities of the NATO Committees. Lord Ismay was Secretary General of NATO from May 1952 to May 1957 when he was succeeded by M. Paul-Henri Spaak, former Prime Minister of Belgium and at that time Foreign Minister. He was succeeded by Mr Dirk Stikker of the Netherlands in 1961 who was in turn followed by Signor Manlio Brosio of Italy in 1964.

The Secretariat, which prepares and organises the work of the Council and its Committees, is 940 strong and is recruited from all the member countries. Members of the Secretariat are international civil servants (may of them seconded from their national civil services for a period and then replaced by other civil servants from their home administrations), who owe their primary allegiance to NATO, which pays them, and not to their national governments. The system of seconding national civil servants gives home governments good contacts with NATO and a good understanding of it and gives the Secretariat close links with the national administrations, but it has a bad effect on the morale of the permanent staff to the extent that it limits their chances of promotion.

The Secretariat is divided into five main sections. The Office of the Executive Secretary provides the Secretariat for the NATO Committees and is responsible for the production of reports, records and other documents to service these Committees. The Civil Emergency Planning Office is also supervised by the Executive Secretary. The Political Affairs Division is responsible for preparing the political discussions of the Council and the discussions of the Committee of Political Advisers. It provides reports and documentation on political matters for the Secretary General and for the Council. Its other tasks are to maintain political liaison with the delegations of member countries and with other international organisations. The Assistant Secretary General for Political Affairs presides over meetings of the Political Advisers and the Committee on Information and Cultural Relations. He is also responsible for the Information and Press Services. The Division directed by the Assistant Secretary General for Economic Affairs and Finance is responsible for studying economic matters of concern to the Alliance, especially those with political effects on defence problems, and maintains a continuing scrutiny of the economic capacities of the member countries in relation to the common defence effort. The Division also studies the general financial aspects of defence by country, in the light of the strategic concepts approved by the Council and the force proposals put forward by the military authorities for their implementation, together with the defence policies and budgets of the member countries. It is further responsible for carrying out the Annual Review (see pp. 408–411) and organises the statistical studies which are required for analysing the NATO defence effort. The Division of Production, Logistics and Infrastructure tries to promote, within the field of armaments, the most efficient use of the resources of the Alliance for equipping its forces. In particular, it studies plans for improvement, standardisation and supply, and organises the exchange of technical information concerning research into armaments, and their improvement and production. This work is carried out under the supervision of the Armaments Committee. It supervises the infrastructure programme under the control of the Infrastructure Committee and the Infrastructure Payments and Progress Committee. The Division of Scientific Affairs advises the Secretary General on scientific matters, prepares meetings of the Scientific Committee and implements its decisions, and maintains contacts in the scientific domain with the military and civil authorities of NATO and of member countries and with international organisations. The Assistant Secretary General for Scientific Affairs is Chairman of the Science Committee. The Secretariat also contains a Personnel and Administration Service and the Service of the Financial Comptroller.

The Council has created a number of subsidiary civil agencies. The Central Europe Operating Agency was set up in 1957 and is responsible for the network of pipelines supplying fuel to NATO forces in Europe. This was constructed after a decision of the Council in 1952, following a request of the Supreme Allied Commander, Europe. The Agency is established near Versailles. The NATO Maintenance and Supply Organisation and Agency were set up in 1958 to provide a common system for the supply of spare parts for the forces of NATO countries. A supply centre was established at Châteauroux, though following the French 'initiative' of 1966 all supply dumps have been moved out of France. The Hawk Agency supervises the Société Européenne de Téléguidage (SETEL) which is a consortium of companies from Belgium, France, the Federal Republic of Germany, Italy and the Netherlands that produces the American designed Hawk missile system in Europe. Each company makes different parts of the system. Further consortia of NATO countries produce other missiles (the 'Sidewinder' and the 'Bullpup'), an anti-submarine torpedo and the multi-purpose F104G 'Starfighter' aircraft. The most ambitious co-operative project so far undertaken is the NATO Air Defence Ground Environment (NADGE), an improved early-warning radar network across the whole of the European NATO land area which will take several years to complete.

THE CIVILIAN BUDGET

The budget for the civilian agencies of NATO which includes the salaries of the Secretariat and the general administrative costs of the organisation is prepared by a committee representing all the member states and paid for by all the members according to an agreed scale. Its total amounts to about £4·4 million, including a scientific programme costing about £1·4 million. The percentages that each member contributes are not published.

The Military Structure and Forces

THE MILITARY COMMITTEE

The chief military authority under the North Atlantic Council is the Military Committee which is composed of representatives of the chiefs of staff of the member states. Iceland, which has no military forces, may be represented by a civilian. The Committee, which meets at top level at least twice a year, provides the Council with military advice and directs the subordinate military authorities. The chiefs of staff appoint permanent military representatives who enable the Committee to work in permanent session.

The Standing Group was the executive of the Military Committee. This body, which sat permanently in Washington until the summer of 1966 when it was abolished by decision of the North Atlantic Council, consisted of representatives of the chiefs of staff of France, the United Kingdom and the United States and the Chairman of the Military Committee. The Standing Group laid down strategic policy and formulated, directed, co-ordinated and integrated the defence plans of the NATO command and the Canada–United States Regional Planning Group, and also controlled the NATO military agencies. The Group was assisted by French, British and American staff teams and sometimes by teams from other member states. On its suppression in the summer of 1966, it was decided that it should be replaced by a suitable structure including an integrated international military staff.

The siting of the Standing Group in Washington, where it established close contacts with the chief American military authorities, was of great importance. The reluctance of the Americans to delegate authority was so great that it was often easier to obtain the decisions of the British and French Governments from London and Paris than American decisions on the spot. Had the Standing Group been sited at Paris it might have been very much more difficult to obtain American decisions.

The Military Committee, which consists of a permanent military representative from each of the other member countries, and used to include the members of the Standing Group, until it was abolished in 1966, keeps all NATO countries informed of one another's national points of view and kept them in touch with the work of the Standing Group. A Standing Group Representative in Paris provided a link between the Standing Group and the North Atlantic Council.

Although the Council is the supreme political and military authority, the Supreme Allied Commander, Europe, the Supreme Atlantic Commander and the Allied Commanders-in-Chief are commanders in the field when the state of NATO alert is reached at which the 'assigned' or 'earmarked' national forces pass under their command. In practice, the Supreme Allied Commander, Europe, wields great authority with regard to military decisions, and deals directly with governments and national delegations, though he is responsible to the Military Committee.

Despite its political powers, the Council seemed to exert little authority over military planning in the Standing Group, and the suspicion of some of the European members of the Alliance that the former Standing Group provided the American Government with a convenient mechanism for dominating the military planning of the Alliance was a disruptive political factor in NATO. The moving of the Military Committee together with the Council to Brussels, strengthened by the creation of an integrated international staff, which was decided in 1966, should have the result, when implemented, of greatly improving the on-the-spot expert military advice given to the Council. This in turn will probably result in some restriction of the advisory role of SACEUR and the separation of the military and political wings of NATO.

THE MILITARY AGENCIES

The specialised military agencies of NATO include the NATO Defence College, established in 1951 at the *Ecole Militaire* in Paris to train officers and government officials in international co-operation and to give them a thorough understanding of the Alliance. It was decided in September 1966 that the Defence College should move to Rome. The Military Agency for Standardisation (MAS) was set up in 1951 to study and encourage the standardisation throughout the forces of the member states of operational and military practice and of war equipment. Little progress has been made in this field on a NATO-wide basis. The Advisory Group on Aeronautical Research and Development (AGARD) was set up in 1952 to encourage co-operation on aeronautical problems and to further research into them. Some of the most valuable work carried out by NATO's military agencies is that carried out by the series of signals agencies that have been set up. These include the Allied Military Communications-Electronics Committee (AMCEC) and the Allied Naval Communications Agency (ANCA), both of which deal with signals matters concerning the defence of the NATO area. The Allied Long Line Agency (ALLA) studies all matters concerning the use of telecommunications facilities in Europe. The Allied Radio Frequencies Agency (ARFA) collects all available information on radio frequencies and allocates them.

THE EUROPEAN COMMAND

The Supreme Headquarters of the Allied Powers in Europe (SHAPE) was first established in Paris in January 1951 and moved to Versailles in June of the same year. In June 1966 it was decided to move SHAPE to Chièvres-Casteau near Mons in Belgium. It has the responsibility for organising the defence of the European member countries against invasion. SHAPE replaced three of the original NATO Regional Planning Groups, and new subordinate commands were set up in their place. The three commands set up are: the Northern European Command, the Central European Command,[1] and the Southern European Command. Also, seven countries have committed forces to a mobile reserve (the ACE Mobile Force) for NATO as a whole, with special reference to an emergency in northern or south-eastern Europe. The Supreme Allied Commander Europe (SACEUR), who has always been an American General,[2] is responsible to the North Atlantic Council for the defence of the allied countries in the area of his command against any attack. He has planning control over all the forces assigned to him by the member states: he is responsible

[1] The three former separate headquarters of the Commander-in-Chief Central Europe and the Commanders-in-Chief of the Land Forces and Air Forces at Fontainebleau were merged into one single headquarters, Allied Forces Central Europe, in November 1966.

[2] The first Supreme Commander was General Eisenhower, who was appointed in December 1950 and was succeeded in June 1952 by General Ridgway. General Gruenther was appointed Supreme Commander in July 1953 and was followed by General Norstad in November 1956. He, in turn, was succeeded by General Lemnitzer in 1962.

for their operational planning and training. In time of war he would command all land, sea and air operations in the European Command. Although defence of coastal waters remains the responsibility of national authorities, the Supreme Commander would carry out the operations he considered necessary for the defence of any part of this area. The reluctance of the national military authorities to integrate arms production and standardise equipment does, however, constitute a considerable obstacle to the effectiveness of SACEUR'S operational control; and the refusal to take joint action on logistics has always been a particular bane to SACEUR. SACEUR is empowered to deal directly with national authorities in all matters concerning the forces assigned to him. He is also responsible for the co-ordination of national arrangements for the logistic support of NATO. He formulates operational plans to meet possible aggression. These internationally agreed plans for military action in different contingencies, worked out by the NATO integrated staffs, are one of the most important elements in the military effectiveness of NATO.

THE ATLANTIC OCEAN COMMAND

The Supreme Atlantic Command Headquarters (SACLANT) was set up in January 1952 in Norfolk, Virginia. It is responsible for protecting the sea lanes in European waters and the Atlantic. There are five subordinate commands: Western Atlantic Command, Eastern Atlantic Command, Striking Fleet Atlantic, Submarines Allied Command Atlantic and the Iberian Atlantic Command. The Supreme Atlantic Commander (also known as SACLANT)[1] controls a staff drawn from the navies, armies and air forces of Canada, Denmark, France, the Netherlands, Norway, Portugal, the United Kingdom and the United States. A representative of SACLANT in Europe maintains direct contact with SACEUR.

Like SACEUR, SACLANT is responsible in peacetime for preparing defence plans and for ensuring that the forces that are 'earmarked' for his command in time of war are adequately trained, organised and equipped by their national authorities. In wartime SACLANT is responsible for ensuring security in the Atlantic area and protecting the sea lanes. Unlike SACEUR, SACLANT has no forces 'assigned' to him in peacetime but certain forces are 'earmarked' for his command in time of war.

[1] The Supreme Atlantic Commanders have been Admiral McCormick (appointed in 1952), Admiral Wright (1954), Admiral Dennison (1960), Admiral Smith (1963) and Admiral Moorer (1965).

THE CHANNEL COMMITTEE

A Channel Committee, composed of the Chiefs of Naval Staff (or their representatives) of Belgium, France, the Netherlands and the United Kingdom, was set up following the establishment of SACEUR and SACLANT, to deal with the special problem of the defence of the Channel. The area controlled by the Committee consists of the Channel itself and the southern waters of the North Sea (with the exception of territorial waters). Directly under the Committee is the Allied Command Channel.

CANADA–UNITED STATES REGIONAL PLANNING GROUP

The Canada–United States Regional Planning Group is the only one of the five original Regional Planning Groups to retain its initial form. It is responsible for planning the defence of North America and for making recommendations on the military requirements of that area. The Group's defence plans are co-ordinated with other NATO plans in the same way as are those of SACEUR and SACLANT.

ARMED FORCES

In 1949 the then member countries of NATO could muster between them less than fifteen divisions, fewer than a thousand operational aircraft and a few hundred serviceable naval vessels: of these twelve divisions, four hundred aircraft and four hundred warships were assigned to the command of the first Supreme Commander, Europe, in 1950. During the 1950s it became an established NATO belief that the Central European Command required some thirty full-strength divisions to provide adequate conventional defence forces for the protection of the Central European sector. In 1966 there was a total of twenty-four divisions[1] assigned to SACEUR for the defence of the key Central front, including twelve German divisions but excluding the two and a half French divisions, previously assigned to NATO, which were withdrawn from this assignment on 1 July 1966, though they remained in Germany. These divisions are equipped with tactical nuclear weapons and supported by air squadrons with a nuclear capacity.[2]

In 1966 the Northern European Command had one German division and all the Danish and Norwegian land, sea and tactical air

[1] Some of the NATO divisions are not at full strength, so that the effective strength is more like the equivalent of twenty divisions.

[2] The information in the following paragraphs is drawn from *The Military Balance 1966–67*, Institute for Strategic Studies, September 1966.

forces assigned to it (though Denmark and Norway refuse to equip their forces with tactical nuclear weapons, or to have nuclear weapons stored on their territory). It also includes German air and naval forces. In the same year the Southern European Command had twenty-nine divisions assigned to it by Italy, Greece and Turkey. The United States 6th Fleet is earmarked for this Command which also has tactical air forces assigned to it. Naval units and maritime air forces of Italy, Greece and Turkey together with a small British naval force are also earmarked for this Command which has absorbed the former Mediterranean Command. Altogether SACEUR has about fifty-eight divisions assigned to him while some thirty more would be brought forward in an emergency if time allowed.

SACLANT has naval forces earmarked to him for training in peacetime and for his command in wartime by seven of the eight NATO naval powers which border on the Atlantic. France does not participate in these arrangements but there are arrangements for co-operation between its fleet and SACLANT's forces. His forces include a strike force, in the form of the attack carriers of the United States 2nd Fleet and missile-firing submarines, and they also include escort vessels and submarines to protect the Atlantic shipping lanes and anti-submarine aircraft and helicopters. Belgium, Britain and the Netherlands provide warships which are earmarked for the Channel Command.

In comparison it was estimated that at the end of 1966 the Soviet Union had some twenty divisions in a high state of readiness in East Germany, four in Hungary and two in Poland, supported by sixty-three divisions of lower efficiency and reliability belonging to the other members of the Warsaw Pact.[1] Soviet and Eastern European divisions are about half the size of the Western divisions. The Soviet divisions are equipped with nuclear weapons, and the forces of the other Warsaw Pact countries are equipped with missiles and aircraft capable of delivering nuclear warheads, though it is generally considered that the warheads themselves remain under Soviet control. As well as the Soviet divisions, the East German, Czech and Polish forces are well equipped with modern, mostly Soviet produced, arms. In recent years considerable emphasis has been placed on the development of close co-operation between the forces of the Warsaw Pact

[1] The bulk of the Soviet Union's armed forces (which total over 3 million men) are deployed between Moscow and the Eastern frontier of the Federal Republic of Germany, the implication being that their primary strategic concern is Western Europe.

countries and an important series of joint manoeuvres has been held.

At the end of 1966 it was believed that the Soviet Union possessed some 300 intercontinental ballistic missiles, 150 fleet ballistic missiles and 750 medium range ballistic missiles. The Western Allies possessed some 934 intercontinental ballistic missiles and 624 medium range missiles.

The principal nuclear striking force which could be used by the Alliance[2] is the United States Strategic Air Command which comprised, in 1966, some 680 bomber aircraft equipped with air-to-surface missiles and nuclear bombs. Some 800 'Minuteman I' and fifty 'Minuteman II' intercontinental ballistic missiles were ready for action in the United States in 1966. The United States Navy had thirty-seven nuclear-powered submarines in commission in 1966, equipped with sixteen missiles apiece.

Problems of Strategy and Nuclear Control

NATO STRATEGY

NATO's basic policy is to prevent war by making it clear that aggression will not pay. With the emergence of thermonuclear weapons, the original concept of direct defence by conventional means was replaced by the concept of indirect defence through the threat of massive nuclear strikes, since which NATO's military planning has therefore been based on the concept of the deterrent. From the beginning NATO had hoped to establish a forward defence strategy, that is to say a strategy involving fighting in order to concede no NATO territory to the enemy at its furthest boundaries (in practice, effectively protecting the eastern frontier of the Federal Republic of Germany), thus fully protecting the NATO peoples against invasion and envisaging no major withdrawal. This was not at first possible, because NATO's force levels were not high enough. While NATO's force levels were gradually being built up the 'tripwire' strategy was therefore adopted. Under this strategy a thin forward screen of NATO forces would register and define any aggressive thrust, which, if it could not be effectively contained, would be met by nuclear retaliation. As forces were built up it became possible to move the forward defence line up to the Rhine. By September 1963 SACEUR had sufficient assigned forces, owing especially to the contribution of

[2] There is no allied command organisation covering strategic nuclear forces but the European and Atlantic Commands participate in the Joint Strategic Planning System at Omaha, Nebraska, where the integrated planning of American and British bomber forces is carried out.

new German divisions, to move it right up to the Federal Republic's eastern frontier.

In 1954 General Gruenther described the strategy of the Alliance in a famous phrase 'the sword and the shield': the sword being the Alliance's capability to retaliate immediately in the event of aggression through a strategic nuclear counter-offensive; the shield consisting of the land, sea and air forces equipped with nuclear weapons, whose task would be to defend the NATO land and sea areas against attack.

The maintenance of strong conventional land forces in Western Europe has always remained an essential part of NATO strategy with the aim of containing any conventional foray or limited regional attack along the boundaries of the Western European area, of avoiding the premature use of nuclear weapons by the allies, and of creating a pause which gives the aggressor time to reflect upon the implications of the demonstrated allied will to resist and so to desist before escalation[1] becomes inevitable.

The nuclear strategy of the United States, which controls the great majority of the nuclear weapons of the Alliance, has changed over the years, from that of 'massive retaliation' (the launching of an all-out nuclear counter-attack on the towns and cities of the Soviet Union in the event of a Russian first strike) in the days when Mr John Foster Dulles was Secretary of State, to that of 'controlled response' under the aegis of the present Secretary for Defence, Mr McNamara. This second strategy provides for the nuclear riposte delivered by the United States to be carefully adjusted in the event of an initially limited Soviet nuclear strike so that only missile sites and military targets would be destroyed. It also allows for the carefully planned and graded conventional response to attacks made by conventional forces—as demonstrated by the military policy of the American forces in the Vietnam war. At all times the nuclear strategy of the United States has remained firmly centred on the idea of the need for a single integrated control and command structure for the Alliance, an idea expounded on many occasions by Mr McNamara.

From 1958 onwards there has been increasing discussion within the Alliance of the questions of policy-making in NATO and the

[1] The rapid progression, through different stages, from the use of conventional to the most destructive nuclear weapons: for instance, the use of tactical nuclear weapons, in reply to purely conventional attack, followed by the use of medium-range and then long-range missiles with nuclear heads in return. A conflict also escalates from attacks on strictly limited military targets and areas to ones on densely populated urban areas of a primarily civilian character.

control of the nuclear deterrent. These problems were first raised by General de Gaulle in 1958 when he proposed that France, the United States and the United Kingdom should co-ordinate their policies in areas not covered by the NATO Treaty and that the use of the nuclear weapons of the Allies should be jointly controlled by the governments of these three countries. Two closely related issues are involved. First, there is a feeling among certain members of the Alliance that the United States has too much influence in shaping NATO's policy and that it does not consult its Allies enough before taking decisions which affect the Alliance as a whole and the individual interests of all its member countries. Second, there is the specific question of the control of nuclear weapons and nuclear strategy.

The French Government has provided the most outspoken and highly developed criticisms of the present structure of the Alliance. President de Gaulle and ministers in his governments have declared on many occasions that France sought the reform of the Alliance and hinted that, unless France was satisfied on this score, it might withdraw from NATO. These criticisms and hints came to a head with the publication of the French Government's two memoranda of March 1966 and the ensuing NATO crisis. The main arguments put forward by the French Government in requesting the reform of NATO are summarised later (p. 402), but the one most relevant here is the French Government's view that, because of the possession by the Soviet Government of intercontinental missiles, the United States Government cannot be relied upon to intervene automatically in a conflict in Europe since this would risk, in reprisal, the launching of Soviet missiles at the great cities of North America. Even, continues this argument, if the European members of the Alliance were confident that the United States would fully commit its military resources, both conventional and nuclear, to the defence of Western Europe in case of need, the Soviet Union might well, in view of the great risk involved for the people of the United States, calculate (however wrongly) that full American commitment was improbable and thus discount it. The question is then posed whether the American Government might not, in certain circumstances, and especially in view of the replacement of its former strategy of 'massive retaliation' by that of 'controlled response', prefer to evacuate or sacrifice its forces in Europe rather than risk the destruction of the United States. The fact that the United States may fear the escalation of any conflict in the European area serves only to heighten this doubt, since Russian fear of such escalation is the Europeans' chief guarantee that the deterrent deters. In effect the Europeans preferred to live under a total nuclear threat and preferred to benefit from total deterrent through the threat of an all-out nuclear war than to run the risk of a limited conflict in which they knew they would be the victims.

The French Government has not been the only government to voice criticisms of thc present control of nuclear strategy and weapons in NATO. In particular, the Government of the Federal Republic of Germany, encouraged by the importance attached by Britain and France to the possession of independent nuclear forces, has shown in the past few years a strong interest in being able to participate in the nuclear counsels of the Alliance and to share in the nuclear decision-making progress in NATO. The Canadian Government has also come out strongly in favour of a revision of the NATO structure, leading to a greater degree of joint nuclear planning and control.

Some European critics have also expressed their concern over a situation in which the North Atlantic Council, which can theoretically meet at short notice and act on behalf of the Council, is located in Europe and thus unlikely to have enough influence on the decisions taken in Washington by the President of the United States.

Leading statesmen and military experts in the European countries of NATO have also expressed the desire to see NATO reorganised in such a way as to give the European countries:

(*a*) a voice in the planning of the way in which nuclear weapons would be used in different eventualities; and,

(*b*) a share in the process of decision making concerning the use of NATO's nuclear weapons at the critical moment of their actual use.

Even before its total withdrawal from the military command structure of NATO in 1966, France's opposition to the principle of 'integration'[1] in NATO led to the withdrawal of its Mediterranean fleet from being earmarked for NATO use in 1959, followed by that of the bulk of its Atlantic fleet in 1963. France had also, from the time of the Algerian war, reduced the number of its divisions assigned to SACEUR from six to two and it refused to allow the nuclear weapons of its allies to be stored on its territory.

The United States Government has taken steps and made proposals in order to appease European criticisms and anxieties. In May 1962, it was decided by the North Atlantic Council to set up

[1] Defined in footnote 1, p. 376.

special procedures which would enable all members of the Alliance to exchange information about the role of nuclear weapons in NATO defence. At the same meeting the United States confirmed that it would continue to make available to the Alliance the nuclear weapons necessary for NATO defence, concerting with its allies on basic plans and arrangements in regard to these weapons. Also in 1962 SACEUR established a liaison staff of European officers at the headquarters of the United States Strategic Air Command at Omaha. In 1963, SACEUR was given a deputy for nuclear affairs, a Belgian General, whose task is to act as a special adviser on nuclear questions to SACEUR and to bring together and synthetise information on major developments in nuclear affairs, though the practical effects of this move have generally been regarded as marginal. The United States Government has also placed three Polaris submarines equipped with nuclear missiles under the command of SACEUR and the British Government has placed its V-bomber force under NATO command.

More serious attempts to give the European countries a greater say in the nuclear policy making and control of the Alliance are represented by the American Government's proposals first put forward in 1963 to set up a Multilateral Nuclear Force (MLF), the British Government's counter-proposals of 1964 to create an Atlantic Nuclear Force (ANF), and the proposals made in 1965 by Mr McNamara to create a permanent committee of certain NATO Defence Ministers to lay down guiding lines for the nuclear policy of the Alliance.

The American Government's proposals for a Multilateral Force envisaged the establishment of a force of twenty-five surface vessels, each armed with eight Polaris missiles, with mixed-manned crews provided by those countries which wished to participate, including the Federal Republic of Germany. The fleet would be commanded by an integrated nuclear NATO command in which all participating countries would be represented. The United States would retain a veto on the use of the fleet, but the European members could obtain a certain degree of control, and the United States did not exclude the possibility of a jointly-exercised European veto—a step which many Europeans saw as leading towards equal partnership in the nuclear field, with a separate European nuclear organisation matching the American one and closely associated with it.

The British Government's proposals for the establishment of an Atlantic Nuclear Force envisaged the creation of a nuclear command which would command and control the Polaris submarines at present being constructed for British use, together with a matching number of American submarines. The force would also include the British V-bombers and would be open to the participation of other members of the Alliance. The national contributions to this force would retain their identity as distinct units and could thus be withdrawn and used as independent national forces under certain circumstances. The United States, Britain and France, if the French Government took part, would have a veto over the use of the force and over changes which might be suggested in the control system. The authority controlling the force would act on the instructions of the participating governments.

In November 1965, the defence ministers of the United States, Britain, Canada, the Federal Republic of Germany, Italy, Belgium, the Netherlands, Denmark, Greece and Turkey decided to form a Special Committee to examine and report on all aspects of nuclear policy and allied consultation, following proposals made in May 1965 by Mr McNamara concerning the creation of a permanent NATO nuclear committee. At this meeting the defence ministers approved the creation of three groups to study nuclear policy, communications and intelligence.

The MLF and ANF proposals have been the subject of detailed studies by the NATO governments and some governments have come out in favour of one or other of them but no general consensus has been reached and in practice, despite American statements to the contrary, both proposals are now moribund. Although the Americans hoped that the adoption of such a scheme could give the European governments the feeling of a greater degree of participation in the nuclear control of the Alliance and although these plans could result in greater consultation between the Allies concerning the planning and execution of NATO's nuclear policy, they do not affect the basic problem of control. This is that so long as the overwhelming majority of nuclear weapons within the Alliance are American owned and their use remains subject to the decision of the President of the United States, European members of the Alliance will not be able to call these forces into use independently.

The American Government claims that Article 5 of the Treaty makes American response to aggression on a member of the Alliance automatic and argues that the integrated planning and control of all the members' nuclear forces is therefore a necessity.

'Our mutual safety demands that the strategic nuclear forces like the theatre nuclear forces must be controlled under a single chain of command. . . . The complex of targets against which such weapons would be used must, as a practical matter, be viewed as a single system. . . . A partial unco-ordinated response could be fatal to the interests of all the members of NATO. That is why in our discussions of the various plans to enlarge the participation of our NATO partners in the strategic nuclear offensive mission we have consistently stressed the importance of ensuring that the Alliance's strategic nuclear forces are employed in a fully co-ordinated manner against what is truly an indivisible target system. The essential point is not that this force must be under exclusive US ownership and control but, rather, that we must avoid the fragmentation and compartmentalisation of NATO nuclear power which could be dangerous to all of us.'[1]

French doubts about the automatic nature of the American response to aggression against other members of the Alliance have already been mentioned. There have been such doubts on the part of other governments too;[2] and European governments tend in particular to be unsure whether, if their countries were subject to a strategic nuclear attack, the full powers of the American strategic deterrent would be brought to bear in their defence.[3]

[1] Statement made by the Secretary of Defence, Mr Robert McNamara, before a joint hearing of the Senate Armed Services Committee on Department of Defence appropriations in February 1966.

[2] The following case shows that such doubts exist (even if the case in point is a very complex and special one). In a letter sent to the Prime Minister of Turkey, Mr Inonu, dated 5 June 1964, President Johnson stated, with reference to the possibility of Turkish military intervention in Cyprus: 'I hope you will understand that your NATO allies have not had a chance to consider whether they have an obligation to protect Turkey against the Soviet Union if Turkey takes a step which results in Soviet intervention without the full consent and understanding of its NATO allies.' In his reply, Mr Inonu wrote: 'Our understanding is that the North Atlantic Treaty imposes upon all member states the obligation to come forthwith to the assistance of any member victim of aggression. The only point left to the discretion of the member states is the nature and scale of its assistance. If NATO members should start discussing the right and wrong of the situation of their fellow-member victim of Soviet aggression . . . the very foundation of the Alliance would be shaken.' These quotations are drawn from a press release issued by Mr Paul Findley, Chairman of the House Republican Committee on NATO and the Atlantic Community, on 18 January 1966.

[3] See, for example, the reply of Mr Christian Herter to a question put to him by Senator Morse during the hearing on his nomination: 'I cannot conceive of any President involving us in an all-out nuclear war unless the facts showed clearly we are in danger of all-out devastation ourselves or that actual moves have been made towards devastating ourselves.' *Hearings on the Nomination of C. A. Herter to be Secretary of State*, Committee on Foreign Relations, U.S. Senate, 86th Congress, First Session, pp. 9–10.

Neither the MLF nor the ANF itself alter the basic and all-important factor of American ownership and control of the great bulk of the Alliance's nuclear weapons. It is because of this that many political groups and leaders in Europe ranging from some British Conservatives, such as Mr Duncan Sandys, and French military experts like General Beaufre, to Herr Franz-Josef Strauss, leader of the Bavarian Christian Social Union Party and Minister for Finance in Chancellor Kiesinger's government, have urged the creation of a European nuclear organisation or even a European nuclear force[1] in which the countries of Western Europe would participate through the merging of their existing nuclear forces or through financial and other contributions. Such a force, its advocates argue, could be an integral part of the NATO defence structure in the way that American nuclear forces are, but its use would depend on the decision of some form of European political authority created for this purpose. They hope that any agreement which might be reached between the United States and the Soviet Union on the non-proliferation of nuclear weapons would allow for the eventual transfer of European nuclear forces to such a European political authority.

Meanwhile Mr McNamara's Special Committee was established and its three working groups met several times in 1966 and made considerable progress. The working group dealing with intelligence agreed that data should be passed to all Heads of State or of Government of NATO countries in an emergency and it worked out a uniform way for presenting this information. This group also came out in favour of the establishment of machinery for crisis-management in all the NATO capitals. In the past very few NATO governments have possessed this kind of mechanism. The working group dealing with communications worked out a sophisticated system by which Heads of State or of Government could communicate with each other and with the Secretary General simultaneously in time of emergency. The third, and most important, working group dealing with nuclear planning met at the level of defence ministers. It enabled the participating countries to gain a detailed view of the whole strategy, planning and targeting of the intercontinental ballistic missile capacity of the United States, which, it was agreed by the participants, was more than sufficient to meet the requirements of the Alliance. In the past,

[1] The view put forward by American political and military leaders that the nuclear delivery systems already in the hands of all the European members of the Alliance who wish to have them already constitutes a 'European nuclear force' tends to exasperate the 'Europeans', since the nuclear warheads themselves remain under American control.

the principle governing the possible use of tactical nuclear weapons by the Alliance has been that once the go-ahead is given by the President of the United States, the field commanders would have complete freedom in using them. These weapons vary from small nuclear mines placed in NATO territory up to powerful missiles which, in time of conflict, would be fired into enemy territory. The working group concluded that the use of such weapons should not be placed indiscriminately in the hands of the Commanders but that strict political controls should be instituted over each stage of escalation from the use of small and primarily defensive weapons to that of larger and more offensive tactical nuclear weapons.

The North Atlantic Council accepted the proposals of the Special Committee, which were submitted to it in December 1966, and it was decided that a permanent Committee on nuclear affairs should be established, open to all members of NATO which wish to participate. This committee will have a general brief to scrutunise the nuclear planning and strategy of the Alliance and also the development of new nuclear weapons systems, in the light of the work of a smaller committee of seven members, the composition of which will be four permanent members (the United States, the United Kingdom, Germany and Italy) and three rotating members, who will serve on the Committee for terms of eighteen months.

Those who supported this proposal hold that it would go far to satisfy the demands of European countries to have a say in the nuclear planning of the Alliance. The implementation of the MLF or ANF plans would have permitted European countries to own and control jointly with the United States a very small proportion of the total nuclear capacity of the Alliance, the use of such a force being in any case subject to the veto of the United States. Under the McNamara proposals the American veto is still retained but the European countries, both nuclear and non-nuclear, now have at least a theoretical opportunity, even though this seems limited in practice, to help shape the planning of the nuclear capacity of the Alliance.

FRANCE AND NATO

(*a*) *The French 'initiative'*

The latent tensions in the Alliance were brought into the open by the publication of the French Government's two memoranda on 11 and 29 March 1966. In its first memorandum the French Government announced its intention of ending its assignment to NATO of all French armed forces and withdrawing French staff from NATO headquarters. It called for the removal from France of SHAPE and AFCENT and the NATO Defence College and also of United States and Canadian forces and military installations, unless these forces and installations were placed under sole French authority.

The memorandum stated that France, while withdrawing from the military organisation, would remain a member of the Alliance and would remain faithful to its Treaty commitments. It assumed that French forces stationed in Germany would be entitled to remain there by virtue of the Convention of 1954.[1]

The second French memorandum stated that French forces would be withdrawn from their NATO assignment on 1 July 1966, and that French personnel would be withdrawn from NATO integrated staffs on the same date. These withdrawals were duly carried out. It also set the time limit of 1 April 1967 for the removal of NATO headquarters and American and Canadian forces from France.

It was announced in September 1966 that the French Government would cease to contribute, with certain exceptions, to the military budget of NATO from 1 January 1967, and also that France would not contribute to the cost of the re-establishment of NATO headquarters in their new sites. It was further stated that France would withdraw from the Military Committee on 10 October 1966.

(*b*) *The arguments of the French Government*

The main arguments set out in the French Government's memorandum and in statements by General de Gaulle were as follows:

(*a*) that 'the threats weighing on the western world, in particular in Europe, which motivated the conclusion of the Treaty . . . no longer present the immediate and menacing character they formerly had';

(*b*) that the growth of Russia's nuclear power and its ability now to strike directly at the United States 'has at least made uncertain the decision of the Americans' to retaliate against Russia with nuclear missiles, in the event of an attack on Europe (see p. 400);

(*c*) that integration in practice implies that in Europe 'everything is commanded by the Americans' and amounts to a form of 'vassalage';

(*d*) that the placing of French forces under joint allied command in peacetime is incompatible with national sovereignty and national dignity, and that, in view of the revival of its

[1] *On the Presence of Foreign Forces in the German Federal Republic.*

economic and military power, 'France must now defend herself by herself, and in her own way'; and

(*e*) that 'while the prospect of world war breaking out on account of Europe is receding, conflicts elsewhere including America . . . are liable . . . to lead to a general flare-up. In this case, Europe . . . would automatically be implicated even against her wishes.'

(*c*) *Problems arising from the French 'initiative'*

Several major problems were posed to the Alliance[1] by the decisions of the French Government. First, the use of French territory and air space is denied to the Alliance. This means that the central sector of NATO is now geographically separated from Italy and the southern flank and hence that difficult problems of communications have arisen, especially concerning the over-flying rights of NATO aircraft over French territory. Second, the land and air forces at the disposal of SACEUR for the defence of the central sector have been, in the absence of an agreement between France and the fourteen on the military role of French forces in time of aggression, effectively reduced by more than two divisions of land forces and by fifteen air squadrons. Another problem has been the need to relocate the military headquarters of the Alliance outside France by 1 April 1967 and to ensure that the Alliance's logistics and communications systems function effectively under the new conditions and that there are adequate infrastructure installations outside France. The problem also arose of the character of the juridical status and military role of French forces stationed in Germany once France had withdrawn from the military structure of NATO on 1 July 1966. Finally, the French decisions aroused doubts on the part of France's partners as to France's readiness to carry out her mutual defence obligations under Article 5 of the North Atlantic Treaty or under the more automatic and rigorous Article 5 of the modified Brussels Treaty of 1954.

(*d*) *The reaction of the Alliance*

Politically, the first reaction of the 'fourteen' was to publish a Joint Declaration on 18 March 1966 which stated:

[1] For a full account of these problems see: *State of European Security*: *France and NATO*, Report presented by Mr Duncan Sandys to the WEU Assembly on behalf of the Committee on Defence Questions and Armaments, Paris, WEU, Assembly Document 375, June 1966.

'The Atlantic Alliance has ensured its efficiency as an instrument of defence and deterrence by the maintenance in peacetime of an integrated and interdependent military organisation in which, as in no previous alliance in history, the efforts and resources of each are combined for the common security of all. We are convinced that this organisation is essential and will continue. No system of bilateral arrangements can be a substitute.

The North Atlantic Treaty and the Organisation are not merely instruments of the common defence. They meet a common political need and reflect the readiness and determination of the member countries of the North Atlantic Community to consult and act together, wherever possible, in the safeguarding of their freedom and security and in the furtherance of international peace, progress and prosperity.'

Separate replies to the French Government were also published by some governments.

On 8 June the North Atlantic Council decided to remove the military headquarters of NATO from France. It was subsequently decided to accept the Belgian Government's offer of a site for SHAPE, which has been referred to earlier in this chapter, and the Dutch Government's offer of a site in the Limburg area for AFCENT, and to simplify the command structure. Accordingly, the three headquarters at Fontainebleau (AFCENT, LANDCENT and AIRCENT) have merged into a single AFCENT headquarters in November 1966. This move has resulted in large personnel cuts and has streamlined the military decision-making process. Finally, in addition to the move of the NATO Defence College from Paris to Rome, the headquarters of United States forces in Europe are being moved from St Germain-en-Laye to Stuttgart.

SACEUR has allotted new defence tasks to the forces assigned to his command so as to take account of the withdrawal of French forces from NATO's integrated command structure in July 1966. The loss of over two French divisions and fifteen squadrons of aircraft in the central sector means, however, that he has had to thin out his defensive screen and has lost a considerable degree of tactical flexibility in the new circumstances in which he has been left with the effective equivalent of twenty divisions. There has therefore been a significant reduction of the 'nuclear threshold' and it is now likely that tactical nuclear weapons would be called into use at an earlier stage, depending on the circumstances of an aggression.

Two separate but parallel sets of negotiations were put in train in June 1966 to resolve the problems arising from the continued presence of French forces in Germany: one between the French and German Governments on the juridical status of French forces stationed in Germany, another between France and the 'fourteen' on the military role to be played by French forces. In November 1966 the North Atlantic Council instructed General Lemnitzer (SACEUR) to represent the 'fourteen' in exploratory discussions on the military role of France with the French Chief of Staff, General Ailleret. In December 1966 the German Government agreed to accept the French Government's argument that the 1954 agreements provided an adequate basis for French forces remaining in Germany, the French Government promising, on its side, that its forces would leave Germany if requested to do so by the German Government.

After a protracted debate during the summer and autumn of 1966 between those countries which considered that the effective political and military functioning of the Alliance required the removal of the North Atlantic Council and the NATO Secretariat from France,[1] and those which considered that the differences between France and the 'fourteen' could be minimised if the Council remained in Paris, the North Atlantic Council decided, in October, that its seat should be moved to Brussels near SHAPE. With the abolition of the Standing Group in Washington, the Council, the supreme political and military body of the Alliance, will thus be close to the military authorities and to its military advisers. After the French 'initiative' the 'fourteen' have used meetings of the Defence Planning Council to discuss and decide on military planning without the presence of France, which takes part in the full Council meetings at the level of the fifteen.

The cost of the moves of SHAPE and AFCENT to new sites, together with that of the North Atlantic Council to Brussels, will be considerable, as will be that of the construction of new infrastructure installations. France will not contribute to any of these costs.

France's allies have sought assurances that France still regards itself as unreservedly committed to fulfil the mutual defence obligations set out in Article 5 of the North Atlantic Treaty and the more fully automatic ones contained in Article 5 of the modified Brussels Treaty. French ministers have declared in general terms that France remains committed to its Treaty obligations and in November 1966

[1] France has continued to participate in the North Atlantic Council and continues to contribute to the budget of the NATO Secretariat. It has also made an '*à la carte*' choice of certain military activities, such as NADGE and the underwater war centre at La Spezia, in which it wishes to continue to take part.

the Council of WEU replied to a question on this specific point contained in a recommendation of the WEU Assembly in the sense that all member governments of WEU continued to accept the commitment set out in Article 5 of the modified Brussels Treaty.[2] Doubts have, however, arisen concerning the French Government's interpretation of its commitments under the North Atlantic and Brussels Treaties following a statement by M. Maurice Couve de Murville, the Foreign Minister, in the French National Assembly on 3 November 1966:

'... the Treaty establishing WEU is not very different from the North Atlantic Treaty, since Article 5 of the former does not, any more than the Washington Treaty, lay down an automatic commitment. If there is an attack against one of the allies, the other governments must take their decisions according to their own constitutional procedure. There is nothing automatic. It is natural, for example, in countries like France where the constitution provides that war is declared by parliament, that constitutional procedures should be respected, that is to say that there should not be any automacity.'[1]

(*e*) *Other problems*

While, at the time of going to press, the Alliance is endeavouring to solve the problems caused by the decisions of the French Government in 1966, new problems concerning the financing of the NATO defence system and related questions of force levels and strategy have come to the fore.

First, Mr Harold Wilson announced in the House of Commons on 20 July 1966 that the British Government might make substantial reductions in British forces in Germany if no agreement were reached with the German Government concerning the offset of the foreign exchange costs to Britain of maintaining these forces.

Second, there were persistent newspaper reports during 1966 that the United States Government was considering a massive withdrawal of its forces from Germany by the end of the 1960s. Although these rumours have been formally denied by Mr Dean Rusk, the Secretary of State, and Mr Robert McNamara, they have been supported by moves in Congress. For example, Senator Mike Mansfield, leader of the Democrat majority in the Senate, tabled a motion in August, signed by thirteen Senators, calling for substantial reductions in American forces in Europe.

[1] *Journal Officiel*, 4 November 1966.

The United States Government, like the British Government, has expressed concern about the balance-of-payments aspects of the stationing of its forces in Germany. In October 1966 tripartite discussions on the financing of American and British forces stationed in Germany and related questions opened in Bonn between the three governments.

Great concern has been expressed by NATO's military authorities and by statesmen from continental European members of the Alliance about possible American and British withdrawals. While large and well equipped and trained Soviet and Warsaw Pact forces remain stationed in Central and Eastern Europe many politicians feel (whatever the present intentions of the Soviet Union concerning their use) that the massive physical presence of American and British forces on the mainland of Europe constitutes an essential part of the NATO defence system, for which the possibility of moving in large scale reinforcements at short notice by operations of the 'big lift' type cannot be a real substitute.[1] There is another school of thought which considers that the nuclear capacity of the West is by far the most significant part of the defence system and that its maintenance, together with that of a comparatively low level of conventional forces, would provide an adequate deterrent, especially in view of the more peaceable attitude now adopted by the Soviet Union towards the West. The supporters of this view argue that if this is the case cuts should be made in the level of conventional forces in Western Europe in view of the economic strains imposed by the effort of maintaining both first-rate nuclear and conventional forces. They look for reductions in force levels, whether reciprocal or unilateral, in the hope that even if they were made unilaterally the Soviet Union would be encouraged to follow suit, particularly as it would seem to have an economic interest in doing so.

These financial problems and their political and strategic consequences are likely to remain one of the main preoccupations of the allies in the near future.

Other Aspects of Military Co-operation in NATO

THE ANNUAL REVIEW

The Annual Review developed out of the work carried out by the Temporary Council Committee in 1951 (see p. 379). The North

[1] Operation 'big lift' moved the personnel and personal equipment of an American armoured division by plane from the United States to Europe within

Atlantic Council decided at Lisbon in 1952 that there should be 'comprehensive Annual Reviews of the requirements for building and maintaining adequate defensive strength on a realistic foundation of political–economic capabilities'. The main purpose of the Annual Review is to assess capacities and to provide goals in building up NATO's military forces. These goals flow from the recommendations of the NATO military authorities, but take account of what countries actually undertake to do, and thus often fail to satisfy the military recommendations. The Annual Review, which is carried out by the Secretariat, in close conjunction with the military authorities and national delegations, is a continuous process. The Annual Review first of all assesses the progress made by member states in reaching the goals already established for that year, then converts the provisional goals of the previous Review into the definite goals proposed for the next year and also prepares 'planning goals' for the subsequent year. It thus provides firm commitments for one year and more general goals covering a three-year period. Through questionnaires the member governments provide detailed information concerning their military, financial and economic position. These questionnaires are analysed by experts and their recommendations for adjustments in national plans are then carried into effect.

An important element in the Annual Review should be the 'reconciliation' between the changes in national plans recommended by the NATO military authorities and the assessment of the capability of national resources to carry out such changes. This reconciliation is prepared and finalised in the Annual Review Committee through the discussion of those changes which can be proposed to governments in the final report. The NATO Secretariat and SHAPE both comment on what each country proposes to do as opposed to what it might be expected to do.

'The comments are circulated and form the basis of a discussion which takes place every autumn in a comprehensive system of cross-examination committees. The national delegates must, on behalf of their countries, run the gauntlet through these committees, answering questions and meeting criticisms from delegates of other countries and from NATO itself. This kind of examination helps to reveal gaps and weaknesses and to see where improvements can be made. It draws attention to the difficulties which particular countries face and

the space of a few hours in the summer of 1964. The division's armour and other heavy equipment was, however, already in Europe.

Evolution of Total Defence Expenditure in NATO Countries 1949–53 and 1961–65

		1949	1950	1951	1952	1953	1961	1962	1963	1964	1965
France	Million Francs	4,787	5,591	8,811	12,531	13,865	20,395	22,184	22,849	24,280	25,300
Federal Republic of Germany*	Million DM	—	—	—	—	6,195	13,175	17,233	19,924	19,553	20,009
United Kingdom	Million £ sterling	779	849	1,149	1,561	1,681	1,709	1,814	1,869	2,002	2,159
United States	Million US Dollars	13,503	14,307	33,059	47,598	49,377	47,808	52,381	52,295	51,213	51,935
Area											
Total Europe†	Million US Dollars	4,825	5,446	7,627	10,231	12,403	15,339	17,408	18,768	19,711	20,687
Total North America	Million US Dollars	13,875	14,801	34,279	49,473	51,347	49,523	54,096	53,884	52,889	53,558
Total NATO†	Million US Dollars	18,700	20,247	41,906	59,704	63,750	64,862	71,504	72,652	72,600	74,245

* Before it acceded to the North Atlantic Treaty Organisation (May 1955), the Federal Republic of Germany contributed to the defence budgets of certain NATO countries by the payment of occupation costs; moreover, it bore certain other costs which also fall within the NATO definition of defence expenditure. The total given in the column for 1953 represents the expenditures made under these various heads for the fiscal year 1953–54 (1 April–31 March). The figures for the years prior to fiscal year 1953–54 have not been communicated to the Secretariat. In addition to defence expenditure (NATO definition), the German authorities are obliged to incur large annual expenditures for Berlin owing to the exceptional situation of this city and the need, in the interests of the defence of the free world, to ensure its viability. This expenditure, which is not included in the figures given above since it does not come within the NATO definition, amounted to DM 1,851 million in 1963.

† The totals for Europe and for NATO do not include defence expenditure of the Federal Republic of Germany for the period prior to 1953, and for this reason they are not directly comparable to the total for the following years.

Source: *Facts about the North Atlantic Treaty Organisation*, Paris, NATO, 1965.

often leads to help from other countries in overcoming these difficulties. Countries frequently do modify their plans to meet the points made at these committees.'[1]

After this cross-examination the recommendations are examined by the Annual Review Committee for multilateral discussion about the changes that can be accepted by or recommended to each government in the final report. The final decisions on recommendations to be made to governments are taken by the Council.

The Annual Review is the principal means of assessing the financial resources of member countries for NATO defence purposes. This technique has proved an effective way of collecting information, analysing it and implementing recommendations based on it. The Annual Review shows where weaknesses lie, where co-operation between members of the Alliance is especially needed and where it can be most effectively deployed.

Since 1961 the system of Annual Review has been modified to a Triennial Review so that member countries can undertake general commitments over a three-year period. Under this revised system, NATO force goals are established and NATO force plans worked out for a period of five years ahead. Each year the plans are revised and are 'rolled forward' one year, but binding commitments are, as before, undertaken for only one year in advance. Since 1964 a group of experts from the major NATO countries have been engaged in an attempt to review the economic capabilities of the Allies over the next five to ten years in order to assess what strategic choices are open to the Alliance as a whole. This is called the Force Planning Exercise.

INFRASTRUCTURE

Under NATO there has been established a 'common infrastructure', that is, a system of fixed installations, such as airfields and communication and fuel networks, without which modern forces cannot operate. Installations for the defence systems of individual countries are called 'national infrastructure' and they are paid for out of national funds. Installations approved for common financing by all the member countries for the maintenance of NATO international forces are known as 'common infrastructure'. Common infrastructure programmes approved up to 1966 comprised projects to the value of approximately £1,200 million.

[1] Anne M. Warburton and John B. Wood, *Paying for NATO*, London, Friends of Atlantic Union, no date, p. 10.

Infrastructure installations are erected or constructed by civilian contractors, who are selected by international competitive bidding. Common infrastructure is financed by the member countries by means of a cost-sharing formula agreed in the North Atlantic Council. In practice this formula has been very difficult to work out to the satisfaction of the member countries. In some years the formula has been no more than a last-minute *ad hoc* agreement to provide the required funds, arranged by the Secretary General and senior members of his staff. On some occasions it has been necessary for the Secretary General to put pressure on national delegations to pay their contributions. Normally, the Supreme Commanders co-ordinate the infrastructure requirements proposed to them by their Subordinate Commanders. The draft programme that they work out is sent to the Infrastructure Committee of the North Atlantic Council. The Infrastructure Committee examines the programme on financial and technical grounds, and the Military Committee on criteria of military necessity and urgency. When the Council approves a project, full responsibility for its implementation is assumed by the country on whose territory the installations are to be placed.

The implementation of these infrastructure programmes has established a network of about 200 NATO airfields and thousands of miles of signals, land-lines and fuel pipelines across Europe. Storage facilities for naval forces have also been constructed and are operational, and training bases for NATO air forces have been constructed in the Mediterranean area. Further training areas are being created to enable land forces to hold joint manœuvres. Whereas the host countries are responsible for the construction of these installations (appointing contractors, for example), NATO supervises engineering standards and costs.

The French 'initiative' of 1966 has resulted in the waste of much of the many years' work to build up an effective NATO infrastructure. New supply dumps, runways and other installations will have to be set up in the Benelux countries to replace the installations which can no longer be based by the Alliance in France. The cost of this will be very high as is shown by the fact that the infrastructure installations in France cost $700 million to install.

DEFENCE PRODUCTION

At the end of the war the armaments industries of most Western European countries had been destroyed or switched to civilian production. Owing to the need for economic reconstruction, outside aid was necessary for large-scale rearmament. Canada and the

United States provided the initial military aid to re-equip the forces of countries that were unable to provide for their own needs.

Western Union and NATO acted as the driving force for the re-development of Western European armaments industries. Various committees co-ordinated national arms programmes so that larger and more rapid deliveries of arms became possible. Member countries were also encouraged to standardise weapons, to make joint studies of technical problems and to exchange relevant information. NATO has established an Armaments Committee which deals with research and development as well as with problems of manufacture and standardisation of defence equipment. Working Groups of the Committee have carried out work on different projects, including types of military aircraft, missiles and anti-submarine torpedoes, the development of steel cartridge cases and specifications for explosives and propellants. But progress that has been made in the key domain of persuading members of the Alliance to adopt standard weapons has, in fact, been limited.

SELF-HELP AND MUTUAL AID

Article 3 of the Treaty states:

'The Parties, separately and jointly, by means of continuous and effective self-help and mutual aid, will maintain and develop their individual and collective capacity to resist armed attack.'

Member countries are not bound to any specified programme of self-help or mutual aid, but they are obliged to develop their own means to resist aggression and to help others.

In 1949 Western Europe was still very weak and various methods were used to provide an adequate defence system. United States and United Kingdom forces on the mainland of Europe were reinforced. United States financial aid, without which some European countries would in 1951 still have been unable to support a defence programme, was continued in the form of 'defence support aid'. Canada and the United States also provided European countries with large deliveries of free weapons and equipment under their military aid programmes. Through the 'offshore procurement programme' the United States provided large sums of money for European member countries to develop their own armaments industries. In this programme (officially the 'Offshore Assistance and Mutual Defence Programme') the United States used part of the credits earmarked for the military aid programme for the purchase of equipment in other countries, and then gave this equipment to one or other of the member countries for the use of its own forces.

Other examples of mutual aid in NATO have been the infrastructure programme, already described, and the granting of rights for the construction and use of military facilities to fellow members by national governments (sometimes on a bilateral basis and in other cases as part of the common infrastructure programme). Further examples of mutual aid have included the provision of airfields by some member countries; loans of ships and aircraft by Britain and the United States to other NATO members; the provision of technical training for specialists by Britain, Canada, France and the United States; the provision of spare parts for military equipment; and the exchange of engineering and industrial information and advice. In contrast, NATO has not yet succeeded in resolving the problem of helping to meet the foreign exchange cost of maintaining British and American forces in the Federal Republic of Germany.

The European member countries of NATO have provided a large share of the conventional military forces assigned to NATO command and have also provided the use of land for training and infrastructure installations and other facilities. The North American powers, in particular the United States, have on their side contributed by far the greater part of the nuclear and conventional weapons, equipment and ammunition needed for the build-up of NATO's forces. The United States has paid up to $400 million a year in military aid to Greece and Turkey. Canada has also given generous military aid to other member countries, though Greek aid was cut off after the 1967 coup.

Thus the strength of NATO forces for the defence of the North Atlantic area has been built up while the financial strains of rearmament of individual states have, in general, been diminished, thanks largely to American aid and to economies resulting from the greater effectiveness of a collective effort. This has enabled NATO to construct a defence system covering all member territories, without a direct relation being necessary between the physical distribution of the forces and the cost of their training and maintenance. These achievements, which are considerable, should not obscure the fact that the progress made in the common financing of the forces of NATO countries and the rationalisation of arms production has been extremely limited. The United States has felt that, following Europe's economic resurgence, the European members should bear a larger share of the financial burden; and fears have been expressed on the European side that unless there can be a fair distribution between armaments production and sales in Europe and the United States, Europe will fall further behind the United States in science and technology. This has led to a series of proposals, put forward recently by General Beaufre, Mr Duncan Sandys, Mr Peter Kirk[1] and others, that an armaments procurement board should be set up to regulate armaments production and sales within the Alliance on a more equitable basis.

The Non-military Role of NATO

In the early days of NATO there were many who considered that the Organisation should develop as a political and economic association between the countries of Europe and North America as well as being a military alliance. However, the development of economic co-operation in OEEC (later OECD) and in the EEC and EFTA meant that the countries of Western Europe had little interest in pursuing comparable activities in the framework of NATO.

The period between the meetings of the North Atlantic Council at Ottawa in September 1951 and at Lisbon in February 1952 was one of conflict in the Organisation over what shape its institutions ought to take and what the economic role of NATO was to be in relation to that of OEEC. The course of events and policies at this time led to the failure to develop the economic side of NATO's work. The main reasons were:

(*a*) The easing of the strains of the Korean war, which removed some of the stimulus for increasing military production and, with this, economic co-operation.

(*b*) The changes of government that took place in both Britain and the United States. Both new governing parties, the Conservatives and the Republicans, had been out of office since before NATO was set up and so were naturally cautious in their approach to it.

(*c*) It was doubtful if governments were ready to allow further large-scale interference by an international organisation in their domestic, economic and defence programmes.

(*d*) Since the French Government did not want Western Germany to become a member of NATO the continued existence of OEEC was essential since it was the only organisation in which countries could discuss economic affairs with Western Germany. The 'Europeans' likewise wanted to retain a purely

[1] A French military expert and two British Conservative former ministers prominent in European affairs.

European economic organisation. At this time, moreover, Britain was coming to attach more value to the work of OEEC and had accepted the Chairmanship of its Council. OEEC also contained the neutrals.

(*e*) The Americans objected to NATO undertaking wide economic commitments since they did not want the multilateral assessment of, and perhaps control of, burden-sharing.

(*f*) Countries did not have enough competent staff available to carry out similar work on economic affairs in both OEEC and NATO.

The decision that the permanent headquarters of the NATO Council was to be in Paris, where the OEEC was also located, further reinforced these arguments and the economic side of NATO's work and establishment was reduced.

There has nevertheless been from the outset some pressure to increase NATO's political, economic and other non-military activities. Mr Lester Pearson, the Canadian Minister for External Affairs, constantly stressed the need. He headed a committee, set up in 1951, to consider 'the further strengthening of the Community and especially the implementation of Article 2 of the North Atlantic Treaty'. Article 2, which is quoted on p. 374 above, provides for economic collaboration. Following the Council meeting of May 1956, a Committee of Three, consisting of Mr Pearson, Mr Lange of Norway and Signor Martino of Italy, was set up to advise the Council on ways and means to improve and extend NATO co-operation in non-military fields and to develop greater unity within the Atlantic Community.

The Committee of Three presented its report in December 1956. The report stated:

'The economic interests of the Atlantic Community cannot be considered in isolation from the activities and policies of the Soviet bloc. The Soviets are resorting all too often to the use of economic measures designed to weaken the Western Alliance or to create in other areas a high degree of dependence on the Soviet world. In this situation it is more than ever important that NATO countries actively develop their own constructive commercial and financial policies. In particular they should avoid creating situations of which the Soviet bloc countries might take advantage to the detriment of the Atlantic Community and of other non-Communist countries. In this whole field of competitive economic co-existence member countries should consult together more fully in order to determine their course deliberately and with the fullest possible knowledge.'

The Committee found that NATO 'has been hesitant' in entering the field of non-military co-operation. The report recommended the adoption of co-operative economic and political policies by the member countries:

'which will demonstrate, under conditions of competitive co-existence, the superiority of free institutions in promoting human welfare and economic progress.'

Specific recommendations of the Committee included the development of common consultation by member countries in the political field, particularly with reference to foreign policy. To achieve this there should be an annual appraisal of the political progress of the Alliance and consideration of the lines along which policy should be directed. There was also need for closer co-operation and mutual consultation in the economic field, and

'in view of the extended range of topics for regular exchange of information and consultation . . . there should be established under the Council a Committee of Economic Advisers'

whose function would be to hold preliminary discussions on matters of common economic interest.

The Committee advised the Council that duplication of the work of other organisations should be avoided:

'The common economic concerns of the member nations will often best be fostered by continued and increased collaboration both bilaterally and through organisations other than NATO.'

The report also stated that increased political co-operation between members of NATO does not conflict with participation in other groups or associations.

'Nor should the evolution of the Atlantic Community through NATO prevent the formation of even closer relationships among some of its members.'

Finally the Committee expressed its opinion that whatever developments of policy might be desirable:

'NATO in its present form is capable of discharging the non-military functions required of it. Structural changes are not needed. The machine is basically satisfactory. It is for governments to make use of it.'

Although minor developments have taken place in cultural co-operation between NATO countries, such as the establishment of a visiting professorship programme, little has been done by the North Atlantic Council to implement the recommendations of the Committee of Three.

NATO and the Politicians

NATO has no official Assembly of its own, but there are two bodies of parliamentarians which concern themselves with the work of the Organisation. The Assembly of Western European Union, which is composed of parliamentarians from seven of the NATO countries, is the only official international parliamentary body that discusses Western defence. The military debates of the WEU Assembly, which are based on the reports of its Committee on Defence Questions, provide an opportunity for detailed consideration of the effectiveness of the NATO defence system. The other body, the quasi-official North Atlantic Assembly, is drawn from all the member states of the Organisation, and in its discussions does not confine itself to the military side of NATO's work.

THE NORTH ATLANTIC ASSEMBLY

In 1954 parliamentarians in both Norway and Canada, prominent among whom were Mr Finn Moe, at that time Chairman of the Norwegian Parliamentary Foreign Affairs Committee, and Senator Wishart Robertson, at that time Speaker of the Canadian Senate, independently came to the conclusion that NATO had not given a sufficiently definite lead in promoting political and economic co-operation among its member countries and that it should be encouraged to develop this side of the Alliance as well as the military. They hoped that a parliamentary conference of the NATO countries might play a useful part in wresting some of the initiative in the economic and political spheres from the countries of the Soviet bloc. The Norwegians took the initiative in creating a NATO parliamentary conference by sending out invitations to certain NATO member countries to discuss the project. The Canadians, after consultation with the Norwegians, suggested that all NATO member countries should be invited to form some such conference and finally the Canadians and Norwegians issued joint invitations to all the other member states.

In 1955 the quasi-official Conference of NATO Parliamentarians (known from 1957 to 1966 as the NATO Parliamentarians' Conference) was established and held its first meeting in Paris in July. At this meeting, which was exploratory, it was decided that further meetings should be held and a 'continuing committee' should be established to organise them. Further meetings have been held in Paris, though the Conference has also met in New York twice. More recently the feeling developed among members of the Conference that it should be put on a more formal footing and in November 1966 the Conference decided to rename itself as the North Atlantic Assembly. Its members now hope that the governments will grant it a more formal consultative status.

The institutions of the Assembly consist of the Standing Committee, which plans the agenda of the annual Conference and generally controls its working and various specialist committees. There is a small secretariat whose headquarters were first in London then in Paris, and moved to Brussels in 1967.

The cost of the Assembly is borne by the member countries of NATO from foreign office grants and parliamentary funds. The national contributions are assessed by the NATO cost-sharing formula. The annual meeting is attended by about 180 delegates who sit in national delegations and are allotted votes on a national basis.

At first some NATO governments regarded the establishment of the Assembly as not altogether desirable and in NATO itself there was some fear of interference from such a body of parliamentarians. It was thought that it might try to assume powers of control but in practice the Assembly has served to develop a frank interchange of ideas concerning the main problems of the Alliance. The Assembly provides a forum in which the parliamentarians of all NATO countries can be given an insight into NATO aims and methods. It also acts as a channel to provide parliamentarians with up-to-date military information about NATO defence measures and strategic plans. SACEUR and SACLANT have regularly addressed closed sessions at the annual meeting.

The Assembly has grown in importance since its early days and it is now no longer regarded with the suspicion which some governments showed towards it in 1955. American participation in the Assembly has contributed to the closer understanding of European problems and points of view by the North Americans and *vice versa.* The Assembly provides the only means of such an exchange of views among the NATO countries, although as far as non-military questions are concerned, the meetings between the Assembly of the Council of Europe and members of the US Congress have served a similar purpose.

Conclusions

The creation by fifteen Western countries of an Alliance with international military headquarters and integrated military planning was unprecedented in time of peace. Three factors combined to make it possible: the weakness of Western Europe, with its economy enfeebled by the war, and in which the strategic potential of each country was in any case slight in relation to that of the United States or the Soviet Union; the military strength of the Soviet Union, deployed under Stalin in a threatening posture in Central Europe; and the military strength and invulnerability of the United States, which was determined to prevent the Soviet domination of Western Europe. These circumstances provided both Western Europe and the United States with the political will to make the alliance work; and through the 1950s it worked well, with strong American leadership based on the dominant strength of the United States.

In the late 1950s these factors changed considerably. The countries of Western Europe, while still strategically weak in comparison with America and Russia, had nevertheless increased their military strength substantially and their economic strength enormously. The posture of Russia seemed less threatening, and this impression was reinforced by the peaceful outcome of the Cuban confrontation. And the United States, while still immensely powerful, was no longer invulnerable, because the Soviet Union possessed long-range nuclear missiles with which it could launch a direct nuclear attack on the US. As a result of these changes the Americans replaced their doctrine of massive retaliation by that of graduated response, and Europeans began to criticise the political and military structure of NATO as unsuited to the new conditions. The main lines of criticism were those of General de Gaulle, who wanted a more influential and more independent role for France, and those of a number of countries, notably Germany, which wanted a real voice in the nuclear planning and control of the Alliance.

The American Government's MLF proposal and the British

proposal for an ANF were intended to satisfy some of these demands, but they did not go to the heart of the problem of nuclear planning and control. Indeed, although the result of the work of Mr McNamara's Special Committee will be to give European countries no more than a consultative role, this should nevertheless allow them more influence in the planning of the nuclear defence of the Alliance than they would gain by taking part in a small joint nuclear force, whose use would be subject to a veto by the United States. But in the long term there is a clear contradiction between the American claim that the complete integration of the nuclear capacity of the Alliance is necessary in order to make a nuclear deterrent credible and effective, and the dissatisfaction of many Europeans with solutions that imply an American veto on the nuclear capacity available for their defence.

Both British and French Governments have resisted the absorption of their nuclear capacities into any system, such as that represented by the MLF, which would be unequivocally subject to an American veto. General de Gaulle has gone much further and withdrawn the French forces from the military structure of the Alliance, because he refuses to accept the limited degree of military integration which exists in NATO, that is to say the integration of the international staffs in NATO headquarters and the internationally agreed planning carried out by those staffs (as distinct from the greater degree of integration which would pertain in wartime when national units would pass, with their governments' permission, under the control of the international staffs under the command of SACEUR). But while this withdrawal of national forces does permit their use without the hindrance of the American veto, the nature of modern warfare is such that the individual forces of the European NATO countries acting in an unco-ordinated way would be helpless in the event of war. Indeed, if the defence of Western Europe is to be assumed independently of ultimate American control, this could be done only through integration between the European allies.

The reorganisation of the Alliance that was induced by the French decisions of 1966 is still in progress. Major problems of force levels, financing and strategy are being reconsidered, and the Secretary General of NATO has been asked to report to the Council at the end of 1967, on a re-evaluation of the long-term objectives of the Alliance. Quite apart from the political and military difficulties caused by the French withdrawal, it will not be easy to adapt the structure and policies of NATO to the changing relationships between the United States, the Soviet Union and the countries of Western Europe.

Chapter Twelve

THE ORGANISATION FOR ECONOMIC CO-OPERATION AND DEVELOPMENT

The Creation of OECD

After the OEEC had completed its immensely important initial task of implementing the Marshall Plan, thus making possible Europe's economic recovery, it helped European countries to get rid of most of the import quotas on trade between them, to move to an advanced degree of currency convertibility and to arrive at a stage where the once formidable dollar gap between its members and the United States had disappeared. But when the EEC had been established and the negotiations in the Maudling Committee to create an OEEC free trade area[1] broke down, it became apparent that Western Europe would be divided into two trading groups, thus undermining the basis for a Western European organisation such as OEEC. The Six were anxious that the United States and Canada should join a transformed OEEC, thus blocking the creation of an OEEC free trade area which might prevent the effective development of the EEC. The United States partly shared the views of the Six and partly felt that it should intervene more directly than in the past to try to assemble the Western countries in a new organisation containing both the individual countries and the two nascent European trade groupings. The members of OEEC outside the Six continued to hope that a general European free trade area could be created. Thus the aims of those who created OECD differed and OECD was, from the start, an amalgam of conflicting purposes. It was also hoped that apart from solving the trade problems which arose following the creation of the EEC, a new organisation of which the United States and Canada were members would make greater efforts to attempt to solve the problems of the less developed countries.

[1] See pp. 105–107.

THE ORGANISATION FOR ECONOMIC CO-OPERATION

A meeting was held in Paris, in December 1959, of the French and United States Presidents, the Chancellor of the Federal Republic of Germany and the British Prime Minister, after which the following communiqué was issued on 21 December:

'The Heads of State and Government have discussed the important changes that have taken place in the international economic situation. Recognising the great economic progress of Western Europe, they have agreed that virtually all of the industrialised part of the free world is now in a position to devote its energies in increased measure to new and important tasks of co-operative endeavour with the object of:

(*a*) furthering the development of the less developed countries; and

(*b*) pursuing trade policies directed to the sound use of economic resources and the maintenance of harmonious international relations, thus contributing to growth and stability in the world economy and to a general improvement in the standard of living.

'In their view these co-operative principles should also govern the discussions on commercial problems arising from the existence of European economic regional organisations which should or will be constituted within the framework of the GATT, such as the European Economic Community and the European Free Trade Association. Their relations both with other countries and with each other should be discussed in this spirit.

'The Heads of State and Government, recognising that the method of furthering these principles requires intensive study, have agreed to call an informal meeting to be held in Paris in the near future. They suggest that the members and participants of the Executive Committee of the OEEC and the Governments whose nationals are members of the Steering Board for trade of the OEEC should be represented at this meeting.

'It is proposed that an objective of such a group should be to consider the need for and methods of continuing consultations dealing with the above-mentioned problems.'

Ministers from Belgium, Canada, France, Denmark, the Federal Republic of Germany, Greece, Italy, the Netherlands, Portugal, Sweden, Switzerland, the United Kingdom and the United States and representatives of the Commission of the European Economic Community met on 12–13 January 1960 as the Special Economic Committee. The Committee adopted a Resolution proposing that a meeting should be held between senior officials of the member and associate member countries of OEEC, and at which the European Communities should be represented, to consider the appropriate institutional arrangements to accomplish the aims of continued economic co-operation, the pursuit of economic policies which would contribute to economic stability in Europe, sound trade policies and increased efforts to aid less-developed countries. The Committee also proposed that a Group of Four should be appointed to prepare the report which would propose draft articles of agreement for the creation of a new organisation, if the Group felt this to be desirable, and to study which activities of OEEC should be continued within the framework of a new organisation. The second Resolution of the Special Economic Committee noted that the Governments of Belgium, Canada, France, the Federal Republic of Germany, Italy, Portugal, the United Kingdom and the United States intended to meet to discuss development assistance questions and invited other capital exporting countries to join with them. The Committee also proposed that the participating governments should form, together with the EEC, a Committee with power to establish informal working groups to discuss trade problems arising from the existence of the EEC and EFTA. These Resolutions were unanimously approved by the Ministers of the twenty OEEC associate and member countries and a representative of the EEC.

The Group of Four was set up shortly afterwards. Its members were Mr Randolph Burgess, the United States Ambassador in Paris, M. Bernard Clappier from France, Sir Paul Gore-Booth from Britain and Mr Xenophon Zolotas from Greece. The Group's Report, *A Remodelled Economic Organisation*, was published in April 1960. The Report proposed the establishment of an Organisation for Economic Co-operation and Development, outlined a structure for it and defined the obligations of membership. It also proposed that a Preparatory Committee for the new organisation, consisting of representatives of the twenty interested governments and the EEC, should be established under the Chairmanship of the Secretary General Designate.

A conference was held in May 1960 to discuss the reconstitution of OEEC in the light of the proposals of the Group of Four. The Conference set up a Working Party to draw up a draft convention remodelling the existing organisation. At a ministerial meeting on

22 and 23 July 1960 a Preparatory Committee was established under the Chairmanship of the Secretary General Designate, Mr Thorkil Kristensen. The Preparatory Committee was instructed to draw up a draft convention and to carry out the necessary structural work involved in reconstituting the organisation into OECD. The Ministers also resolved that the new body should include a Trade Committee and that the Development Assistance Group which had been established in January 1960 should become the Development Assistance Committee of OECD. They also agreed that the European Nuclear Energy Agency (ENEA) and the European Monetary Agreement should be continued under OECD.

The Preparatory Committee began work on 14 September 1960 and met almost continuously until the end of November. During this period it completed the draft convention, defined the structure of the transformed organisation and drew up a list of those Acts of OEEC which were to be recommended to the Council of OECD for approval.

On 13 December 1960 the ministerial meeting decided to 'approve the report of the Preparatory Committee and accept the recommendations contained therein'. On 14 December the Convention on the Organisation for Economic Co-operation and Development was signed by Ministers of the twenty member countries at the *Quai d'Orsay*. During 1961 work on the transformation of OEEC into OECD still continued but by 30 September seventeen member countries had ratified the convention, thus enabling the new organisation to come into being officially. All the members of OEEC were founder members, together with Canada and the United States. Japan became a full member of OECD in 1964, and Australia is a member of the Development Assistance Committee.

In December 1961 the Council of OECD met for the first time at ministerial level at the Château de la Muette. At this meeting the economic prospects of all member nations were surveyed, a collective growth target of 50 per cent in real gross national product was set to be achieved during the decade 1960–70, and the future work and aims of OECD were reviewed.

The Convention

The Convention of OECD sets out the three main functions of the Organisation: economic policy co-ordination; aid to developing countries; and the expansion of world trade.

Article 1 of the Convention states:

'The aims of the Organisation for Economic Co-operation and Development shall be to promote policies designed:

(*a*) to achieve the highest sustainable economic growth and employment and a rising standard of living in Member countries, while maintaining financial stability, and thus to contribute to the development of the world economy;

(*b*) to contribute to sound economic expansion in Member as well as non-member countries in the process of economic development; and

(*c*) to contribute to the expansion of world trade on a multilateral, non-discriminatory basis in accordance with international obligations.'

Article 2 of the Convention states that member countries both individually and jointly agree to:

(*a*) promote the efficient use of their economic resources;

(*b*) in the scientific and technological field, promote the development of their resources, encourage research and promote vocational training;

(*c*) pursue policies designed to achieve economic growth and internal and external financial stability and to avoid developments which might endanger their economies or those of other countries;

(*d*) pursue their efforts to reduce or abolish obstacles to the exchange of goods and services and current payments and maintain and extend the liberalisation of capital movements; and

(*e*) contribute to the economic development of both Member and non-member countries in the process of economic development by appropriate means and, in particular, by the flow of capital to those countries, having regard to the importance to their economies of receiving technical assistance and of securing expanding export markets.

Article 3 of the Convention obliges members of OECD to:

(*a*) keep each other informed and furnish the Organisation with the information necessary for the accomplishment of its tasks;

(*b*) consult together on a continuing basis, carry out studies and participate in agreed projects; and

(*c*) co-operate closely and where appropriate take co-ordinated action.

Articles 5 and 6 provide for the taking of 'decisions which except as otherwise provided shall be binding on all the Members' by a unanimous vote of the Council and empower the Organisation to 'make recommendations to Members' and to 'enter into agreements with Members, non-member States and international organisations.'

The Institutions

The institutional structure of OECD is essentially the same as that of OEEC (which is described on pp. 82–87) except for two main changes. First, the powers of the Secretary General were notably increased with the transformation of OEEC into OECD by his being empowered to preside over the Council at the level of permanent representatives. In OECD the Secretary General has maintained his important right to submit proposals to the Council or to other bodies of the Organisation. He is also able to propose items for inclusion on the agenda of meetings of the Council. In general, the constitutional position of the Secretary General, who has been Mr Thorkil Kristensen from Denmark since the creation of OECD, has become somewhat more important in view of these changes. The Secretariat of OECD totals about 1,300.

The other main structural change which took place when OEEC was transformed into OECD was the replacement of the Technical Committees by a new group of committees dealing with the main activities of the new Organisation. These committees and their work are described later in this chapter. Further, in OECD the Executive Committee consists of the representatives of ten member states.

The budget of OECD is paid for by contributions from all member countries according to an agreed scale, and at present amounts to about £8 million a year.

The Nature of OECD

The fact that OECD was, from the very beginning, conceived as an Atlantic organisation with the United States and Canada playing a full part alongside the European former members of OEEC has had the effect of both widening the responsibilities of the old Organisation and diminishing the community of interest which was shared by the members of OEEC. The scale of OECD's interests and responsibilities is enormous. The trade of its members constitutes a very high proportion of the total of world trade, and about 90 per cent of all aid to the developing countries comes from its members.

In the introduction to the 1963 report of OECD to the Consultative Assembly of the Council of Europe, even before Japan became a member of the Organisation, the Secretary General, Mr Thorkil Kristensen, wrote:

'The new organisation no longer has a purely European character. It comprises 500 million human beings and covers a geographical area which extends from the coast of the Black Sea to the middle of the Pacific Ocean. It is no longer solely concerned to ensure the prosperity of its members, but rather, to bring about an improvement in the economic situation throughout the whole world. . . . When they decided to create it [OECD], the twenty governments . . . determined to act in such a way that the new organisation should constitute an instrument of progress not only in the geographical area of OECD but throughout the whole world.'

The very diversity both of geographical membership and of industrial trading and development activity, while it demonstrates Europe's renewed capacity to play a full worldwide role in trade and aid matters in co-operation with the North American countries and Japan, and with Australia in the case of aid, has caused a loosening of the links which bound the members of OEEC together in the days of Marshall aid and the liberalisation of intra-European trade. In setting up OECD the United States and Canada were even less prepared than Britain, in the days of OEEC, to agree to delegate some of their national powers. They stressed that OECD should be used mainly for mutual consultation and information and should not be a decision-making executive institution. These views have been reflected in the convention and activities of OECD. Although the active participation of the United States in OECD's work on economic policy has given the organisation some influence in this domain, there are some activities that are mainly of interest to the European member states, in which the presence of the United States has tended to delay the despatch of business. OECD's scale of geographical coverage may grow even further. At the Council meeting of November 1966, the Ministers instructed the Secretary General to study, in co-operation with the permanent representatives, the possibilities of greater co-operation in the area of East–West economic relations. This is understood to involve the possibility of Eastern European countries being invited to take part in some of the Organisation's activities.

In the more liberal and prosperous context of the 1960s, OECD is no longer asked to carry out dramatic programmes, such as the administration of Marshall aid, or to stave off crises such as acute shortages of raw materials. Instead, OECD, by trying to help governments to prepare national economic policy decisions in the light of the policies of their partners, is attempting to achieve the highly sophisticated aim of making all the many separate facets of its members' economic lives fit together into a complementary international structure.

The extension of the geographical area of OEEC to the enormous area covered by OECD is a symptom of the growing interdependence of the developed trading countries of the non-communist world. With the realisation of this interdependence there has also come an awareness of new responsibilities and new tasks. When Europe was poor and its economy dislocated in the immediate postwar years, European recovery was naturally the overriding aim. When Europe became equipped to take part in an international economic structure on more equal terms with the United States it was, however, clearly able to do more to aid the poorer countries of the world. Something of the scale of this particular task can be seen if it is realised that if 'we succeed in having a per capita increase in production of 3 per cent a year in the developing countries, while the rate of increase in industrialised countries is 2 per cent' which 'would be an enormous difference in growth rates in favour of the developing countries, and it is certain we shall not see it in the near future, it would still take a little more than 200 years for the two average income levels to be the same'.[1] Thus although President Kennedy's idea of a 'Decade of Development' provided an impulse towards solving the problem of narrowing the gap between the living standards of the rich and the poor countries, it is clear that this problem will remain for many decades.

Even within its own area of membership, OECD faces new and complex problems. The very success of Europe's economic recovery since the days of 1946–47 has, in turn, created a whole new range of problems concerning the correlation and adjustment of national economic plans. A typical instance is the need to rationalise farm structures in Europe, where too many people eke out a poor livelihood from small and inefficiently exploited farms. If in solving this problem the member governments of OECD encourage farm workers to leave the land to work in industry, this in turn creates new social and human problems of adaptation which must be solved.

When OECD was created it was widely expected that the new organ-

[1] From a lecture given at the Christian Michelsens Institute, Norway, by Mr Thorkil Kristensen.

isation would be both a forum in which the United States would discuss and solve the main problems of its economic relations with Western Europe and also a dynamic instrument in which the North American countries could join together with European countries to help the developing countries. It soon became clear that neither of these aims would be fully realised. The United States has tended to deal directly with the EEC Commission or individual European governments over major economic issues, for instance in trying to settle differences over tariffs and quotas. As far as aid is concerned, although the Development Assistance Committee of OECD quickly proved itself to be a lively body within the limits of the mandate given to it by member governments, this mandate has been too restricted to enable OECD to respond fully to the problems posed by the developing countries to the industrialised countries of the West. Thus OECD is not so much a decision-taking body as a decision-influencing body that undertakes research and to some extent influences the economic policies of its member governments, which, while themselves remaining finally responsible for economic policy-making, can act in the full knowledge of the views and problems of their partners.

The Work of OECD

ECONOMIC POLICIES

The first of the aims of OECD is the achievement of the 'highest sustainable economic growth and employment and a rising standard of living in Member countries while maintaining financial stability'. The main specific objective of OECD in trying to achieve this general aim has been set by the decision of its Council, in 1961, to set a collective growth target for its members of a 50 per cent rise in their gross national product during the decade 1960–70.

The Economic Policy Committee is concerned with this problem of growth and it is the forum in which current economic trends are reviewed and ideas, advice and information on economic developments in member countries and their national economic policies are exchanged. The Committee pays particular attention to the international repercussions of national policy decisions. Work on economic growth is closely related to the equilibrium of international payments, the external balance of payments of member countries, the maintenance of price stability, and the idea of an incomes policy for its members.

The Economic Policy Committee, which is responsible for advising member governments how they can best achieve the target of a 50 per cent rise in their collective gross national product, is composed of senior national civil servants responsible for formulating economic policy and representatives of the central banks. It meets three or four times a year. Its reports and recommendations are given close attention by the great majority of member governments. The United States, for instance, sends very high level representatives to this Committee and its economic policy-making is influenced by the Committee's work. In its work concerning payments problems and monetary matters the Committee collaborates with the International Monetary Fund and the Bank for International Settlements. The Committee has established various working parties, of which the most important are working party No. 2, which deals with longer-term problems of economic growth, and working party No. 3, which is concerned with the promotion of a better equilibrium in international payments. Another working party studies the problem of rising costs and prices.

The continuing review carried out by the Economic Policy Committee and its working parties is aimed not only at promoting better informed policy-making by member governments, but may also help to solve urgent problems facing member countries. Countries with temporary balance-of-payments difficulties have been able to raise financial assistance quickly from other members because these other governments have known, through previous discussions and the interchange of information in OECD, that they approved of the policies being applied. On other occasions, the Economic Policy Committee's recommendations to a member in severe economic difficulties has helped the government or the ministers concerned to gain acceptance for an unpopular solution which would otherwise probably have proved unacceptable. Discussions in the Economic Policy Committee have also helped governments to understand the lessons to be drawn from policy decisions which have produced unexpected results.

The Economic Development and Review Committee is responsible for continuing the practice, developed in OEEC, of carrying out an annual economic survey of individual member countries (and of Yugoslavia). Following the 'confrontation' technique evolved in OEEC, the economic situation and policies of each country are examined by a group of representatives of other member governments and the results of each examination, which carry considerable weight and obtain wide publicity, are published. These surveys are highly respected by member governments. The Committee is also responsible for advising the Council on the special growth problems of the less industrialised member countries.

The annual country-by-country reviews work in the following way. Each member country submits a memorandum explaining its economic situation and the methods and aims of its government's policy. Members of the Secretariat then prepare a draft report based on this material and two examining countries draw up a list of questions in consultation with the Secretariat on the problems, policies, short-term and medium-term prospects of the country concerned. Government officials of the country being examined reply to these questions before the Committee and discuss the emergent issues with the other members. These discussions are confidential and are noted for their frankness. The Secretariat's draft report is amended in the light of the discussions and is finally published in the form of a factual analysis and policy recommendations. Policy recommendations are sometimes concerned with immediate policy issues, but sometimes include longer-term appraisals of the strength and weaknesses of a national economy and of the policies used by the government in dealing with its problems.

The work of the Economic and Statistics Department of the Secretariat in sifting and analysing economic data provides the factual and statistical basis for OECD's system of discussion, confrontation and recommendation. OECD also makes much of its data publicly available in an internationally comparable form. It publishes the monthly 'Main Economic Indicators' giving a detailed picture of the production, trade and finance of each member country, together with other bi-monthly and annual statistical records of the international trade figures of its members and bulletins on individual subjects. Some idea of the scale of the Organisation's role as a producer of economic statistics can be gained from the fact that OECD produces over 10,000 statistical tables every year.

In 1965 a Mid-term Review was carried out to determine how far members of OECD were succeeding in achieving their aim of a 50 per cent collective rise in their gross national product by 1970. Its conclusions, which were published in November 1966,[1] were optimistic. The Review stated that it appeared 'that the output target will be achieved or surpassed. However, since inflationary strains and external imbalances have been encountered by almost all Member countries in recent years, an important task for policy during the

[1] *Economic Growth: 1960–1970—A Mid-decade Review of Prospects*, Paris, OECD, 1966.

remainder of the decade will be to place growth on the more balanced and sustainable basis that was contemplated when the target was established.' The Review established that for OECD members taken together, the total output of goods and services increased at an annual rate of 4·9 (and 4·7 per cent excluding Japan, which was not a member in 1960) per cent a year during the period 1960–65 and that the expansion of production was much faster than the growth of population. Growth was thus 'significantly faster than the average rate of 4·1 per cent needed to reach the 1970 target'. The Review forecast: 'Provided the right policies are adopted by countries and are adequately harmonised among them, there is every reason to expect that something like the present rate of expansion can be continued. This would imply reaching or even exceeding the 50 per cent growth target for the decade as a whole.' The table, shown overleaf, shows the expansion of total output of OECD countries between 1960 and 1965 and projects this expansion to 1970.

In making its recommendations to governments on how to increase growth rates OECD has continuously studied the complex interrelation between economic growth and the balance of payments and costs and prices. The Economic Policy Committee set up its working party on the problem of rising costs and prices to study, on a continuing basis, methods of resisting the tendency for wages to outstrip productivity. The emphasis of the work of OECD in the domain of economic policy has been to try to enable its members to achieve financial stability at the same time as increased growth. In 1964 OECD laid special stress on the need for its members to develop effective incomes policies in response to the rapid rate of expansion achieved in the second half of 1963 and the earlier months of 1964, which had led to considerable price increases. Several member countries started, with varying degrees of success, to put incomes policies into operation in 1964 and 1965. Consultation between countries engaged in this operation is carried out in Working Party No. 4 of the Economic Policy Committee.

In setting general aims and laying down guiding principles for their achievement OECD has helped to improve the quality of economic planning and policy-making in member countries. The 'confrontation' carried out in the Organisation can enrich the economic policies of its members by supplementing the traditional instruments available to them, in the light of experience gained by other countries. OECD has, moreover, helped to dilute motives of national self-interest in the making of economic policies, where these are likely to damage other countries.

The Expansion of Total Output in OECD Countries, 1960–70

	Share of OECD output in 1963 (*per cent*)	*Annual average percentage rates of increase* Decade 1960–70	1st half-decade 1960–65 actual	2nd half-decade 1965–70 projected
Major countries:				
Canada	3·6	5·2	5·5	4·8
France	7·3	4·9	5·1	4·8
Federal Republic of Germany	8·6	4·2	4·8	3·5
Italy	4·1	5·1	5·1	5·0
Japan	5·4	8·5	9·6	7·5
United Kingdom	7·7	3·7	3·3	4·1
United States	53·3	4·5	4·5	4·5
Total above	90·0	4·7	4·8	4·6
Smaller industralised countries:				
Austria	0·7	4·0	4·3	3·8
Belgium	1·3	4·3	4·5	4·0
Denmark	0·7	4·7	4·9	4·4
Iceland	0·1	—	5·6	—
Ireland	0·2	—	3·8	—
Luxembourg	0·1	3·0	2·9	3·2
Netherlands	1·3	4·7	4·8	4·5
Norway	0·5	5·0	5·2	4·8
Sweden	1·4	4·7	5·1	4·3
Switzerland	1·0	4·5	5·3	3·7
Total above	7·3	4·5	4·8	4·2
Developing countries:				
Greece	0·4	8·1	8·7	7·5
Portugal	0·3	6·2	5·8	6·6
Spain	1·4	—	9·2	—
Turkey	0·6	—	4·3	—
Total above	2·7	—	7·7	—
Total OECD	100·0	4·7	4·9	4·6
Total OECD, excluding Japan	94·6	4·5	4·7	4·4
The collective objective		4·1	—	—

Source: Economic Growth: 1960–1970—A Mid-decade Review of Prospects, op. cit., p. 11.

DEVELOPMENT ASSISTANCE

Development assistance has been one of the main preoccupations of OECD. Article 2(e) of the OECD convention states that members will 'contribute to the economic development of both member and non-member countries in the process of economic development by appropriate means and, in particular, by the flow of capital to those countries, having regard to the importance to their economies of receiving technical assistance and of securing expanding export markets'. OEEC had already established a Development Assistance Group in January 1960. This body has extended its work, under OECD, as the Development Assistance Committee (DAC). All the major capital-exporting countries other than the communist countries are members of DAC.[1] The aims of DAC are, first, to increase the volume of financial aid provided by its member countries to the developing countries and, second, to improve the quality and efficiency of aid through the harmonisation of the aid efforts and policies of its members. DAC also tries to ensure that the recipient countries use their aid in the most effective way. Much of DAC's activity is devoted to basic fact-finding, which includes the exchanging of the experience of members in dealing with various specific problems. DAC also tries to develop common policy positions concerning, for instance, the softening of terms of financial aid. It also tries to bring moral suasion to bear on its members, through mutual criticism to improve their performance in such matters. DAC is serviced and staffed by the Development Department of OECD which has often originated new approaches taken up by the DAC members.

DAC has no funds of its own to pay out to the developing countries. It tries, however, to influence the aid policies of its member countries. Something of the scale of its task is indicated by the fact that the flow of official and private funds in various forms from the members of DAC to the developing countries amounted to some $10,000 million in 1965. Most of DAC's work is carried out by means of its Annual Aid Review which examines, using once again the technique of confrontation, the effectiveness of the individual national aid programmes of its members. It has been within the context of confrontation that most of the major policy pressures, for instance for softer terms for loans, have been exerted by individual member countries. Although DAC has been found a useful place in which to

[1] The members of DAC are: Australia, Austria, Belgium, Canada, Denmark, France, the Federal Republic of Germany, Italy, Japan, the Netherlands, Norway, Portugal, Sweden, the United Kingdom, the United States of America and the Commission of the EEC.

exert such pressures, its own corporate identity has not been very strong and its influence has been less than its well-wishers had hoped. The findings of the Aid Review are summarised in an annual report published by the Chairman of DAC[1] and much of the statistical information about aid totals and the terms in which aid is provided by the donor countries is published in annual OECD reports entitled *The Flow of Financial Resources to Developing Countries.*

The recent reports of the Chairman of DAC have shown that, apart from the constant efforts of DAC to increase the total sums devoted to aid by its members on a mutually equitable basis, there are four main tasks which confront the donor countries: the elimination of aid-tying (insisting that aid must be spent in the donor country); the improvement of the terms and conditions on which aid is given; the provision of aid in ways which increase the effective use by less developed countries of their own resources; and the co-ordination of aid from various sources.

Although some governments claim that they might have to make considerable cuts in their aid unless they can point to the effects of tying in reducing their balance-of-payments deficits and providing contracts for their home industries, the opinion of the Chairman of DAC is that aid-tying is an undesirable practice. In July 1960, under the terms of the Bonn Agreement, the members of DAC agreed to move to untied aid, bearing in mind their balance-of-payments situation. Despite this agreement, much of the aid provided by the members of DAC is still tied. The report of the DAC Chairman for 1963[2] stated 'almost all DAC countries tie parts of their aid, but the proportion of directly tied aid is particularly high for Japan, the United States of America and Canada. About two thirds of bilateral aid extended by DAC combined is subject to procurement restrictions.' The 1966 report revealed no significant improvement in this situation. Amongst the suggestions made by DAC in its attempts to do away with aid-tying is that restrictions should be relaxed by a number of donor countries simultaneously so that trade losses might be matched by comparable gains for each donor country.

DAC has shown a continuing preoccupation with the harmonisation, in a more generous direction, of the terms and conditions on which aid is granted. First of all, 'hard' loans at high interest rates can saddle developing countries with a debt-burden which they cannot support. At the beginning of 1965, for instance, three

[1] The first Chairman was an American, Mr James W. Riddleberger, who was succeeded by another American, Mr Willard L. Thorp, in February 1963.

[2] *Development Assistance Efforts and Policies—1963 Review, Paris,* OECD.

recipient countries—Brazil, Chile and Turkey—reached a position in which they were unable to continue the repayment of their debts together with the accumulated interest. In April 1963 a resolution was adopted at a meeting of DAC recommending to members that they should relate the terms of their aid to the individual circumstances of the recipients and setting as an object 'the achievement of a significant degree of comparability in the terms and conditions of the aid coming from different members'. In general, DAC has managed to persuade its members to 'soften' interest rates and lengthen repayment periods. Thus, in 1965, 78 per cent of the total aid commitments of DAC members, whether grants or loans, carried 3 per cent interest or less: a considerable improvement on the situation at the beginning of the sixties. There has also been a general move towards lengthening repayment periods and over half the loans made by DAC members since 1962 have repayment periods of twenty years or more. However, the debt-burden of the developing countries still remains formidable and it threatens to eat up much of the new aid given to the more indebted recipient countries. DAC has emphasised in its reports that insistence on high interest rates by some donor countries is unfair to those donor countries which charge low interest rates, since these countries are in practice subsidising, by their loans at low interest rates, the high interest rates charged by their fellow donors. In July 1965 DAC recommended that its members should try to provide 80 per cent of their aid either as grants or as loans with a repayment period of not less than twenty five years at interest rates of not more than 3 per cent and with, on average, a grace period of seven years. In his 1966 report the DAC Chairman stated that eight of the DAC members had already met these objectives.

Finally, there are considerable disparities between the efforts made by the individual donor countries. DAC is, therefore, trying to achieve a fairer distribution of the burden of aid.

DAC is well aware that financial aid is only one of three main ways in which the industrialised countries can help the developing countries, the others being trade and technical assistance. DAC itself has no direct mandate concerning the commercial policies adopted by its members towards the developing countries, questions of this kind being dealt with primarily in GATT and the United Nations Conference on Trade and Development (UNCTAD),[1] but in July 1964, following the first meeting of UNCTAD, DAC created a working

[1] OECD, however, takes a lively interest in trying to increase the export earnings of the less developed countries. See pp. 442–43.

party to study problems arising out of the Conference and instructed it to investigate the recommendations adopted by UNCTAD regarding the financing and expansion of international trade. The Trade Committee of OECD is also concerned with UNCTAD's recommendations on trade.

DAC's work in trying to increase the total aid given by its members to the developing countries has become increasingly difficult since 1961 in view of the worsening payments problems of some of the principal donor countries, in particular the United States and the United Kingdom. Further, while (partly owing to the efforts of DAC) the quality and efficiency of aid-giving have greatly improved in recent years, public opinion in the donor countries has become to some extent disenchanted with aid policy in the knowledge that in the past large sums of public money have been inefficiently spent or have vanished into the hands of corrupt administrations or individuals. The combination of these circumstances has made it difficult for DAC, along with other bodies concerned with aid, to receive the degree of governmental and public support that its work deserves.[1] One instance of an improvement in the transmission of aid, involving both donors and recipients, has been the establishment of an Inter-American Committee (CIAP) by the Alliance for Progress which hopes to achieve for Latin America what OEEC did for Europe during the days of Marshall aid. CIAP plans to hold an annual review and use the 'confrontation' technique to make the best of the financial aid which the Latin American countries receive. This adaptation by Latin America of the techniques of European cooperation is a striking tribute to OECD and its predecessor.

The part played by private investment in development is of great importance. The governments of capital-exporting countries are trying, therefore, to improve the climate of confidence which is

[1] Commenting on this situation at the ministerial meeting of the Council on 25 November 1966 Mr Kristensen stated:

'If we look for an explanation, it can be found partly in the developing countries and partly in our own Member countries. No doubt several developing countries have made mistakes in their development planning, partly because of ignorance and in some cases perhaps also because of ambitions that are not justified. It is also true that their administration has not always been efficient and these factors are used in public discussions as arguments against an increase in aid.

'However, one has of course to recognise that the tasks which the governments of developing countries have to tackle are immense and their resources in terms of qualified administrators and so on are extremely small. In spite of that it seems that on the whole planning is becoming better in a number of these countries and progress is being made concerning the implementation of the plans.'

necessary to attract private investment. One way which may help to do this is the 'Draft Convention for the Protection of Foreign Property' which has been drafted by the OECD Committee for Invisible Transactions, which could govern the behaviour of host countries concerning foreign investment and business activities. The Draft Convention has been studied by donor and recipient governments who have formulated their comments on it. The text was transmitted to the World Bank, which has now opened a Convention for signature.

In 1963–64 DAC introduced the technique of holding meetings between the representatives of the donor countries and representatives of the different regions in which aid is received, such as the Middle East, Latin America and East Africa, to discuss the economic requirements of the recipient areas.

DAC is also concerned with the provision of technical assistance by its members to the developing countries. It tries to increase the flow of teachers, administrators and technicians, and management personnel from its members to the developing countries. It also tries to ensure that the experts sent to developing countries have appropriate qualifications to be of use in the particular conditions of the countries where they go to work.

DAC reviews the technical assistance policies of its members and tries to co-ordinate them so that the best use is made of the money spent.[1] It is trying to find ways in which the governments of the donor countries can more easily attract and recruit qualified experts who are willing to interrupt their careers to work in the developing countries, and to ensure that experts are not penalised in their careers on account of such interruptions. DAC has set up an Expert Group on Requirements for and Supply of Technical Assistance.

Most of the work of OECD as a whole concerning technical assistance and educational aid has been concentrated on the Mediterranean countries and Iceland, although work in the member countries does not come within the scope of DAC. OECD has carried out development programmes for Sardinia, the Epirus, Turkey, Portugal and Yugoslavia.[2]

DAC has recently laid great stress on the need to teach the peoples of the less developed countries to exploit their agriculture in a modern and scientific way. This vast task involves changing the whole social structure of the countries concerned.

[1] The cost of bilateral technical aid provided by DAC members in 1965 was $1,115 million.

[2] For details of the OECD Consortia for Greece and Turkey see p. 444.

In 1963 OECD published an important report (prepared by the agricultural division of the Secretariat) on the role of food aid in economic development, which showed how food aid could be used to complement other forms of aid in limited and specific ways, but which also underlined the dangers to the balanced development of recipient countries, especially to their agriculture, which unplanned food aid could cause. India's food problems of 1965 and 1966 dramatically focused attention on the food needs of the developing countries and at its high-level meeting (attended by ministers and senior civil servants) in July 1966 DAC adopted a recommendation on the food problems of the less developed countries recommending its members to 'encourage developing countries to give greater emphasis to the agricultural sector of their economies with the aim of raising the level of food production' and 'to give more emphasis to capital and technical assistance designed to support domestic policies in the developing countries which would lead to increased productivity in the agricultural sector'.

In 1963 OECD established a Development Centre to help the developing countries to bring all available economic knowledge and experience to bear upon their development policies. The Centre tries to do this by: research on urgent economic policy problems of the developing countries; advanced training for civil servants from these countries; and provision of documentary information in reply to specific questions raised by the policy-makers of these countries.

In its research activities, the Centre has given priority to the research projects which, it is hoped, will be of the greatest use to policy-makers in the developing countries. One of the main subjects of the research programme is the relationship between international aid and economic development. The Centre tries to evaluate the efficiency of different forms, techniques, methods and objects of aid through case studies. It has also carried out case studies on the impact of technical assistance on economic development. The Centre hopes to obtain systematic co-operation between organisations engaged in similar work and in December 1963 organised a meeting in Palermo attended by representatives of development and research institutes in Europe, the United States of America and Japan as well as of the United Nations and its regional economic commissions. Follow-up meetings have been held.

The Centre has sent teams of experts to some of the smaller developing countries to discuss with senior civil servants, during seminars lasting a month, development problems of special concern to these countries. These seminars are prepared in close consultation with the regional economic commissions of the United Nations. The Centre also holds courses in Paris for civil servants from developing countries.

TRADE, PAYMENTS AND CAPITAL MOVEMENTS

The aim of OECD concerning trade is 'to contribute to the expansion of world trade on a multilateral, non-discriminatory basis in accordance with international obligations.'

With the transformation of OEEC into OECD, the Code of Liberalisation was not continued, since the United States and Canada were not prepared to accept, within the framework of OECD, any obligation of the 'Code of Liberalisation' type. The quotas originally imposed by members of OEEC had, more or less, been almost entirely abolished and convertibility attained. It was felt that there was no need for OECD to set precise legal obligations governing trade since the international trade of member countries was governed by the rules of GATT. Since it was also considered that tariff negotiations were best conducted within GATT, two of OECD's main aims in the field of trade have been to eliminate any remaining quotas, and to extend the liberalisation already achieved among the OECD countries to the other members of GATT. Another major concern of OECD has been the elimination of restrictive technical and administrative regulations which unnecessarily hamper trade, and OECD has tried to simplify and standardise the administrative measures governing trade in its member countries. Finally, OECD has sought to complement the aid given by its members to the developing countries by seeking to obtain easier access to the markets of its member countries for the developing countries' exports.

The Trade Committee of OECD is the Organisation's principal body working on trade problems. The Committee, which is composed of high-level national civil servants responsible for trade matters, confronts the general trade policies and practices of member countries. It examines those trade problems which are of particular interest to its members and considers urgent problems which may arise such as, for instance, the imposition of the 15 per cent import surcharge by the British Government in October 1964.[1]

Between March and October 1962, the Trade Committee held a confrontation concerning the quantitative restrictions still in force in member countries, excluding those affecting trade in agriculture.

[1] After discussions in the Trade Committee and elsewhere, OECD expressed its concern that this measure should be of a temporary and non-discriminatory nature.

By October nearly 30 per cent of the restrictions which had been identified in March had been eliminated. Further confrontations have been held on specific groups of industrial and agricultural products.

With the initial elimination of quotas, tariffs now remain the main obstacle to international trade. OECD has no mandate to deal with tariff problems which are the concern, on a European regional basis, of the EEC and EFTA, and, on a world basis, of GATT. OECD has, however, endeavoured to co-ordinate the attitude of its member countries towards the trade and tariff problems discussed and negotiated within GATT and the United Nations Conference on Trade and Development (UNCTAD). In particular, OECD has tried, though with little apparent success, to persuade its members to adopt common positions in the Kennedy Round of tariff negotiations in GATT which opened in May 1964.[1] Further, OECD realised, in view of the unco-ordinated approach adopted by its member countries during the first meeting of UNCTAD, which was held in 1964, that the developed countries of the world should seek to establish common positions at future meetings of UNCTAD so as to be able to reply to the joint demands formulated by the developing countries concerning their aid and trade problems. OECD has therefore set up special working parties to study the problems concerned. At its meeting of December 1964, the Ministerial Council of OECD encouraged this development in the Organisation's work and emphasised the need for OECD to continue its work in 'co-ordinating member countries' efforts to formulate constructive policies designed to further the economic expansion of the developing countries'.

Restrictive administrative regulations are also a major and continuing obstacle to the expansion of international trade. Many of these regulations are concerned primarily with security, public health, quality control, the prevention of fraud and the rationalisation of production rather than with trade, but they may have the effect of hampering trade. OECD, while recognising that countries need to impose rules of this kind, has tried to eliminate their commercially restrictive effects as far as possible. Thus, OECD holds consultations on specific restrictions which are brought to its attention by countries whose exports meet with difficulties. It also organises country-by-country surveys of different types of regulations and examines regulations imposed on different groups of products. Following its investigations into administrative regulations, OECD has drafted several model rules and regulations in the hope that member states, in accepting them, will adopt uniform practices.

[1] The aims of the Kennedy Round are outlined on p. 143.

OECD has also tried to eliminate, or to mitigate the effects of, certain national regulations which are directly related to international trade. Thus OECD has carried out examinations of anti-dumping legislation, import licences, customs formalities and rules governing the classification and valuation of goods for tariff purposes. Moreover, it has studied and tried to alleviate the unfavourable effects in foreign trade of certain national laws and practices, such as those governing purchases of goods by government departments and agencies. In the course of the study of anti-dumping arrangements in member countries which OECD carried out in 1964, the United States invited OECD to comment on certain proposed changes in its anti-dumping legislation, and the American Government made certain modifications in its new regulations, in the light of OECD's comments, before they were put into effect.

OECD, whose members buy about two thirds of the exports of the developing countries,[1] has consistently worked for the adoption of more liberal trading policies by its members towards the less-developed countries. OECD aims to help the developing countries to increase their receipts from sales of primary products while simultaneously encouraging their industrialisation and providing easier access to the markets of the developed countries for their exports of industrial products. The Council of OECD adopted a Ministerial Resolution in November 1962 on the co-ordination of aid and trade and urged its members to give urgent attention to the problem of providing adequate access to the exports of the developing countries. Following this Ministerial Resolution, OECD stepped up its studies on the economic relations of its members with the developing countries. These studies have been closely connected with the principal issues which have been the subject of the work of GATT and UNCTAD in this domain. In particular, OECD has studied the ways in which the developing countries can increase their export earnings.

In view of the payments difficulties of the developing countries there has, in recent years, been a tendency to lengthen the credits extended by the industrialised countries to finance their exports to the less-developed countries. Since there are certain dangers in this practice, OECD established, at the end of 1963, a Group on Export Credits and Credit Guarantees to hold policy confrontations among the member countries. This group works in close co-operation with DAC.

Since the International Monetary Fund, the 'Group of Ten' and other primarily monetary organisations are responsible for the

[1] The great bulk of which are agricultural products or raw materials.

monetary problems of the free world, OECD's role in monetary and payment matters is limited.[1] OECD has, however, established financial Consortia to handle credits and technical assistance to two member countries, Greece and Turkey,[2] in order to help them to carry out their development plans. OECD has, since 1964, persuaded its members to make special arrangements to help Turkey overcome its very difficult external financial situation and to repay its foreign debts. The Turkish Consortium is the outstanding example of OECD bringing members together to provide a country with a concerted assistance programme.

The OECD Fiscal Committee has continued the work begun under OEEC on the subject of double taxation leading, in 1963, to a draft convention on the avoidance of double taxation with respect to taxes on income and capital. By this time twenty three bilateral conventions on the subject had been concluded between member states. As a result of this work the fiscal position of tax payers in any one member country who are engaged in business activities in other member states can now be clarified and standardised. A complementary draft convention for the avoidance of double taxation with respect to taxes on estates and inheritances has been prepared.

The group of experts on Restrictive Business Practices (which became a full Committee in 1961) has published a *Guide to Legislation on Restrictive Business Practices in Europe and North America*, which is a comprehensive survey of legislation and administrative and court decisions and includes the relevant legal dispositions of the European Economic Community and the European Coal and Steel Community. The Guide is kept up to date by supplements. In 1964 OECD published a 'Comparative Summary' dealing with the main aspects of legislation on restrictive business practices in Europe and North America.

OECD has continued OEEC's work concerning the liberalisation of invisible transactions.[3] About a quarter of payments between OECD member countries are for services of this kind, so this programme, which has now eliminated practically all restrictions on current invisible operations between OECD member countries,[4] has been of considerable importance. The Committee for Invisible Transactions administers the Code of Liberalisation of Current Invisible Operations

[1] The structure and operation of the European Monetary Agreement are described on p. 98.

[2] At present only the Turkish Consortium is in operation.

[3] See p. 102.

[4] Except on the film industry, insurance and land transport.

which lists over fifty kinds of transaction which the member countries have agreed to liberate from restrictions. One of the main tasks of the Committee is to examine cases where states which are confronted with economic difficulties suspend their application of the Code or make reservations concerning particular transactions. The Committee for Invisible Transactions has recently devoted considerable attention to the film industry, which many governments still protect (for political, cultural or prestige reasons) through restrictions on the importing and distribution of foreign films. The Committee is also studying restrictions on insurance and land transport which governments have been reluctant to eliminate.

The Committee for Invisible Transactions also provides a forum for OECD members in their efforts to liberalise international capital movements. The Committee administers the Code of Liberalisation of Capital Movements, which was drawn up by OEEC in 1959. Since 1959 international financial operations have increased considerably and the scope of the Code was accordingly enlarged in July 1964. In particular, the working of this Code helps manufacturers or businessmen to invest across frontiers. The operations which have been freed under the Code include: direct investment and its liquidation, personal capital movements, commercial credits, dealing in securities and dealing in real estate. A number of member governments have not been able to free all the types of operation laid down in the Code and have lodged a number of reservations which OECD is encouraging them to remove.

A separate committee of OECD, the Maritime Transport Committee, works to remove obstacles to the freedom of shipping throughout the world. In 1964 the Committee succeeded in ending persistent differences between the United States and the European maritime member countries over the organisation of ocean liner services.

The Tourism Committee of OECD works for the improvement of tourist facilities in member countries and tries to persuade them to remove restrictions on tourism, such as currency restrictions. In 1964, for instance, the OECD Council agreed that the minimum tourist allowance in foreign currency should be raised from $500 to $700 per person per journey.

MANPOWER AND SOCIAL AFFAIRS

In June 1964, the Council of OECD recommended its member countries to reconsider their manpower policy with a view to promoting economic growth. Governments were asked to report back to OECD within a year about the action they were taking. For the guidance of member governments, the Manpower and Social Affairs Committee prepared a report, which was approved by the Council, setting out the main elements necessary for a dynamic manpower policy. The report stated:

'Along with the basic programme for education and training of youth there is need for training programmes for persons of all working ages to help meet demands for new skills and adaptation to changes in the industrial structure. Along with scientific and technical progress there is need for measures to promote acceptance of new techniques by all concerned. Along with fiscal and monetary policies designed to maintain high levels of employment and business activity in general terms, there is need for more specialised and selective measures, creating jobs in labour surplus areas and encouraging the flow of manpower from such areas to expanding and productive industries.'

The report also summarised the underlying philosophy of OECD concerning manpower:

'Countries sometimes accept the burden of large direct or indirect subsidies or measures of protection to maintain employment in declining and less productive sectors. Public money could often be better used to facilitate and stimulate workers' moving and retraining for better jobs or the establishment of industries with positive prospects in areas facing employment difficulties. Expenditure of the types envisaged here for the improvement of human resources and their readjustment should not be regarded as a cost to society, but rather as a sound "investment in adaptation". At the same time they promote important social values by increasing the individual's freedom in the choice of an occupation or workplace and his security against loss of income.'

During 1965 member governments reported to OECD on the ways in which they had applied the recommendation made in June 1964 and, in particular, explained the methods which they intended to adopt in readjusting their national manpower policies along the lines indicated by the Manpower and Social Affairs Committee.

The Manpower and Social Affairs Committee carries out annual surveys on employment policies in the member countries and makes special studies of individual countries. The annual reports which member countries make to the Committee deal mostly with policy changes and developments in administration concerning manpower and related social policies. It is hoped that members will make use of each other's experience in their own policy-making and administrative practice. Sweden was the first country to be the subject of a special manpower study, but reviews have also been made of the United States, Greece, Italy, Austria and Canada.

The Manpower and Social Affairs Committee carries out studies of specific problems which are of general concern. Studies of this kind have examined: the problems of the public employment services; the demographic, cultural, psychological and social factors influencing geographical mobility; the adaptation problems of rural workers moving into industry; the location of industry; the employment of elderly workers; office automation; and the re-development of distressed areas.

Some governments have developed 'early warning systems' to provide information about prospective changes in the demand for labour. The Manpower and Social Affairs Committee is comparing these systems and has worked on employment forecasting methods. A report on this subject was published in 1963 and a pilot study of the employment structure of the cotton textile industry has been carried out in several member countries. Thus OECD aims at achieving a flexible system of employment in which changes in patterns of employment can be forecast and workers moved from one sector of the economy to another with adequate readaptation training for their new jobs. Manpower policy is clearly closely linked with social policy so that OECD is concerned with improving the relevant aspects of social policy, such as social security and redundancy benefits. Industrial relations and the effects of automation and technological change on relations between management and workers are also studied.

In its varied activities the Manpower and Social Affairs Committee works in close contact with trade union and employers' organisations and the major international organisations concerned with social and manpower problems such as the International Labour Organisation and the EEC.

INDUSTRY AND ENERGY

A Council Resolution of 1962 established that the Industry Committee and the Energy Committee of OECD were responsible for the co-ordination of the work of a group of Special Committees concerned with individual industries and energy. In the industrial domain there were at the outset Special Committees for iron and steel, non-ferrous metals, timber, pulp and paper, textiles, chemical products, machinery, hides and skins and cement. At that time, there were also Special Committees in the field of energy, dealing with coal, electricity, oil and gas.

By virtue of a Council Resolution of July 1965, concerning future activities in the fields of energy and industry, the Organisation now has an Industry Committee and an Energy Committee established on a permanent basis, as well as the Special Committee for Oil, and, for a five-year period, five Special Committees for Iron and Steel, Textiles, Chemical Products, Machinery and Pulp and Paper.

The Special Committees are composed of civil servants, and, in a number of cases, of representatives of industry appointed by member governments. They keep a close watch on developments in a particular industrial or energy sector, and try to detect changes in economic conditions which will have repercussions on that industry. They study obstacles to growth, investment trends, and the future growth and demand prospects of the industry concerned. They also relate developments in a specific industry or energy sector to industrial and economic developments as a whole. The work of these Committees is of great value to the Economic Policy Committee in surveying the whole range of the economic activity of OECD's member countries. Finally, their work concerning industrial employment by sector complements the studies made by the Manpower Committee.

The Industry and the Energy Committees as well as the Special Committees obtain a constant flow of information from member countries by use of the 'confrontation' technique and detailed questionnaires. Their studies are useful to member governments in formulating their own national policies concerning industrial and energy developments. Sometimes the confrontations or replies to questionnaires on particular industries reveal that the position of a whole industry requires urgent attention throughout the OECD area. This was found to be the case with the shipbuilding industry where the Industry Committee set up a working party to examine the effectiveness of the governmental and private measures that had been taken to improve the situation of this industry.

The main questions dealt with by the Industry Committee are the adaptation of industry to technological changes and market trends, policies for regional development and policies for industrial investment. The industrial problems of the developing member countries are also given special attention.

This work is carried out with the help of working parties and commissions set up by the Industry Committee. Until 1965, and in accordance with the instructions of the Council, the Committee also carried out a programme to stimulate productivity, including activities in the field of management development and education, modern marketing and distributing techniques, productivity measurement and arranging meetings of the Heads of National Productivity Centres. In 1965, however, following a report by the Secretary General concerning operational activities, the Council decided that the results of these activities in the industrial field had been satisfactory, and that it was now up to the various national bodies or to the industries of member countries to take over the responsibility for them.

In the Energy Committee the energy policies of the member countries are examined through country-by-country confrontations and problems requiring co-operation among member governments are studied and discussed. The chairman of the Special Committee for Oil can take part in these meetings and close contacts concerning developments in the different energy sectors are maintained. Whereas during the first half of the 1950s the development of an 'energy gap' was feared, a number of technical developments have since helped to create a more optimistic climate. *Towards a new Energy Pattern in Europe*, a report published by OECD in 1960, was the first official recognition of this changed position. In the new context, member countries have been re-thinking their energy policies, and the Energy Committee now prepares a general energy report for the OECD area as a whole, dealing in particular with national energy policies and the scope for harmonisation which they offer.

Following initiatives taken in the early 1950s by OEEC's Electricity Committee, a European electricity network has been created. Austria, Belgium, France, the Federal Republic of Germany, Italy, Luxembourg, the Netherlands and Switzerland have developed and put into operation, since 1951, the Union for the Co-ordination and Production and Transportation of Electricity. Since then, France has linked its electricity systems with the Spanish and British grids and links with a grid of the Scandinavian countries are being developed.

AGRICULTURE AND FISHERIES

Agriculture in the OECD area faces many critical problems. Farming has not kept pace with industrial and technological developments; in several countries too many people are trying to gain their living from small and inefficient farms; and agricultural incomes have risen more slowly than industrial incomes. International trade in agriculture is hindered both by short-term problems such as seasonal fluctuations in production and prices and by such long-term problems as excessive protection. Administrative and health rules, which vary from country to country, and lack of adequate international co-ordination concerning definitions and quality-grading of agricultural produce are also hindrances to international trade.

The OECD Committee for Agriculture promotes international co-operation concerning the agricultural problems of its members. OECD has, however, always emphasised that the agriculture of its member countries cannot be considered in isolation from world agricultural problems, which include the food needs of less-developed countries. In 1963 OECD published a major study on *Food Aid.*

The central features of OECD's work on agriculture are its 'confrontations' of national agricultural policies, with the aim of harmonising these policies, and the publication of a series of reports. OECD has tried to promote a basic long-term adjustment in the agricultural sector. Publication in 1964 of the report on *Low Incomes in Agriculture* was followed in 1965 by major reports, prepared by six experts, on *Agriculture and Economic Growth.*

OECD carries out detailed studies of individual agricultural problems. Studies of this kind have dealt with: the more efficient use of land; the allocation of land as between agricultural and other uses; the identification of the economic, legal, social and other obstacles to shifts in land use within agriculture and from farming to other purposes; obstacles to the mobility of agricultural manpower; and the planning and implementation of development schemes for rural areas.

OECD has been trying to encourage its member governments to put greater emphasis on measures to induce farm workers and small farmers to leave the land to work in other sectors of the economy. An OECD report, 'Intellectual Investment in Agriculture for Economic and Social Development', has led to pilot projects in several countries for education in agricultural areas. OECD also brings together agricultural scientists and economists from different countries to exchange their experiences and ideas.

The International Centre for Advanced Mediterranean Agronomic Studies was set up by seven countries[1] under the joint auspices of OECD and the Council of Europe to promote agricultural progress in the Mediterranean region. The Centre has two institutes, at

[1] France, Greece, Italy, Portugal, Spain, Turkey and Yugoslavia.

Montpellier and Bari, which train agricultural scientists and experts and carry out research into the special agricultural problems of the Mediterranean area.

The Committee for Agriculture has worked for the elimination of unnecessary administrative and health regulations, and tries to achieve the harmonisation, wherever possible, of those regulations whose continuance is regarded as necessary. The administrative practices arising out of the new regulations or preferential arrangements introduced by the EEC and EFTA have also been studied. Working parties have been set up to study the current situation and short-term prospects in 'sensitive' agricultural products: meat, dairy produce, fruit and vegetables. These follow production and market trends, and monthly bulletins are published by OECD setting out the most up-to-date information on harvest forecasts. Work is also being carried out on quality-grading and OECD has been responsible for international agreements on seed certification and the grading of fruit and vegetables and on the testing of farm tractors. Uniform standards for fruit and vegetable containers are being worked out as is an international system of identification of beef, veal and pork carcases. Studies aimed at improving marketing methods and modernising food transport and distribution are also under way.

The fishing industry has lagged behind other sectors of the economy in the OECD area. Old-fashioned methods and structures have held back modernisation in many countries, while ill-considered financial support has often discouraged the shift of manpower to more profitable industries. Little has so far been done to explore the possibilities of a rational exploitation of the resources of the sea. Over-fishing by fishermen from non-member countries has increased the difficulties of the fishing industry and various legal problems and disputes concerning fishing rights have stood in the way of an international approach to the development of the fishing industry. The development of international trade in fish is hindered by import restrictions, and some countries refuse to allow direct landings of foreign-caught fish in their harbours.

The OECD Committee for Fisheries tries to find co-operative solutions to these problems. Member countries have held a country-by-country confrontation on the use of financial supports for national fishing industries, and the Committee has made recommendations for the reduction and eventual elimination of support measures which are inconsistent with rational production and the free development of competition between member countries. Members of OECD are also studying the reduction of import quotas and customs duties on fish and the establishment of common rules on such questions as minimum landing prices and bans.

The Committee for Fisheries has launched a study of the economic factors involved in the exploitation of the resources of the North Atlantic. The Committee is also encouraging member countries to promote modern distribution and marketing techniques for the export of fish and is encouraging the development of 'cold chains' so that quick frozen fish can be moved rapidly by refrigerated transport to inland markets. The Committee is also trying to establish common quality standards for fish and to harmonise sanitary regulations.

SCIENCE AND EDUCATION

Since economic growth is closely linked to scientific research and education, and governments are increasingly aware of the need for policies for science and education which complement their economic and social plans, OECD tries to relate scientific and educational planning to economic policies and, in particular, tries to encourage its countries to share the benefits of scientific research by developing joint programmes wherever appropriate. OECD has two Committees, the Committee for Scientific and Technical Personnel and the Committee for Scientific Research, which deal with these problems.

OECD organised a Conference of ministers of science in October 1963. The Ministers agreed on the need to establish priorities in scientific research and technological development and considered how OECD member countries could work together to make the best use of their resources. The Ministers established an Interim Committee which promotes the exchange of information between member countries and prepared a second Ministerial Conference, held in 1966. The three main subjects discussed were: the place of the social sciences and of fundamental research in science policy; international scientific co-operation; science and economic growth. To make parliamentarians more aware of the importance of science and technology in the modern world and in the hope of achieving a closer relationship between scientists and national parliaments, OECD and the Council of Europe have jointly organised two Parliamentary and Scientific Conferences (see p. 157).

In 1964 OECD extended its Country Review Programme to cover science policy, and the science policies of Sweden and Greece were examined. Reviews have since been made of science policy in France, Belgium, the Federal Republic of Germany and the United

Kingdom. The importance of education, for both scientific development and economic growth, has led OECD to establish a programme on long-term educational planning. At a conference held in Washington in 1961, educational targets were set, up to 1970, for the European members of OECD. OECD has also surveyed the scientific and technical manpower resources available in its member countries.

Under its Mediterranean Regional Project, which covers Greece, Italy, Portugal, Spain, Turkey and Yugoslavia, OECD consultants have stimulated these countries to work out how and to what extent national education programmes need to be developed during a fifteen-year period in such a way as best to help them achieve their aims for long-term economic development. Under this programme, national educational needs have been worked out up to 1975, as have their financial implications. The building of schools and colleges in these countries is being carried out on a co-operative basis.

The success of the Mediterranean Project has led Latin American countries as well as some industrialised OECD member countries to carry out similar schemes. Thus fourteen OECD countries take part in an Educational Investment and Planning Programme in which they exchange information about their educational programmes. The techniques worked out by OECD in its Mediterranean Regional Project have been applied in these later developments. In 1964 the Conference of European Ministers of Education invited OECD to set out, in a model handbook, the factors involved in planning educational investment, and this is being prepared.

OECD considers that the future scientific success of its member countries depends on the basic quality of science education in schools. It has accordingly launched a programme designed to make school curricula in science up to date and effective. A series of books has been published suggesting modern curricula for chemistry, physics, biology and mathematics. Pilot projects have been carried out in certain OECD countries along the lines suggested in these books. In Greece and Turkey, centres have been set up to manufacture scientific equipment paid for jointly by OECD and these countries. Travelling units for teaching physics have also been jointly financed for use in Italy, Greece and Turkey, and the use of television in science teaching is being studied.

OECD's interest in the pooling of scientific research and technological development has encouraged the growth of a large number of co-operative research projects in which about 300 scientific institutes are engaged. Under this system, elaborate research projects, which would otherwise be beyond the means of individual countries, can be carried out by several states working together, using existing laboratories. Metal fatigue, road research and water pollution are amongst subjects on which work of this kind is being carried out.

NUCLEAR ENERGY

To help meet Europe's growing energy needs, the Council of OEEC established the European Nuclear Energy Agency (ENEA), which has been continued by the eighteen European members of OECD. The United States, Canada and Japan are associate members. Because of the enormous cost of developing atomic fission as a source of industrial and domestic power ENEA tries, wherever possible, to pool research and development projects among countries which are prepared to work together.

ENEA is directed by the Steering Committee for Nuclear Energy which tries to harmonise the nuclear programmes of the member countries and promotes joint undertakings for the application and use of nuclear energy. The Steering Committee has set up a number of sub-committees and study groups including a top level group on co-operation in the field of research, together with study groups or groups of experts on the long-term role of nuclear energy in Western Europe, the production of energy from radio-isotopes, food irradiation, heavy-water production, third party liability and a Health and Safety Committee. A control bureau watches over the application of the Security Control Convention of December 1957, under which a European Nuclear Tribunal was set up to decide on questions and disputes arising from the application of the Convention.

Together with Euratom, the United States and Canada, ENEA set up a European–American Nuclear Data Committee in 1959 to review and co-ordinate the work of the member countries on the measurement of the nuclear properties of materials. To make the information on these measurements available to the nuclear centres and experts which need them, ENEA has established a Neutron Data Compilation Centre at Saclay in France which works in co-operation with American centres of this kind. A Computer Programme Library has also been set up by ENEA at the Euratom Joint Research Centre at Ispra in Italy. Another committee, the European–American Committee on Reactor Physics, was set up in 1961 to achieve co-operation between member states in their work on the neutron aspects of reactor physics. In addition, in 1965, a Committee on Reactor Safety Technology (CREST) was established.

Three major joint undertakings are sponsored by ENEA. One is the boiling heavy-water reactor at Halden in Norway, which began work on a joint ENEA Research and Development Programme in 1958. The original programme, which was twice extended, ended in 1964, but a new programme has begun in which the reactor is being used for long-term fuel element testing, and research into chemical reactions between the boiling water and the reactor fuel elements and core.[1]

The 'Dragon' reactor project at Winfrith in England is developing a high-temperature reactor with helium gas-cooling and graphite as a moderator. The Dragon project, which started in 1959 as a five-year Agreement, was extended to eight years in 1962.[2]

The third joint project which operates under the sponsorship of ENEA is the European Company for the Chemical Processing of Irradiated Fuels (Eurochemic), which was created by an international convention signed in 1957. This is a company owned by governments and industrial organisations in thirteen countries.[3] Eurochemic is concerned with the recovery of unburnt nuclear fuel from used fuel elements and has carried out research on the chemical treatment of these elements in order that unused fissile material may be recovered. It is also studying the separation of useful by-products of the fission process. Eurochemic's plant at Mol in Belgium began operation in 1966.

Members of ENEA have adopted common basic norms for protection against radioactive contamination. Radioactivity measurements are taken in all member countries so that countries can be warned of any extraordinary increase in the rate of radioactivity. Sixteen member countries of ENEA have signed a convention establishing a special regime to ensure that persons suffering personal or property damage as the result of a nuclear accident are properly compensated. Although work is done in ENEA concerning the transport of radioactive materials, no regulations have been established since it has been felt preferable that this should be regulated at a world level in the International Atomic Energy Agency.

[1] The countries taking part in this project are: Denmark, Finland, the Federal Republic of Germany, Norway, the Netherlands, Sweden, Switzerland and the United Kingdom. Italy and the United States take part through separate agreements.

[2] Countries taking part in this project are: Austria, Denmark, Norway, Sweden, Switzerland, the United Kingdom and Euratom (on behalf of its members).

[3] Austria, Belgium, Denmark, France, the Federal Republic of Germany, Italy, the Netherlands, Norway, Portugal, Spain, Sweden, Switzerland and Turkey.

Conclusions

Whereas OEEC set and achieved definite programmes and often acted as a decision-making body, its successor is primarily an organisation in which efforts are made to harmonise national economic policies and economic research is undertaken on an international basis. By virtue of the membership of the North American Countries and Japan and the participation of Australia in the work of DAC, OECD is an organisation of the industrialised countries, excluding the Soviet bloc, rather than a European grouping. With this wide membership there has been a dilution of that common interest which bound the members of OEEC closely together in the early 1950s, and hence of the capacity to formulate policies and take decisions in common. The preponderant influence of the United States in OECD has reinforced this trend, since the United States is opposed to the idea of being bound by decisions taken internationally in OECD. The American predominance has, moreover, led some Europeans to consider that it is in any event desirable for the Organisation's role to be strictly limited to that of carrying out studies and organising mutual consultation until the members of the EEC (or eventually of an enlarged EEC) can be represented in it as a unit on a basis of approximate equality with the United States. The OECD's constitutional limitations, which centre on the unanimity rule in the Council, are appropriate to these conceptions of its role as a research and consultative body.

The problems which have faced the members of OECD since its creation in 1961 have been different from those which OEEC tackled during the 1950s. Stemming from the economic circumstances of the 1960s, these problems include the acceleration of growth while minimising inflation, the development of new structures for agriculture and fisheries, the adaptation of manpower policies to cope with technological change and automation, and the unsatisfactory economic growth of the world's less developed countries. Most of these problems do not lend themselves to short-term, dramatic or direct solutions, and it is therefore hard to say how effective OECD has been in helping member countries to solve them, and to formulate their individual economic policies in a way which takes account of their partners' needs. As a clearing centre for the exchange of ideas and research and for the pooling of experience, however, OECD makes for the smoother, better informed and more forward-looking conduct of international economic and commercial relations. OECD's studies, which are generally of a high standard (thanks largely to the ability of the Secretariat), and its recommendations carry considerable weight and stimulate the member governments to rethink different aspects of their national economic policies; in this respect, the importance attached by the American Government to the work of the Economic Policy Committee has been of some significance. Finally, one of the most useful achievements of OECD is its work in discovering and presenting basic information on a comparable basis and thus making it possible to evaluate economic developments more effectively.

Part 7

CONCLUSIONS

Chapter Thirteen

CONCLUSIONS

Ten regional organisations have been examined in the previous chapters, and it is now possible to draw some conclusions that seem likely to apply to international organisations in general as well as some about these European organisations in particular.

The Membership and Political Orientation of the European Organisations

Europe is defined in geography as the land between the Atlantic and the Urals. Politically, however, it has come to mean different things to different people. The most important of these concepts of political Europe are defined in the membership of one or other of the European organisations, and have corollaries in the political orientation of these organisations, particularly in relation to the two great powers, Russia and the United States.

IDEOLOGY AND THE DIVISION OF EUROPE

Traditionally, political Europe has consisted of the European powers including Russia, that is to say Europe from the Atlantic to Vladivostok. This Europe was the basis for the first European organisation to be established after the Second World War, the ECE, where the use of the term 'all-European' is still stressed.

Stalin's ideological struggle and his crude use of Russia's power in Eastern European countries divided Europe, and this stood in the way of ECE's taking decisions of any importance. The experience confirmed a lesson that should be obvious enough, although it has not always been understood by those who wish to build a better world. Ideological and power conflicts among the members tend to hamstring an international organisation. The members must share a common political will if their organisation is to take political action;

and excessive political hostility is likely to stand in the way of any substantial joint action by the members even in a technical domain.

The most recent experience of ECE has, however, demonstrated the converse: an international organisation can become a useful vehicle of technical co-operation as political hostility declines. It is, moreover, reasonable to suppose that such co-operation can do something to reinforce the trend towards political convergence.

But for the division of Europe, Marshall aid might well have been channelled through ECE. As it was, the next major European organisation to be established was OEEC, which was concerned with the distribution of Marshall aid to the non-communist countries of Western Europe; and all the other organisations examined in this book consisted of groups of Western countries, and excluded the Eastern Europeans. In a number of cases the desire to enable Western Europe to resist the pressure of Stalin's Russia was an important motive for the establishment of an organisation; in the case of NATO it was, of course, the dominant motive.

As Russia after the death of Stalin became less intransigently hostile, détente with Eastern Europe became one of the themes underlying the work of Western organisations. The Council of Europe and OEEC, followed by its successor, OECD, have associated Eastern European countries with their work in various ways; and while NATO, as a defence organisation, has shown much greater reserve, it puts considerable energy into the exchange of information between its members about their contacts with the East, and has been seriously considering how it could, as an organisation, contribute to East–West détente.

The restriction of the membership of European organisations to Western Europe has posed particular problems for the Germans, for the division of Europe is at the same time the division of Germany. It is therefore not surprising that one of the main points of controversy about the organisations of which the German Federal Republic is a member has concerned the effect of these organisations on the prospects for German reunification. This question tends to be divisive in the main organisations of which Germany is an important member, that is the EEC and NATO.

There are three main lines of thought. There are those, including particularly the Gaullists and the communists, who are opposed to integration whether at European or Atlantic level and would regard it as hindering a solution of the German problem. There are the 'Europeans', who hold that the integration of Western Germany in a European Community, both for economic and defence purposes, is a precondition for the establishment of any stable system in Central Europe, of which a satisfactory solution of the German problem must be a part. And there are the Atlanticists, who include some of the 'Europeans' as well as others, particularly in Britain, who believe that continued military integration in NATO, together with American political support and almost certainly an American initiative, are essential if the German problem is to be solved. The interaction between these lines of thought will clearly have an important bearing on the future of the European organisations and on the concepts of political Europe that they represent.

RELATIONS WITH THE UNITED STATES

Relations with the United States are, indeed, one of the main axes around which the European organisations have turned. The Second World War and its aftermath demonstrated decisively that there were only two great powers in the world: America and Russia. Faced by Russian hostility, it was natural that Western European governments should depend upon America's financial support for their economic reconstruction and its military support for their defence. The similarities between the economic and political systems in America and in postwar Western Europe, and their sharp contrast with the systems of Eastern Europe, provided an ideological basis for this relationship.

Two organisations stemmed directly from the relationship with America: OEEC and NATO. The United States was not a full member of OEEC but, as the source of Marshall aid funds, it caused OEEC to be set up and had much influence over its form. On this as on many later occasions, American influence was exerted in favour of closer European unity: the Americans, supported by the French, were thinking in terms of a customs union and a supranational organisation. This degree of unity was blocked by the British, but OEEC nevertheless represented a closer unity than had previously been achieved by European states. When the OEEC countries later split into two economic groups—the EEC and EFTA—the United States and Canada became full members of the OECD, which succeeded it.

Just as the driving force for unity in OEEC was American money, so that in NATO was American strategic power. America undertook responsibility for both the conventional and the nuclear defence of Western Europe, and in return the European countries agreed to a measure of integration in terms of command structure, infrastructure and strategic planning, in which American generals, finance and policies were inevitably dominant.

Thanks to Marshall aid the economy of Western Europe recovered quickly; and having established the EEC, with the full support of America, the economic strength of the Six was further reinforced. The initial purpose of NATO was likewise shown to have been fulfilled when the Russian posture became gradually less aggressive. Thus the postwar American initiatives in Western Europe and the organisations that resulted from them had succeeded in their prime objectives.

Since, however, this relationship depended on Western Europe's weakness, which these organisations were intended to remove, their success carried within it the seeds of their own transformation. The conversion of OEEC into OECD has already been mentioned. As the Continent regained its strength, moreover, first France and then Germany began to ask for a greater say in the running of NATO.

Faced with these insistent demands as well as the great weight of the EEC in world trade in general and in America's trade in particular, President Kennedy, in his Independence Day speech in 1962, urged the idea of reorganising the relations between Western Europe and North America in the form of a partnership.

In the economic domain the first steps in partnership were clearly worked out. A tariff negotiation, which came to be known as the Kennedy Round, was proposed with a view to securing massive tariff cuts on both sides of the Atlantic, most particularly on those products that are important in transatlantic trade. The EEC, with its great importance as a trading unit, would be a powerful participant in the Kennedy Round, so that the proposal fully recognised Europe's newly-found economic strength.

Western Europe's economic strength had, however, not been reflected in any great access of strategic strength. In particular, the nuclear capacity of Western European countries was negligible when compared with that of the United States. Here, where no sort of equality existed, President Kennedy's proposal, although it was often qualified as 'equal' partnership, gave no clear indication as to how far it was intended that inequality between the two sides of the Atlantic should be reduced. The MLF proposal would have allowed European countries to participate in the financing and manning of a substantial nuclear force; but the possibility that Europeans would gain an effective share in the control of the force was only hinted at, while the main stress of American nuclear doctrine continued to be laid upon the need for centralised control of all nuclear forces, which meant in practice control by the President of the United States.

Many leading 'Europeans' were inclined to accept the MLF

proposal, regarding it as a step on the road to full equality with America and hence as a valid element in the proposals for equal partnership. For General de Gaulle, unfettered control of a national nuclear force was an essential part of his concept of independence; far from accepting the MLF as a step towards partnership, he decided to withdraw France from the military structure of NATO and thus to assert national independence from America. The British appeared to prefer the existing military structure; they did not object to American dominance, nor did they wish to be placed on a footing of nuclear equality with Germany either by losing the national deterrent altogether or by merging it within a collective force in which Germany's role would be the same as their own. They therefore proposed the ANF, in which the British deterrent would have been a separate component that could have been withdrawn by the British government if so desired.

These divergent reactions to the questions of nuclear control and status made agreement on the MLF and ANF plans impossible and, following an American initiative, the McNamara Committee was set up, where European members of NATO are informed and consulted about questions of nuclear strategy, but which is not intended to lead to any changes in the control of the deterrent that might make a reality of the concept of equal partnership.

The experience of postwar relations between Western Europe and America has shown that a hegemony can be effective under certain conditions. (The word hegemony is used, here and elsewhere in this book, as the most convenient to describe a relationship between a strong state and weaker states associated with it. As the word sometimes carries pejorative connotations, it may be worth adding that this does not necessarily imply that the strong state is abusing its power.) Thus there has to be on both sides a strong political motive for the relationship. This was provided by the desire in both Western Europe and America to prevent Russian domination of Europe, and by the fact that American military and economic support for Western Europe was the only way to ensure this, especially during the decade following the war. The dominant partner must also promote policies strong enough to fulfil the shared political objectives, while paying enough attention to the special interests and views of the weaker partners.

To the extent that the political motive is weakened on one side or the other, however, or the power balance between the dominant state and the others changes, the difficulties of this kind of relationship increase. As a consequence of the economic resurgence of Western Europe, the high degree of economic unity achieved by the

EEC in the heart of this area, and the reduction of tension in East–West relations, such difficulties arose in the Atlantic relationship. The policies that have emerged for meeting them are of three types, corresponding broadly to the reactions to the MLF proposal that have already been noted. One policy has been to conserve the existing relationship and its institutional forms (NATO and OECD) as far as possible. The second has been to maintain as close a relationship as possible between America and Western Europe while increasing the relative power and position of the latter by strengthening the institutions of European unity: the concept of partnership. The third has been deliberately to loosen the relationship between America and the countries of Western Europe. The results of these conflicting policies have been to create confusion in the Atlantic relationship and, in Britain at least, focus attention on the question of unity in Western Europe where, even if there are major problems, they do not stem from the great strains inherent in the relationship between small powers and a great power.

UNITY IN WESTERN EUROPE

The relations between the states of Western Europe are, by contrast, not much distorted by ideological divergences or by the imbalance caused by the presence of a dominant power among their number. The economic, social and cultural differences between the peoples of these states are in general small when compared with the differences between these peoples taken together and the peoples in other regions of the world. In these circumstances organisations designed to promote unity in Western Europe have flourished, and seven of the ten organisations examined in this book have exclusively Western European membership, though one of these, the OEEC, had Canada and the United States as associate members.

The Council of Europe contains all the democratic states of Western Europe and besides these OEEC also included Portugal and Spain among its members, but the membership of the other five organisations reflects divisions between these states. The three Communities, the EEC, the ECSC and Euratom, represent those states that decided, in the decade following the war, to move towards the establishment of a union with supranational or federal form. WEU consists of these states together with Britain, which was in 1954 the only European country with the military weight to make the construction of some sort of European framework for German re-armament possible, following the failure of the Six to provide this on a supranational basis in the form of a European Defence Community.

EFTA groups together, for trading purposes, most of the countries of Western Europe that did not join the supranational Economic Community. Thus the division of Western Europe into different groups of states centred around conflicting views about the relative merits of supranational and intergovernmental forms of organisation in Europe, which reflected divergences as to the intensity of political collaboration that would be desirable in the future.

The Form of European Organisations

The nature of international relations is such that it is impossible to provide scientific proof that one form of organisation is more effective than another. Since the relevant factors are never equal, a controlled experiment is not possible. The effectiveness of the different forms is therefore a matter for judgement rather than for conclusive proof. Given this limitation, it is possible to draw some conclusions on the basis of the studies of individual organisations in the preceding chapters.

THE CHARACTERISTICS OF INTERGOVERNMENTAL ORGANISATIONS

Apart from the three Communities, all the organisations examined in this book may be classed as intergovernmental. This is, indeed, the traditional form of international organisation. The taking of decisions is the exclusive responsibility of a Council of Ministers, one Minister representing each member government, and unanimity is the normal voting procedure, at least where decisions of political importance are concerned. The Council of Ministers is served by a secretariat which has in general little scope for initiative. In two of the European intergovernmental organisations, the Council of Europe and WEU, there are in addition assemblies consisting of members of the national parliaments, whose functions are consultative.

The scope for major achievements by such organisations is limited by the difficulty of securing agreement between the members. This applies not only to major new departures of policy. It is also hard to reach agreement on how to adapt policies to meet changing circumstances; and the detailed execution of policies by a number of governments, each responding to its own public opinion and perhaps interpreting the policies in various ways and with varying degrees of enthusiasm, is not generally conducive to efficiency. Substantial achievements are nevertheless possible in certain conditions.

One such condition has already been considered in examining relations between Western Europe and America: the presence of one state that is much more powerful than the others, and which is accepted as the leader of a coalition that may take the form of the organisation in question. It has been shown that such a relationship of hegemony has existed as between the United States and the European members in NATO. It was also present in the early years of OEEC in two forms: during the Marshall aid period, though the United States was not a full member, its dominant influence was very strongly felt as American agreement had to be secured for the distribution of aid in each of the first four years; and for a rather longer period Britain, being at that time easily the strongest of the full members, was able to exercise a form of leadership from within the organisation. Finally, when France, Germany and Italy, the other large members of OEEC, joined together in establishing the EEC, which Britain declined to join, the EFTA grouping which was set up by Britain and six of the small members of OEEC also took the form of an intergovernmental group led by one predominant member.

A second condition that tends to make intergovernmental organisations more effective is the existence of objective or external pressures, which may well take the form of crises that can be surmounted only by common action. One example was Europe's postwar economic weakness and the offer of Marshall aid to cure it provided that the allocation of such aid was jointly agreed upon by the European countries. Another was the fear of Stalin and the consequent reliance on America for defence. A third was the EFTA countries' fear of economic disadvantage should each country have to face the powerful EEC alone.

A third condition that can help to make intergovernmental organisations effective is the development of suitable institutions and procedures. The strength of the secretariat is a critical factor. Thus OEEC could not have dealt with difficult problems of economic reconstruction had it not had a staff large and able enough to master the technicalities involved and to hold its own in these matters with the national government machines. The effectiveness of a secretariat can also depend on the extent to which it is allowed to take initiatives and on the status of the Secretary General. Much of the ECE's best work, for example, has been embodied in its economic reports, since the first Secretary General established a high degree of independence for the secretariat in its research and publication policy. And the role of the political institutions of NATO was considerably enhanced when it was decided, in 1957, that the Secretary General should preside at all Council and ministerial meetings.

Two procedural devices that were evolved in OEEC have proved their value both in OEEC and in other international organisations: confrontation and the restricted group. The confrontation procedure was described on p. 83, whereby officials of the countries involved in a contentious problem have to justify their policies to officials of the international organisation and of the other member countries, at successive levels of the governmental hierarchy, so that the possibilities of reaching agreement have been thoroughly explored by the time a decision has to be taken at ministerial level. This procedure has not only been carried over from OEEC into OECD, but is also the basis of NATO's Annual Review of defence capabilities and military force goals; some of the process of decision-taking in the EEC also resembles the confrontation procedure.

The use of the restricted group was developed by OEEC (see p. 89) to overcome the difficulty of reaching unanimous agreement on a clear policy in an organisation with over a dozen members. The group usually consisted of representatives of the most important members and of one or two of the smaller countries, including those particularly concerned with the problem at issue. Agreement was more readily obtained in such a group and, given the membership of the group, their proposals were likely to be acceptable to the organisation as a whole. The technique has also been used from time to time in NATO, where it has been called the 'Wise Men' technique when the members of the restricted group have been particularly distinguished people. There is clearly less need for it in organisations with smaller membership, such as the EEC and EFTA; but if the EEC is enlarged so as to include, say, ten or more members, some such device may be found necessary.

The Council of Europe, too, has developed a useful device in the Partial Agreement, whereby a number of the member states can co-operate particularly closely on specific matters.

Two of the intergovernmental organisations examined, the Council of Europe and WEU, have consultative parliamentary assemblies, and two more, NATO and EFTA, have unofficial bodies of parliamentarians associated with them. It is clear that the assemblies and the unofficial bodies have some influence in relating the work of the organisations to opinion in the parliaments and to some extent to that of the peoples of the member countries. But the degree of that influence, which varies from time to time and as between the different assemblies and unofficial bodies, depending on various factors such as the roles of the several national parliaments with respect to the issues in question, the types of members selected to attend the sessions of the assemblies, and the importance of the work of the organisations themselves, cannot be confidently assessed in the absence of sufficient empirical research on the subject.

Although the presence of certain structural and institutional conditions can increase the effectiveness of intergovernmental organisations, however, there are rather strict limits to what they can achieve with respect to issues that are held by governments to be politically important. The existence of a dominant member in the organisation and of strong external pressures can overcome for a period the centrifugal forces inherent in a coalition of states, but over time the external pressures or the relationship of hegemony are liable to be reduced, and the organisation's period of real political importance is therefore likely to be of limited duration, probably associated with the existence of an economic or strategic crisis.

It is obvious enough that external pressures strong enough to cause crises will not last for ever; and certain causes of instability in relationships of hegemony have already been remarked upon. First the dominant member can fail in its role of leadership. This has on the whole been the case in OECD, in most of whose activities America, as the dominant member, has not shown itself to be deeply interested. It was the case of Britain in OEEC after the end of the Marshall aid programme, when the British resisted the common action at Western European level which most of the Continental members sought. It was the case in EFTA when Britain imposed the import surcharge against other members without the stipulated consultations. And it was the case when Britain, during the time of the EEC negotiations and of the establishment of WEU, failed to offer more than a minimal defence organisation at European level, although a powerful community was eagerly desired by the Six. Secondly, the weaker members can increase their strength and thus change the balance of power. This happened as between the Six and Britain in OEEC and later, in defence terms, in WEU; and it happened between Western Europe and America in OECD, and to a much lesser extent, in NATO.

Institutions and procedures designed to counter the centrifugal forces can certainly increase the effectiveness of intergovernmental organisations, by making it possible to take political decisions more efficiently while the crisis lasts and by facilitating smooth operation with respect to more routine matters when work of political importance is no longer possible; but it does not appear likely that such devices can in themselves overcome the resistance to common action in important political matters when the external pressures or the relationship of hegemony are no longer strong enough.

Such at least was the conclusion reached by those who decided to establish the supranational European Communities.

THE CHARACTERISTICS OF THE SUPRANATIONAL COMMUNITIES

The intention of the founders of the EEC, the ECSC and Euratom was to overcome these centrifugal tendencies of groups of sovereign states to the extent that would enable the members to act together on a sustained basis in matters of political importance. The institutions were designed to make this possible.

Before the institutional characteristics that have tended to lead to this result are analysed, it is necessary to remember that the relative economic strength of the six member countries is such that there is no relationship of hegemony in the EEC and the ECSC. France, Germany and Italy have populations of similar size and, while the Italian economy is still much the least developed of the three, those of France and Germany are not dissimilar, Germany's somewhat more powerful economy being compensated by France's greater political weight. It is, indeed, a basic characteristic of the EEC and the ECSC that they do not depend on the hegemony of one naturally dominant member. A serious, and perhaps the critical, weakness of Euratom on the other hand has been that in the field of nuclear energy France is predominant among the Six and has not chosen to exercise leadership in such a way as to put life into the organisation—quite the contrary, in fact. There was some fear, on the part of the four weaker countries, that the Franco-German Treaty would lead to joint domination of the EEC by France and Germany; but this Treaty has proved to be considerably less effective in unifying the policies of the governments than most of the inter-governmental arrangements examined in this book. It may be noted that the entry of Britain into the Community would not introduce any further danger of hegemony. On the contrary, a third member with the weight that now only France and Germany have would tend to improve the political balance within the Community, avoiding the alternatives of deadlock when France and Germany disagree and fears of domination when they act together.

It is also necessary to bear in mind that the institutions are but one element in a political context that includes not only the power relationship between the member states but also factors such as the degree of economic integration, the degree of 'social community', similarity of political institutions, geographical contiguity and a previous experience of working together.[1] All these may be of great importance in determining the success or failure of international organisations. But in this book, which is about the working of the institutions, it is the institutional factors that are naturally stressed.

The central feature of the Community institutions as they have worked so far is the relationship between the Commission and the ministerial Council of the EEC (see pp. 174–77).

The Commission differs from the secretariats of the intergovernmental organisations in three main ways. First, it has very important powers of initiative; for although the Council has to take decisions on many of the most important matters, it can do so only on the basis of proposals from the Commission, and can amend the Commission's proposals only by a unanimous vote. Except, therefore, in circumstances where all the governments agree with each other and disagree with the Commission, the Community's decision will have been drafted by the Commission. Second, the Commission is responsible for the direct execution of many aspects of policy and for checking that agreed decisions are in fact carried out where they are to be executed by national governments. Third, the Commission not only disposes of a civil service strong enough to carry out its tasks and to hold its own with the national civil services, but the Commissioners themselves have been men of political weight as well as administrative ability, the mixture of political and administrative scope having proved attractive to men of this calibre and having given them the opportunity to exercise their talents. Thus the Commission can speak and act for the general interest of Community Europe a great deal more effectively than the secretariats of the intergovernmental organisations could do with respect to the common interests of their member states.

In the Council, the main innovation is the wide provision for the use of majority votes. After the first two stages of the transitional period, which ended at the end of 1965, little scope remains under the provisions of the Treaty for the vetoing of decisions by individual member governments. The system of weighted majority voting is such that, in order to block a decision, one of the big countries (France, Germany or Italy) has to have at least Belgium or the Netherlands on its side. These constitutional provisions are of course subject to the statement of the French Government, at the Luxem-

[1] For a discussion of these factors see Karl W. Deutsch *et al.*, *Political Community and the North Atlantic Area*, Princeton University Press, 1967; and K. C. Wheare, *Federal Government*, Oxford University Press, 1951.

bourg meeting of foreign ministers in 1966, that it would not accept a majority decision which it believed to run counter to a vital national interest. The other five members agreed that a majority decision should not be applied where this would prejudice a vital national interest, but did not agree that each national government should be the judge as to which of its national interests were in fact vital ones. The Luxembourg meeting did not result in any changes in the rules for majority voting, but the French Government's declaration, if applied in a restrictive manner, may reduce their effectiveness in precisely those matters that are of greatest political importance.

The provision for majority voting in the Council greatly enhances the potential effectiveness of the Commission's right to initiate policy, because it reduces the scope for a small minority of member governments to block a measure that is held by the Commission to be in the general interest and is agreed by the majority of members. This relationship between initiatives from the Commission and the possibility of majority votes in the Council is, indeed, the key innovation in the Community as a policy-making body.

A second major factor that has enabled the Community to undertake politically important action is its wide range of competence. The chapter on the ECSC showed how that organisation was handicapped by being confined to only two industrial sectors; many of the ECSC's problems were related to larger problems of economic or of energy policy, and valid decisions could not be taken without securing agreement in these wider fields, which the institutions of the ECSC had no power to do. The EEC has, however, responsibilities over a large part of the vast range of economic policy. This not only removes many of the conflicts, of the type that have arisen in the ECSC and have helped to weaken that organisation, between the interests of sectors for which the Community is responsible and the interests of sectors for which it is not. It also gives the EEC a political weight that is denied to organisations operating on a narrower front. And it facilitates the taking of politically important decisions, because decisions on a range of subjects can be combined in a package deal which comprises some benefits as well as some disadvantages for each member country, whereas each of the decisions taken separately would be liable to be excessively disadvantageous for one or more members. The package deal has in fact become an essential element in the working of the EEC.

A third important element in the effectiveness of the EEC has been the precise and detailed provisions agreed in the Treaty with respect to a key issue: the removal of tariffs and quotas on the trade between the members and the establishment of the common external tariff. While the Treaty merely offered an outline with respect to other policy issues, leaving the details to be decided within the institutions, the detailed prior agreement on this issue ensured that the Community would act effectively in this very important matter, even if there were difficulties and delays in taking decisions on other questions. The momentum thus generated has been in itself a major political factor in carrying the Community forward. EFTA itself has also benefited from similar provisions regarding the removal of tariffs and quotas, although it has lacked most of the other characteristics that have given strength to the Community.

A fourth characteristic, whose presence has been a source of strength to the ECSC and its absence a source of conflict in the EEC, is the right to raise its own revenue. The ECSC can levy a small percentage of the turnover of coal and steel enterprises in the member countries, and this has enabled it to play an important role in investment policy and social policy in these industries, even at a time when it has lost political momentum. On the other hand, the 1965–66 crisis in the EEC, which exposed the difference between the governments of France and of the other five over the balance between national and Community interests and powers, was triggered off by the proposal that the revenue from agricultural import levies and also from customs duties on industrial imports should go to the Community, thus endowing it with a financial independence similar to that of the ECSC.

A fifth important characteristic of the Community is the provision, in the Court of Justice and the European Parliament, for the juridical and the representative aspects of government. Neither of these has yet played a major role in the development of the Community, because cases of great political importance have not yet come to the Court for decision, and because the Parliament lacks the standing of a directly elected assembly and most of the powers of a national parliament. Thus the Commission and Council have so far continuously been the central decision-taking bodies while the Parliament and Court have been peripheral. But if the Community is to continue to be responsible for taking decisions that may arouse acute political controversy in the member states, this situation may eventually change. National parliaments and supreme courts are likely to lie at the centre of such controversies. It may well be found that parliamentary and juridical institutions at Community level have an essential role in their resolution. The European Parliament could hardly fulfil such a role on the basis of its present powers and status; but it does provide a starting point if it is found that a stronger representative element in the Community institutions is required.

These five characteristics of the Community are among those that make its institutions stronger than those of intergovernmental organisations. Yet it is frequently said, and it has been said in this book, that the institutions of the Community will work only if the member governments share the necessary political will. What, then, is the difference between the Community and the intergovernmental organisations, for the effective working of which a similar condition was posed?

In the last analysis all political institutions depend on the political will of the citizens and groups within their jurisdiction. If the will to uphold the institutions disappears there is anarchy or civil war. The more homogeneous the citizens, the more firmly established the institutions, and the less controversial the problems they have to solve, the less the effort of political will required to make the institutions work. With heterogeneous groups of citizens, shallow-rooted institutions and deeply divisive problems, much greater political will is required. Moreover, the satisfactory operation of institutions in itself reinforces the political will required for their satisfactory operation in the future, thus engendering a benign circle, in contrast with the vicious circle of institutional failure causing political alienation which in turn causes further weakening of the institutions. The performance of the EEC institutions tends to show that they have approached more closely to the benign circle of mutually reinforcing institutions and political will than the intergovernmental organisations have been able to do. For the Community has managed to sustain the will to take effective decisions in such politically important questions as agricultural policy, external policy and cartel policy, over a period when political relations between the members have been otherwise strained, and without the compulsion of overriding external pressures. In similar circumstances the intergovernmental organisations have tended to deal only with politically unimportant issues or to develop rifts, particularly where they were not or ceased to be effectively led by a dominant member.

The question of tension between the formation of policies within those domains for which the Community has competence and policies in domains that still pertain exclusively to the national governments has already been raised. This tension, combined with the mutual reinforcement of the community institutions and the political will of the member states, is the basis for the theory of 'spillover'. In its crude form, this theory asserts that the tensions between matters of Community competence and matters of national competence will be reduced by the absorption of more and more subjects into the sphere of Community competence, at least until the whole of defence and foreign policy have been so absorbed. But the difficulties of the Community, faced with Gaullist opposition to the supranational elements in its institutions and to the extension of the Community method, have shown that belief in the automaticity of spillover depends on very favourable assumptions about the relationship between the existence of Community institutions and the political will to unite within the framework of such institutions. If the will to unite is not strong, it is possible that the tension between areas of Community competence and areas of national competence might remain unresolved over a long period; and if there is a strong will *not* to unite by means of the Community method, the tension may have the reverse effect of provoking an attack on the working of the Community method in the domains where the Community already has competence, as indeed happened when the French Government party boycotted the EEC institutions during the crisis of 1965–66. The spillover theory is useful, so long as it is modified to allow for a sober assessment of the member governments' political will to unite and their consequent reactions to the tensions that stem from the co-existence of community and national competences. The sufficiency of the political will for further measures of integration can never be taken for granted, at least until integration has taken place in the field of defence, and the armed forces are therefore at the disposal of Community institutions and not at that of the member states; and it is also necessary to keep under review the question of whether the will to unite, reinforced though it may be by the existing institutions, is sufficient to enable the institutions to carry out their existing functions effectively.

Even if the progress of the Community is less automatic than its enthusiasts have sometimes believed, the achievements of the EEC's first decade are still very impressive. The creation of a single market within a customs union has proceeded faster than was originally planned and is now nearly complete. Despite the complex and intractable problem of agriculture, a coherent Community agricultural policy has been evolved, and national policies have been harmonised or common policies have been formed in a mass of questions such as indirect taxation, transport policy and cartel law.

The Community's obvious success in practice has been reflected in efforts to establish economic groupings in other regions of the world, notably Latin America, and has attracted a number of those European countries that originally stood aside from the venture. Greece and Turkey have become associates; all the EFTA countries, Ireland and Spain applied for membership or association during the period of the British negotiations in 1961–63; the Austrians have since gone far in negotiating for an association agreement; and the British were at the time of writing once more moving towards the Six.

Britain and its Place in Europe

From 1945 to about 1960, one form or another of the concept of the three circles was the basis of established British doctrine about Britain's place in the world. Britain, as the best ally of the United States, the leader of the Commonwealth, and a leading European state, was the point where the three main circles of the free world intersected. The judicious exploitation of this fortunate position would give Britain an influence out of all proportion to its power.

Initially there may have been some hope that the relationship with the Commonwealth was the most important of these circles, but it was not long before it became clear that the national centrifugal tendencies of independent sovereign states with diverse interests were stronger than the traditional links, and that it was an illusion to suppose that the Commonwealth could give Britain the economic and strategic power and influence that had been derived from the Empire. This being so, the relationship with America was accorded much higher priority than that with either the Commonwealth or Europe.

This priority for the American alliance was a natural extension of the wartime partnership and rested comfortably on the common language and on many personal and historical links. It was, moreover, almost inevitable against the background of the cold war and in the absence of British belief in the possibility that a strong European union might be created in alliance with America.

Although the British wanted good relations with Western Europe and a certain amount of organised co-operation, there was no doubt that Europe came last among the three circles. The Commonwealth still loomed large in British minds; the alliance with America was a reality that made sense by the criteria of traditional diplomacy; and there was a pronounced lack of confidence in the prospects for the Continent of Europe. There was in the first place no realisation that the shattered economies of continental countries could within twenty years be rebuilt and surpass the British in prosperity and strength;

and for some years after the economic growth rates on the Continent could no longer be ignored, the British remained very sceptical about the general political capacity of the continental countries and in particular about their ability to unite effectively.

In these circumstances, the British Government strongly resisted any attempts to establish supranational organisations of which Britain would be a member. The British Government neither saw the need for radically changing the relations between states in a world which still seemed to offer it scope for the exercise of outstanding influence, nor would it have chosen Europe as the location of any supranational experiments in which it might have been persuaded to take part. OEEC and the Council of Europe were therefore established as intergovernmental organisations, after conflicts between the federally-minded governments of the Six supported by the United States on the one hand and the remaining countries of Western Europe, led by the British, on the other. Britain stood aside from the supranational ECSC and after the proposal for a supranational European Defence Community had been rejected by the French Parliament, substituted for it the intergovernmental WEU. The British response to the establishment of the EEC was the proposal to form an intergovernmental free trade area of all the OECD countries, which, while not being intended to destroy the EEC, certainly did not take much account of the conditions under which a supranational economic union might be expected to flourish. Finally, when the negotiations for a free trade area to embrace the whole of Western Europe broke down, Britain and Sweden took the lead in establishing the intergovernmental EFTA.

The end of the 1950s was, however, a watershed in British policy towards Europe. It was becoming clear that the Commonwealth was not a source of power for Britain and that it provided her with much less influence than had been hoped. At the same time respect for the achievements of the Continent of Europe was rising rapidly. Not only was it evident that the greater part of the EEC would shortly overhaul the formerly much superior British economy; but there was a growing appreciation of the political success of the Six in their drive towards unity, and of the practical effectiveness of the community method that they had developed.

Attitudes towards the Commonwealth and Europe were the independent variables in this reorientation of the British point of view. The attitude towards America changed largely as a function of the new attitudes towards Europe: if an effective union in Europe was feasible, the relationship with America would not necessarily have the same exclusive priority as it had before. The readjustment was, however, helped by official encouragement from the United States to regard a link with America through a European union as healthier than an attempt to maintain an Anglo-American 'special relationship', which tended to get in the way of American relations with other European countries, Germany in particular. The idea of giving Europe a higher priority was, however, confined in the thinking of the British Government largely to the economic domain. The evidence that Europe could unite was confined to this sphere, and there was little disposition in Britain to reconsider the exclusive priority for relations with America in matters of defence.

The first major evidence of a radical change in the British Government's thinking about Europe was the attempt of Mr Macmillan's Government to negotiate entry into the three Communities during 1961–63. The change had been sudden and, when General de Gaulle unilaterally broke off the negotiations against the protests of his partners in the Community, it was still not certain that, with the Labour Party effectively opposing the completion of the negotiations, British public opinion had accepted the prospect of membership.

Despite the veto, however, the British reorientation continued, and by the time that Mr Wilson began, in 1966, to explore the possibility of renewing the British application, acceptance of the principle that membership was desirable was much more widespread, both in Parliament and among the general public. Ironically enough at the same time as General de Gaulle had weaned French policy and much of French opinion away from its attachment to the Community's institutions, British opinion appeared to have evolved to the point of a ready acceptance of those institutions as they had been shown to work in practice.

As this book goes to press, it is far from certain that a British application will result in membership. If Britain does remain outside the Community, the structure of European organisations seems likely to remain for some years in much the same form as at present, although it is likely that the three Communities will be merged into one and possible that the Six will set up some kind of political union.

If, however, Britain joins the European Communities, certain important changes may follow for the other European organisations. EFTA would be wound up, with perhaps three of its members becoming members of the Communities and the others probably becoming associates. The prospect that the three existing Communities will be merged would be unaltered by British accession; and steps would no doubt also be taken to establish the beginnings of a European Political Community for foreign policy and defence. If such steps are successful, they are bound to affect both the Council of Europe and WEU. The former would no doubt continue to serve as a political forum in which the members of the Community would meet with non-members; but if Britain and other countries were at that time members, such political work as the Council of Europe now performs would tend to shift towards the Community nucleus. The political tasks of WEU would gradually be assumed by the Community, and WEU itself would lose its separate *raison d'être* if the Community developed defence competences.

The EEC, which is already represented in the meetings of the appropriate organs of OECD, could be expected to increase its importance in the proceedings relating to those matters for which the Community has competence, until OECD eventually becomes, with respect to these subjects, an organisation bringing together one large economic unit from each side of the Atlantic together with Japan and a number of smaller industrial states. If political union of the members of the enlarged Community were to develop into an effective Political Community with major responsibilities in defence as well as foreign policy, a similar development could take place in NATO. And any evolution in the relationship of Russia and other Eastern European countries with Western Europe and America might be reflected in relationships not only within the ECE, but also with other European and Atlantic organisations.

The precise form of any such developments cannot be foreseen. But it is at least necessary to remember that the existing structure of European organisations has been governed by three basic conditions: the political division of Europe into East and West; the alliance between the American great power and the relatively small countries of Western Europe; and the conflict between Britain and the Six over the priority to be given to union in Europe and whether the form of that union was to be supranational or intergovernmental. In so far as these basic conditions change, the structure of the organisations themselves can be expected to change as well.

SUMMARIES OF CHAPTERS ON ORGANISATIONS

This Section briefly assesses how far each of the organisations examined earlier in this book has succeeded in carrying out the tasks it was originally alloted or later undertook.

THE ECONOMIC COMMISSION FOR EUROPE

The Economic Commission for Europe was the first regional agency established under the United Nations Charter. Its terms of reference were widely drawn and it was given a considerable degree of independence from its parent body. The original objectives of the Commission were to initiate and to participate in concerted action for the economic reconstruction of the whole of Europe, to raise the level of European economic activity, and to strengthen the economic relations of the European countries with each other and with the rest of the world. When the Marshall offer to underwrite a full-scale European recovery programme was made, relations between the Soviet Union and the West had already deteriorated to such an extent that there was no real possibility of all-European economic co-operation. The Soviet rejection of the Marshall offer and the division of Europe into two political and economic camps meant that, for political reasons, ECE could not become an effective means for the economic reconstruction of Europe. Thus the political and economic differences between the two halves of Europe led to the development of Western European economic co-operation in OEEC (later OECD), the EEC and EFTA and of Eastern European economic co-operation in COMECON (later CMEA). Despite the Cold War ECE has been successful in obtaining all-European co-operation in research and in the exchange of technological and statistical information. In its early years the Technical Committees played a useful role in solving the problems caused by postwar shortages and, more recently, taking advantage of the atmosphere of *détente* which developed in the mid-1950s, ECE has removed many of the legal and administrative obstacles which restricted East–West trade. The economic research carried out by the Commission is of high quality and its Research Division's publications provide useful studies and statistics concerning the prospects for industrial and agricultural products.

It is likely that ECE will increase technical co-operation between Eastern and Western European countries and that it will continue to facilitate the growth of East–West trade. ECE cannot hope to achieve far-reaching measures of economic harmonisation because of the great differences in the political and economic systems of its Eastern and Western members, but it can help to further, in a practical way, the development of better relations between Eastern and Western Europe.

THE ORGANISATION FOR EUROPEAN ECONOMIC CO-OPERATION

OEEC's handling of Marshall aid laid the foundations for the subsequent development of European unity. The $11,500 million which the United States provided to enable Western European countries to restore their war-shattered economies, effectively allocated by OEEC, was the cornerstone of Europe's subsequent economic prosperity. The other main achievements of OEEC were the freeing of intra-European trade from quota restrictions and the establishment of an effective multilateral European payments system.

When faced with specific 'crisis' type tasks OEEC was seen at its best, particularly in its early years when the need to distribute and administer Marshall aid, and the leading role played by Britain in the Organisation, largely offset the institutional limitations of OEEC, notably the rule of unanimity for taking decisions in the Council. Thus when the member governments of OEEC shared a common and urgent problem, the Organisation was highly successful.

The creation of the European Economic Community in 1958 meant, however, that even before OEEC's transformation into OECD the major role of promoting European economic integration, through the establishment of a customs and eventually an economic union, had passed to the six states which were prepared to go beyond intergovernmental co-operation. Following the establishment of the EEC, it became clear that the basis for OEEC as a Western European organisation no longer existed, and it was transformed into an Atlantic organisation, the OECD (see p. 490).

THE COUNCIL OF EUROPE

If the Council of Europe is measured against the intentions of its founders it has clearly failed to achieve its main original aim: the political unity of Europe. For this the character of the original statute is to some extent responsible. The limited powers of the Committee of Ministers, which can only make recommendations, by unanimity, to member governments and cannot take binding decisions, prevented political progress. Further most member governments have shown little will to achieve political unity.

The Council of Europe has, however, served as the main parliamentary forum for the discussion of political and economic affairs by the countries of Western Europe as a whole. In particular, the Assembly has proved a valuable meeting-place in which parliamentarians from the EEC and EFTA countries have been able to discuss the problems of the economic division of Europe, and has provided the opportunity for leading politicians of European countries that are not members of the EEC to gain a clearer appreciation of the Communities' aims and methods.

On the intergovernmental side, the Committee of Ministers has built up a wide and complex structure of co-operation which has made the Council of Europe the principal framework for co-operation at Western European level in cultural, legal and social affairs. The Conventions established by the Council have been useful in harmonising national practices and standards on many subjects and have laid the foundations for a corpus of commonly applied European laws. The Council of Europe has also played an important moral role by pioneering its widely accepted Human Rights Convention, and it is the symbol of European democratic standards.

The Council will continue to have a role as the main international political forum in Europe until such time as the European Communities may be enlarged to include Britain and some other countries. The Council has moreover already started to develop contacts on a technical basis, between Western European countries and the countries of Eastern Europe.

THE EUROPEAN ECONOMIC COMMUNITY

Based on the experience of the working of the European Coal and Steel Community, the aim of the EEC was to apply the Community method to the whole range of industry and agriculture within the six member countries by, first, the establishment of a customs union and, eventually, the establishment of a full economic union. Since its creation in 1958, the EEC has practically achieved, ahead of schedule, its initial aim of setting up the customs union. Tariff reductions have been carried out without difficulty and the common external tariff is being established smoothly. Trade within the area has, as a result of the progressive creation of a single market, increased very rapidly.

The Treaty of Rome, which established the EEC, is a skeleton treaty which has left the institutions of the EEC with the task of formulating and putting into effect detailed common policies on a wide range of subjects such as agriculture and transport. Partly at the insistence of the French Government the EEC has also made great efforts to ensure that the single market for agricultural products will be completely established according to schedule. This illustrates a principle that has been fundamental to the work of the Community, that a fair balance must be found between the differing interests of the individual member countries and different facets of the economy, in the context of a growing awareness of a common interest.

The development of the Community method by the ECSC, the EEC and Euratom has been the most significant institutional development in the whole process of European unity. This method consists essentially of dialogue between an independent Commission representing the collective interests of the Community and a Council of Ministers representing the interests of each member state (in which provision is made for majority voting over many issues). It goes far beyond the institutional arrangements devised in the purely intergovernmental organisations such as the Council of Europe, WEU or OECD, in which decisions of the ministerial bodies can be taken by unanimity only and in which there is no independent executive representing the collective interests of the whole. Although the subject matter of the work of the EEC is economic, many community decisions on matters of major economic policies, such as food prices and tariff levels, are of considerable political significance.

Of the EEC's other institutions, the European Parliament and the Court of Justice are of substantial political importance, and are shared with the other two Communities, the ECSC and Euratom.

The scale of the Community's success was such that in 1961, the British Government, followed by Denmark, Norway, and the Irish Republic, posed its candidature for membership of the EEC. The breaking off of the negotiations between Britain and the EEC in January 1963 by the French Government led to a crisis of confidence within the EEC, and in 1965 the French Government precipitated a further crisis, concerned superficially with the financing of the common agricultural policy but essentially with the question of majority voting in the Council and the supranational character of the Community. Despite these two major crises, the EEC has continued to make progress towards the achievement of the customs union and an economic union, but since 1963 the EEC has been somewhat vitiated by a tendency for each agreement to be bargained over and closer watch to be kept on the respective sacrifices involved in each 'package deal'.

At present it is not clear whether the Community method, which has been successfully applied to tariffs and to some other economic matters in the creation of an industrial and agricultural common market, will eventually be applied to foreign policy and defence matters as well. Many 'Europeans' hope that this will happen. But it is unlikely while General de Gaulle is President of France, because of his fundamental opposition to the pooling of national sovereignty within the structure of supranational institutions. The hopes of 'Europeans' for the progressive construction of a federal United States of Europe on the basis of existing Community institutions must therefore wait on the General's departure. Whether the idea will then recover its momentum depends on whether the member governments can recapture the necessary will to unite.

THE EUROPEAN COAL AND STEEL COMMUNITY

The main value of the European Coal and Steel Community has been as the initiator of the Community method, which is now fully proved and which has been extended to the two subsequently created Communities, the EEC and Euratom. Although the formal powers of the High Authority of the ECSC are greater than those of the executives of the EEC and Euratom, all share the essential Community machinery of a continuing dialogue between an independent executive representing the common interest and a Council of Ministers whose members represent their national interests, within the framework of a Treaty that lays down common rules and procedures.

Politically the establishment of the ECSC was a practical and successful means of bringing about the reconciliation of France and Germany which was essential for the construction of the European Community. The ensuing political relations between these two countries in particular and the six members of the Community in general were governed by the fact that, in the vitally important coal and steel sectors of the economy, they had agreed to exercise jointly powers that had previously been wielded separately by national governments. The experience of the ECSC showed, moreover, that the working of important industries could be controlled and made subject to common policies across national frontiers and that a supranational executive could run the day-to-day official business relating to large and complex industries facing different problems in different countries.

The integration of the coal and steel industries of the Six was achieved quickly and successfully, and even though crises, particularly in the coal industry, have confronted ECSC with difficult economic and human choices affecting the long-term viability of the coal industry, wherever the member governments were willing to act in common these problems were overcome. Community action was, however, severely limited on those occasions when the member governments refused to work in common. In more recent years it became clear that the limitations of the sector approach to integration were considerable and, especially in view of the development of industrial and agricultural common markets within the EEC, that the ECSC should be merged together with the two other Communities of the Six.

THE EUROPEAN ATOMIC ENERGY COMMUNITY

When Euratom was established, it was generally considered that Western Europe was heading for a grave fuel shortage which the joint development of nuclear energy by the Six could help to offset. In fact conventional sources of power have become more efficient and new sources have been developed in Western Europe, so that Euratom's role has been less significant than was originally expected.

Within the comparatively limited context of encouraging and rationalising nuclear research and development concerning the peaceful use of atomic energy, Euratom has enabled its six members to organise their research and development programmes in a relatively economic way and has also enabled the results of large-scale research internationally planned and carried out to be made available to its separate member countries, which would have found it much more expensive to finance individual national research and development programmes on a comparable scale. The great emphasis placed by the French Government on the development of an autonomous French nuclear energy programme and its reluctance to co-operate with its five partners in Euratom have, however, been largely responsible for Euratom's potentialities not being fulfilled.

Many of the most important decisions affecting Euratom's future research and development programmes will not now be taken until the single merged Commission of the three Communities is established.

WESTERN EUROPEAN UNION

The primary reason for the creation of WEU arose from the defeat of the European Defence Community project in the summer of 1954, and the urgent need to provide a framework in which the Federal Republic of Germany could be rearmed and enabled to make a contribution to the defence of Western Europe, in response to the strong fears felt at that time of Soviet military power. The creation of WEU enabled the Federal Republic to build up armed forces which now constitute a substantial proportion of the conventional forces at the disposal of NATO Commanders. It is, however, one of the greatest ironies of the history of European unification that the fears which led the French National Assembly to reject the EDC Treaty, and with it the prospect of rapid progress to federal-type political and military institutions by the Six, led to the establishment of a separate German army within the loose framework of WEU instead of a German contribution to an integrated European force under common military and political institutions.

WEU was also intended to promote political, economic and social co-operation between its seven member countries. In view, however, of the economic work being carried out in OEEC, and of the fact that the Council of Europe offered a wider and more appropriate framework for the development of intergovernmental co-operation in other spheres, WEU has had little opportunity to develop such co-operation. In the spring of 1960 the social and cultural expert committees of WEU were transformed into committees of the Council of Europe.

Although the members of WEU are linked together by military commitments of a rather more binding nature than those set out in Article 5 of the NATO Treaty, there is no separate military command structure controlling the forces of the WEU countries. In practice, therefore, the main functions of WEU have been twofold: on the ministerial side there has been a degree of political consultation within the Council; and the WEU Assembly has provided a degree of parliamentary supervision over the work of NATO and of defence policy in general, and its committees' reports constitute a rich source of documents on subjects inadequately treated elsewhere.

THE EUROPEAN FREE TRADE ASSOCIATION

EFTA was established, following the breakdown in November 1958 of the negotiations within OEEC to set up a wider European free trade area, to enable European countries which were not members of the EEC to develop their mutual trade in industrial goods. The seven members of EFTA set out to demonstrate that trade can be freed from tariff restrictions, and the advantages of an expanded domestic market secured, with few common rules and minimal and flexible institutional arrangements. By means of a system of certificates of origin, the EFTA countries have shown that their industrial free trade area is workable. On the commercial front, trade between the EFTA countries in both industrial and agricultural products has risen markedly and tariff reductions have been carried through, without the members having adopted common policies or far-reaching institutional mechanisms. The Council of Association between EFTA and Finland has enabled Finland, whose Government faces political problems in taking part in the process of European unification, to participate in European economic co-operation.

Politically, although EFTA has enabled the European countries which are not members of the EEC to strengthen their position in some ways *vis-à-vis* the common market, it has also hampered their individual freedom in dealing with it. It has also given them a useful forum in which to consult on and concert their respective policies towards the EEC. There has, however, been a fundamental division within EFTA between countries such as Austria (which has already started negotiations with the EEC Commission concerning its association with the EEC), desiring to use EFTA as a means of easing and accelerating their eventual entry into the EEC and those, such as Portugal and Switzerland, which have considered that EFTA should concentrate primarily on the development of intra-area trade expansion. It has been a principle in EFTA that members should adopt a common attitude towards the EEC and that no one member of EFTA should take steps to join or associate itself with the EEC without full prior consultation with its partners. During 1966 there were signs that some EFTA countries, in particular Denmark, were restless about the continued discussions between the EEC and EFTA and considered that Britain had been too reticent over the reopening of negotiations with the EEC.

EFTA's commercial success has been qualified not only by the difference between its members in the ways in which they have sought to develop the Organisation, but also by the failure to create a single agricultural trading area within EFTA. This has meant that the more agriculturally orientated members, in particular Denmark, have had less opportunity to obtain commercial benefits from EFTA than the industrial members, such as Britain and Sweden. Finally, it is clear that EFTA's success is only relative and that EFTA is primarily a holding operation pending the eventual extension of the EEC. Meanwhile, the fact that EFTA consists of diverse and geographically separated countries, one of which, Britain, is preponderant while the other six are much smaller, makes it unlikely that EFTA will develop more ambitious aims. The difficulties of the imbalance within EFTA were clearly demonstrated by the disruptive effects of the British Government's imposition of a 15 per cent import surcharge in October 1964, without prior consultation with its EFTA partners.

THE NORTH ATLANTIC TREATY ORGANISATION

The establishment of NATO, at a time when Western Europe was threatened by Soviet military powers, has discouraged any attempt by the Soviet Union to exert effective military pressure on any member of the Alliance. The United States has inevitably predominated both politically and militarily over the European members of NATO by virtue of its size and resources and in the absence of a European union in the field of defence. The military structure of the alliance, both in the early years, before the Soviet Union acquired nuclear weapons, and more recently, has been essentially under American command, with American Supreme Commanders both on the European mainland and in the North Atlantic Area, and with the ultimate decisions on the use of the nuclear capability of the Alliance in the hands of the President of the United States.

This situation, although unsatisfactory to many Europeans, worked well while Europe was weak and divided and while the fear of Soviet military aggression persisted. With changing circumstances, however, notably Europe's economic recovery, the development of European unity, and the emergence of new strategic factors such as the ability of the Soviet Union to bombard American cities with nuclear missiles, American predominance has in recent years become increasingly irksome to European members of the Alliance, who feel that they should have some say in nuclear planning and control and would like to see greater equality between the American and European sides of the Alliance.

The proposals made by the American and British Governments respectively for a Multilateral Force and for an Atlantic Nuclear

Force did not prove acceptable to enough members of NATO, though the system of nuclear consultation worked out in Mr McNamara's Special Committee of Defence Ministers has met with a warmer response. The French Government has meanwhile asserted its independence by withdrawing from the military structure of NATO and insisting on the autonomous command of its own national forces. On the other hand it is widely believed in Europe that separate national forces are now incapable of providing either effective deterrence or defence, so that if Europe's defence is to be assured independently of the United States it must be through military integration between the European allies. Official proposals for integration have not, however, been made since the collapse of the project for a European Defence Community in 1954, nor does there seem to be any prospect of an early reform of NATO along these lines, following the French withdrawal from its military structure.

Although the political danger posed by the Soviet Union seems to have receded, fears of possible military pressure remain and the NATO governments consider that a Western military alliance will be necessary, at least so long as relations between Eastern and Western Europe remain unstable, in the absence of peaceful settlement of the German problem.

THE ORGANISATION FOR ECONOMIC CO-OPERATION AND DEVELOPMENT

The membership of OECD includes the United States, Canada and Japan, besides Western European countries. The main purpose of the Organisation is to influence the member governments to frame their economic policies in such a way that they fit in with and take account of those of their partners.

The economic problems with which OECD is concerned are, however, different from those that were dealt with by OEEC in the 1950s. They are mainly long-term problems such as economic growth, price stability, structural changes in agriculture and fisheries, manpower policy, automation, and relations with the developing countries.

Most of these problems are such that it is hard for an intergovernmental organisation to make a major contribution to their solution, and the role of the Organisation has been that of a useful economic research laboratory, rather than of a body that commits the member governments to clearly defined or far-reaching common policies on major economic issues.

The research studies carried out by OECD are of high quality and they give governments a detailed knowledge of each other's policies.

The Organisation has been a clearing house for the exchange of ideas and research and for the pooling of the separate economic experiences of its different members, As such, OECD has exerted a certain beneficial influence over national economic policy-making and in particular over the conduct of international economic and commercial relations by its members.

Appendix I

LIST OF ABBREVIATIONS

ACE	Allied Command Europe
AFCENT	Allied Forces Central Europe
AGARD	Advisory Group on Aeronautical Research and Development, of NATO
AIRCENT	Air Forces Central Europe
ALLA	Allied Long Line Agency, of NATO
AMCEC	Allied Military Communications—Electronics Committee, of NATO
ANCA	Allied Naval Communications Agency, of NATO
ANF	Atlantic Nuclear Force
ARFA	Allied Radio Frequencies Agency, of NATO
ATIC	Association Technique de l'Importation Charbonnière
BENELUX	Belgium, Netherlands and Luxembourg Customs Union
BIS	Bank for International Settlements
CCC	Council for Cultural Co-operation, of the Council of Europe
CCRN	Consultative Committee for Nuclear Research, of Euratom
CEA	Commission de l'Energie Atomique
CEEC	Committee for European Economic Co-operation
CERN	European Nuclear Research Centre
CIAP	Inter-American Committee for Progress
CID	Information and Development Centre, of Euratom
CMEA	Committee for Mutual Economic Assistance (formerly COMECON)
COBECHAR	Comptoir Belge du Charbon
COCOR	Co-ordinating Committee, of ECSC
COPA	Comité des Organisations de Producteurs Agricoles
CREST	Committee on Reactor Safety Technology, of ENEA

CST	Scientific and Technical Committee, of Euratom
DAC	Development Assistance Committee, of OECD
ECA	United States Economic Co-operation Administration
ECE	Economic Commission for Europe
ECITO	European Central Inland Transport Organisation
ECO	European Coal Organisation
ECSC	European Coal and Steel Community
EDC	European Defence Community
EEC	European Economic Community
EECE	Emergency Economic Committee for Europe
EFTA	European Free Trade Association
ELDO	European Launcher Development Organisation
EMA	European Monetary Agreement
ENEA	European Nuclear Energy Agency
EPA	European Productivity Agency
EPC	European Political Community
EPU	European Payments Union
ESRO	European Space Research Organisation
EURATOM	European Atomic Energy Community
EUROCHEMIC	European Company for the Chemical Processing of Irradiated Fuels
FAO	Food and Agriculture Organisation
FDP	Freie Demokratische Partei
FEB	Financial and Economic Board, of NATO
FINABEL	Meetings of Chiefs of Staff of the Six EEC Countries
FINEFTA	Finland-European Free Trade Association Agreement of Association
GATT	General Agreement on Tariffs and Trade
GEORG	Gemeinschaftsorganisation Ruhrkohle
IAEA	International Atomic Energy Agency
IBRD	International Bank for Reconstruction and Development
ILO	International Labour Organisation
IMC	International Materials Conference, of OEEC
IMF	International Monetary Fund
LANDCENT	Land Forces Central Europe
MAS	Military Agency for Standardisation, of NATO
MLF	Multilateral Nuclear Force
NADGE	NATO Air Defence Ground Environment
NATO	North Atlantic Treaty Organisation

OECD	Organisation for Economic Co-operation and Development
OEEC	Organisation for European Economic Co-operation
OKU	Oberrheinische Kohlenunion
PDSI	Partita Democratica Socialista Italiana
PSI	Partita Socialista Italiana
SAC	United States Strategic Air Command
SACLANT	Supreme Allied Commander, Atlantic
SACEUR	Supreme Allied Commander, Europe
SETEL	Société Européenne de Téléguidage
SHAPE	Supreme Headquarters Allied Powers in Europe
SWNCC	United States State-War-Navy-Co-ordinating Committee
TCC	Temporary Council Committee, of NATO
UN	United Nations
UNCTAD	United Nations Conference on Trade and Development
UNICE	Union des Industries des Communautés Européennes
UNR	Union pour la Nouvelle République
UNRRA	United Nations Relief and Rehabilitation Administration
WHO	World Health Organisation

Appendix II

MEMBERSHIP OF EUROPEAN ORGANISATIONS

	ECE	OEEC	Council of Europe	EEC	ECSC	Euratom	WEU	EFTA	OECD	NATO
Austria	M	M	M	—	—	—	—	M	M	—
Belgium	M	M	M	M	M	M	M	—	M	M
Cyprus	M	—	M	—	—	—	—	—	—	—
Denmark	M	M	M	—	—	—	—	M	M	M
Finland	M	—	—	—	—	—	—	AM	S	—
France	M	M	M	M	M	M	M	—	M	†
Fed. Rep. of Germany	M	M	M	M	M	M	M	—	M	M
Greece	M	M	M	A	—	—	—	—	M	M
Iceland	M	M	M	—	—	—	—	—	M	M
Ireland	M	M	M	—	—	—	—	—	M	—
Italy	M	M	M	M	M	M	M	—	M	M
Luxembourg	M	M	M	M	M	M	M	—	M	M
Malta	M	—	M	—	—	—	—	—	—	—
Netherlands	M	M	M	M	M	M	M	—	M	M
Norway	M	M	M	—	—	—	—	M	M	M
Portugal	M	M	—	—	—	—	—	M	M	M
Spain	M	M	S	—	—	—	—	—	M	—
Sweden	M	M	M	—	—	—	—	M	M	—
Switzerland	AM	M	M	—	—	—	—	M	M	—
Turkey	M	M	M	A	—	—	—	—	M	M
United Kingdom	M	M	M	—	S	—	M	M	M	M
Yugoslavia	M	S	—	—	—	—	—	—	S	—
Canada	—	AM	—	—	—	—	—	—	M	M
United States	M	AM	—	—	—	—	—	—	M	M

M represents full membership, and AM associate membership; A represents an agreement of association with the organisation. S represents participation in certain activities of an organisation or a special relationship with it. The Soviet Union and other Eastern European countries are members of ECE. Japan is a member of OECD and Australia is a member of its Development Assistance Committee. All the countries listed above are members of the United Nations with the exception of the Federal Republic of Germany and Switzerland. †In 1966 France withdrew from the military structure of NATO while remaining a member of the Alliance and continuing to take part in the political activities of the Council.

SELECTED BIBLIOGRAPHY

This bibliography is not comprehensive but indicates certain books and articles which the authors of this report consider to be particularly useful. Further information about individual organisations can be obtained from their information services whose addresses are set out below. Most of the organisations publish both detailed annual reports which give a full picture of their activities and also information magazines or bulletins. *The European Yearbook*, published by Nijhoff, The Hague, is a most valuable source of information and documentation as is *The Annual Register*, published by Longmans, Green, London and *L'Année Politique* published by the WEU Assembly, Paris. PEP has published, both alone and in conjunction with the Royal Institue of International Affairs, a series of specialised studies on different aspects of the work of the European Communities and other European problems: further details may be obtained from PEP, 12 Upper Belgrave Street, London SW1.

GENERAL

Albonetti, Achille, *Préhistoire des Etats-Unis de l'Europe*, Paris, Sirey, 1963.

Aron, Raymond (ed.), *La Querelle de la CED*, Paris, Armand Colin, 1956.

Ball, M. Margaret, *NATO and the European Movement*, London, Stevens, 1959.

Beever, R. Colin, *European Unity and the Trade Union Movement*, Leyden, Sythoff, 1959.

Beloff, Max, *Europe and the Europeans*, London, Chatto and Windus, 1957.

Beloff, Max, *New Dimensions in Foreign Policy*, London, Allen and Unwin, 1961.

Beloff, Max, *The United States and the Unity of Europe*, London, Faber, 1963.

Benoit, Emile, *Europe at Sixes and Sevens*, New York, Columbia, 1961.

Brugmans, Henri, *L'Idée Européenne 1918–65*, Bruges, de Tempel, 1965.

Buchan, A., and Windsor, P., *Arms and Stability in Europe*, London, Chatto and Windus, 1963; New York, Frederick A. Praeger, 1963.

Cleveland, Harold van B., *The Atlantic Idea and Its European Rivals*, New York, McGraw-Hill, 1966.

The Economist Intelligence Unit, *The Commonwealth and Europe*, London, 1960.

Ganshof van der Meersch, W. J., *Organisations Européennes*, Brussels, Etablissements Emile Bruylant, 1966.

Granbord, Stephen, R. (ed.), *A New Europe*, London, Oldbourne, 1965.

Haines, C. Grove (ed.), *European Integration*, Baltimore, Johns Hopkins University Press, 1957.

Hay, Peter, *Federation and Supra-National Organizations*, Illinois. University of Illinois Press, 1966.

Horsfall Carter, W., *Speaking European—The Anglo-Continental Cleavage*, London, Allen and Unwin, 1966.

Kitzinger, U. W., *The Politics and Economics of European Integration*, New York, Praeger, 1963.

Kleiman, Robert, *Atlantic Crisis*, London, Sidgwick and Jackson, 1965.

Kraft, Joseph, *The Grand Design*, New York, Harper, 1962.

Lapie, O., *Les Trois Communautés*, Paris, Fayard, 1960.

Lindsay, Kenneth, *European Assemblies*, London, Stevens, 1960.

Marchal, André, *L'Europe Solidaire*, Paris, Cujas, 1965.

Massip, Roger, *De Gaulle et l'Europe*, Paris, Flammarion, 1963.

Mayne, Richard, *The Community of Europe*, London, Gollancz, 1962.

Meade, James, Leisner, H. H., and Wells, S. J., *Case Studies in European Economic Union*, Oxford, Oxford University Press, 1962.

Passeron, André, *De Gaulle Parle—1962–66*, Paris, Fayard, 1966.

Pickles, Dorothy, *The Uneasy Entente—French Foreign Policy and Franco-British Misunderstanding*, London, Royal Institute of Internationa-Affairs, 1966.

Pinder, John, *Europe against de Gaulle*, London, Pall Mall for the Federal Trust, 1964.

Pinto, Roger, *Les Organisations Européennes* (2nd edition), Paris, Payot, 1964.

Reuter, Paul, *Institutions Internationales* (revised edition), Paris, Presses Universitaires de France, 1955.

Robertson, A. H., *European Institutions* (revised edition), London, Stevens, 1966.

Sannwald, R. F., and Stonle, J. *Economic Integration*, New Jersey, Princeton, 1959.

Schuman, Robert, *Pour l'Europe* (2nd edition), Paris, Nagel, 1964.

Tracy, Michael, *Agriculture in Western Europe—Crisis and Adaptation since 1880*, London, Cape, 1964; New York, Frederick A. Praeger, 1964.

Trempont, Jacques, *L'Unification de l'Europe*, Amiens and Brussels, Editions Scientifiques et Littéraires, 1955.

Triffin, Robert, *Europe and the Money Muddle*, New Haven, Yale University Press, 1957.

Uri, Pierre, *Partnership for Progress*, New York, Harper, 1963.

Von Geusau, Alting, *European Organizations and Foreign Relations of States*, Leyden, Sythoff, 1962.

Worswick, C. D. N. (ed.), *The Free Trade Proposals*, Oxford, Blackwells, 1960.

ECE

Rostow, W. W., The Economic Commission for Europe, in *International Organization*, Volume 3, 1949.

Wightman, David, *Economic Co-operation in Europe—A Study of the*

United Nations Economic Commission for Europe, London, Stevens and Heinemann, 1956.

ECE—The First Fifteen Years, Geneva, the International Secretariat, 1962.

For further information write to: The Director of Information,
ECE,
Palais des Nations,
Geneva.

OEEC

Diebold, William, Jr., *Trade and Payments in Western Europe*, New York, Harper, 1952.

Gordon, Lincoln, The Organization for European Economic Co-operation, in *International Organization*, Volume 10, 1956.

Jones, Joseph M., *The Fifteen Weeks*, New York, Viking Press, 1955.

Roll, Sir Eric, Ten Years of European Co-operation, *Lloyds Bank Review*, April 1958.

Ninth Annual Report, *A Decade of Co-operation*, Paris, the International Secretariat, 1958.

For further information write to: The Director of Information,
OECD,
2 rue André Pascal,
Paris XVI.

COUNCIL OF EUROPE

Carstens, Karl, *Das Recht des Europarats*, Berlin, Duncker and Humblot, 1956.

Duclos, Pierre, *Le Réforme du Conseil de l'Europe*, Paris, Bibliothèque de textes et études fédéralistes, 1958.

Duclos, Pierre, *Le Conseil de l'Europe*, Paris, Presses Universitaires de France, 1960.

Haas, Ernst B., *Consensus Formation in the Council of Europe*, Berkeley, University of California Press, 1960.

Leuprecht, Peter, Der Europarat, *Jahrbuch des Offentlichen Rechts der Gegenwart*, New Format, Volume XV.

Lindsay, Kenneth, *Towards a European Parliament*, Strasbourg, Council of Europe, 1958.

Rencki, Georges, *L'Assemblée Consultative du Conseil de l'Europe*, Paris, Union fédéraliste inter-universitaire, 1956.

Robertson, A. H., *The Council of Europe* (2nd edition), London, Stevens, 1962.

The Consultative Assembly—Procedure and Practice (5th edition), Strasbourg, Council of Europe, 1965.

Man in a European Society—Programme of Work for the Intergovernmental Activities of the Council of Europe, Strasbourg, Council of Europe, 1966.

Selected Bibliography

For further information write to: The Director of Information,
The Council of Europe,
Strasbourg.

THE EUROPEAN ECONOMIC COMMUNITY

Beloff, Nora, *The General Says No*, London, Penguin, 1963.

Campbell, A., and Thompson, D., *Common Market Law*, London, Stevens, 1962.

Camps, Miriam, *Britain and the European Community 1955–63*, London, Oxford University Press, 1965.

Camps, Miriam, *What Kind of Europe?*, London, Oxford University Press, 1965.

Camps, Miriam, *European Unification in the Sixties—From the Veto to the Crisis*, New York, McGraw-Hill, 1966.

Clark, Colin, *British Trade in the Common Market*, London, Stevens, 1962.

Clerc, François, *Le Marché Commun Agricole*, Paris, Presses Universitaires de France, 1964.

Deniau, J. F., *The Common Market* (3rd edition), London, Pall Mall, 1962.

Drouin, Pierre, *L'Europe du Marché Commun*, Paris, Julliard, 1965.

Frank, Isaiah, *The European Common Market . . . An analysis of Commercial Policy*, London, Stevens, 1961.

Hallstein, Walter, *United Europe—Challenge and Opportunity*, London, Oxford University Press, 1962.

Houben, P. H. J. M., *Les Conseils de Ministres des Communautés Européennes*, Leyden, Sythoff, 1964.

Kitzinger, U. W., *The Challenge of the Common Market* (4th edition), Oxford, Blackwells, 1963.

Lemaignen, R., *Europe au Berceau*, Paris, Plon, 1964.

Lindberg, Leon, *The Political Dynamics of European Economic Integration*, Oxford University Press, 1963.

Pinder, John, *Britain and the Common Market*, London, Cresset Press, 1961.

Pryce, Roy, *The Political Future of the European Community*, London, Marshbanks, 1962.

Shanks, Michael and Lambert, John, *Britain and the New Europe: the future of the Common Market*, London, Chatto and Windus, 1962; New York, Frederick A. Praeger, as *The Common Market, Today—And Tomorrow*, 1962.

Valentine, D. G., *Court of Justice of the European Communities*, London, Stevens, 1965.

Van Oudenhove, Guy, *The Political Parties in the European Parliament*, Leyden, Sythoff, 1965.

The Negotiations on Political Union, London, PEP, 1962.

The Parliament of the European Communities, London, PEP, 1964.

For further information write to: The Official Spokesman,
European Economic Community,

23–27 avenue de la Joyeuse Entrée,
Brussels 4,
Belgium.

or: Head of Information Service,
European Communities Information Service,
23 Chesham Street, London SW1.

THE EUROPEAN COAL AND STEEL COMMUNITY

Diebold, William, *The Schuman Plan*, New York, Praeger, 1959.

Haas, Ernst B., *The Uniting of Europe*, London, Stevens, 1958.

Mason, Henry L., *The European Coal and Steel Community*, The Hague, Nijhoff, 1955.

Monnet, Jean, *Les Etats-Unis d'Europe ont Commencé*, Paris, Laffont, 1955.

Scheingold, Stuart, *The Rule of Law in European Integration*, New Haven, Conn., Yale University Press, 1965.

Wigny, Pierre, *Un Témoignage sur la Communauté des Six*, Luxembourg, ECSC, 1957.

For further information write to: Official Spokesman,
The European Coal and Steel Community,
High Authority,
2 Place de Metz,
Luxembourg.

or: Head of Information Service,
European Communities Information Service,
23 Chesham Street, London SW1.

EURATOM

Errera, Jacques and others, *Euratom, Analyses et Commentaires*, Brussels, Bibliothèque de l'Institut Belge de Science Politique, 1958.

Moore, Ben T., *Euratom—The American Interest in the European Atomic Energy Community*, New York, Harper, 1958.

Polack, Jaroslav, *Euratom*, Dobbs Ferry, N.Y. Oceana Publications, no date.

Euratom's Second Five-Year Research Programme (Topic No. 23) Brussels, The Press and Information Service of the European Community, no date.

Euratom Joint Research Centre (Topic No. 16), Brussels, The Press and Information Service of the European Community, no date.

Répertoire des Installations Nucléaires de la Communauté Européenne de l'Energie Atomique (4th edition), Brussels, Euratom Commission, 1966.

Selected Bibliography

For further information write to: The Official Spokesman,
European Atomic Energy Community,
51–53 rue Belliard,
Brussels,
Belgium.

WEU

Borcier, P., *The Contribution of the Assembly of WEU to Western Defence*, Paris, WEU Assembly, 1959.

Fesseri, E., L'Agence de l'UEO pour le Controle des Armements, in *The European Yearbook*, Volume 5, 1959.

Fischer, P., Dreijährige Bilanz der Westeuropäischen Union, in *Europa Archiv*, Volume 2/3, 1959.

Robertson, A. H., The Creation of the Western European Union, in *The European Yearbook*, Volume 2, 1956.

Britain in Western Europe—WEU and the Atlantic Alliance, London, Royal Institute of International Affairs, 1956.

Ten Years of Seven-Power Europe, Paris, WEU Assembly, 1964.

For further information concerning (1) The Council write to:
The Librarian,
Western European Union,
9 Grosvenor Place,
London SW1.
(2) The Assembly write to:
The Press Counsellor,
WEU Assembly,
43 Avenue du President Wilson,
Paris XVI.

EFTA

Baumgartner, Max, *Das Zollrecht der Europäischen Freihandels-assoziation*, Basle, Verlag für Recht und Gesellschaft, 1960.

Figgures, Frank E., Legal Aspects of the European Free Trade Association, *The International and Comparative Law Quarterly*, October, 1965.

Green, S. A., and Gabriel, K. W. B., *The Rules of Origin*, Geneva, EFTA, 1965.

Jantzen, Torben, *The Operation of a Free Trade Area*, Geneva, EFTA, 1964.

Lambrinidis, John S., *The Structure, function, and law of a free trade area: the European Free Trade Association*, London, Stevens, 1965; New York, Frederick A. Praeger, 1965.

Long, Olivier, *The European Free Trade Association*, Geneva, EFTA, no date.

Meyer, F. V., *The Seven: A provisional appraisal of the European Free Trade Association*, London, Barrie and Rockliffe, 1960.

Mori, Roland, *Rechtssetzung und Vollzug in der Europäischen Freihandels-assoziation*, Winterthur, P. G. Keller, 1965.

Building EFTA—A Free Trade Area in Europe, Geneva, EFTA, 1966.

Legal Problems of the European Economic Community and the European Free Trade Association: A Report of a Conference, British Institute of International and Comparative Law, London, Stevens, 1961.

The European Free Trade Association, EFTA, London, Central Office of Information, 1963.

Further information may be obtained from: The Department of Press and Information,
EFTA,
32 Chemin des Colombettes,
Geneva.

OECD

Kristensen, Thorkil, Two Conditions for Solving our New Economic Problems, in *The European-Atlantic Review*, Autumn 1966.

Kristensen, Thorkil, OECD in the Years Ahead, *OECD Observer*, October 1966.

Rubin, Seymour J., *The Conscience of the Rich Nations—DAC and the Common Aid Effort*, New York, Harper and Row, 1966.

La Mission de l'OCDE—Conclusions du Groupe de Liaison du Conseil des Fédérations Industrielles d'Europe avec l'OCDE, Paris, Patronat Français, 1962.

The Organization for Economic Co-operation and Development, Washington, Senate Committee on Foreign Relations, 1961.

Organisation for Economic Co-operation and Development—History, Aims and Tasks, Structure and Functions, Paris, OECD, 1963.

For further information write to: The Director of Information,
OECD,
2 rue André Pascal,
Paris XVI.

NATO

Beaufre, General, *L'OTAN et l'Europe*, Paris, Calmann-Lévy, 1966.

Buchan, Alastair, *NATO in the 1960s*, London, Chatto and Windus, 1960; Revised edition, New York, Frederick A. Praeger, 1963.

Buchan, Alastair and Windsor, Philip, *Arms and Stability in Europe*, London, Chatto and Windus, 1963; New York, Frederick A. Praeger, 1963.

Ismay, Lord, *NATO—The First Five Years*, Paris, NATO, 1954.

Kahn, Herman, *On Escalation*, New York, Praeger, 1965.

Kissinger, Henry A., *The Necessity for Choice*, New York, McGraw-Hill, 1961.

Kissinger, Henry A., *The Troubled Partnership*, New York, McGraw-Hill, 1965.

Moore, Ben T., *NATO and the Future of Europe*, New York, Harper, 1958.

Mulley, Frederick, *The Politics of Western Defence*, London, Thames and Hudson, 1962.

Munk, Frank, *Atlantic Dilemma*, Dobbs Ferry, N.Y., Oceana Publications, 1964.

Osgood, Robert, *NATO: The Entangling Alliance*, Chicago University Press, 1962.

Richardson, James, *Germany and the Atlantic Alliance*, Cambridge, Mass., Harvard University Press, 1966.

Stanley, T., *NATO in Transition*, New York, Praeger, 1965.

Facts About the North Atlantic Treaty Organisation (latest edition), Paris, NATO, 1965.

For further information write to: The Director of Information,
NATO, Brussels 39.

INDEX